Mysteries
of the
Bible

READER'S DIGEST

Mysteries
of the
Bible

The Enduring Questions
of the Scriptures

The Reader's Digest Association, Inc.
Pleasantville, New York/Montreal

Mysteries of the Bible

Editor: Alma E. Guinness
Art Editor: Penny Larrick
Senior Editor: David Rattray
Assistant Editor: Jennifer Moses
Research Editor: Maymay Quey Lin
Research Associate: Megan Newman
Editorial Assistant: Jean Ryan

Supervising Art Editor: Robert M. Grant
Contributing Associate Editor: Suzanne E. Weiss

FREELANCE CONTRIBUTORS:

Picture Researcher: Marion Bodine
Researchers: Mary Hart, Mary Lyn Maiscott,
    Jo Reidy
Art Assistants: Joe Dyas, Susan Desser Haggin
Proofreader: May Dikeman
Indexer: Sydney Wolfe Cohen

READER'S DIGEST GENERAL BOOKS

Editor in Chief: John A. Pope, Jr.
Managing Editor: Jane Polley
Art Director: David Trooper
Group Editors: Norman B. Mack, Joel Musler (Art),
    Susan J. Wernert
Chief of Research: Monica Borrowman
Copy Chief: Edward W. Atkinson
Picture Editor: Robert J. Woodward
Rights and Permissions: Dorothy M. Harris
Head Librarian: Jo Manning

Jonah and the whale, page 250.

The Scripture quotations contained herein are from the Revised Standard Version of the Bible, copyright 1946, 1952, 1971 by the Division of Christian Education of the National Council of the Churches of Christ in the U.S.A. Used by permission.

The credits and acknowledgments that appear on pages 383–384 are hereby made a part of this copyright page.

Library of Congress Cataloging in Publication Data

Mysteries of the Bible.

    At head of title: Reader's digest.
    Includes index.
    1. Bible—Criticism, interpretation, etc.
I. Reader's Digest Association.   II. Reader's digest.
BS538.M97   1988   220.6   87-32402
ISBN 0-89577-293-0

Reader's Digest Fund for the Blind is publisher of the Large-Type Edition of *Reader's Digest*. For subscription information about this magazine, please contact Reader's Digest Fund for the Blind, Inc., Dept. 250, Pleasantville, N.Y. 10570.

Printed in the United States of America

About this book

"Religion without mystery ceases to be religion"
—*Bishop William Thomas Manning*

MYSTERIES OF THE BIBLE is your invitation to understand more about one of the world's most treasured books. The Bible is a whole library of history, adventure, great people, great places. It was written across a thousand eventful years, in three languages, by writers ages and worlds apart from us. No wonder the Bible can seem mysterious! MYSTERIES OF THE BIBLE is intended as a companion to your family Bible, a means of delving deeper, a way to enrich your understanding.

In articles ranging in length from a half page to several pages, in an easy-to-read, informal style, MYSTERIES OF THE BIBLE takes you on an amazing journey. Guided by theologians, historians, archaeologists, and other specialists, this book explores mysteries such as the search for the Garden of Eden. But at the heart of this book are mysteries too profound for explanation—mysteries to ponder, to enter into, to cherish.

Special Commentary pages give the viewpoints of distinguished thinkers on such intensely personal subjects as prayer and God's love. We hope you will enjoy reading our pages on the meaning of the Ten Commandments, the 23rd Psalm, and the Our Father. Scattered throughout the book are quotes that offer inspiration and insight. Scores of box features give word origins and modern interpretations of Bible subjects.

We trust that the many beautiful illustrations in MYSTERIES OF THE BIBLE will help fix biblical events in your mind and that our specially commissioned maps and concise Time Line will aid your understanding. We hope this book will give you and your family many hours of pleasure.

—The Editors

PRINCIPAL CONSULTANTS AND EDITORIAL ADVISERS:
The editors are deeply grateful for the generous assistance of Professors David Noel Freedman and Thomas L. Robinson at every stage in the preparation of this volume.

David Noel Freedman
Professor of Biblical Studies and Director of Program on Studies in Religion
The University of Michigan

Thomas L. Robinson
Department of Biblical Studies
Union Theological Seminary

CONTRIBUTING CONSULTANTS AND WRITERS:
The theologians listed here provided us with both articles and guidance in their specialties.
Particular thanks are due to Thomas L. Robinson, who provided more than a third of the articles in this book.

Oded Borowski
Department of Modern Languages and Literatures
Emory University

Michael David Coogan
Department of Religion
Wellesley College

Richard W. Corney
Professor of Old Testament
The General Theological Seminary

David Noel Freedman
Professor of Biblical Studies and Director of Program on Studies in Religion
The University of Michigan

Deirdre Good
Assistant Professor of New Testament
The General Theological Seminary

Herbert G. Grether
Former Principal and Teacher
McGilvary Theological Seminary Thailand

Lawrence Grossman
Director of Publications
The American Jewish Committee

Richard L. Jeske
Professor of New Testament
Lutheran Theological Seminary at Philadelphia

John Koenig
Professor of New Testament
The General Theological Seminary

Donald R. Miesner
Professor of Religion and Classics
Concordia College

Roland E. Murphy, O. Carm.
Professor Emeritus of Biblical Studies
Duke University

Jerome H. Neyrey
Associate Professor of New Testament
Weston School of Theology

William H. Propp
Visiting Lecturer in Judaic Studies
University of California at San Diego

Thomas L. Robinson
Department of Biblical Studies
Union Theological Seminary

Robin Scroggs
Professor of New Testament
Union Theological Seminary

Gerald T. Sheppard
Associate Professor of Old Testament
Emmanuel College of Victoria University in the University of Toronto

Graydon F. Snyder
Dean and Professor of New Testament
Chicago Theological Seminary

Bruce E. Willoughby
Editor
The University of Michigan

David slays Goliath, page 139.

CONTRIBUTING WRITERS:
Charles Flowers
Lois Gottesman
David Green
Norman Green
Norman Kotker
Claudia McDonnell

Jean McKeon
Wendy Murphy
Philip Ressner
Eleanor Schwartz
Bryce Walker

Contents

The beloved city of Jerusalem *evoked the cry: "let my right hand wither . . .if I do not set Jerusalem above my highest joy!"*

The enduring mysteries of the Bible

Exploring ambiguities, contradictions, and depths

"Lo! I tell you a mystery." When Paul the Apostle wrote those words to the Christian community in the ancient city of Corinth, he sounded a note that resonates throughout the Bible. Paul was expressing amazement at the mystery of resurrection. In 1 Timothy, the writer stated "Great indeed, we confess, is the mystery of our religion." Those who have sought God through the ages have responded "Amen."

The Bible is concerned with the mystery of the human quest for God. Written by scores of people across centuries, it bears witness to the depth and variety of mankind's longing for God. It peers into the mystery of human existence and proclaims its beauties, its tragedies, and its hopes.

The Scriptures vividly capture a perception of the divine which some in our century consider central to all religious experience. One widely influential scholar, Rudolf Otto, called the religious experience *mysterium tremendum et fascinans*—a mystery that causes one to tremble with awe and at the same time evokes fascination and love.

But what do we find when we examine the mysteries? Although in antiquity the word "mysteries" might have referred to secret rites and teachings, today it refers to the deepest, most difficult questions with which human beings grapple.

The Bible is indeed mysterious. Mysteries arise from the chasm of time that separates the language, culture, and history of these ancient writings from modern life. Indeed the languages from which the Bible was translated have presented readers with textual difficulties since ancient times. And biblical texts raise many historical questions as well. For example, all four Gospels tell the story of Jesus, so one might expect that the chronology of his life would be known exactly. However, the opposite is true. No date in Jesus' life is known with precision.

The Gospels do not provide us with an answer to one of the most basic questions: When was Jesus born? In western culture, historical time has traditionally been reckoned using the birth of Christ as the key date. "B.C." refers to events before the birth of Christ; "A.D.," meaning *anno domini* or "Year of the Lord," refers to years after the birth of Christ. In the sixth century, when this reckoning began, the monk who made the calculations may have been wrong by at least four years and possibly more.

The "star of Bethlehem," which Matthew says the Magi followed, is another mystery. Some have sought to establish the date by identifying it astronomically. An exploding supernova or a brilliant comet has been proposed as an explanation for the star. However, no astronomical data have been found to support such theories.

Several scholars have suggested that the star was actually a brilliant conjunction of the planets Jupiter and Saturn that occurred in 7 B.C. But this explanation is not compatible with Matthew's description of a miraculous moving star that "came to rest over the place where the child was."

The Gospels of Matthew and Luke indicate that Jesus was born before the death of King Herod the Great, in 4 B.C. And Matthew's narrative suggests that Jesus may have been two or three years old when Herod died. Thus Jesus may well have had his sixth or seventh birthday in the year that we would count as A.D. 1.

How long was Jesus' ministry? Though it changed the course of history, none of the Gospels spells out when the ministry began or how long it lasted. Luke gives the start of John the Baptist's ministry as about A.D. 28. Jesus was baptized by John some time later. Luke says that Jesus was "about" 30 years old when his ministry began, but when that number is correlated with the information that the Gospels give concerning his birth, it appears that Jesus was perhaps 33 to 35 years of age when he began his public ministry.

The Gospels provide diverse hints concerning the length of his ministry. The Gospel of John mentions that Jesus went to Jerusalem for the Passover three times—at the beginning, middle, and end of his ministry. That could indicate a period of just over two years. In the Gospels of Matthew, Mark, and Luke, however, it was quite clearly implied that the ministry in Galilee was brought to a climax by a single journey to Jerusalem for the Passover. Thus, these Gospels suggest a one-year ministry.

Such historical puzzles and problems are very real, but it is important to notice that the Gospels—like much of the rest of Scripture—are relatively unconcerned with these difficulties. Their attention is on mysteries deeper than the intricacies of chronology or consistent reporting.

The meaning of a single word can often affect the image conjured up in a reader's mind. Take, for example, Jesus' famous saying, "Consider the lilies of the field, how they grow" (Matthew 6:28). What flower were his disciples to consider? Was it the beautiful white Madonna lilies which decorate many churches at Easter time? Such flowers did indeed flourish in Palestine, but they were not common as wildflowers in the field. The Greek term translated "lilies" is broad enough to cover a variety of blossoms, and many researchers think that Jesus was referring to the scarlet crown anemone, also known as the windflower, that blooms abundantly on the hillsides of Palestine in spring.

What is the meaning of Jesus' saying: "It is easier for a camel to go through the eye of a needle than for a rich man to enter the kingdom of God" (Mark 10:25)? The camel was the largest animal commonly found in Palestine and stands in stark contrast to a tiny needle's eye.

One popular explanation that arose in the Middle Ages was that the "eye of the nee-

"Behold the lilies of the field." These anemones may be the "lilies" cited in Matthew's Gospel.

dle" was actually a small gate in the wall of Jerusalem that was difficult, but not impossible, for a camel to pass through. Unfortunately, no remnants of this gate have been found. Even earlier, interpreters had noted the similarity of sound between the Greek word for "camel" (*kamelos*) and that for "rope" (*kamilos*) and suggested that Jesus was referring to squeezing a strand of rope through a needle.

The very attempts to explain or soften the mystery of Jesus' words reflect the continuing force of his paradoxical statements. Scholars now recognize that Jesus' words must not be softened, but allowed their full force if one is to understand his meaning. As he himself explained it, "With men it is impossible, but not with God; for all things are possible with God."

A yet more profound difficulty of language arises when Jesus repeatedly describes himself in the Gospels as "the Son of man." Why does he use this phrase? Why does practically no one else use it? A commonsense approach to the phrase is that it refers to the humanity of Jesus, as contrasted to the title "Son of God." However, the two phrases are very seldom used in contrast to each other in the Gospels.

Jesus describes himself as "Son of man" in different contexts within the Gospels. One is when he claims extraordinary authority, as, for example, to forgive sins. Another is when he speaks of the son of man in glory, coming from heaven on the clouds. These passages echo a similar reference to "one like a son of man" in Daniel 7:13. A third context is when Jesus discusses his coming suffering and death. This enigmatic epithet in some ways captures the interplay of authority, glory, and suffering that lay at the core of Jesus' life and teaching.

Tantalizing questions arise on practically every page of the Gospels. Jesus was baptized by John. Where did this rite, which was to be

With the help of the Lord, *Moses was able to perform miracles great and small, as when he brought forth water from the rock at Kadesh.*

so important for Christianity, come from? Was it unique to John? Purification rituals had a long history in Israel; the priests had to perform ritual washing in preparation for sacrifice. John perhaps knew of the elaborate ablutions performed by the Essenes at Qumran. But he seems to have been the first to call for a single ritual of immersion as a sign of repentance and preparation for coming judgment. Jesus and his disciples continued John's distinctive practice, but gave it new meaning.

Few elements of the Gospels are stranger to modern readers than Jesus' encounters with people possessed by unclean spirits. Though the Hebrew Scriptures say hardly anything about the existence of demons, belief in their malevolent work was widespread by the time of Christ. In the Gospels, the presence of supernatural spirits gave the possessed the ability to recognize Jesus' divine identity when others could not. But Jesus commanded the demons to be silent as a sign of control and conquest over these evil powers. Jesus' exorcisms appear as part of the conflict between God and Satan.

Enigmas can arise from many quarters.

One question revolves around the Gospel references to Jesus' brothers and sisters. Did Jesus have siblings? Some suggest that these relatives were step-siblings or cousins, but most scholars think they were, in fact, brothers and sisters.

Sometimes a reference to prophecy can seem quite mysterious. Matthew tells that when people demanded a miraculous sign from Jesus, he responded that he would only give them "the sign of the prophet Jonah." He interpreted this sign in two different ways: linking it to Jonah's sojourn in the belly of the fish, and to Jonah's marvelously successful preaching. Did Jesus understand the story of Jonah as literal fact? What is clear is that the story was a well-known part of Scripture and could be readily used as a point of reference.

Passage after passage—not only in the Gospels but throughout the Bible—tantalize, fascinate, puzzle. Ultimately, all of the smaller enigmas of the text point back to the enduring mystery of God. The Bible is not a quiet narrative—it stirs the mind. Perhaps these mysteries are present for just this purpose—to cause us to ponder. ✦

11

Origins of the Bible

From ancient Hebrew and Aramaic scrolls to present-day texts

HO WROTE THE BIBLE? Many books of the Bible contain no claims of authorship. For example, the first five books of the Hebrew Scriptures, called the Pentateuch or Torah, are anonymous. Tradition ascribed the writing of the Pentateuch to Moses, although Moses is often referred to in the third person, and the fifth book, Deuteronomy, reports his death.

Modern biblical scholarship has confirmed the great antiquity of many of the traditions of the Pentateuch. The books are believed to be the product of many writers. In fact, most scholars argue that the text, as it has come down to us, is an interweaving of several ancient traditions. The process of combining the traditions began by the end of the second millennium B.C. and was completed nearly 500 years later.

Through the centuries, Israel was influenced by the cultures around her. For example, just as the Bible told how the infant Moses was laid by his mother in a basket lined with bitumen and set upon the Nile River, so Babylonian legend recounted a similar story about Sargon I, founder of the Akkadian dynasty. Sargon's mother carried him down to a riverbank: "She set me in a basket of rushes, with bitumen she sealed my lid. She cast me into the river. . . ." Scholars have found scores of such links between Israel's literature and that of surrounding nations.

While Israel clearly was influenced by some of the traditions of her neighbors, the Hebrew prophets and religious leaders abhorred other aspects of these cultures. First and foremost, they condemned such religious practices as idolatry, common in Canaan and in the surrounding regions. The Hebrews called a pagan deity to whom child sacrifices were often made by the contemptuous title *Molech*. This name combines the Hebrew consonants for "king" with the vowels from the word meaning "shame."

It is difficult for people today to imagine the world in which the Bible was produced. It emerged from the experiences of a people over centuries and is more like a living growth than an ordinary book. Much of both the Hebrew Scriptures and the New Testament was written anonymously, and often one author used the work of another or of some lost source. In addition, every copy was laboriously produced by hand. No two copies were exactly alike.

The Hebrew Bible comprises many different types of literature. Traditionally, it is divided into three sections, the law, *Torah*; the prophets, *Neviim*; and the writings, *Ketuvim*. The first letters of these designations produce the traditional Jewish acronym for the Scriptures, "Tanak." The three groups reflect the process of "canonization" in which these writings were recognized as Scripture. The five books of the Torah were universally recognized by about the middle of the fifth century B.C. But it was not until the first century of the modern era that the final versions of both prophets and writings were canonized.

The Christian Church continued to group the five books of Torah together as the Pentateuch, but established a different order for the books of history, prophets, and writings. In the Christian version, the narratives from Genesis to Esther were brought into a rough chronological sequence. However, the books of poetry and prophecy were not arranged chronologically. This lack of historical sequence can be confusing for a reader of the prophets, since their words often refer to specific historical events. For example, the Book of Amos falls eighth among the prophets. But chronologically, he predated Isaiah by more than a generation, and predated Jeremiah, Ezekiel, and Daniel by many generations.

When a reader comes to the New Testament, some of the same chronological confusion can arise. Although the four Gospels describe the earliest period of Christianity, they were not the first part of the New Testament to be written. The letters of Paul were the earliest, dating principally from about the middle of the first century A.D. The Gospels and most of the other writings, on the other hand, were evidently written between A.D. 70 and 100.

Most modern readers know the Bible through translations, as did many ancient readers. By the third century B.C. there were many Jews, especially in Egypt, who desired to read their Scriptures but knew little Hebrew. To meet their needs the great task began of translating the ancient Hebrew text into the Greek language commonly spoken throughout the Hellenistic world. Legends grew up around the translation that attributed it to 70 inspired sages, and thus it was dubbed the "Septuagint," Latin for "70."

When the Septuagint was produced, the Hebrew text was not yet standardized. Several works of history, wisdom, and prophecy in the Greek Scriptures did not become part of the Jewish canon. However, early Christians accepted the Septuagint as the official form of the Old Testament.

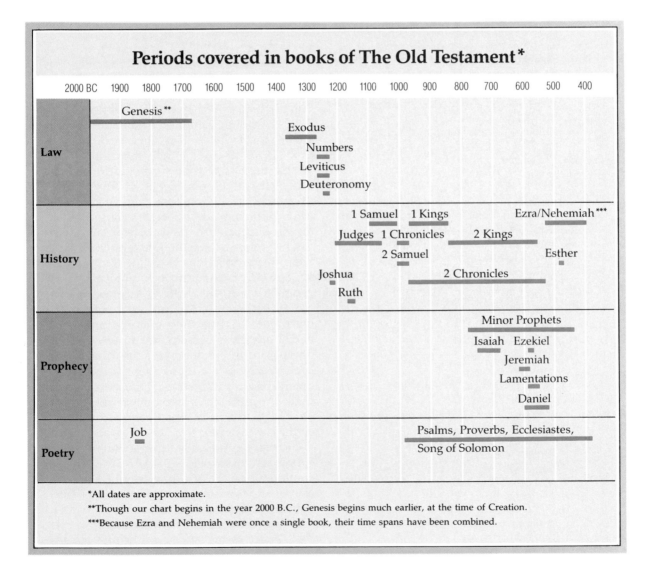

Periods covered in books of The Old Testament*

| | 2000 BC | 1900 | 1800 | 1700 | 1600 | 1500 | 1400 | 1300 | 1200 | 1100 | 1000 | 900 | 800 | 700 | 600 | 500 | 400 |

Law
- Genesis **
- Exodus
- Numbers
- Leviticus
- Deuteronomy

History
- 1 Samuel
- 1 Kings
- Judges
- 1 Chronicles
- 2 Kings
- Ezra/Nehemiah ***
- 2 Samuel
- Esther
- Joshua
- 2 Chronicles
- Ruth

Prophecy
- Minor Prophets
- Isaiah
- Ezekiel
- Jeremiah
- Lamentations
- Daniel

Poetry
- Job
- Psalms, Proverbs, Ecclesiastes, Song of Solomon

*All dates are approximate.

**Though our chart begins in the year 2000 B.C., Genesis begins much earlier, at the time of Creation.

***Because Ezra and Nehemiah were once a single book, their time spans have been combined.

Facts about
☙ the Bible ❧

Most of this information is generally agreed upon by Bible scholars. However, some of these statements are the subject of debate.

• Number of books in the Hebrew Bible: 24. These books are traditionally categorized under three headings: Torah (or Law), Prophets, and Writings.

• Number of books in the Protestant version of the Old Testament: 39.

• Number of books in the Catholic version of the Old Testament: 39, plus seven books of Apocrypha.

• The Bible was not a single book but a collection of scrolls or stacks of volumes until the fourth century A.D.

• The Bible was divided in the 16th century, long after the printing of the first Bible, into the chapters and verses we use today.

• Number of chapters in the 39 books of the Old Testament: 929; verses: 23,314; words: 593,493.

• Number of books in the New Testament: 27; chapters: 260; verses: 7,959; words: 181,253.

• Shortest book in the Old Testament: the Book of Obadiah.

• Shortest book in the New Testament: 2 John. Shortest verse: John 11:35, "Jesus wept."

• The longest verse of the Bible: Esther 8:9, consisting of 90 words describing the Persian Empire.

• Middle verse of the Bible (Old and New Testaments): Psalm 118:8, "It is better to take refuge in the Lord than to put confidence in man."

• Oldest verses in Bible: fragments of "The Song of Deborah."

• Newest verses: Gospel of John, dating from around 100 A.D.

• The name *Yahweh* or *Lord* appears in the Bible 855 times.

• The name *Jesus* appears 700 times in the Gospels and Acts, fewer than 70 times in the Epistles. The name *Christ* occurs 60 times in Gospels and Acts, 240 times in Epistles and Revelation.

When in the fourth century A.D. Jerome produced his Latin translation, which became known as the Vulgate, he translated from Hebrew manuscripts and relegated the additional books that were in the Septuagint to a secondary status. He labeled them "Apocrypha," meaning "set aside" or "hidden" from full canonical authority.

It wasn't until the 14th century that the theologian John Wycliffe produced the first complete English translation of the Bible. For over a century thereafter, the Wycliffe translation was the sole vernacular edition (written in the common language of a region) available. But with the advent of the printing press in the mid-15th century, other vernacular editions began to appear.

King James commissioned the Bible that bears his name. After assuming the throne in 1603, he appointed 54 scholars to produce a Bible that would satisfy his subjects, both Protestant and Catholic. The fruits of their labor, the beloved King James Bible, was published in 1611. While the King James Bible combined artistry with accuracy, the discovery of more ancient manuscripts of the Bible called into question many of its translations. In addition, its language became increasingly remote from everyday speech. For instance, in the King James version, Jesus tells his disciples, "Suffer little children to come unto me." This sentence may be confusing for the modern reader, who thinks of suffering as synonymous with pain. At the time of King James, the word *suffer* was used to mean "allow." Still, for nearly three centuries, the King James Bible was the standard Bible in most English-speaking churches. However, it was never completely accepted by the Roman Catholics, who used the Rheims-Douay version (a translation from the Vulgate).

It wasn't until 1870 that a Revised Version was commissioned. And in 1952, the National Council of Churches of Christ produced the Revised Standard Version (RSV), which sought to retain the literary quality of the King James version while updating the text. Since then, several other fine translations have been made. ✦

PART I

The Pentateuch

The Books of Genesis, Exodus,
Leviticus, Numbers, and Deuteronomy

*Christians call the first five books of
the Bible the Pentateuch (Greek for "five
scrolls"); Jews call them the Torah.
Vigorously direct in narrative and law,
these books are at the same time deeply
mysterious. We ponder the enigma of the
fall and redemption of mankind. We are
awed by God's regard for his creatures.*

*"**And God saw that the light was good;** and God separated the light from the darkness."*

Where time began

God speaks . . .

WHY ARE WE HERE? What are our origins? How can we understand our world? Down through the ages, religion, philosophy, and even science have delved into such mysteries, and the questions never cease to rise in the human heart.

In Genesis 1, the Bible confronts those fundamental mysteries and conveys a vision of God, the world, and humanity. The narrative is astoundingly peaceful—without the titanic battles characteristic of so many ancient accounts. The world in its magnificent order and goodness emerges from the creative word of God.

"In the beginning God created the heav-

ens and the earth. The earth was without form and void, and darkness was upon the face of the deep; and the Spirit of God was moving over the face of the waters." Genesis begins with majestic prose that almost bursts into poetry. It evokes a sense of awe and wonder before the miracle of being.

In the first part of the creation drama, the stage is prepared for life. God created light and separated the light from the darkness of chaos (1:3–4). This was not the light of heavenly bodies, but a cosmic light which flashed at God's command. God named the light *day* and the darkness *night*. Genesis shows the mysteriousness of God's work, for time began before there was a sun to rise

16

and set: "And there was evening and there was morning, one day."

On the second day (1:8), God created space. He separated "the waters (above) from the waters (below)" by placing a "firmament," a solid barrier, between them.

On the third day of creation, the waters were gathered together into bounded places (lakes and seas) and dry land appeared (1:9–13). Then God called on the mysterious fertility of the earth to take part in creation (1:11–13). "Let the earth put forth vegetation, plants yielding seed, and fruit trees bearing fruit in which is their seed, each according to its kind, upon the earth."

Then, on the fourth day, God created the luminaries (sun, moon, stars). They were created to "separate the day from the night," to mark times and seasons, and "to give light upon the earth." The sun, moon, and stars, Genesis emphasizes, are simply lights set in the firmament, and possess no divinity or power—traits many ancients often assigned to them. Vegetation, created on the previous day, is normally dependent upon the light and warmth of the sun. But in Genesis, light, time, and vegetation were brought into being by God's word; their existence is based on his continuing care.

On the fifth day, God created animal life, or *nefesh hayyah* ("living being"). A living being was characterized by breath, flesh, blood, mobility, and sexual reproduction. The latter was dependent on a special blessing from the Creator. These creatures were to live in lakes, streams, and oceans, while the birds would take to the sky.

On the sixth day, land animals and human beings were created. While all animals are considered equal, the Bible uses the Hebrew term *adam* to describe humankind. "Let us make man in our image, after our likeness; and let them have dominion over the fish of the sea, and over the birds of the air, and over the cattle, and over all the earth . . . " (1:26). The story stresses the close relation between animals and humans, who were created on the same day. Man's dominion was to be benevolent and peaceful, and until the time of Noah, he was only to eat the plants of the earth. God said, "And to . . . everything that has the breath of life, I have given every green plant for food" (1:30).

The seventh day, the Sabbath (a word based on a Hebrew verb for "rest"), was declared to be holy or sacred time; a time that belongs especially to God. The Sabbath was "hidden in creation" only to be disclosed to the people of Israel later at Mount Sinai. This day of worship was to endow all other days with meaning.

The hallowing of the Sabbath at the very climax and conclusion of the creation story suffuses the whole account with the atmosphere of worship. It also provides an invitation to human beings to give praise to their Creator, even as other creatures do by living as God ordained.

The creation story has some parallels in earlier myths and legends that were recited in the temples of the ancient world—in Babylonia, Egypt, Canaan. One of the best known of these ancient myths is the Babylonian creation epic, known by its opening words, *Enuma elish* ("When above . . . "). According to this myth, the universe was created after a fierce struggle between the creator god and the powers of chaos, which were symbolized by a monster of the deep, variously called Tiamat, Leviathan, or Yamm ("Sea"). The body of the slain monster was divided, forming a barrier between the watery parts, thereby making a space between the celestial and terrestrial water.

There are distinct differences between

On reading the Bible

"The greatness of it [the Bible] lies just in the fact that it is a mystery—that the passing earthly show and the eternal verity are brought together in it. In the face of the earthly truth, the eternal truth is accomplished. . . .What a book the Bible is, what a miracle, what strength is given with it to man. It is like a mould cast of the world and man and human nature, everything is there, and a law for everything for all the ages."

—**Fyodor Dostoyevsky**
The Brothers Karamazov

The fourth day of Creation, in a woodcut from an old Venetian Bible.

🐚 Firmament 🐚

The second day of Creation begins with God's enigmatic command, "Let there be a firmament in the midst of the waters." What is a "firmament"? This little-used English word is a translation of the Hebrew word *raqia*, but it captures little of the color of the original. The Hebrew *raqia* derives from the verb *raqa*, meaning to beat out or hammer out, and it conveys the vivid image of a metal surface hammered out like a copper or golden bowl.

God used this solid expanse to divide the waters of chaos from the lower waters of the earth. God called the solid dome "heaven," connoting "the skies." As the Book of Job observed, God "spread out the skies, hard as a molten mirror" (Job 37:18). It was in this dome that God set the sun, moon, and stars, and across this firmament that the birds flew (Genesis 1:17; 20). Under the firmament God pronounced the creation good; above it lay chaotic waters that could pour through the windows of heaven to destroy creation. Thus, the mighty firmament, visible day and night as the dome of heaven above the earth, proclaimed the glory and "handiwork" of God (Psalm 19:2). The world was enclosed and protected, since God's immeasurable power had spread the heavens "like a tent to dwell in" (Isaiah 40:22).

these myths and the Genesis creation story. For one thing, Genesis deals with the mystery of the beginning of all things. God created a habitable world out of chaos. Thus, the universe was created in God's purpose, even as it will end with the consummation of God's purpose.

Prevailing scientific theory proposes that the universe was created in a flash of light. This "big bang," or cosmic explosion, is believed to have occurred some 16 billion years ago. Some see parallels between this modern, scientific theory and the biblical account which opens with God's command, "Let there be light."

Repeatedly the creation story is punctuated with the refrain, "God saw that it was good," and over the whole stands God's final evaluation: "God saw everything that he had made, and behold, it was very good" (1:31).

The Creator not only originated, but also constantly maintains the cosmos. In the Genesis story, the waters of chaos were not eliminated, but were only pushed back and assigned their proper boundaries so that the dry land might appear and creatures might exist. The habitable world is surrounded on all sides by these waters, which are held in check by the Creator's power.

Were God's sustaining power to be withheld, as in the flood story, the chaotic waters would surge in through "the windows of the heavens" and spring up from "the fountains of the great deep." The "laws" of nature are manifestations of God's dependability or "covenant faithfulness," as expressed in his pledge to Noah at the end of the Deluge: "While the earth remains, seedtime and harvest, cold and heat, summer and winter, day and night, shall not cease" (Genesis 8:22).

When the psalmists read Genesis they were filled with awe at the grandeur of creation. They wrote poems extolling God's handiwork. These were meant to be read alongside Genesis, and they ask the reader to celebrate the joy of creation and the mastery of Yahweh. Psalm 90 exclaims: "from everlasting to everlasting thou art God." ✦

On the fifth day, God created birds, fish, and all manner of beast; *the unicorn, at center, symbolized Christ. God commanded his creation to be fruitful and multiply.*

19

❧ Psalms of Creation ❧

THE BOOK OF PSALMS contains many "songs of praise" to God, Creator of the universe. These hymns extol the greatness of the Lord, his goodness, and his majesty. The psalmists wonder at the awesome power of God. They give thanks for man's place in the divine order. Although the Priestly Code of the Israelites sets forth no requirements for hymns, in fact singing played an important part in Israelite worship.

When I look at thy heavens, the work of thy
    fingers,
      the moon and the stars which thou hast
      established;
what is man that thou art mindful of him,
    and the son of man that thou dost care for him?

Yet thou hast made him little less than God,
    and dost crown him with glory and honor.
Thou hast given him dominion over the
      works of thy hands;
    thou hast put all things under his feet,
all sheep and oxen,
    and also the beasts of the field,
the birds of the air, and the fish of the sea,
    whatever passes along the paths of the sea.

O LORD, our Lord,
    how majestic is thy name in all the earth!
❧ ❧ ❧ ❧ ❧ ❧ ❧ ❧   Psalm 8:3–9

The heavens are telling the glory of God;
    and the firmament proclaims his
      handiwork.
Day to day pours forth speech,
    and night to night declares knowledge.
There is no speech, nor are there words;
    their voice is not heard;
yet their voice goes out through all the
      earth,
    and their words to the end of the world.
❧ ❧ ❧ ❧ ❧ ❧ ❧   Psalm 19:1–4

By the word of the LORD the heavens
      were made,
    and all their host by the breath of his
      mouth.
He gathered the waters of the sea as in a
      bottle;
    he put the deeps in storehouses.
❧ ❧ ❧ ❧ ❧ ❧ ❧   Psalm 33:6–7

Bless the LORD, O my soul!
    O LORD my God, thou art
      very great!
Thou art clothed with honor and majesty,
    who coverest thyself with light as with
      a garment,
who hast stretched out the heavens like
    a tent,
    who hast laid the beams of thy
      chambers on the waters,
who makest the clouds thy chariot,
    who ridest on the wings of the wind,
who makest the winds thy messengers,
    fire and flame thy ministers.
❧ ❧ ❧ ❧ ❧ ❧   Psalm 104:1–4

O LORD, how manifold are thy works!
    In wisdom hast thou made them all;
    the earth is full of thy creatures.
Yonder is the sea, great and wide,
    which teems with things innumerable,
    living things both small and great.
There go the ships,
    and Leviathan which thou didst form
      to sport in it.
These all look to thee,
    to give them their food in due season.
When thou givest to them, they gather
      it up;
    when thou openest thy hand, they are
      filled with good things.
When thou hidest thy face, they are
      dismayed;
    when thou takest away their breath,
      they die
    and return to their dust.
When thou sendest forth thy Spirit, they
      are created;
    and thou renewest the face of the
      ground.
❧ ❧ ❧ ❧ ❧ ❧   Psalm 104:24–30

The enigmatic "we" of Genesis

Did God have a heavenly court?

THE CLIMAX of Genesis 1 and the heart of its mystery comes in the description of the creation of *adam*, the Hebrew term meaning "human being" or "humanity." God had said, "Let there be light." But now, God does not say, "Let there be man." Instead he says, "Let us make man (*adam*) in our image, after our likeness" (Genesis 1:26). Every other act of creation had been a singular act—a word spoken and carried out. Now it would appear that God is surrounded by others like himself.

This passage has long been a puzzle for interpreters of the Bible. The ancient Jewish philosopher Philo admitted that only God knows the reason for it, but argued that it reflected the mixed character of humanity, combining both good and evil. Early Christian interpreters thought of it as a reference to the presence of Christ at creation.

The image of God surrounded by a heavenly council is not uncommon in the Old Testament. The book of Job mentions the "sons of God" (*Elohim*) presenting themselves before Yahweh (Job 1:6). Isaiah saw a vision of God surrounded by his seraphim. "And I heard the voice of the LORD saying, 'Whom shall I send, and who will go for us?'" (Isaiah 6:1–8). The prophet Micaiah saw "the LORD sitting on his throne, and all the host of heaven standing beside him on his right hand and on his left" (1 Kings 22:19). Modern ideas about these beings—angels, seraphim, and the host of heaven—are clouded by the elaboration of later ideas. However, the Bible itself does not go into detail about them.

It may be that Genesis 1 refers to "*our* image" and "*our* likeness" in order to suggest a link between humanity and the whole realm of the divine. In a similar way Psalm 8 says that Yahweh made the human "little less than" *Elohim*, a word which interpreters have taken to mean either God himself or the angels.

The "image" and "likeness" of God is not precisely defined. The Book of Genesis does not, unlike many later interpreters, link the words only to human intelligence or moral capacity. Rather, Genesis links it to human dominion over the nonhuman world and responsibility for it. Genesis evokes a vision in which the human being is the instrument and representative of God's creative and caring rule over the world.

The moment of human creation is given dramatic emphasis by repetition. "God created *adam* in his own image, in the image of God he created him; male and female he created them." The word "create," which had not been used since the opening phrase of Genesis, is here used three times. The human being is created in a web of relationships—related to God and the world, as expressed by the double emphasis on the "image" of God, and related to one other (this is expressed in part by the differences between male and female).

By evoking this vision at the climax of creation, Genesis touches the mystery of who and why we are. It sets humanity on a quest for a responsible life, which is the very image of God's creative rule. ✦

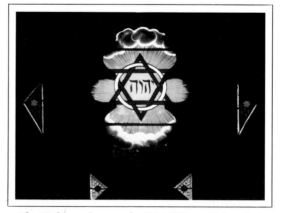

***The Hebrew letters for* YHWH,** *or Yahweh, in Winchester Cathedral. This word is called the Tetragrammaton, Greek for "four letters."*

21

The end of innocence

Adam and Eve taste the fateful fruit

THE BIBLICAL STORY of the creation of man, of paradise and paradise lost, holds depths and mysteries that have fascinated readers and challenged scholars throughout the centuries. Its vivid images of basic relationships—between man and God, between man and nature, and between man and woman—have profoundly affected the way people understand their lives to this day.

The story of creation in Genesis 1 is majestic and austere, while the account that begins in Genesis 2:4 is more human and less cosmic. The latter is introduced with "These are the generations of the heavens and the earth when they were created."

Two important elements mark the Genesis 2 account. The first is the rendering of the name of God. Throughout Genesis 1, the creator was designated by the word "God" (Hebrew, *elohim*). But in Genesis 2 the mysterious personal name "Yahweh" was introduced, and used along with the word "God." Most English translations of the Bible follow the convention for the reverent use of the name of God and render *Yahweh-elohim* as LORD God.

Genesis 2 is also distinguished by the fact that it places the creation of man before that of plants and animals. It states that man

While Adam slept, *the Lord created Eve.*

was created "when no plant of the field was yet in the earth and no herb of the field had yet sprung up" (Genesis 2:5). The narrator made no effort to correlate this description with the story of creation in Genesis 1.

Then the LORD God "formed man of dust from the ground, and breathed into his nostrils the breath of life; and man became a living being" (Genesis 2:7). The Hebrew word for "formed" was regularly used for a potter working clay. Thus, these words suggest an image of God gathering the dust of the earth and shaping it into a human form. When God blew his own breath into the nostrils of the man he had formed, the figure became a "living being."

The Hebrew word for man was *adam*, the same word used as the name for the first human. Occurring more than 500 times in the Hebrew Scriptures, this word was also used to distinguish man from other living things. Its etymology is uncertain, but Genesis used a wordplay to reveal a special aspect of its meaning. The *adam* was formed from *adamah*, "the ground." Thus, the human was an earthling, one whose existence was tied to the soil from which he came.

The body of man, shaped from the ground, was animated by the Lord God's breath. Genesis does not differentiate between body and soul, as was so often done in later centuries, but between the body and the vitality in the breath. The human became a *nephesh hayyah* (living being), a Hebrew phrase used for both beasts and humans. But man was distinguished by the way the gift of life was bestowed. The breath never ceased to belong to God, for he sustained life. Later generations speculated that if God should "gather to himself his breath, all flesh would perish together."

Once man was formed, God created his environment. Yahweh "planted a garden in Eden, in the east" (Genesis 2:8). The ancient Greek translation of the Scriptures used the word *paradeisos* to mean "garden"—hence the description of Eden as "paradise."

The garden was filled with trees, some of which provided food. At the center of the garden were the mysterious tree of life and the fateful tree of the knowledge of good and evil. Yahweh forbade man to eat of the tree of the knowledge of good and evil, "for in the day that you eat of it you shall die" (Genesis 2:17). Genesis does not explain why the knowledge of good and evil should be forbidden to man. Perhaps the fateful tree simply expressed God's mastery over his creation, and man's duty to obey him.

From the beginning, man was a worker whose task was to till and maintain the garden. But Adam was alone. "Then the LORD God said, 'It is not good that the man should be alone; I will make him a helper fit for him' " (Genesis 2:18). Yahweh formed the beasts and birds and brought them to man so that he could name them. Adam gave names to all the creatures, but no fit helper was found for him.

Finally, Yahweh caused Adam to fall into a deep sleep. While he slept, the Lord God took one of Adam's ribs and formed woman. Yahweh led the woman to the man, who said, "This at last is bone of my bones and flesh of my flesh; she shall be called Woman (*ishshah*) because she was taken out of Man (*ish*)" (Genesis 2:23).

Genesis implied that the attraction between man and woman was a result of the original unity between male and female. Genesis stated, "Therefore a man leaves his father and his mother and cleaves to his wife, and they become one flesh." It is remarkable that although the actual practice in most ancient patriarchal cultures, including Israel, was for the woman to leave her family and join the clan of her husband, the reverse was decreed here.

Man and woman were naked and unashamed, thus symbolizing the innocence of Eden and their pure relation to God. Within a short time, however, man and woman encountered the serpent.

Although in later centuries the serpent was seen as demonic and was identified

The beguiling serpent tempted Eve to eat of the tree of knowledge, saying that "God knows that when you eat of it your eyes will be opened, and you will be like God."

Has the Garden of Eden been found?

So specific is the biblical description of Eden that scores of people have sought to locate it. The Bible tells of a land in the east, out of which a single river divided into four: the Pishon, the Gihon, the Tigris, and the Euphrates. Locating the Tigris and the Euphrates rivers is not difficult, of course, because they still exist. But in the absence of data concerning the Pishon and Gihon, the search for the location of Eden has been unsuccessful. Places that have been suggested include Ethiopia, Turkey, and even India. But in recent years, Dr. Juris Zarins, of Southwest Missouri State University, has concluded that the Garden of Eden lies beneath the waters of the Persian Gulf. For thousands of years, starting at the time of the Great Ice Age, what is now the Persian Gulf was dry land. Over the centuries, the climate varied, but by around 6000 B.C., the rains were heavy and the riv-

Before the Fall, Eden was a lush and lovely paradise, in which man and woman dwelled peacefully.

with Satan, the Genesis narrative referred to it simply as a "wild creature" (Genesis 3:1). What distinguished the serpent from other animals was that it was "subtle." The narrator does not explain how this creature had the gift of speech or came to be more knowledgeable and clever than the human pair.

The serpent began a conversation with the woman, asking, "Did God say, 'You shall not eat of any tree of the garden'?" She replied, "God said, 'You shall not eat of the fruit of the tree which is in the midst of the garden, neither shall you touch it, lest you die.' " The two had not questioned the limit God had set on their freedom.

The serpent challenged God's authority. "You will not die," the serpent said, "for God knows that when you eat of it your eyes will be opened, and you will be like God, knowing good and evil" (Genesis 3:4–5). Was God jealously guarding his prerogatives from human beings? The woman reflected and decided to eat the fruit, giving some to the man. Just as man had unquestioningly obeyed God, now without a hint of reflection he disobeyed.

Man and woman ate from the tree, but did not die. Was the serpent right after all? According to the Book of Genesis, God had never promised immortality to humankind. However, it has often been suggested that it was through this act of disobedience that man became mortal.

Thus, the temptation was subtle and had a hint of truth. God did not follow through on his threat of death, revealing his divine grace and forbearance. However, by disobeying God the two had separated themers ran full. Watered by four rivers, such a place would be a natural paradise. Thousands of animal remains found in the Gulf area suggest that game was abundant. Furthermore, the presence of stone tools provides evidence of human habitation.

Geological investigations indicate that two gulleys, known today as the Wadi Rimah and the Wadi Batin, trace the course of ancient rivers. Zarins believes that these are the remains of the Pishon River, and that the Gihon is the modern Karun, emptying into the Gulf.

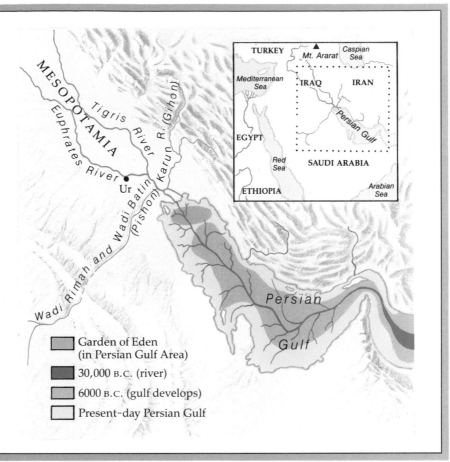

Garden of Eden (in Persian Gulf Area)

30,000 B.C. (river)

6000 B.C. (gulf develops)

Present-day Persian Gulf

selves from him, and were no longer entitled to the perfect enjoyment of life that the garden offered. "The eyes of both were opened, and they knew that they were naked." The shame at their nakedness signified their broken relationship with God.

"And they heard the sound of the LORD God walking in the garden in the cool of the day, and the man and his wife hid themselves from the presence of the LORD God among the trees in the garden." When confronted by Yahweh, the man blamed the woman, and the woman blamed the serpent—they knew cowardice.

Yahweh's judgments came swiftly. The serpent was condemned to be a belly-crawling animal hated by humans. As for the man and woman, their eyes were opened, and Yahweh said that they had "become like one of us, knowing good and evil" (Genesis 3:22). According to Genesis, woman would now feel the pain of childbirth; she also would become subservient to her husband. For some, this divine judgment provided an explanation for woman's subordinate place in ancient society. The man would continue as a tiller of the soil, but suddenly the soil would be poor and thorn-infested. "In the sweat of your face you shall eat bread till you return to the ground" (Genesis 3:19).

Adam and Eve were cast out of the garden, never to return. Without ever using the words "sin," "fall," "disobedience," "freedom," or "punishment," this fascinating narrative sketched the boundaries of human existence. The story of mankind's struggle in the world now began. ✦

Apocryphal tales of Adam and Eve

Elaborating on the words of the Lord

OW DID ADAM AND EVE ADAPT to the hostile world to which they were exiled? The Book of Genesis gave no information about man's first days outside paradise, but later legend attempted to follow him.

According to one apocryphal story, after they were cast from the garden, Adam and Eve built a hut and spent seven days lamenting their sin. Then Adam arose, and for the next seven days wandered about

In shame and despair, *Adam and Eve went forth from Paradise into a harsh world.*

looking for food. His search produced nothing. Finding only fodder for beasts, Adam proposed that he and his mate do penance, in the hope of forgiveness.

For her part, Eve stood on a rock in the midst of the Tigris River, the water flowing up as high as her neck. There she was to stand in silence for 37 days. Similarly, Adam was to stand on a rock in the Jordan River for 40 days. After 18 days, Eve was beguiled by Satan. Disguised as an angel, Satan beseeched Eve to join him on the riverbank, where he would find food for her. Unable to resist, Eve stepped from the water. Realizing at once the devil's true identity, Adam cried to Eve, "How is it that you have been again ensnared by our adversary?" Overwhelmed by this new deception, Eve fell to the ground in sorrow.

The devil spoke to Adam: "It is on account of you that I was thrown out of heaven. When you were formed I was expelled from the presence of God and banished from the company of angels." Upon hearing this, Adam pleaded with the Lord to put this adversary, who sought to destroy his soul, far away from him. With that, Satan vanished, and Adam finished his penance.

The inclination to embroider Bible stories also prompted the creation of tales about a creature named Lilith. According to legend, God had originally given Lilith to Adam as his first wife. Like Adam, Lilith had been formed from dust, and as a result she demanded full equality. Refusing to submit to Adam's authority, she disappeared. God sent angels to find her, but Lilith refused to return. The angels vowed to punish her by killing 100 of her demon children each day.

Lilith was said to have taken her revenge by injuring human babies, and in ancient times some parents wore amulets to protect their children from her rage. In other legends, Lilith joined with the serpent to help bring about the fall of Adam and Eve. ✦

26

"The fear of the LORD is the beginning of wisdom."
—Proverbs 9:10

TIME AND AGAIN, the Bible urges us to fear God. By "fear" is meant that healthy mix of love and dread that is awe. The theologian A.J. Heschel says: "The Bible does not preach awe as a form of intellectual resignation; it does not say, awe is the end of wisdom. Its intention seems to be that awe is a way to wisdom."

"God said to Moses: 'Do not fear' (Numbers 21:34), and yet it says in Proverbs 28:14, 'Happy is the man who fears always.' It is a quality of the righteous that although they have received God's assurance, they never cast off the fear of Him."
—C. G. Montefiore and H. Loewe
A Rabbinic Anthology

"He who has knowledge of the Law, but no fear of God, is like a keeper of a treasury, who has the inner keys, but not the outer keys. He cannot enter." **—*Talmud***

"Do not withdraw your hand from your son or your daughter, but from their youth teach them the fear of God. Do not, when embittered, give orders to your slave, male or female, for they hope in the same God; otherwise, they might lose the fear of God, who is the Master of both of you. He surely is not coming to call with an eye to rank and station in life; no, He comes to those whom the Spirit has prepared."
**—*The Teaching of the Twelve Apostles*
(First century A.D.)**

"The holy fear of the Lord expels all evil fear and protects those good things which cannot be expressed in words or even thought of. It is not given to all to have this fear, for it is a very great gift. The fear of God rules and governs a man and makes him come into the grace of the Lord. If a man has that grace, the fear of the Lord preserves it, and if he does not have it, it leads him to it. . . .For it is impossible for someone to ascend to the grace of God or to persevere in it without a holy fear and a holy dread. . . . Again, the more fear we have, the more we pray. And it is no small thing to be given the grace of holy prayer. No matter how great they seem, the works of men are not to be judged according to the opinion of men but according to the judgment and pleasure of God. And so it is good for us to have holy fear at all times." **—Ugolino di Monte Santa Maria**
The Sayings of Brother Giles

"What can better take away the love of sinning from one's life than a real fear of death? And what moves one to live more fervently and to do good more than confident hope in the mercy and goodness of God? . . . When these two are combined they provide a sure staff of hope to hold on to in all your good works. . . .For reverence is nothing but dread and love blended together by the staff of a sure hope."
—Anonymous 14th-century English mystic
The Epistle of Prayer

"Perhaps if we feared God more we would fear everything else less. We can rightly fear the consequences of violating the physical and moral laws through which the creative power of God works. There is something to fear in our flouting of the basic structure of the universe. The foundation of wisdom lies in knowing what we ought to fear."
—Rolland W. Schloerb
The Interpreter's Bible

Cain's murderous rage

The baffling death of Abel

THE STORY OF THE Garden of Eden ended with great sorrow. Adam and Eve, by their own sin, had been banished from a world that was wholly good. They were united as man and wife, but their union was clouded by their sin.

"Adam knew Eve his wife, and she conceived." Two sons were born to them. The firstborn, Cain, became "a tiller of the ground" like his father; the second son, named Abel, became a shepherd.

The name *Cain* may be a play on a Hebrew word meaning "get," as in Eve's statement, "I have *gotten* a man with the help of the LORD." The name *Abel* is also a Hebrew word. It means "vapor, breath, futility," and may suggest that his life was cut short.

The struggle between the first brothers has mystified generations of Bible readers. Yet the deeper meaning of the story has shone through the Bible's brief account.

It is remarkable that this powerful drama, so influential in our thinking and so well known throughout the world, should occupy only 54 lines of text (in the Revised Standard Version of the Bible).

The two sons brought offerings to Yahweh. Cain brought "the fruit of the ground," and Abel "the firstlings of his flock and of their fat portions." In the ancient world, there was often conflict between farmers and semi-nomadic shepherds. Many scholars believe that the story of Cain and Abel reveals the tension between these two ways of life.

Yahweh "had regard for Abel and his offering, but for Cain and his offering he had no regard" (Genesis 4:4). Why would God prefer Abel's offering over his brother's, and how did he make his preference known? The silence of Genesis left a mystery for later generations. A passage in the New Testament attributed God's choice to the faith of Abel (Hebrews 11:4).

Theorizing about this mystery, the Jewish historian Josephus spoke of Abel's respect for justice and virtue, and of Cain's complete depravity. According to Josephus, God preferred what grew according to nature (animals) over what man forced from nature (crops). Interestingly, the Torah commanded sacrifices of both animals and grain crops.

Cain was furious at God's disregard of his offering. Genesis reported that "Cain was very angry, and his countenance fell" (Genesis 4:5). Yahweh responded to Cain, counseling him that all was not lost; Cain's fate was in his own hands. He was a man in danger; he could "do well" and be accepted, or "not do well."

The Lord said to Cain, "Sin is couching at the door; its desire is for you, but you must master it" (Genesis 4:7). The moral struggle of humanity was vividly portrayed as a life-and-death struggle with a savage beast within.

The "beast" pounced, and, like many others after him, Cain was unable to master it. In the field one day, "Cain rose up against his brother Abel, and killed him" (Genesis 4:8). Cain so resented God's preference for his younger brother's offering

Jealously Cain watched the acceptance of Abel's offering.

Cain slew Abel, *but was protected from retribution by the "mark of Cain."*

that he could not control himself. Their differences had led to bitter resentment and, finally, to murder.

When Yahweh appeared and asked about Abel, Cain responded, "Am I my brother's keeper?" This question has echoed through the centuries, and has come to represent man's inhumanity to man.

No longer just struggling together in a harsh world, humans were now fighting one another. The Lord's anger burned as he said to Cain, "What have you done? The voice of your brother's blood is crying to me from the ground." Now Cain was cursed to be "a fugitive and a wanderer on the earth." Fearing that he had been forsaken by God, Cain said, "My punishment is greater that I can bear . . . and whoever finds me will slay me" (Genesis 4:13–14).

In his mysterious graciousness, Yahweh did not abandon the murderer. Instead the Lord said, "If anyone slays Cain, vengeance shall be taken on him sevenfold" (Genesis 4:15). He gave him a mark, perhaps like a tattoo or a tribal mark, to protect his life. "Then Cain went away from the presence of the Lord, and dwelt in the land of Nod, east of Eden" (Genesis 4:16). ✦

The bizarre lineage of mankind

Seth, Enoch, and the giants

AFTER MURDERING his brother Abel, Cain became a fugitive. He founded a city, and had numerous descendants—it is noted that these included musicians and metalsmiths and those who dwell in tents and have cattle (Genesis 4:17–22). But this fugitive murderer was not to be the ancestor of the rest of mankind.

Adam and Eve had a third son named Seth, and through him came "the generations of Adam" that continue the biblical story. Among these descendants, the name of Enoch stands out. "Enoch walked with God; and he was not, for God took him" (Genesis 5:24). Many interpreters have taken that statement to mean that Enoch did not die. The possibility that he did not die provided a mystery for later generations.

In the second century B.C., the Book of Jubilees reported that Enoch was "conducted into the Garden of Eden in majesty and honor, and behold there he writes down the condemnation and judgment of the world." Numerous apocalyptic writings were attributed to him, and in some, he was perceived as the angel closest to God.

Genesis also reported that "the sons of God saw that the daughters of men were fair; and they took to wife such of them as they chose." From these marriages were born the *Nephilim*, or "giants," also known as "the mighty men that were of old." This mysterious statement was taken up in later apocalyptic writing. In one of the books that has been attributed to Enoch, for example, the "sons of God" were seen as fallen angels. These angels corrupted the earth and produced evil giant children.

According to Genesis, the birth of the giants was an indication of how wicked the earth had become. "The LORD saw that the wickedness of man was great . . . so the LORD said, 'I will blot out man whom I have created from the face of the ground.' " ✦

Corrupt humanity drowns in the flood

Why Noah was saved

THE STORY OF NOAH and his family, riding out the flood in an ark filled with birds and other animals, is among the Bible's most cherished episodes. At the same time, the description of the cataclysmic inundation that covered the earth is among the most terrifying.

Ten generations after the creation of Adam and Eve, God announced his intention to erase all life from the earth and start anew. Humanity had grown corrupt, so much so that God resolved to unleash a flood that would destroy mankind.

"The LORD saw that the wickedness of man was great in the earth, and that every imagination of the thoughts of his heart was only evil continually. And the LORD was sorry that he had made man on the earth, and it grieved him to his heart" (Genesis 6:5–6). Man, granted free will to live either righteously or wickedly, had chosen the evil path. What sins had been committed?

Corruption and violence—the breakdown of human society—were what sealed the world's fate. According to the Bible, even the lower animals were somehow guilty. "So the LORD said, 'I will blot out man whom I have created from the face of the ground, man and beast and creeping things and birds of the air, for I am sorry that I have made them.' " There was but one man who was "righteous . . . blameless in his generation," a man who "walked with God." This one man was Noah.

God told Noah of his intention to destroy the world, and instructed him, for his salvation, to build "an ark of gopher wood; make rooms in the ark, and cover it inside and out with pitch." God specified the dimensions of the ark, the need for three decks in it, and the location of the door. Only after giving these instructions did God explain: "For behold, I will bring a flood of waters upon the earth, to destroy all flesh in which is the breath of life from under heaven. . . .But I will establish my covenant with you; and you shall come into the ark, you, your sons, your wife, and your sons' wives with you" (Genesis 6:17–18).

In order to ensure the survival of all living species, Noah was to take into the ark seven pairs—male and female—of all animals and birds known in Israelite tradition as "clean" (permissible to eat), and one pair each of all "unclean" creatures. He stocked the ark with food for all of them. Without comment, Noah "did all that the LORD had commanded him."

The coming of the flood is described graphically. "All the fountains of the great deep burst forth, and the windows of the heavens were opened." As time went on, "the waters increased, and bore up the ark, and it rose high above the earth. . . .And the waters prevailed so mightily upon the earth that all the high mountains under the whole heaven were covered." Other than fish, all living creatures outside the ark drowned—"birds, cattle, beasts, all swarming creatures that swarm upon the earth, and every man" (Genesis 7:11–21).

Archaeologists have found tantalizing evidence of flooding in the Mesopotamian area. In 1929, the English scientist Leonard

Charged with care of man and beast, *Noah built the ark according to God's word.*

31

Woolley, tunneling into a Sumerian burial pit at the site of Ur on the Euphrates, struck a layer of water-deposited silt, over eight feet thick, and below it the relics of an earlier, more primitive culture. Woolley declared that a great flood had swept through the region late in the fourth millennium B.C., wiping out the existing culture. Centuries later, he said, a new culture had taken shape on the site. Later researchers uncovered evidence of flooding at a number of other locations in Mesopotamia. Archaeologists believe, however, that these flood layers were formed during the third millennium B.C. Thus, scholars today reject Woolley's conclusion regarding the Great Flood.

It rained for 40 days and 40 nights. Then God "made a wind blow over the earth, and the waters subsided; the fountains of the deep and the windows of the heavens were closed, the rain from the heavens was restrained, and the waters receded from the earth continually." After 150 days, the ark came to rest upon solid ground, on Mount Ararat—thought to be in modern Turkey.

Still, Noah did not know how much the flood waters had receded. So he opened the window and sent out a raven, which "went to and fro until the waters were dried up from the earth." He next released a dove, "but the dove found no place to set her foot, and she returned to him to the ark, for the waters were still on the face of the whole earth" (Genesis 8:9).

A week later, Noah again released the dove. This time, it brought back an olive branch, "so Noah knew that the waters had subsided from the earth." The image of a dove clutching an olive branch has been a symbol of peace and harmony ever since. Waiting another week, Noah sent out the dove once more. It did not return.

When Noah opened the door of the ark, the world was once again pristine. All wickedness had been purged from it. God reiterated the command made to his original creation: Noah and his family, as well

Assyrian *relief of Gilgamesh.*

as the surviving animals and birds, were to "be fruitful and multiply upon the earth." Noah expressed his thanks for the deliverance by offering sacrifices to God.

Later Jewish folklore, elaborating on the account with a wealth of detail, described the troubles Noah encountered with the animals in the ark. The patriarch and his sons labored day and night to feed them, hauling fodder for the zebras and gazelles, dried meat for the tigers and other carnivores. At one point, the lion, grumpy and seasick, bit Noah in the leg, laming him.

According to these legends, filth piled up and rats proliferated. Noah solved these problems by creating two new animals. Passing his hand over the elephant, he caused it to give birth to a pig, which soon devoured the filth. Then, when he rubbed the lion's nose, the beast produced a cat, which began to eliminate the rats. Special attention was given to two creatures too large for the ark to accommodate: a gigantic beast called the *reem* that swam behind, tethered by a rope; and the giant Og, who straddled the roof, and whose food was passed to him through a hatchway.

Interestingly, many cultures around the globe have preserved ancient folklore about a primeval flood that destroyed everything and everyone except one lucky man, or one chosen family. Many people today believe that the very universality of such sagas proves that they are based on fact. Others suggest that the existence of these traditions among so many different cultures illuminates a deep human fear of nature's destructive power.

One early version of the story comes from Babylon, located in what is now Iraq. It forms an episode in the classic *Epic of Gilgamesh*. Its counterpart to Noah is Utnapishtim of Shuruppak. One night, as Utnapishtim slept, the god Ea whispered a warning through the reed walls of his house: Enlil, the chief god of the Babylonian pantheon, was about to send a flood that would destroy humanity.

32

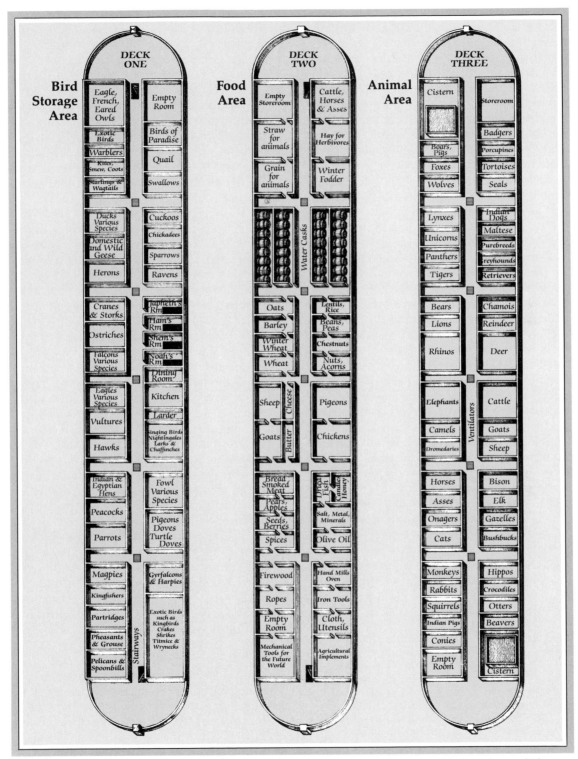

DECK ONE

Bird Storage Area

Eagle, French, Eared Owls	Empty Room
Exotic Birds	Birds of Paradise
Warblers	Quail
Kites, Smew, Coots	
Starlings & Wagtails	Swallows
Ducks Various Species	Cuckoos
Domestic and Wild Geese	Chickadees
	Sparrows
Herons	Ravens
Cranes & Storks	Japheth's Rm
	Ham's Rm
Ostriches	Shem's Rm
Falcons Various Species	Noah's Rm
	Dining Room
Eagles Various Species	Kitchen
Vultures	Larder
Hawks	Singing Birds Nightingales Larks & Chaffinches
Indian & Egyptian Hens	Fowl Various Species
Peacocks	Pigeons Doves Turtle Doves
Parrots	
Magpies	Gyrfalcons & Harpies
Kingfishers	
Partridges	Exotic Birds such as Kingbirds Crakes Shrikes Titmice & Wrynecks
Pheasants & Grouse	
Pelicans & Spoonbills	

Stairways

DECK TWO

Food Area

Empty Storeroom	Cattle, Horses & Asses
Straw for animals	Hay for Herbivores
Grain for animals	Winter Fodder
Water Casks	Water Casks
Oats	Lentils, Rice
Barley	Beans, Peas
Winter Wheat	Chestnuts
Wheat	Nuts, Acorns
Sheep	Cheese	Pigeons
Goats	Butter	Chickens
Bread Smoked Meat	Dried Fish	Candles Honey
Pears, Apples	Salt, Metal, Minerals	
Seeds, Berries		
Spices	Olive Oil	
Firewood	Hand Mills Oven
Ropes	Iron Tools
Empty Room	Cloth, Utensils
Mechanical Tools for the Future World	Agricultural Implements

DECK THREE

Animal Area

Cistern	Storeroom
	Badgers
Boars, Pigs	Porcupines
Foxes	Tortoises
Wolves	Seals
Lynxes	Indian Dogs
Unicorns	Maltese
Panthers	Purebreeds
Tigers	Greyhounds
	Retrievers
Bears	Chamois
Lions	Reindeer
Rhinos	Deer
Elephants	Cattle
Camels	Goats
Dromedaries	Sheep
Horses	Bison
Asses	Elk
Onagers	Gazelles
Cats	Bushbucks
Monkeys	Hippos
Rabbits	Crocodiles
Squirrels	Otters
Indian Pigs	Beavers
Conies	
Empty Room	Cistern

Ventilators

From dimensions given in Genesis, *the 17th-century Jesuit Athanasius Kircher devised this floor plan of the ark. Kircher envisioned three decks, each containing 300 stalls.*

Ea gave instructions for building an ark, and Utnapishtim arranged for its construction. He then embarked with his family and servants, a supply of silver and gold, and "the seeds of all living things." The rains came, the waters rose, and the storm raged six days and six nights. On the seventh day the ark came to rest on a mountaintop. The land below, shrouded in silt and debris, lay "flat like a roof," the chronicle states, "and all of mankind had returned to clay."

Utnapishtim opened a shutter and, to make sure that the earth was dry, released first a dove, then a swallow, and finally a raven. Then, on the mountaintop, he offered up a sacrifice to the gods. Enlil's rage was eventually appeased, and he conferred immortality on Utnapishtim and his wife.

The Gilgamesh narrative resembles an even older Babylonian source, which in turn is similar to an extremely ancient Sumerian text. A fragment of the Sumerian *Epic of Ziusudra*, written on a clay tablet, was excavated in 1890 in Nippur, holy city of Sumer.

Thus, many cultures preserved the story of a flood that killed all but a favored few. In addition, Bible scholars, closely examining the verses in Genesis, have noted some interesting patterns in the biblical text. The Genesis account may in fact derive from two separate sources that were pieced together to make a single story.

The first version, dating from around the time of King Solomon, reads like a folktale. Noah loaded the animals—seven pairs each of ritually acceptable animals and birds that the Israelites used in their sacrifices, and one pair apiece of the other animals. The rains fell just 40 days and 40 nights; when the flood subsided (this version does not

say where), Noah first sent out the raven and then the dove. Then, he went forth from the ark, and sacrificed to God.

The second, probably later, account is both more sweeping and more precise. In it, only single pairs of animals entered the ark. The narrative shows a careful concern for detail, giving Noah's age (600 years) and the lengthy duration of the flood. The deluge itself was not just a rainstorm, but a return to the primordial chaos of creation, when God parted the waters to differentiate heaven from earth. The ark came to rest on Ararat. And when the crisis was ended, God established a covenant with Noah.

What is finally so marvelous about the biblical account is neither its literary value nor its historicity, but its moral force. Indeed, Genesis raises the story to new levels of dramatic power and moral insight.

The Bible story is concerned not only with the salvation of the world that occurs after the cataclysm, but also with moral law. God resolved that he would never "again destroy every living creature as I have done. While the earth remains, seedtime and harvest, cold and heat, summer and winter, day and night shall not cease" (8:21–22).

God then provided other means to deal with corruption and violence. Whoever was guilty—man or beast—would be punished individually for his crime. God told Noah and his family, "for your lifeblood I will surely require a reckoning; of every beast I will require it and of man; of every man's brother I will require the life of man. Whoever sheds the blood of man, by man shall his blood be shed." God set forth a theological basis for the significance of every human life: "for God made man in his own image." Thus, whoever spills blood attacks God.

God then established a covenant with Noah, which extended to all of his progeny—all people forever after. He promised that he would never destroy the world by a flood again. A rainbow in the sky symbolized this pledge: "when the bow is in the clouds, I will look upon it and remember the everlasting covenant." Upon emerging from the ark, Noah began to till the soil. ✦

On the search for Noah's Ark

"Does it make a difference really if the ark is found? By now it is immortal. If it did not find refuge in the heart of this mountain [today called Mt. Ararat], it has found a safer refuge in the human heart. Here it has lived for thousands of years, and here it will live forever."
—**Gordon Gaskill**
"**Have They Found Noah's Ark?**"

Desperate people and animals *struggled in vain to save themselves from the raging waters of the Great Flood. But only those who found refuge in the ark escaped the wrath of God.*

Has Noah's ark been found?

Controversy on Mount Ararat

IN 1955, FERNAND NAVARRA, a French explorer, pulled a five-foot-long wooden beam from beneath the glacial cap of the Turkish mountain Agri Dag. Could this mountain, often identified as the biblical Mount Ararat, have yielded the remains of Noah's ark?

After performing a battery of scientific tests, experts determined that this was not the case, for the beam was no more than 1200 years old. What, then, was the origin of this beam and other wooden pieces retrieved from the mountain?

In the Middle Ages, pilgrims were attracted to a monastery at the foot of Agri Dag, for the monks there had relics reputed to be from Noah and his family. These monks, in their zeal, may have constructed an ark-like structure on the mountaintop. The remains uncovered by Navarra could have been part of this medieval ark.

In spite of this disappointment, biblical researchers have continued to comb the region and to reexamine the data. They hope to find evidence that Noah's ark does lie atop this icy pinnacle. ✦

The mysterious transformations of wine

"Giver of gladness," "poison of serpents"

THE ANCIENT ISRAELITES were quite aware that drinking wine could bring comfort or disgrace, joy or despair. On one hand, Joshua ben Sira, the second-century B.C. Jewish scribe, asked, "What is life to a man who is without wine? It has been created to make men glad" (Sirach 31:27). On the other hand, Proverbs 20 stated, "Wine is a mocker, strong drink a brawler; and whoever is led astray by it is not wise."

In the first biblical anecdote involving wine, the drink's attraction, power, and danger were all presented. Noah "drank of the wine, and became drunk, and lay uncovered in his tent" (Genesis 9:21). The Bible reported that his son Ham saw him and ran to tell his brothers, Shem and Japheth. Circumspectly, the two brothers backed toward their father. Keeping their eyes averted, they covered their father's nakedness.

This passage was meant to illustrate Ham's disrespect. The Israelites found public nakedness shameful. Adam and Eve sought clothing after committing the first sin; thus, there was a strong symbolic tie between nakedness and impiety. Ham not only looked upon his father's nakedness but also watched as Noah was under the influence of this destructive force.

Over-all, the ancients were mystified by wine's paradoxical character. In later Jewish folklore, this mystery was explored. One story relates that Noah learned viticulture from Satan himself. Satan used blood from a lamb, a lion, an ape, and a pig as fertilizer. This is legend with an ironic twist, for the heavy drinker may go through four stages: meek as a lamb, fierce as a lion, awkward and silly as an ape, and at last piglike, wallowing in the mud.

The Genesis story of Noah and other early biblical writings indicate an antagonistic attitude toward the use of wine. However, by the 10th century B.C., wine had apparently become accepted as part of the fabric of Old Testament life. Though there were still warnings against drunkenness, the tendency was to stress moderation, not total abstinence. Proverbs predicted that "the drunkard and the glutton will come to poverty" (23:21), but also recommended "give strong drink to him who is perishing, and wine to those in bitter distress" (31:6).

Wine became a staple of daily life—the most common beverage at meals and a prominent feature at weddings, banquets, and festivals.

Wine was acceptable, and in some cases required, in religious ritual. Although never presented as a sacrifice by itself, it was used as a libation with offerings to God. Because wine in ancient times was almost always red, it seemed symbolic of the blood of sacrificial animals.

At the Sukkoth—the principal harvest festival of the year—celebrants traveled to Jerusalem for seven days of feasting and drinking. In Hellenistic times, the Passover feast, which commemorated the Israelites' escape from Egypt, involved the ritual drinking of wine.

As a main agricultural occupation, the growing of grapes rivaled the cultivation of olives and figs in Israel. The vine's fertility was proof of God's power. Wine, a product of the vine, was evidence of God's generosity to man, especially since water was not always available throughout Palestine.

In the New Testament, drinking per se was not condemned, though immoderation was still disdained. Jesus' first miracle in the Gospel of John involved wine—when the wine gave out at the wedding feast at Cana, he changed water into wine. Obviously, Jesus accepted the prudent use of wine, and appreciated its role in celebrations.

Just as wine marked Jesus' first public miracle, it was central to his last private meeting with his apostles. According to the Gospels of Matthew, Mark, and Luke, this last meal was a Passover supper. Jesus explained that the wine they shared in convivial company should be understood symbolically. According to St. Paul, at the supper Jesus proclaimed, "This cup is the new covenant in my blood." He then enjoined them to "drink it, in remembrance of me." ✦

How was wine made in ancient times?

When the Hebrews settled in Canaan, they must have picked up the finer points of viticulture from their more sophisticated neighbors. The basic structure of the wine-press was a pair of large pits or basins cut into the rock, one above the other. Workers crushed the grapes in the upper chamber with their feet. The juice ran through a channel to the lower basin, where it was then left to ferment in the late summer heat.

Achaemenid drinking vessel, made of seven pieces of joined gold.

Egyptian tomb art was thought to provide the dead with everything, such as vineyards, for their afterlife.

"He who tills his land will have plenty"

What archaeology reveals

AS THE MAIN OCCUPATION, agriculture was the driving force behind daily life in ancient Israel. It influenced not only the economy, but also religious life, law, social life, and art.

Archaeology has greatly increased our knowledge of agricultural practices. Several ancient texts, including the Bible itself, contain references to farming methods. In addition, farm implements and organic remains (such as seeds and animal bones) have been unearthed throughout the biblical lands.

Because ancient Israel was under the political and cultural influence of foreign powers, the Israelites undoubtedly adopted the agricultural practices of other peoples. We can learn about these methods from the art and writings of surrounding countries. For example, remains from ancient Egyptian tombs—wall paintings, papyri, statues, and reliefs—offer glimpses of daily life that include descriptions of agricultural activities. Mesopotamian archives and other remains also provide information about agriculture in antiquity. Within their own country, Israelite farmers inherited a large variety of domesticated plants and animals from their Canaanite neighbors.

From biblical and archaeological information, scholars have learned that the Israelite farmer cultivated mainly field crops and fruit trees. Cereals, (such as wheat and barley), legumes (such as lentils and chickpeas), flax, and sesame were among the field crops. The biblical orchard produced grapes, used also for wine and raisins; olives (used for oil); figs; pomegranates; and dates. Many farmers also raised nuts—almonds, pistachios, and walnuts—and herbs—onions, leeks, and garlic. Spices included cumin and coriander.

The ancient farmer gradually replaced his copper and stone plows and other implements with iron ones. However, he continued to use flint for sickle and knife blades, although it lacked durability. Desiring greater efficiency, he learned to fertilize and rotate his crops for better yield and pest-control. He also built agricultural terraces, harnessed runoff rainwater—collecting it in cisterns or diverting it through channels to water his fields.

Though tilling the land was his main concern, the Israelite farmer kept some animals. Goats and sheep were raised mostly

Assyrian stone carving depicting an ancient method of raising water for irrigation; from Nineveh.

This Egyptian funerary model of a granary shows men loading grain.

This Egyptian wall painting shows men inspecting cattle; 15th century B.C., Thebes.

for milk and wool. Oxen, mules, donkeys, and camels were used as draft animals in the field and for transportation. Animals were seldom slaughtered for food, since meat was generally reserved for such special occasions as festivals or visits of important guests.

The harvest was stored in private and public facilities, in silos or jars above ground and dry cisterns underground. In addition, storage pits and rooms were constructed in or near the farmer's house to accommodate the daily needs of the family—flour for baking bread, oil for cooking and lighting, and wine for drinking. Dried fruit was stored in jars, mashed into cakes, or hung on strings.

The Bible said that it was the responsibility of the community to take care of the needy—the poor, the sojourner, the orphan, and the widow. Laws were therefore established to this end. These laws allowed the poor to participate in harvesting the seventh-year growth (Exodus 23:11; Leviticus 25:6); gave them an unharvested corner of the field (Leviticus 19:9; 23:22); allowed them to glean in the fields (Leviticus 19:9; 23:22), the vineyards (Leviticus 19:10; Deuteronomy 24:21), and the olive groves (Deuteronomy 24:21); left the small bunches of grapes for them in the vineyards (Leviticus 19:10); allowed them to have any sheaves left behind in the fields at the end of the day (Deuteronomy 24:19).

Agriculture was a major influence on the cultic calendar. The three main festivals were celebrated at the beginning and end of the growing season. Passover marked the beginning of spring, while the Feast of Weeks, 50 days later, marked the completion of the cereal harvest. *Sukkoth*, or the Feast of Tabernacles, was observed at the end of the growing season.

Indeed, agriculture was so important that blessings and curses were spelled out in terms of the success and failure of crops. The Israelite dream was to be able to dwell "in safety, from Dan even to Beersheba, every man under his vine and under his fig tree"(1 Kings 4:25). The hope for the future was an age of peace in which the nations would "beat their swords into plowshares, and their spears into pruning hooks." ✦

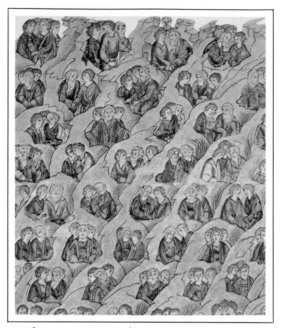

The generations of Genesis are portrayed in this 16th-century Russian manuscript.

Bloodlines of Genesis

The famous "begats" of the Bible

GENEALOGIES WERE OF great interest to the writers of the Bible. From the story of Adam to the birth of Jesus, the Bible provided elaborate lists of lineage. But perhaps the best-known of the biblical genealogies are those in the Book of Genesis. They link the generations of Adam, as the Bible calls them, to Abraham. These are the "begats" of the King James translation of the Bible.

There were ten generations from Adam to Noah, and another ten from Shem, Noah's son, to Abraham. Before the flood, men lived incredibly long lives: Adam, 930 years; Seth, his son, 912; Enosh, 905; Kenan, 910, and so on, with Methuselah, Noah's grandfather, living an astounding 969 years (Genesis 5). Noah's descendants, however, did not live as long. Shem, for example, died at the age of 600, and Abraham's father, Terah, lived to be 205. Abraham died "in a good old age" after a mere 175 years.

Noah had three sons: Shem, Ham, and Japheth. Shem is understood to be the progenitor of the "Semitic" peoples of the Middle East. From Ham came Egyptians, Canaanites, and Africans. Japheth's descendants included the Sea Peoples and the inhabitants of Asia Minor. "These are the families of Noah . . . and from these the nations spread abroad on the earth after the flood" (Genesis 10:32).

Why all this interest in names and national origins? There are several possible answers. First, from these passages the Israelites gained an understanding of their rich heritage. Second, by this method the Bible stressed that Hebrew culture did not develop in a vacuum. Israel's history was tightly linked with that of its neighbors. Finally, the equality of all people was underscored through these genealogies, since all of mankind, regardless of race or religion, could trace its ancestry back to Noah. ✦

The Tower of Babel

God punishes man's arrogance

THE GREATNESS OF MAN and the insignificance of man both have their place in the Bible. The famous story of the Tower of Babel vividly illustrates this dualism. This is also a story of man's defiance. Contrary to God's command that mankind disperse and fill the earth, vainglorious men strove to unite, building a city in celebration of their own greatness.

The Book of Genesis places the story during an indefinite period when "the nations spread abroad on the earth after the flood" and "the whole earth had one language and few words" (Genesis 11:1). However, the region where the events occurred is more certain: "And as men migrated from the east, they found a plain in the land of Shinar and settled there."

The land of Shinar, according to Genesis 10, was the location of the Mesopotamian cities of Babel, Erech, and Accad. Some scholars think that the opening of the Babel narrative constitutes a record of prehistoric tribal migrations that brought the Hebrews into the Fertile Crescent.

Erech, called Uruk in the Akkadian language, was a great temple city of ancient Mesopotamia, located southeast of Babylon. Its ruins have revealed the earliest known examples of writing, a kind of pictograph dating back to the fourth millennium B.C. Its legendary hero was the great Gilgamesh, whose epic adventures were celebrated in stirring poetry.

Akkad, (spelled *Accad* in Genesis), is truly a lost city. Archaeologists believe it lay near modern-day Baghdad, but have never discovered its remains. Still, it gave its name to an empire during the third millennium B.C., a whole region of ancient Mesopotamia, and to the Akkadian tongue, a Semitic language related to Hebrew.

Genesis recounts that these two cities of Shinar, along with the city of Babel, formed the original kingdom of Nimrod. This king was "the first on earth to be a mighty man" and "a mighty hunter before the LORD" (Genesis 10:8–9). The search for the historical identity of Nimrod has proved fruitless, although some scholars think the name may be connected with the Babylonian god Ninurta. Genesis linked the region around Babel (Babylon) to the origin of powerful rulers—later Mesopotamian kings who would play a destructive role in the history of the Israelites.

Thus the story of the Tower of Babel is firmly rooted in history. At the same time, it is symbolic of the larger story of humanity, originally united by one common language. Though it is a story of man's pride, no individual is ever mentioned.

The deep fertile soil of the land between the rivers provided no stone for building, but the people "had brick for stone, and bitumen for mortar." They made mud bricks, baked them, and held them together with bitumen, a natural asphalt found near the surface of the earth.

"Come," they said, "let us build ourselves a city, and a tower with its top in the heavens, and let us make a name for ourselves, lest we be scattered abroad upon the face of the whole earth" (Genesis 11:4). This summons is the heart of the story. It focuses on human ambition, expressed by the great artifacts of human culture. Here Genesis emphasizes the longing for renown symbolized by the city and its tower.

> "The function of religion is to confront the paradoxes and contradictions and the ultimate mysteries of man and the cosmos; to make sense and reason of what lies beneath the irreducible irrationalities of man's life; to pierce the surrounding darkness with pinpoints of light, or occasionally to rip away for a startling moment the cosmic shroud."
> —**Lewis Mumford**
> *The Conduct of Life*

Punished by an angry God, *builders of the Tower of Babel were scattered over the earth.*

The image of the city of Babel stood in sharp contrast to the nomadic life of Israel's patriarchs. Moreover, the episode at Babel foreshadowed the dangers Israel faced as it settled among the Canaanite cities, with their long-established cultures, rich temples, and inviting deities.

As the story of Babel was retold throughout the generations, the image of a tower "with its top in the heavens" was emphasized. It was said that the tower-builders attempted to reach well beyond earth to the realm of God—an extreme expression of man's pride. The Hebrew word for "heavens" (*shamayim*), however, also simply means "sky." Many scholars believe that the description of the tower in the Book of Genesis simply evoked a structure that was very tall in comparison to others.

Yahweh "came down to see the city and the tower which the sons of man had built." Displeased by mankind's arrogance, the

42

Lord said, "Behold, they are one people, and they have all one language; and this is only the beginning of what they will do; and nothing that they propose to do will now be impossible for them." Genesis does not imply that God was threatened by the tower itself, but rather that he saw some future extravagance of human action that needed to be prevented. God decided to restrain the ambition of humanity by introducing confusion and division.

"Come, let us go down," Yahweh said, "and there confuse their language" (Genesis 11:7). By making people "not understand one another's speech," God not only thwarted man's plans to build "a tower with its top in the heavens," but he caused the scattering of mankind throughout the world. "And they left off building the city."

Genesis states that the tower was built in Babel, which has been identified with Babylon—one of the most magnificent cities of the ancient world. The city's name in Akkadian evidently meant "Gate of God," but Genesis transformed its meaning by a wordplay on the Hebrew word *balal*, "confuse." "Its name was called Babel, because there the LORD *confused* the language of all the earth" (Genesis 11:9).

Was there really such a magnificent tower? Archaeologists point to the existence of one particular *ziggurat*, or "pinnacle," dedicated to the god Marduk. This ziggurat, which stood in the city of Babylon, was a massive stepped structure with a square base, nearly 300 feet tall. According to some estimates, there were some 30 lesser towers in Babylon. So marvelous was the ziggurat of Marduk that Babylonian legend attributed its construction to the gods.

The Babylonians indeed intended it to reach the skies, but not as a symbol of rebellion. Rather, it was an exalted altar by which the Babylonians served their deity. ✦

The dawn of civilization

Lost peoples of the ancient world

THE GREEKS CALLED the long, fertile valley between the Tigris and Euphrates rivers *Mesopotamia*, meaning "the land between the two rivers." Here the various cultures of the region flourished for three millennia. And it was here, in this fertile valley, that the world of the Bible slowly took shape.

Today the Middle East is characterized by vast deserts, harsh climates, and little rainfall. But during the last Ice Age, some 10,000 years ago, the entire valley was bordered by grasslands, where large herds of grazing animals roamed.

When the ice sheets retreated, much of the region became parched and barren. But the land between the rivers, which remained verdant, attracted nomadic tribes. As the rivers emerged from the mountains of Armenia, they carried a burden of silt, which produced great alluvial plains.

The Sumerians were among the nomadic tribes attracted to this fertile strip, with its abundant game. Over time, they built small settlements and learned to plant seeds and harvest grain. Thus began the domestication of crops and early glimmerings of civilization. Bronze tools have been unearthed by archaeologists, which give evidence of the development of culture.

Accomplished farmers, the Sumerians built canals for irrigation, which carried water from the slightly higher Euphrates to the lower Tigris. As the society flourished, the Sumerians established city-states, such as Ur and Uruk (known in the Bible as *Erech*). By the beginning of the third millennium, rivalries among these cities led to the establishment of a kingship.

Archaeology has revealed that the Sumerians were skilled in art, especially sculpture, and music. But their most important contribution was probably the invention of pictographic writing. Samples, dating from the

43

latter part of the fourth millennium, have been unearthed at Uruk. It was from this early form of writing that the distinctive cuneiform sign systems developed. Composed of wedge-shaped lines impressed in clay, cuneiform was widely used for centuries.

About a thousand years after its first settlements were built, Sumer and its cities were conquered by the armies of Sargon I, the ruler of a great Semitic empire centered in Akkad. The Akkadians left behind a rich literature, including a creation epic known as "Enuma Elish" and the famous "Epic of Gilgamesh." However, this empire lasted only four generations.

During the following decades, a resurgence of Sumerian culture took place. The Sumerian city of Ur became the center of a new Mesopotamian empire, under the rule of its former governor, Ur-Nammu. However, the dynasty he founded collapsed at the beginning of the second millennium B.C., when the Amorites invaded from the west and the Elamites from the east.

The Amorites established an empire in Babylon, and the city rose to great prominence. Hammurabi, the famous lawgiver who reunified Mesopotamia, was the sixth king of the First Dynasty of Babylon.

It was perhaps during the period of the Amorite invasion that Abraham's family moved to Haran in upper Mesopotamia. For centuries, this region was the contested site of powerful empires. Beginning in about 1600 B.C., it was dominated by the Mitanni empire, which, in its struggle with Egypt for power, pressed southward. The Mitanni subjugated the inhabitants of Canaan. Then they were, in turn, conquered by the Hittites, an Indo-European people who had established a strong kingdom in central Asia Minor in the second millennium B.C. Some 300 years later, the Hittite empire fell to invaders from the Greek islands.

Egyptian culture was already well established as early as the end of the fourth millennium B.C. By the middle of the third millennium, the pharaohs of Egypt's fourth dynasty, seeking immortality, had built the great pyramids. Around the beginning of

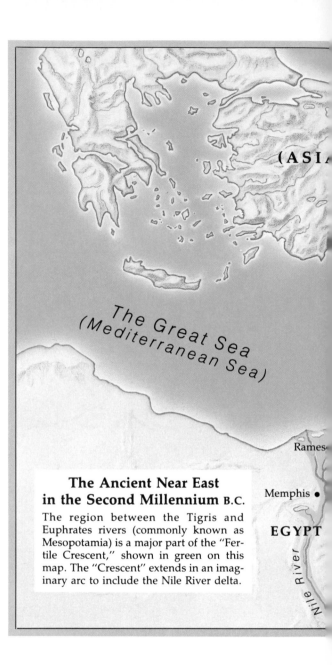

The Ancient Near East in the Second Millennium B.C.

The region between the Tigris and Euphrates rivers (commonly known as Mesopotamia) is a major part of the "Fertile Crescent," shown in green on this map. The "Crescent" extends in an imaginary arc to include the Nile River delta.

the second millennium, possibly during the 12th dynasty, Abraham sojourned in Egypt.

Egypt flourished for many of the same reasons that Mesopotamia did. The Nile River, fed by rainfall in the interior highlands, made the Nile Valley and the delta fertile. The annual flooding of the Nile has nourished the region since antiquity.

However, Egypt was repeatedly beset by war and strife. Around the 17th century

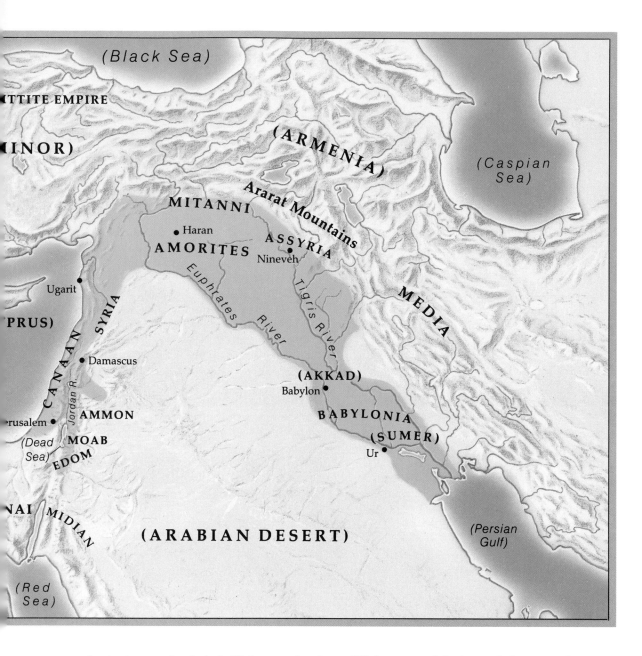

(Black Sea)

TTITE EMPIRE

INOR)

(ARMENIA)

(Caspian Sea)

MITANNI

Ararat Mountains

AMORITES

• Haran

ASSYRIA

Nineveh •

MEDIA

Ugarit •

Euphrates River

Tigris River

PRUS)

SYRIA

CANAAN

• Damascus

Jordan R.

(AKKAD)

Babylon •

rusalem •

AMMON

BABYLONIA

(Dead Sea)

MOAB

(SUMER)

EDOM

Ur •

NAI MIDIAN

(ARABIAN DESERT)

(Persian Gulf)

(Red Sea)

B.C., for instance, the Asiatic Hyksos gained domination. It may have been during this period that Joseph, Jacob's favorite son, rose to prominence by Pharaoh's side.

A rain-watered corridor along the eastern coast of the Mediterranean provided a link between the two fertile regions of Mesopotamia and Egypt. Known as the Via Maris, it supported farming and forests, and formed a commercial highway as well.

With parts of Syria and Assyria, these regions formed the famous "fertile crescent."

Thus, it was among these empires and ancient cultures that the people of Israel emerged. Semi-nomads living in the land of Canaan, the Israelites derived their identity and their strength from the single God they worshipped. Emerging from the ruins of now vanished empires, the Israelites forged a new vision for all mankind. ✦

Cities of the patriarchs

Exploring ancient Ur and Haran

THE BIBLE OUTLINES with precision the genealogy of the patriarchs. It reports that Terah, the father of Abraham, was a ninth-generation descendant of Shem, the oldest of Noah's three sons. There is no historical record other than the Bible itself that tells of Abraham. Nevertheless, we have no reason to doubt that Abraham and his descendants were real figures, and not merely symbols created hundreds of years later to help explain the origins of the Hebrew people. Many of the details of the patriarchal account in the Book of Genesis are supported by the political, cultural, and religious history of the second-millennium B.C. Near East.

Archaeological findings of the last century, most of them textual, have shed new light on the truth of the Genesis narrative. The story begins in Ur, which the Bible calls *Ur of the Chaldeans*. This name is an anachronism because Ur was not occupied by the Chaldeans, who were from the Persian Gulf area, until the 11th century B.C. Scholars are in general agreement that the events described in Genesis, chapters 12–50, took place much earlier—probably between the 20th and 16th centuries B.C.

Ur, located in southern Mesopotamia, was one of the largest cities in the kingdom of Sumer and later in Babylonia. Some scholars claim that Ur of the Chaldeans was a different place altogether from the Mesopotamian Ur, but most agree that Abraham and his family were from the Sumerian city, situated in what is today southern Iraq.

The city of Ur reached its peak of development during Sumer's Third Dynasty, around the 22nd–21st centuries B.C. The founder of the dynasty was Ur-Nammu, who, with his son Shulgi, extended the dominion of Sumer north to Akkad. Ur-Nammu compiled the oldest known collection of laws in the world, and he built the great temple, or ziggurat, in Ur.

A ziggurat (from the Akkadian word for pinnacle) was a temple built in the form of a stepped pyramid. The ziggurat of Ur had three steps, with the first providing the massive base. The shrine to the moon god, Nanna (*Sin* in Akkadian), was at the summit. It was reached by an outside stairway.

From the royal tombs at Ur, *this mosaic, made of lapis lazuli and shell, depicts peacetime.*

The ruins of this ziggurat have been partially restored, based on a reconstruction by the British archaeologist Leonard Woolley.

Woolley conducted excavations between 1922 and 1934 at the site of ancient Ur. One of his discoveries was a layer of red soil, over eight feet deep, that separated two distinct layers of remains. On the basis of this silt, which had been deposited by water, Woolley postulated that most of the settlements in a 38,610-square-mile (100,000-square-kilometer) area in the southern region of the Tigris and Euphrates rivers had been covered by a great flood.

He believed that this was the Great Flood of Genesis. But later researchers found similar flood layers in this region, dating to around 2800 to 2600 B.C.—too late to have been caused by the biblical flood.

Woolley's excavations of Ur's royal cemetery uncovered artistic treasure from about the 25th century B.C. The Standard of Ur, for example, consists of two mosaic panels, one portraying "war"—the triumph of the king over his enemies—and the other portraying "peace"—the celebration of victory.

This work not only reveals the artistic achievement of the Sumerians but also certain aspects of their society. The soldiers depicted on the war panel drive chariots with wooden wheels; they wear helmets and fringed skirts and capes. The peace panel indicates a love of music; a man plays the lyre, as a woman, perhaps a singer, follows. Many animals appear in this panel: a bull, an oryx, asses, and goats.

Another important find at the cemetery was a statue of a male goat—made of gold, silver, lapis lazuli, and white shell—standing upright against a flowering tree. To the Sumerians the natural world was invested with an array of supernatural forces, and this handsome statue may have had religious significance.

Near the beginning of the second millennium B.C., Ur went into an economic decline, and was invaded by the Amorite people from the West. Evidence suggests that during this period many families migrated from Ur. It may have been at this time that Abraham and his family left Ur for Canaan; however, when they reached Haran, some 600 miles (965 kilometers) away, they settled there instead of moving on. In ancient times Haran, located in northern Mesopotamia, was on a caravan route from Babylon, just north of Ur, to Asia Minor.

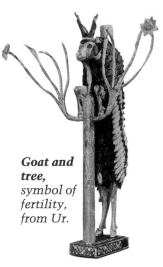

Goat and tree, symbol of fertility, from Ur.

The names of various members of Abraham's clan are reflected in the geography of the region: Haran and Nahor (the latter a town probably southeast of Haran) were the names of Abraham's two brothers, and Serug (identified with Sarugi, west of Haran) was the name of his great-grandfather. Both Ur and Haran were centers of the moon cult, which also seems to correlate with family names. *Terah*, the name of Abraham's father, may be related to the Aramaic word for moon. *Laban*, the name of Jacob's uncle and father-in-law, means white and was an epithet of the moon god.

In Haran, Abraham received and obeyed God's call to continue the journey to Canaan. Two generations later, Jacob, Israel's third patriarch, traveled from Canaan to Haran to seek refuge with Laban. These wanderings have an authentic ring, echoing the known movements of people in the second millennium B.C.

The extra-biblical evidence tends to corroborate the biblical account of the ancestors of Israel, and places it into historical context. In addition to the factors already cited, the legal and social traditions of various ancient Near Eastern cultures are similar to those conveyed in the Bible. So, although there will probably never be absolute proof of an historic Abraham, there is reason to believe that there was such a man, and that he is well served by his description in the Book of Genesis. ✦

*"**Behold, three men** stood in front of him."*

"A stranger and a sojourner"

Abraham: Father of the Israelites

ACCORDING TO THE BIBLE, God chose Abram (later to be called Abraham) to father the nation of Israel. "Now the LORD said to Abram, 'Go from your country and your kindred and your father's house to the land that I will show you. And I will make of you a great nation, and I will bless you, and make your name great.' "

The fact that the 75-year-old Abram was willing to uproot himself and give up his home suggests a man accustomed to obeying God. However, Genesis simply revealed that Abram's father was Terah, he had two brothers, and his wife's name was Sarai. Originating in the land of Ur in Mesopotamia, the family migrated toward the west.

Genesis gave so little explanation for the choice of Abram that later generations were inspired to fill in the gaps. For example, the Book of Jubilees, a second-century B.C. Jewish text, greatly elaborated on Abram's early years. At the age of 14, Abram already abhorred the idol-worship of his father.

For decades he urged his family to renounce this practice. When he was 60 years old, he set fire to the house of idols. As his kin scrambled to save their gods from destruction, Abram's brother Haran was burned in the flames. The Book of Jubilees shows that God called Abram because he had crusaded against idolatry.

According to Genesis, Abram took his

family to the city of Shechem, in the land of Canaan. God promised, "To your descendants I will give this land" (Genesis 12:7). However, Abram found that the land was already inhabited, and even more ominously, famine struck; Abram had to emigrate in order to survive. He journeyed to Egypt.

As he traveled, Abram had a strange thought. He feared that his wife Sarai was so beautiful that the Egyptians would kill him to possess her. Abram asked Sarai, "say that you are my sister that it may go well with me because of you, and that my life may be spared on your account." When the Egyptians saw Sarai they were struck by her beauty, and Pharaoh desired her for his harem. Abram did not protest when Sarai was taken into Pharaoh's household. Posing as Sarai's brother, Abram accepted gifts from the king.

But by surrendering Sarai to another, Abram endangered his relationship with the Lord. Rather than punishing Abram, Yahweh brought plagues upon Pharaoh and his house. Discovering the truth, Pharaoh returned Sarai to her husband, and sent them both away.

Later interpreters grappled with the moral dilemma the story presented. How could Abram, God's chosen, compromise his own wife? The Book of Jubilees omitted Abram's role and stated that Pharaoh tore Sarai away from Abram. Other interpreters laid great blame on Abram. Moses Nahmanides, a 13th-century Jewish scholar, suggested that Israel's later enslavement in Egypt was punishment for Abram's sin. However, the story in Genesis implied that God preserved and defended his promises even in the face of betrayal by Abram.

Once back in Canaan, Abram and his nephew Lot, who was traveling with him, "had flocks and herds and tents," and "the land could not support both of them dwelling together" (Genesis 13:5–6).

Abram offered Lot his choice of the land. "Is not the whole land before you?" he asked: "Separate yourself from me. If you take the left hand, then I will go to the right; or if you take the right hand, then I will go to the left." Lot chose to live near Sodom, in the plains of the Jordan Valley. His choice seemed sound, for the land was fertile, "like the garden of the LORD."

After Lot's departure, God reaffirmed his promise to Abram. "All the land which you see" would belong to his descendants, who were destined to be as numerous "as the dust of the earth" (Genesis 13:15–16).

Soon a war beset the region around the Jordan. The hostilities were of no concern to Abram, until he discovered that his nephew Lot had been taken prisoner. Despite their decision to part company, the ties of blood were strong. Abram organized an army of 318 men and, with them, defeated the enemy and recovered the prisoners.

On his return from battle, Abram met King Melchizedek of Salem, a "priest of God Most High." Abram donated a tenth part of the booty to the priest-king.

Who was Melchizedek, and where was Salem? How did Melchizedek become a priest of God; and why did Abram, God's chosen, give a title to this priest-king? The silence of Genesis left a mystery.

Apocryphal stories

Gaps in Bible narratives have inspired an impressive collection of legends, composed by those rich in faith and imagination. In the Middle Ages, many of these legends took so firm a hold that to this day many believe they are part of the Bible itself. For instance, the young Abraham has often been depicted smashing his father's idols, though the story does not appear in Genesis. When the mysteries of the Bible made a reader uneasy, legend often provided details that were less ambiguous. Thus, according to another legend, while Eve was pregnant with Cain, she succumbed again to the temptations of Satan. After she had given birth to both boys, Eve had a dream: she saw the blood of Abel flow into the mouth of Cain, who drank it greedily, though Abel beseeched him not to.

Psalm 76:2 identified Salem with Zion and Jerusalem. Psalm 110:4 linked the kings of Israel to Melchizedek, calling them priests "after the order of Melchizedek." It has been suggested that the Messiah in Psalm 110 was linked to Melchizedek. In the New Testament, the letter to the Hebrews speaks of Melchizedek as "resembling the Son of God" because he is "without father or mother or genealogy and has neither beginning of days nor end of life." Thus Melchizedek, it was argued, provided a pattern for the priesthood of Jesus as Messiah.

Having survived the ordeal of war, Abram received another pledge from God. "Fear not, Abram, I am your shield; your reward shall be very great." But Abram despaired of ever having children. He and Sarai were aging. God said, "Look toward heaven, and number the stars . . . So shall your descendants be."

As the sun set, Abram fell asleep, "and a dread and great darkness fell upon him." God told him about the future enslavement of his descendants and their eventual redemption. "Know of a surety that your descendants will be sojourners in a land that is not theirs, and will be slaves there and they will be oppressed for four hundred years; but I will bring judgment on the nation which they serve, and afterward they shall come out with great possessions." Why must Abram's people wait so long to inherit the Promised Land? God explained that it would be unjust to punish the Canaanites until their own actions warranted dispossession.

Ten years had passed since God's original call to Abram. On numerous occasions Yahweh had promised that Abram's considerable progeny would inherit the land of Canaan. Yet the patriarch and his wife remained childless.

While Abram seemed to have been satisfied with God's reassurances, Sarai was not. Following a common custom of the time, she gave Hagar, her Egyptian maid, to Abram, saying, "go in to my maid; it may be that I shall obtain children by her." Abram complied, and took Hagar as a concubine.

When Hagar conceived, however, she began to treat Sarai with contempt. The mistress lashed out with bitterness. "And Sarai said to Abram, 'May the wrong done to me be on you! I gave my maid to your embrace, and when she saw that she had conceived, she looked on me with contempt. May the LORD judge between you and me!' " Abram gave Sarai permission to discipline Hagar. "Then Sarai dealt harshly with her and she fled from her."

God had compassion on the mistreated servant. He sent an angel to her in the wilderness, advising her to return. The angel told Hagar that she was destined to produce many descendants through this son, who was to be called Ishmael. However, the angel stated, Ishamel would "be a wild ass of a man; his hand against every man and every man's hand against him" (Genesis 16:12). Hagar returned to Abram, and gave birth to her child.

Thirteen years passed before God appeared to the patriarch with more promises for the future. God wished to renew his covenant with Abram, and he renamed him Abraham, which means "father of a multitude of nations." God also gave Sarai the name Sarah. "I will make you exceedingly fruitful," said God to Abram, "and I will make nations of you."

Circumcision was part of God's renewed covenant with the patriarch. "Every male among you shall be circumcised . . . it shall be a sign of the covenant between me and you." Failure to fulfill the obligation brought severe sanctions, "any uncircumcised male . . . shall be cut off from his people; he has broken my covenant."

Thus, Abraham, Ishmael, and every male in Abraham's household were cir-

Abraham (left) met *Melchizedek.*

The agony of Hagar and Ishmael
in the wilderness.

cumcised "that very day." The people of ancient Israel were aware that many nations around them also practiced circumcision, but the origin of the rite is unknown. For the Israelites, however, circumcision was the sign of God's covenant with them.

God also informed Abraham that Sarah would have a son of her own. Abraham could only laugh. "Shall Sarah, who is ninety years old, bear a child?" He asked God to favor Ishmael, his first-born. But God repeated the promise. He said the son would be called Isaac, and asserted that Isaac, not Ishmael, would be the heir to Abraham's covenant with God.

As Abraham sat before his tent, he saw three men approaching. Assuming that they were travelers, he hastened to fulfill the duty of hospitality to the strangers. He bowed in greeting. "Let a little water be brought, and wash your feet," said Abraham, "and rest yourselves under the tree, while I fetch a morsel of bread . . . and after that you may pass on." He was unaware that the strangers were angelic messengers.

With Sarah's help, Abraham prepared a sumptuous meal for the guests. Sitting down to eat, the angels informed Abraham that Sarah would give birth to a son the following spring. Listening at the tent door,

Sarah laughed, "after I have grown old, and my husband is old, shall I have pleasure?" (Genesis 18:12). "Is anything too hard for the LORD?" was God's response.

The miracle that God had promised, the birth of a son to Abraham and Sarah, finally occurred. In keeping with the divine covenant, Abraham circumcised his son at the age of eight days. But the two sons in Abraham's family, Ishmael, son of Hagar the slave, and Isaac, son of Sarah, brought tension to the household.

Sarah insisted that Abraham dispose of "this slave woman with her son." But Abraham refused to cast out his own son. However, God himself intervened, explaining that Abraham's great mission would be continued through the progeny of Isaac. He reassured the patriarch, "I will make a nation of the son of the slave woman also, because he is your offspring."

God did indeed sustain Ishmael. The next morning Abraham sent Hagar and her son away with a supply of food and water. The water gave out in the middle of the wilderness, and "the child lifted up his voice and wept." But God "opened her eyes," enabling Hagar to see a well that saved both mother and son from death. From then on, "God was with the lad and he grew up." ✦

When Lot's wife glanced back at the burning city of Sodom, she turned into a pillar of salt.

Obliteration of the sinful cities

The crimes of Sodom and Gomorrah

THE ANGELS WHO visited Abraham took their leave and, with their host showing the way, set out for the city of Sodom. As they walked, God deliberated with himself: "Shall I hide from Abraham what I am about to do . . . ?" (Genesis 18:17). Since he had already chosen the patriarch "to keep the way of the LORD by doing righteousness and justice," God decided to reveal to Abraham his decision to carry out "righteousness and justice." He informed Abraham that Sodom and its sister city Gomorrah were suspected of grave sins. Their inhabitants were to be judged, and, if found guilty, punished (Genesis 18:19–21). Two of the angels were to be God's agents of punishment.

Abraham's response was astounding. Up to now so passive in accepting God's will and following his commands, Abraham suddenly protested. He defended the people of Sodom and Gomorrah, communities of undoubted wickedness, and sought some

way to convince God to spare them. "Wilt thou indeed destroy the righteous with the wicked?" he asked God. Surely there must be 50 righteous people living in these cities. Would not their merit suffice to prevent destruction? Abraham had the effrontery to challenge God, "Far be it from thee to do such a thing, to slay the righteous with the wicked, so that the righteous fare as the wicked! Far be that from thee! Shall not the Judge of all the earth do right?"

Abraham continued his protest. If there were not 50, were there 45 righteous, or 40? Perhaps 30, or at least 20? Surely there were 10? If even 10 could be found, God conceded, he would not destroy the cities. "And the LORD went his way, when he had finished speaking to Abraham; and Abraham returned to his place" (Genesis 18:33).

As Abraham set out for home, the two angels proceeded to Sodom where, "sitting in the gate," was Lot, the patriarch's nephew, who had gone to live there some years before. Lot, unaware that the strangers were angels, rose to meet them. He bowed with his face to the earth, and said, "My lords, turn aside, I pray you, to your servant's house and spend the night, and wash your feet; then you may rise up early and go on your way" (Genesis 19:1–2). The angels accepted his invitation, entered his home, and ate the meal that Lot had prepared.

Up to this point, the Bible has not revealed what sins the Sodomites had committed. But the specific nature of their guilt becomes clear. The visitors had been seen entering Lot's house, and "the men of the city, the men of Sodom, both young and old, all the people to the last man, surrounded the house; and they called to Lot, 'Where are the men who came to you tonight? Bring them out to us, that we may know them' " (Genesis 19:4–5).

In ancient custom, the responsibility of a host to protect guests was considered to be nearly absolute. Genesis could give no more vivid demonstration of Sodom's depravity than by describing the attempt of "all the people" to assault these guests. The wickedness of Sodom that condemned it to destruction was a lack of basic human decency: infringement on the sacredness of the host's hospitality.

Lot's desperate efforts to protect his guests are described in Genesis. He offered his two virgin daughters to the men of Sodom. "Let me bring them out to you, and do to them as you please," he said. But the people insisted on the visitors (Genesis 19:8). Angered by Lot's refusal to let them in the door, they turned their ire against him: "This fellow came to sojourn, and he would play the judge! Now we will deal worse with you than with them" (Genesis 19:9).

Since Lot was Abraham's nephew, the angelic visitors meant to save him and his family while destroying all the others. They brought Lot into the house, shut the door, and struck the Sodomites with blindness so that they could not see the door. Then they ordered Lot to gather his family before the coming catastrophe. When morning came, the angels pulled Lot, his wife, and two daughters out of the city, advising them, "Flee for your life; do not look back or stop anywhere in the valley; flee to the hills, lest you be consumed" (Genesis 19:17).

With Lot and his family safe, the punishment came. "The LORD rained on Sodom and Gomorrah brimstone and fire from the LORD out of heaven; and he overthrew those cities, and all the valley, and all the inhabitants of the cities, and what grew on the ground" (Genesis 19:24–25).

Lot's wife, unable to resist the temptation of looking back to see what had happened to her home, "became a pillar of salt" (Genesis 19:26).

Lot and his two daughters were the sole survivors of Sodom's destruction. When Abraham rose early in the morning, he could see the smoke rising from where the city used to be, "like the smoke of a furnace" (Genesis 19:28).

Archaeologists have discovered that the southern part of the Dead Sea was once dry and fertile, the home of flourishing societies. Scholars have suggested that an earthquake could have caused the Dead Sea to spread southward, covering the existing cities and leaving the land barren. Thus the account of Sodom's destruction may be based on an actual event. Even today visitors are amazed at the salt deposits in the area, and recall the account of Lot's wife being turned into a pillar of salt. ✦

"Pillars of salt" in the Dead Sea.

53

The angel of the Lord *stayed Abraham's hand, saving Isaac.*

The sacrifice of Isaac

The Lord requires an awful obedience

AS TERRIBLE AS IT WAS for Abraham to send his son Ishmael away, his final, most excruciating test was yet to come. This test was to involve Isaac, the son of his old age. God called on him to "take your son, your only son Isaac, whom you love, and go to the land of Moriah, and offer him there as a burnt offering upon one of the mountains of which I shall tell you."

What was Abraham to make of this? From the initial call to leave his homeland and set out for the Promised Land, his entire life had been based on the seemingly impossible hope of having sons to carry on his line and inherit his patrimony. With Ishmael gone, Isaac was his sole heir. And now the same God who had miraculously granted a son to Abraham and Sarah was insisting on the sacrifice of that child. What could this awful demand mean? And what kind of a father would heed it? Surely the man who had negotiated with God to forestall the destruction of the wicked cities of Sodom and Gomorrah would question the justice of sacrificing an innocent child.

Yet the Bible does not portray Abraham as outraged against such a horror, but rather as an obedient and silent servant of the Lord. Rising early in the morning, he saddled his ass, took wood to be used at the

54

sacrifice, and brought Isaac along with two servants "to the place of which God had told him" (Genesis 22:3).

After traveling for three days, they saw the place from afar. Leaving the servants with the ass, "they went both of them together," Isaac carrying the wood on his back, and Abraham carrying the fire and a knife. But Isaac's suspicions were aroused. "Behold, the fire and the wood," he said, "but where is the lamb for a burnt offering?" With simplicity, beneath which one senses the kind of hope against hope that had moved him throughout his life, Abraham responded, "God will provide himself the lamb for a burnt offering, my son."

When they reached the appointed place, hope was waning. Abraham built an altar, laid the wood on it, and in grim silence tied Isaac down. As Abraham was about to plunge the knife into his son, an angel stopped him, calling "Abraham, Abraham! . . . Do not lay your hand on the lad or do anything to him; for now I know that you fear God, seeing you have not withheld your son, your only son, from me."

Abraham untied Isaac from the altar and replaced him with a ram. "And the angel of the LORD called to Abraham a second time from heaven, and said, 'By myself I have sworn, says the LORD, because you have done this, and have not withheld your son, your only son, I will indeed bless you, and I will multiply your descendants as the stars of heaven and as the sand which is on the seashore. And your descendants shall possess the gate of their enemies, and by your descendants shall all the nations of the earth bless themselves, because you have obeyed my voice' " (Genesis 22:15–18).

This powerful story, which the Bible conveys in stark, unembellished prose, has fascinated countless readers through the ages. Bible scholars have sought to pierce the mystery, theorizing that the story was meant to show a transition from child sacrifice to animal sacrifice. Yet nowhere in the account is child sacrifice discussed. And later stories in the Bible recount instances of it, which casts doubt on this interpretation.

In fact, Abraham's final test is exactly that—a trial of his devotion to God. For Jews, the binding of Isaac has been a powerful theological symbol. The Jew's devotion to God, it was taught, should be modeled on Abraham's unquestioning obedience and Isaac's meek acquiescence.

In the Christian tradition, Abraham's willingness to sacrifice his son Isaac prefigures God the Father's willingness to let his son Jesus die on the cross for the salvation of all mankind. In the Islamic religion (the word "Islam" means "submission" in Arabic), this narrative plays a pivotal role. Interestingly, Moslem tradition holds that it was Ishmael, progenitor of the Arab people, and not Isaac, who was brought to be sacrificed.

Tradition equates the mountain of the sacrifice with the Mount Moriah on which the Jerusalem Temple was built. Thus, Israel's worship through the centuries was linked to Abraham's trial. To this day, Moriah is considered to be sacred by millions. Capped by the Dome of the Rock, a Moslem holy site, Mount Moriah looms above the modern, sprawling city of Jerusalem.

When Isaac came of age, the elderly Abraham, eager to see him married in his own lifetime, sent a servant to Mesopotamia to find a suitable wife for him. Loaded with "choice gifts," the servant arrived at the city of Nahor and sat down by the town well to wait for a sign. Rebekah appeared, "very fair to look upon, a virgin, whom no man had known." Moreover, she was Isaac's cousin. Meeting Rebekah's father and brother, the servant explained his mission. Rebekah's father said: "The thing comes from the LORD . . . Behold, Rebekah is before you, take her and go, and let her be the wife of your master's son." ✦

"The great thing was that he loved God so much that he was willing to sacrifice to Him the best. . . . Where is the man with a soul so bewildered that he would have the presumption to weep for Abraham? . . . for how could Abraham do anything but what is great and glorious?"
—S. Kierkegaard
Fear and Trembling

55

A stolen blessing

The schemer who wrestled with God

THE ACCOUNT OF JACOB in the book of Genesis tells the story of a complex man who lived in a world vastly different from our own. With a wonderful realism, punctuated by historical and religious mysteries, the narratives take a modern reader back nearly 4,000 years into the early second millennium B.C.

It has been said that the Book of Genesis tells but one story, that of a younger son surpassing an elder. And nowhere is that pattern more vivid than in the powerful story of Jacob and Esau.

Rebekah, the wife of Isaac, was barren— like Sarah before her and Rachel after her. Yahweh intervened to allow her to conceive, but the babies in her womb so turned and struggled that she wondered if she could survive. She obtained an oracle from Yahweh, however, that gave the kicking in her womb epic meaning: "Two nations are in your womb, and two peoples, born of you, shall be divided; the one shall be stronger than the other, the elder shall serve the younger" (Genesis 25:23).

Twin boys were born, but they were hardly identical twins. The first to emerge, a red, hairy baby, was named Esau. The chance of birth had made him the firstborn, bearer of the birthright. In ancient times, the firstborn enjoyed a number of advantages. From a religious standpoint, the firstborn of any species possessed a degree of sanctity. Indeed, in Jewish law even today, a male firstborn must be "redeemed" from a priest at the age of 30 days. Before the initiation of the Israelite priesthood, it was the firstborn who performed all cultic functions. Finally, the eldest also received a double share of the father's inheritance.

But before the first infant was fully out, the hand of his brother emerged grasping his heel (Hebrew, *ageb*). Thus the second twin was named Jacob (*Yaaqob*).

Jacob's name illustrates the delight that the narrator repeatedly takes in audacious wordplays that can illuminate the characters in the story. The etymology of the name Jacob is "God protects." But in the context of the story, the pun on the word for "heel" and the closely related word meaning "defraud" or "supplant" (*agab*) best reveals the character of Jacob.

The twins grew up to be very different from one another. Isaac's favorite was Esau, "a skilful hunter, a man of the field," while "Jacob was a quiet man, dwelling in tents," and the favorite of Rebekah (Genesis 25:27–28). Family conflict was inevitable.

Our next glimpse of the twins reveals Jacob cooking pottage, a thick red lentil soup. In came Esau, famished after a luckless day of hunting. "Let me eat some of that red pottage," he begged. Jacob saw an opportunity and immediately grasped it. "First sell me your birthright," he demanded. Esau could not see beyond his momen-

---

THE STORY BEHIND THE WORD

✑ Israel ✑

It is curious that the first appearance of the word *Israel* is in one of the most deeply mysterious passages in the Bible (Genesis 32:28). The exact meaning of the word is not certain. *Israel* may mean "he who fights Gods," "he who fights for God," "he whom God fights," "he whom God rules," "the upright one of God," or "God is upright."

When the kingdom of Israel was divided in 922 B.C., the northern kingdom remained *Israel*, while the southern one was called *Judah*. The land itself, as bordered on the west by the Mediterranean Sea, and on the east by the Jordan River, is called *Erez Israel*, the Land of Israel.

tary hunger and swore that Jacob could have it. For a bowl of soup Jacob had gained the right to become leader of the clan and had brought the oracle given to Rebekah a step nearer fulfillment. Later Esau was angry with Jacob, but though Jacob might be criticized as opportunistic and self-serving, no apparent deceit was involved. The narrator condemns Esau because he "despised his birthright" (Genesis 25:29–34).

Time passed. Esau married two Hittite women. Isaac, more than a century old, grew blind and was apparently near death, and he wished to give his patriarchal blessing to his beloved Esau. Such a blessing was thought of not just as a prediction of the future but as a powerful statement that would determine the future. It has been compared to an arrow; once shot it could not be called back.

Isaac told Esau: "Behold, I am old; I do not know the day of my death. Now then . . . hunt game for me, and prepare for me savory food, such as I love, and bring it to me, that I may eat; that I may bless you before I die." But Rebekah overheard, and in one of the most striking displays of female initiative in the Bible, took matters into her own hands. She knew well the savory spices Isaac loved, and conspired to ensure that Jacob receive the valued blessing. She dressed Jacob in Esau's robes, and put the skins of kids on his hands and neck because "Esau is a hairy man."

Isaac was suspicious when Jacob, posing as Esau, arrived so soon, sounding so different from Esau. But the disguise worked. "I am Esau your first-born," Jacob said. So Isaac spoke the powerful words over Jacob rather than his favorite: He would have the "fatness of the earth and plenty of grain and wine . . . Let peoples serve you, and . . . be lord over your brothers."

With dramatic poignancy, the narrator describes how Esau arrived just a moment after Jacob left. When he realized that the

With his mother's help, *Jacob disguised himself as his brother Esau. Thus, by deception, Jacob gained his father's blessing.*

blessing had been given to his brother, "he cried out with an exceedingly great and bitter cry" and begged for any remnant of a blessing that might remain. Isaac could only tell him, "By your sword you shall live, and you shall serve your brother; but when you break loose you shall break his yoke from your neck" (Genesis 27:40).

Hatred flared in Esau, and in desperation he made plans to break Jacob's yoke by killing him. Rebekah heard of his threats but knew that her son's anger would be short-lived. She urged Jacob to "flee to Laban my brother in Haran . . . until your brother's fury turns away" (Genesis 27:44).

There follows a puzzling episode. After urging Jacob to "flee," Rebekah arranged for Jacob to travel to Haran with Isaac's full blessing to find a wife. Such a trip would have involved a caravan of gifts like the 10 camel loads that were sent when Rebekah was found for Isaac (Genesis 24:10). Later, however, it becomes clear that Jacob left home as a fugitive with only his staff in his hand. Such puzzles within the story indicate that more than one source may have contributed to the present narrative.

As Jacob traveled north, one phase of his life was ending, and another one, an uncertain future, was beginning. While he pos-

sessed both the birthright and the patriarchal blessing, he owned nothing but the staff he was carrying. At nightfall he lay down where he was. Using a stone as a pillow, he fell into an exhausted sleep.

It was then that Jacob had the famous dream, where he saw "a ladder," or more properly, "a staircase" reaching to heaven and "angels of God were ascending and descending on it!" Without realizing it, Jacob had come to "none other than the house of God, and this is the gate of heaven" (Genesis 28:12–17). Jacob evidently understood that he had come to the sacred spot where angels move between earth and heaven on their missions for God.

From above the staircase Yahweh spoke: he renewed the promises God had made to Abraham and Isaac. The land of Canaan would belong to him and his multitudes of descendants, and Yahweh would be with him and return him to this land.

To mark the presence of God in the place, Jacob set up his stone pillow as a pillar, sanctified it with oil, and he called the place Bethel, which means "house of God." He vowed that if God would bless him, Yahweh would be his God.

The tradition regarding God's appearance to Jacob helps explain the importance of the ancient sanctuary at Bethel. Archaeo-

The dream of Jacob's ladder *signified that Jacob would be the father of the nation of Israel.*

Jacob loved Rachel at first sight.

logical excavations have indicated that it was a flourishing city throughout the period of the patriarchs, and Genesis 12:3 indicates that Abraham lived outside Bethel for a period. During the time of the judges, Bethel was an important sanctuary, and when the kingdom split it was one of the principal temple cities of the north.

Jacob traveled some 400 miles north across the Euphrates River to Haran, the home of his uncle Laban in "the land of the people of the east" (Genesis 29:1). Just as his mother Rebekah had been discovered at a well, so Jacob immediately met and aided his cousin Rachel at a well near Haran. The well was covered by a huge stone that normally required several people to remove. But "when Jacob saw Rachel . . . Jacob went up and rolled the stone from the well's mouth, and watered the flock of Laban."

For a month Jacob enjoyed the hospitality of Laban and his daughters Leah and Rachel (whose names mean "cow" and "ewe" respectively). Rachel was lovely, but "Leah's eyes were weak," evidently meaning they lacked luster. Laban is possibly one of the most subtly drawn villains in the Bible. His very name, which in Hebrew means "white" and connotes purity, conceals an exploitative personality. But Jacob agreed to work for Laban—for very special wages. Jacob had fallen in love: "I will serve you seven years," he promised, "for your younger daughter Rachel." The proposal illustrates well how, in that ancient society,

daughters literally belonged to their fathers: they could be paid out as wages for labor.

Laban agreed, and the seven years passed like days for the love-struck Jacob. The wedding night arrived. His veiled bride was brought to him, and the marriage was consummated. But when the veils were lifted, Jacob discovered not Rachel but Leah. With cold-blooded treachery, the man who was his benefactor had betrayed him.

Jacob was outraged. But Laban explained: "It is not so done in our country, to give the younger before the first-born." He offered to give Jacob Rachel also—in exchange for another seven years of service.

Jacob now had two wives, one imposed upon him by fraud. And since "he loved Rachel more than Leah," his second seven-year term of service to Laban was not marked by domestic bliss. The beloved Rachel—like Sarah and Rebekah before her—could not bear a child. Leah, on the other hand, had four sons very quickly. Scripture attributes her fertility to God's compassion: "When the Lord saw that Leah was hated, he opened her womb." Indeed, the names Leah chose for her first three sons—Reuben, Simeon, and Levi—have Hebrew derivations that refer ruefully to her unfavored status. Her fourth son was Judah, which means, "I will praise the Lord."

Rachel, watching helplessly as Leah bore son after son, "envied her sister." "Give me children, or I shall die!" she cried to Jacob.

These Syrian household gods—*small, portable statues of ancestors—are like the ones that Rachel stole.*

Rachel adopted a tactic used by Sarah before her, resorting to concubinage. She gave her maidservant Bilhah to Jacob, with the understanding that the children would be considered hers. Bilhah bore two sons, Dan and Naphtali. Then Leah gave her maidservant Zilpah to Jacob, and out of this union came Gad and Asher. Shortly thereafter, Leah gave birth to two more boys, Issachar and Zebulun, and a girl, Dinah. Finally, "God remembered Rachel, and God hearkened to her and opened her womb. She conceived and bore a son, and said, 'God has taken away my reproach'; and she called his name Joseph" (Genesis 30:22–24).

While the unintended marriage to Leah produced strife, it also helped to produce the bounty that would be the 12 tribes of Israel. In fact, two of Leah's sons, Judah and Levi, would later become two of the most important figures of Judaism. From Judah would come the Davidic kingdom, and from Levi, the priesthood.

After the second seven years of labor, Jacob struck another strange bargain with Laban. He would continue to serve Laban, but only if he could begin to build his own flocks. He would take the black lambs and the speckled or spotted sheep and goats. Laban agreed, but then he quickly removed from Jacob's care any such animals that were already in the flocks. But this handicap did not stop Jacob. In front of the watering troughs where the animals mated, he set up wooden rods with white streaks on them,

believing that what the animals saw as they mated would affect the coloring of their offspring. Incredibly, the scheme worked, "the flocks bred in front of the rods and so the flocks brought forth striped, speckled and spotted" (Genesis 30:39). Jacob "grew exceedingly rich" and God told him to leave Laban and return to Canaan.

Jacob's two wives agreed to leave their father, and while Laban was off shearing his sheep, they fled with all their possessions across the Euphrates. As they left, Rachel secretly stole her father's household gods (Genesis 31:19). Laban was incensed. He pursued them almost all the way into Canaan and would have done them harm except that God warned him in a dream to "say not a word to Jacob, either good or bad" (Genesis 31:24).

When Laban confronted Jacob he said that he could understand his desire to return to his home, "but why did you steal my gods?" Unaware of Rachel's deed, Jacob swore that "any one with whom you find gods shall not live." Laban began ransacking the tents: Jacob's, Leah's, the maidservants', and finally Rachel's. By that time Rachel had hidden the gods (in Hebrew, *teraphim*) in her camel saddle and was sitting on them. She said she could not rise for her father, "for the way of women is upon me."

What were these *teraphim* that Laban was so desperate to regain? They were probably small, rather common looking figurines, not valuable as objects, but valuable for what they represented. Some ancient texts suggest that they symbolized the legal right to an estate. Laban would have handed them down to his eldest son; so for Rachel to take them was tantamount to stealing the symbol of the birthright, if not the birthright itself.

In any case it is clear that the *teraphim* had important religious functions. They were widely used to obtain various kinds of oracles about the future and played a role in a clan's worship. Throughout most of the history of ancient Israel, such *teraphim* continued to be widely used in spite of prophetic condemnations of them. The prophet Hosea listed them among the common religious institutions of the nation (Hosea 3:4).

Once Laban's anger had abated, the two schemers were able to make a covenant between them. They set up a heap of stones as a "witness" that each would treat the other justly and that Jacob would not ill-treat his wives, the daughters of Laban. And the two men parted in peace.

As Jacob turned his attention toward Canaan, he was overwhelmed with fear. He had expected that Esau would meet him with great hostility. When his messengers brought word that Esau was coming with four hundred men, Jacob prepared for the worst. He divided his company so that at least half might escape destruction, prayed to God for deliverance, and strung out in front of him a procession of different droves of animals as gifts to appease Esau.

The night before Esau's expected arrival, Jacob sent his family to safer ground across the Jabbok River, and he remained alone. That night he experienced one of the most mysterious manifestations of God ever described in the Bible. The Book of Genesis simply says "a man wrestled with him until the breaking of the day," but he could not overcome Jacob. The man "touched the hollow of the thigh;

and Jacob's thigh was put out of joint," but still Jacob would not release him. "I will not let you go unless you bless me," he said. The man asked his name, and he replied, "Jacob." "Your name shall no more be called Jacob," the stranger said, "but Israel, for you have striven with God and with men, and have prevailed." Still Jacob wanted to know his name. The man refused but gave Jacob, now Israel, the blessing he desired (Genesis 32:30).

Jacob could hardly believe what had happened. He called the place Peniel, meaning "face of God," because, he said, "I have seen God face to face, and yet my life is preserved" (Genesis 32:24–32).

Esau's wrath, which Jacob feared, turned out to be graciousness, welcome, and forgiveness. By now Jacob had learned the value of such qualities; indeed, meeting Esau was the fitting conclusion to his wrestling with God and men. "To see your face," Israel told his brother, "is like seeing the face of God, with such favor have you received me" (Genesis 33:10). Jacob was ready to continue the line of patriarchs to whom God had promised so much. ✦

The last thing Jacob expected was Esau's greeting him with gladness.

*"**And they took him** and cast him into a pit."*

Joseph: Master of dreams

Rising above betrayal

CAN HARSH CIRCUMSTANCES and malicious intentions be turned to good account? The story of Joseph answers with an emphatic yes. As William Cowper's 18th-century hymn says, "God moves in a mysterious way, his wonders to perform." The belief that God's providence may be at work even in human evil is one of the perennial mysteries of the Bible.

Joseph suffered from the hatred of his brothers, which led to his enslavement. Later, he was imprisoned on false charges and forgotten in prison even by those whom he helped. Still, as he looked back on his life, he was able to say to his brothers, "You meant evil against me; but God meant it for good, to bring it about that many people should be kept alive, as they are today" (Genesis 50:20).

The ancient Hebrew language has no word for the concept of "providence." But in the story of their people, the Israelites saw again and again the hand of God guiding events toward his own ends.

The story of Joseph is the longest of the patriarchal narratives of Genesis, longer than the accounts of Abraham and Isaac together. Within the story are woven numerous themes and historical elements.

The older brothers portray crime and guilt, repentance and reconciliation; Joseph in Egypt is the very embodiment of the wise man. Even in the greatest adversity he was true to his master and to himself. His piety and wisdom brought him success. The story of Joseph's travail reveals how the Israelites were separated from the land they had been promised by God, and how Israel grew to be a nation in a foreign country.

Joseph was the eleventh of Jacob's 12 sons by four women. But he was the first son of Rachel, the wife whom Jacob really loved. Like Sarah before her, and the mothers of Samson and Samuel after her, Rachel had been barren. Thus the birth of Joseph is described as an act of God, who opened her womb (Genesis 30:22). Rachel died giving birth to a second son, Benjamin. So it was that Jacob lavished all his love on her sons.

Joseph was portrayed as the favored and pampered 17-year-old son of a doting father, who "loved him more than all his brothers." As a result "they hated him, and could not speak peaceably to him."

Jacob's favoritism was expressed by his gift to Joseph of a "coat of many colors," as the King James version of the Bible described it. The exact meaning of the Hebrew phrase is a puzzle, however, and no one knows for sure just what made this garment so special. The ancient Greek translators of the Bible took the Hebrew word *passim* to mean "multicolored," and that provided the basis for the King James translation. Studies in modern times have suggested a range of meanings, such as "a long robe with sleeves" or "an ornamented ceremonial robe." Thus, the coat was not the rough tunic that his brothers would have worn, but a luxurious robe that spoke clearly of his privileged status.

Joseph's dreams were another important facet of the story. Dreams were assumed to be a means of a divine communication that indicated the future. In Joseph's first dream the family was binding sheaves of grain. Joseph's sheaf stood upright, and his brother's sheaves bowed to it. In his second dream Joseph said, "the sun, the moon, and eleven stars were bowing down to me." Even Jacob took offense, "Shall I and your mother and your brothers indeed come to bow ourselves to the ground before you?" (Genesis 37:5–10).

After Joseph revealed these dreams, the jealousy and hatred of his brothers became implacable. But Joseph only reported the dreams God had sent; he did not interpret them. The narrator seems careful to attribute no excessive pride to Joseph. He appeared oblivious to the hatred his father's favoritism and his dreams had aroused.

Joseph's brothers showed his bloodstained coat to their father Jacob.

The older brothers were grazing Jacob's flock north of Hebron, where the family dwelled at the time. Jacob sent Joseph, wearing his decorated coat, to see how they were faring. When Joseph reached Shechem, where his brothers were supposed to be, he was told that they had gone to the town of Dothan—well outside the reach of his father's protection. As he approached Dothan, the brothers saw him in the distance. "Here comes this dreamer" (literally, "master of dreams"), they said, and their hostility became murderous. "Come now, let us kill him . . . and we shall see what will become of his dreams."

But Reuben, the eldest, said, "Shed no blood; cast him into this pit here in the wilderness, but lay no hand upon him." Thus they stripped off the robe and threw Joseph into an empty cistern. Reuben secretly hoped to return later, rescue Joseph, and bring him back to his father.

Dothan was on a major trade route, and soon there came a camel caravan from Gilead carrying luxury items of gum, balm, and myrrh to Egypt. These items were extracts from plant resins, used for their fragrance or healing qualities. Joseph's brother Judah immediately saw the opportunity for profit that these traders offered, and said, "What profit is it if we slay our brother and conceal his blood? Come, let us sell him to the Ishmaelites." Thus they sold Joseph for 20 shekels of silver.

When the brothers returned home they went to their father and showed him Joseph's robe, which they had spattered with goat's blood. Jacob fell into their trap no less than Joseph: "A wild beast has devoured him," he cried, "I shall go down to Sheol to my son, mourning" (Genesis 37:33–35). The brothers thought that they had permanently rid themselves of Joseph.

In Egypt, Joseph was sold to a nobleman, Potiphar, a name meaning "he whom Re [the sun god] has given." Potiphar is described in Hebrew as a *saris*, literally a eunuch, but, since he was married, it probably meant that he was a royal official. He was called "captain of the guard" and was one of the chief officials of Egypt.

Joseph was an immediate success under Potiphar. This was because Yahweh was with him. He quickly rose from foreign slave to Potiphar's overseer "in charge of all that he had" (Genesis 39:2–4). But Joseph could progress no further in Potiphar's service. To rise higher, he had first to fall.

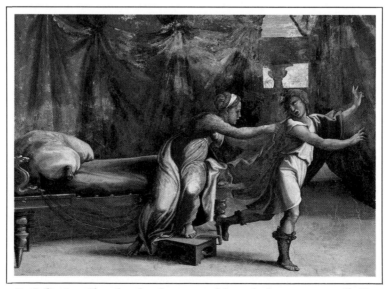

Potiphar's wife relentlessly pursued Joseph, but to no avail. He repelled her, refusing to dishonor his master and his God.

The instrument of his fall was Potiphar's wife. Joseph's near-tragedy bears a remarkable likeness to the events described in the ancient Egyptian story "The Tale of the Two Brothers." The wife of the elder brother attempted to seduce the boy Bata. When she failed, she lied to her husband, who set out furiously to kill his brother. Miraculously, he discovered the truth—and slew his dishonest wife. Potiphar's wife repeatedly tried to seduce Joseph, who was shocked at the proposition: "How then can I do this great wickedness and sin against God?" Angry at being spurned, the woman tore part of Joseph's garments and accused him of trying to rape her.

Potiphar was angry, but he did not execute the slave, which was the standard punishment for the offense. Instead, he placed him in the royal prison. There, as before, Joseph was successful and quickly became overseer of the other captives.

Joseph was put in charge of two special prisoners—Pharaoh's butler and baker, who had committed some offense. They each were troubled by dreams. When they complained that they had no one to interpret their dreams, Joseph asserted that "interpretations belong to God." However, he implied that he had access to that secret knowledge: "Tell them to me, I pray you" (Genesis 40:8).

Like Joseph's, the prisoners' dreams predicted the future. The butler had dreamed that in three days he would be squeezing the grapes into Pharaoh's cup once again. But the baker's dream indicated that in three days he would be executed. With knowledge of the future, Joseph begged the butler to remember him to Pharaoh when he was restored to his position. Though everything occurred just as Joseph had predicted, the butler forgot him.

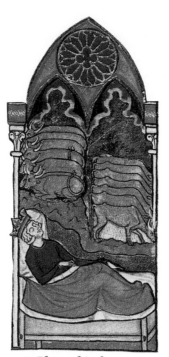

Pharaoh's dream.

Joseph passed two more years in prison. One morning the royal court was in a stir. Pharaoh had dreamed two portentous dreams, and "all the magicians of Egypt and all its wise men" were baffled by their meaning (Genesis 41:8). The Egyptians thought themselves to be able interpreters, but when faced with Pharaoh's dreams, they were at a loss. Finally the butler remembered Joseph, and he was brought, shaved and cleaned, before Pharaoh.

Pharaoh's dreams were straightforward, but their meaning was obscure. First, seven well-fed cows emerged from the Nile, but they were followed and devoured by seven gaunt cows that grew no fatter. Then, seven plump heads of grain growing on a single stalk were swallowed by seven blighted heads of grain.

With God-given confidence, Joseph reported the meaning of the dreams. Seven years of plentiful harvest would be followed by seven disastrous years of famine. The doubling of the dream indicated that the future was "fixed by God" (Genesis 41:32). Wisdom dictated a prudent policy of storing grain against the famine, and Joseph advised that the whole of Egypt's agricultural economy be marshaled behind his interpretation of Pharaoh's dream.

Pharaoh was immediately convinced. He elevated Joseph, a foreign prisoner, to be viceroy of Egypt, with a mandate to control its grain supply. Joseph was given Pharaoh's signet ring and a long Egyptian name meaning "God speaks: he is living!" (Genesis 41:45). He married the daughter of an Egyptian priest, and she bore him two sons, Manasseh and Ephraim.

At the end of seven plentiful years, Joseph had stored more grain than could be measured. When famine struck, the grain that had been stored was sold back to the

Joseph could no longer *refrain from revealing his true identity, and cried aloud, "I am your brother, Joseph, whom you sold into Egypt."*

people, and Pharaoh's economic control of the land was strengthened.

When the effects of the famine reached Canaan, Jacob sent 10 of his sons to Egypt to buy grain. As Joseph's brothers bowed before him, not only was his original dream fulfilled but his brothers were in his power. The story is told with pathos. Joseph recognized his brothers, but they did not realize that the Egyptian viceroy was the brother they had sold into slavery.

Joseph devised a number of trials to test the character of his brothers. First, he accused them of being spies. Then he impris-

oned them, held Simeon as a hostage, and demanded that they send for Benjamin, the youngest brother. Now, the brothers, in their own language, expressed regret at having sinned against young Joseph. "So now there comes reckoning for his blood," Reuben said. Hearing Reuben's remorse, Joseph turned away and wept.

On their return to Egypt with Benjamin, Joseph treated the brothers with unexpected graciousness, but as soon as they had left for Canaan, with Simeon restored to them, he had them arrested for the theft of a silver goblet. To their complete consternation, the cup was discovered in Benjamin's sack of grain. Though innocent of the theft, he was condemned to death.

But Joseph was soon convinced that his brothers had changed, for they begged him to pardon Benjamin for their father's sake. Judah made a moving plea that he be allowed to substitute his life for that of Benjamin (Genesis 44:18–34). "Joseph could not control himself before all those who stood by him." In a scene of joyous tears, he revealed himself to them. "I am your brother, Joseph," he wept, "whom you sold into Egypt. And now do not be distressed . . . for God sent me before you to preserve life" (Genesis 45:5).

The patriarchal narratives of Genesis conclude with scenes of reunion, blessing, and prosperity in Egypt. Jacob brought his entire clan to settle in the land of Goshen in the Nile delta, which Joseph obtained for them. Jacob adopted Joseph's Egyptian sons as his own, so that Joseph's inheritance was in their names. But as Jacob blessed the boys, he crossed his hands so that his right hand, signifying the greater blessing, rested on the head of the younger Ephraim, another instance of the younger son gaining precedence over the elder. The nearly blind father foretold that the tribe of Ephraim would be one of the greatest in Israel.

When he had given an appropriate blessing to each of his sons, Jacob "breathed his last, and was gathered to his people," at the age of 147. Joseph and his brothers continued to prosper in Egypt, but they did not forget their heritage. "God will visit you," the dying Joseph told his children, "and bring you up out of this land to the land which he swore to Abraham." Centuries were to pass before the time of God's visitation, and the return to Canaan. ✦

The season of starvation

Clues to famine in Egypt

THE FERTILITY OF the land of Egypt depends on the Nile floods that inundate the river valley each year. A low flood, resulting from sparse rainfall in the highlands of Ethiopia, or elsewhere in the Nile watershed, can bring about the failure of an entire year's crops. Ancient Egyptian texts have frequent references to such "years of misery," when the life-giving river failed to reach its normal levels.

Egyptian archaeology has produced no evidence of the specific famine described in the Book of Genesis. Nor do ancient texts make mention of a high official of Hebrew birth. Nor do these sources make reference to a man named Joseph. There is, however, an ancient tradition of seven-year-long failures of the Nile floods.

A rock inscription from the second century B.C. records the plaint of Pharaoh Djoser, the first of the pyramid builders, in the 28th century B.C. He said, "I was in distress on the Great Throne, and those in the palace were in heart's affliction from a great evil, since the Nile had not come in my time for a space of seven years. Grain was scant, fruits were dried up, and everything which they eat was short. Every man robbed his companion."

A low level of flooding means not just crop failure in a single season, but long-term damage as well. A scorching equatorial sun compounds the effects of a drought, shriveling existing vegetation. The waters of the Nile are essential to keep the desert at bay. In a dry season, the sands of the Sahara encroach upon the narrow alluvial plain and then suffocate the vegetation.

So crucial was the Nile's flooding that the Egyptians studied its rhythms. This led to the development of a very accurate calendar in the third millennium B.C. For seven or eight months each year, the Egyptians watched the waters recede. But, by their calculations, they could count on a return of the life-giving floods each summer. ✦

From the Patriarchs to the Twelve Tribes

BRAHAM WAS THE FIRST of the Patriarchs, his son Isaac was the second, and his grandson Jacob was the third. This is the line of descent for the 12 tribes of Israel. Jacob had 12 sons and a daughter. However, his favorite son, Joseph, had no tribe; instead, his two sons, Manasseh and Ephraim, received his birthright. Because the tribe of Levi had a priestly role and did not bear arms, it was neither counted in the general census of the Israelites in the wilderness nor allotted tribal territory in the land of Canaan.

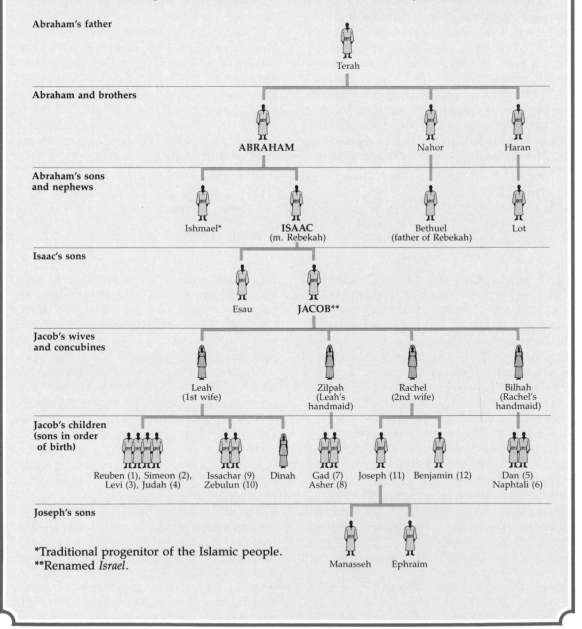

Abraham's father
Terah

Abraham and brothers
ABRAHAM Nahor Haran

Abraham's sons and nephews
Ishmael* ISAAC (m. Rebekah) Bethuel (father of Rebekah) Lot

Isaac's sons
Esau JACOB**

Jacob's wives and concubines
Leah (1st wife) Zilpah (Leah's handmaid) Rachel (2nd wife) Bilhah (Rachel's handmaid)

Jacob's children (sons in order of birth)
Reuben (1), Simeon (2), Levi (3), Judah (4) Issachar (9) Zebulun (10) Dinah Gad (7) Asher (8) Joseph (11) Benjamin (12) Dan (5) Naphtali (6)

Joseph's sons
Manasseh Ephraim

*Traditional progenitor of the Islamic people.
**Renamed *Israel*.

In a desperate effort to save her child, Moses' mother placed him in the reeds, where he was found by Pharaoh's daughter.

Preparing for deliverance

The reluctant rise of Moses

IN THE STORY of their exodus, their departure out of Egypt to freedom, the people of Israel found the heart of their faith. It was the one story above all others in their rich tradition that told them who they were and how they had come to be. It dramatically portrayed their responsibilities to God and embodied their continuing covenant and law.

When an Israelite brought the offering of first fruits to the Temple each year, he recited a confession that some scholars consider to be one of the most ancient in the Hebrew language. It is an encapsulation of the story of Exodus: "A wandering Aramean was my father; and he went down into Egypt and sojourned there, few in number; and there he became a nation great, mighty, and populous. And the Egyptians treated us harshly, and afflicted us, and laid upon us hard bondage. Then we cried to the Lord the God of our fathers, and the Lord heard our voice, and saw our affliction, our toil, and our oppression; and the Lord brought us out of Egypt with a mighty hand and an outstretched arm, with great terror, with signs and wonders; and he brought us into

this place and gave us this land, a land flowing with milk and honey."

The strange wonder and mystery of that story has grasped and held the heart of Israel and its descendants to this day. It told them that their God, the creator who revealed himself by giving freedom to an enslaved people, was different from the gods of other nations. And because their God was different, Israel was also different.

Exodus begins by scanning the centuries of Israelite prosperity in Egypt: "Then Joseph died, and all his brothers, and all that generation. But the descendants of Israel were fruitful and increased greatly; they multiplied and grew exceedingly strong; so that the land was filled with them."

However, a new presence loomed that threatened their prosperity. "Now there arose a new king over Egypt, who did not know Joseph. And he said to his people, 'Behold, the people of Israel are too many and too mighty for us'" (Exodus 1:8-9). The new pharaoh, whom some scholars identify as Seti I (1308-1290 B.C.), feared that the unity and fruitfulness of the Israelites threatened the safety of his nation and

Fearful of the Israelites' growing numbers, *Pharaoh made slaves of them: "Therefore they set*

that the Israelites would "join our enemies and fight against us" (Exodus 1:10).

The Pharaoh's solution was to conscript the Hebrews into labor brigades. He had an ambitious building program, and by forcing the Hebrews to construct new cities for him, he hoped to gradually kill off their young men and thus reduce their numbers. When this failed and the Hebrew population continued to grow, Pharaoh ordered that their work include "all kinds of work in the field." And even though their lives were

"bitter with hard service," this too did nothing to stem the tide of their numbers.

Pharaoh decided on more direct measures to limit the Hebrew birthrate. He called in the two midwives who attended Hebrew births and ordered them to kill all male Hebrew babies. "But the midwives feared God, and did not do as the king of Egypt commanded them." With considerable boldness, they told Pharaoh that, unlike Egyptian women, Hebrew women were so vigorous that they delivered before the

taskmasters over them to afflict them with heavy burdens, and they built for Pharaoh store-cities.''

midwife arrived (Exodus 1:17–19). In frustration, Pharaoh commanded all his people to cast any son born to a Hebrew into the Nile. The slave nation was forced to struggle for the survival of its people.

Hebrew families lived in fear of having their babies drowned. One family from the tribe of Levi hid their newborn son for three months. Finally, in desperation, the baby's mother "took for him a basket made of bulrushes, and daubed it with bitumen and pitch; and she put the child in it and placed it among the reeds at the river's brink. And his sister stood at a distance, to know what would be done to him" (Exodus 2:3–4).

Pharaoh's daughter came to bathe in the water, and she saw the basket. Peering into it, she saw the crying babe and took pity. "This is one of the Hebrews' children," she said. The baby's sister offered to find a Hebrew woman to nurse him, and she brought their mother to look after him.

Not only was the child saved, but his mother was paid wages by Pharaoh's house to nurse her own baby. After he was weaned, the child was returned to Pharaoh's daughter, who called him Moses. The name is related to the Egyptian word for "child" or "be born," found in such royal names as Rameses or Tutmose. However, in Hebrew, the word can refer to the fact that Moses was "drawn out" (from the Hebrew *mashah*) of the water.

Exodus says nothing of Moses' education, but later tradition filled the void. The Jewish historian Josephus told of his precociousness and his exploits as an Egyptian general. The philosopher Philo told how Moses quickly surpassed teachers brought in from all parts of the world and mastered every branch of knowledge. In later stories the young Moses was credited with many achievements, from inventing hieroglyphics, to teaching philosophy to the Greeks, to engineering irrigation machinery.

Despite his Egyptian upbringing, Moses knew of his Hebrew origins. One day he saw an Egyptian beating a Hebrew, and he killed the aggressor. The next day he saw two Hebrews fighting and tried to pacify them. One of them asked, "Do you mean to

The bush burned, but was not consumed by the flames.

kill me as you killed the Egyptian?" Realizing that his attack on the Egyptian was now a matter of common knowledge, Moses fled Egypt, and his life was completely changed. He became a shepherd among the nomadic Midianites of the Arabian peninsula. There he married Zipporah, the daughter of the priest called Jethro.

During Moses' years away as a desert nomad, a new Pharaoh arose. The ruler Seti I died, and Rameses II succeeded him; the plight of Israel worsened. However, a crucial event occurred. Israel's "cry under bondage came up to God. And God heard their groaning, and God remembered his covenant with Abraham" (Exodus 2:23–24). The exodus began with God's response to cries of suffering.

One day as Moses came to a place called "Horeb, the mountain of God" (elsewhere identified with Mount Sinai), he saw flames in the center of a bush (in tradition, a blossoming green thornbush). But as he watched, "the bush was burning, yet it was not consumed" (Exodus 3:2).

One later theory about this miracle proposes that the burning bush was a desert plant named *fraxinella*. This plant contains an oil so volatile that it can be ignited by the sun. The oil quickly burns off, and the bush itself is not damaged.

However, from the point of view of the narrative, what is most significant is that this was the first of a series of marvelous theophanies—appearances of God to humans—that occur throughout the book of Exodus. The presence of God had made the spot into "holy ground," a place of power and danger for humans. In the presence of the palpable power, Moses had to keep his distance and remove his shoes.

Yahweh addressed Moses: " 'I am the God of your father, the God of Abraham, the God of Isaac, and the God of Jacob.' And Moses hid his face, for he was afraid to look at God" (Exodus 3:6). Yahweh told Moses how he had heard the cries of suffering Israel. " 'I have come down to deliver them out of the hand of the Egyptians,' " he said. " 'Come, I will send you to Pharaoh

*"**Aaron cast down** his rod before Pharaoh . . . and it became a serpent."*

that you may bring forth my people, the sons of Israel, out of Egypt.' "

One might have expected Israel's great hero, who had long ago struck a blow against the Egyptians, to rise eagerly to the mighty task of deliverance. But the decisiveness of God contrasts sharply with the reticence and resistance of Moses: " 'Who am I that I should go to Pharaoh?' " he asked (Exodus 3:11). Moses made excuses and raised objection after objection until it had become clear that the power for delivering the Israelites from bondage lay not with its human leader but with God.

For each of Moses' weaknesses, God added a strength. He gave him marvelous signs to prove his commission: his rod became a serpent; his hand became leprous and then clear; he could pour Nile water on the ground and it would turn to blood. To compensate for Moses' lack of eloquence, God commissioned his brother Aaron to speak for him (Exodus 4:1–17).

First and foremost God assured Moses of his presence. In an elusive phrase that is variously translated "I am who I am" or "I shall be what I shall be," God interpreted his Hebrew name "Yahweh" to Moses. " 'This is my name for ever,' " he said, " 'and thus I am to be remembered throughout all generations' " (Exodus 3:15).

Moses returned to Egypt with his family. On the way, Yahweh met Moses and "sought to kill him." But Zipporah circumcised their son with a flint knife and thereby saved Moses' life, saying, " 'You are a bridegroom of blood to me!' " (Exodus 4:24–26). Many have proposed that the incident referred to a long-forgotten rite. Indeed this strange incident has baffled scholars. However, the story served to reinforce the importance of the covenant of circumcision that God had made with Abraham.

When Moses and Aaron reached Egypt, the battle with Pharaoh began. They challenged the king with powerful prophetic voice, "Thus says the Lord [Yahweh], the God of Israel, 'Let my people go' " (Exodus 5:1). But Pharaoh proved a hard enemy. He had never heard of this Yahweh they spoke of and saw no reason to obey him. Further, if the slaves had time to worship, they must need more work, and Pharaoh ordered that their labor loads be increased.

The Israelites who initially welcomed Moses and Aaron now accused them of putting a sword into Pharaoh's hand to kill them (Exodus 5:21). But the hard struggle was just beginning. " 'Now you shall see,' " Yahweh told Moses, " 'what I will do to Pharaoh . . . yea, with a strong hand he will drive them out of his land.' " ✦

The plague of locusts *from a 15th-century German Bible.*

From the hand of God: Pestilence, darkness, death

The ten plagues of Egypt

THE BOOK OF EXODUS stressed that the Israelites' deliverance from Egypt was an act of God. This was demonstrated through miracles that touched almost every detail of the Exodus story. The awesome might of Yahweh, who had mysteriously chosen the enslaved and downtrodden people of Israel as his own, was the focus of the story.

Egypt was an ancient empire whose mighty gods were well known, and whose Pharaoh was worshiped as divine. But the divine Pharaoh was as nothing to Yahweh. Future generations would tell, Yahweh said, "how I have made sport of the Egyptians and what signs I have done among them; that you may know that I am the LORD" (Exodus 10:2).

When Moses and Aaron again asked Pharaoh to free the Israelites, he demanded a demonstration of power from them. Aaron cast down his rod, "and it became a serpent." But "the magicians of Egypt did the same by their secret arts." Then "Aaron's rod swallowed up their rods."

"Still," Exodus continues, "Pharaoh's heart was hardened." As the conflict began, Yahweh had told Moses, "I will harden Pharaoh's heart, and though I multiply my signs . . . Pharaoh will not listen to you" (Exodus 7:3–4). Thus, even Pharaoh's opposition to Moses was within Yahweh's control. Pharaoh thought that he had the Israelites trapped, but he was the one who was trapped.

That God both saved Israel and hardened Pharaoh's heart posed a theological problem for later generations regarding the nature of human freedom. Rabbinic commentaries on Exodus explained that Pharaoh's refusal to repent caused God to close Pharaoh's heart so that he could not repent. In the New Testament, Paul used the example of Pharaoh to assert God's absolute power: "he has mercy upon whomever he wills, and he hardens the heart of whomever he wills" (Romans 9:18).

The Book of Exodus itself does not dwell on the mystery of human freedom, but simply states that Yahweh told Pharaoh, "For this purpose have I let you live, to show you my power, so that my name may be declared throughout all the earth."

God's power was manifested in the ten plagues. The first four plagues were severe trials. First Aaron stretched out his hand and turned the Nile and other sources of water to blood (Exodus 7:19–21). The life-line of Egypt became a river of death! But Pharaoh's magicians could do the same, and the Egyptians' wells still provided water. Therefore, Pharaoh ignored it.

Then hordes of frogs covered the land; but they too could be produced by the magicians. The frogs were such a nuisance, however, that Pharaoh appeared to give in. He recanted when the frogs died (Exodus 8:1–15). Next Aaron turned the dust into swarms of gnats. The magicians could not perform this trick, and they concluded that it was "the finger of God." Pharaoh, however, was unmoved (Exodus 8:16–19). When the flies of the fourth plague struck, Pharaoh again appeared to concede. But again he recanted when the plague had passed.

The next four plagues injured the Egyptians and their property, but spared the Israelites. The fifth plague killed their cattle; the sixth covered the people with boils so that even the magicians could not stand up. But "the LORD hardened the heart of Pharaoh" (Exodus 9:12). The seventh brought lightning and hail, destroying crops and cattle. Pharaoh said, "I have sinned this time . . . I will let you go" (Exodus 9:27–28). But when the storm ceased, "he sinned yet again, and hardened his heart."

The eighth plague darkened the land with locusts so that "not a green thing remained." Pharaoh again confessed his sin against Yahweh; but when the locusts passed, "the LORD hardened Pharaoh's heart" (Exodus 10:14–20).

The ninth plague brought a "thick darkness," a "darkness to be felt" over Egypt for three days. Pharaoh offered several partial concessions to the Israelites, but Moses refused to compromise. Thus, Pharaoh drove him out with threats, "in the day you see my face you shall die" (Exodus 10:28).

Passover

God told Moses that the Israelites were to slaughter a lamb and mark their doors with its blood. He would smite the firstborn of the Egyptians, but, seeing the blood of the lamb on the Israelites' doors, the angel of death would pass over their houses. Furthermore, God commanded the Israelites to observe a "feast to the LORD" throughout their generations.

Thus, on the 15th day of the Jewish month of *Nisan*, in March or April, Jews the world over commemorate the Exodus from Egypt by celebrating Passover, so called because God passed over the houses of the Jews. (It is also called *the feast of unleavened bread*.)

Passover is observed at home in a first-night ceremony called the *Seder*. The slaughter of the *paschal lamb* is symbolized by the display of a shankbone; the tears of slaves by a dish of salt water; the mortar that the Israelites used for Pharaoh's building projects by a sweet paste of apples, nuts, and raisins, called *haroset*, and the flight from bondage by *matzot*, or unleavened bread. Throughout the *Seder*, the Passover *Haggadah*, a book of prayers and benedictions recounting the Exodus, is read aloud.

In medieval times, Passover was celebrated standing up.

Interpreters have often noticed that many of these plagues correspond to relatively common phenomena in Egypt. Some have suggested that the reddening of the Nile was not blood, but an annual infestation of minute organisms in the water or the clogging of the river with reddish silt. Often when the Nile receded, hordes of frogs remained in the riverbed. Dead and dying frogs brought gnats and flies, which in turn led to diseases of cattle and people. Hail, locusts, and the "thick darkness" of sandstorms were also common. Such a coincidental sequence of disasters is, of course, impossible to prove. However, the narrator of Exodus described each plague as a direct action of God.

The final plague was unique in its severity. It became the basis for the most important festival in Israel's calendar—the Passover. On the evening of the fourteenth day of the month, later called Nisan, each family in Israel was to kill a lamb and smear its blood on the doorposts and lintel of their house. The lamb was to be roasted whole and eaten in haste with unleavened bread and bitter herbs.

This was Yahweh's passover. He said, "for I will pass through the land of Egypt that night, and I will smite all the first-born in the land of Egypt, both man and beast; . . . and when I see the blood, I will pass over you" (Exodus 12:11–13).

God commanded Israel to reenact this meal annually "throughout your generations." They were to explain it to their children so that it would be a perpetual memorial of the salvation God had given them (Exodus 12:25–27).

When the horror of the tenth plague struck that midnight, "there was a great cry in Egypt." Both Pharaoh and his subjects "were urgent with the people, to send them out of the land in haste" with their cattle and any silver or gold they wanted (Exodus 12:30–36). That night, we are told, more than 600,000 left slavery, 430 years after the arrival of Jacob. The great Exodus of the Israelites had begun. ✦

Miraculous path to freedom

Moses parts the Red Sea

THE LORD KNEW that freedom would be difficult for these people conditioned by years of servitude. "Moses took the bones of Joseph with him; for Joseph had solemnly sworn the people of Israel, saying, 'God will visit you; then you must carry my bones with you from here.' " Yahweh made his presence clearly known among them, traveling before them by day in a "pillar of cloud" and by night in a "pillar of fire" (Exodus 13:21).

"In God's own time these exiles, taught by sorrow and disciplined by suffering, were to usher in a new day not only for their own people but for all mankind."
— **Raymond Calkins**
The Interpreter's Bible

The Lord did not send the Israelites over the shortest route into the Promised Land of Canaan. He wished to avoid undue hardship "Lest the people repent when they see war, and return to Egypt." Thus he chose a route that would take them "round by the way of the wilderness toward the Red Sea," avoiding hostile tribes.

Yahweh had another purpose in avoiding the most obvious road out of Egypt. When Pharaoh heard that the Israelites had fled, he resolved to recapture and enslave them once again. Pharaoh did not realize that he was being drawn into a trap that would glorify the Israelite God more than all the ten plagues put together. The Lord said, "I will get glory over Pharaoh and all his host; and the Egyptians shall know that I am the LORD" (Exodus 14:4).

Pharaoh and his army quickly caught up

Pharaoh's forces, chariots mired in mud, were drowned in the rushing waters of the sea. Many scholars believe that the Israelites may in fact have crossed the "Sea of Reeds."

with the fleeing Israelites, who were camped at "the sea, by Pihahiroth, in front of Baal-zephon." The Hebrew phrase *yam suph*, traditionally translated "Red Sea," actually means "Sea of Reeds." The exact location of this "sea" remains a mystery, but many scholars think that it was a marshy area or a lake, such as the Bitter Lakes near Baal-zephon between the Gulf of Suez and the Mediterranean.

Upon seeing the approaching army, the Israelites lost faith and "cried out to the LORD." But Moses said to them "fear not, stand firm, and see the salvation of the LORD" (Exodus 14:13). As God's pillar of cloud blocked the Egyptians' path, Moses lifted his rod, "and the LORD drove the sea back by a strong east wind all night, and made the sea dry land, and the waters were

divided" (Exodus 14:21). Was it a storm whose winds drove back the shallow waters of the sea, as some have suggested? Or did a volcanic eruption cause the sea to part, as others have proposed? For the Israelites it was the final, miraculous door that Yahweh opened to freedom.

The Israelites marched right through the sea, "the waters being a wall to them on their right hand and on their left" (Exodus 14:22). The Egyptians attempted to follow, but as they struck the seabed, their chariots became mired in the mud. In a panic, they tried to retreat. "Let us flee from before Israel; for the LORD fights for them against the Egyptians." Before they could do so, God told Moses to raise his rod again, and this time "the sea returned to its wonted flow," covering the chariots, horsemen, and "all the host of Pharaoh that had followed them into the sea."

The Israelites sang a hymn of triumph and praise to the Lord for delivering them from the Egyptians. The song predicted that just as God had triumphed over the Egyptians, so too would he defeat other nations that might try to prevent Israel's entry into Canaan. In celebration of God's absolute power, the hymn joyously concluded, "The LORD will reign for ever and ever."

The state of exalted devotion quickly deteriorated into bickering and recrimination once the people left the sea and began their journey into the wilderness. Their supply of water ran out, and when they did find water, it was bitter. The people grew angry, and murmured. Yahweh's remarkable response was to show Moses a certain tree, "and he threw it into the water, and the water became sweet" (Exodus 15:25).

But water was not their only need. The Israelites had been out of the land of Egypt for a month, and food was in short supply. Again the people lost faith and murmured

The Israelites were sustained *on manna from heaven, "the bread which the* LORD *has given you to eat."*

against Moses: "you have brought us out into this wilderness to kill this whole assembly with hunger." They wished for the "fleshpots" and bread they had enjoyed in Egypt. But God intervened to satisfy them. "Behold, I will rain bread from heaven for you; and the people shall go out and gather a day's portion every day, that I may prove them, whether they will walk in my law or not." In addition to bread, God also sent flocks of quail, so they could have meat.

The Israelites called the bread manna. The Bible says, "it was like coriander seed, white, and the taste of it was like wafers made with honey." Greek monks living in the region early in our era believed that the manna was a secretion from insects burrowing in the bark of the tamarisk tree, a desert shrub. The insects excrete a sugary substance that dries into a sticky solid. To this day, desert Bedouins eat it.

The Israelites also faced a military threat in the wilderness. The Amalekites, a desert tribe, attacked. Moses sent men out to defend the people under the leadership of Joshua. Watching the battle from a hill, Moses was able to control the course of hostilities. When he raised his hands, holding the "rod of God," the Israelites prevailed, but when he wearied and lowered his hands, the Amalekites seized the initiative. The Israelites finally won the day when Moses sat down on a rock and had two others hold up his hands until the sun went down.

This battle marked the first of Israel's holy wars. Yahweh told Moses, "Write this as a memorial in a book . . . I will utterly blot out the remembrance of Amalek from under heaven." The Amalekites had attacked the sacred encampment of Yahweh, and thus Yahweh "will have war with Amalek from generation to generation" (Exodus 17:16).

Three months after the Israelites left Egypt, having withstood Pharaoh's army, the Amalekites, and privation, "on that day they came into the wilderness of Sinai." ✦

Bull cults in the ancient world

WHY DID AARON CHOOSE to make a golden calf as an idol for the people? The word translated "calf" in the narrative refers more specifically to a young bull. Thus the choice may well have related to the practice of bull worship, which was prevalent in ancient Egypt and Canaan. Fearsomely strong, notoriously quick-tempered, bulls were revered throughout much of the ancient world as symbols of strength and fertility. The bull appears in the art and sacred texts of Syria, Mesopotamia, and Egypt.

Early records from Memphis, in Egypt, reveal that the Egyptians worshiped a live bull known as Apis. The animal was thought to be a manifestation of the city's patron deity, Ptah, creator of the universe. Apis became identified with Osiris, legendary god of the sun and of immortality.

Egypt's goldsmiths turned out finely wrought effigies of Apis-Osiris and of his wife, Isis, represented by the head of a cow. When an Apis bull died at Memphis, its body was mummified. It was entombed in splendor during a period of mourning that lasted 70 days. In later centuries, the Apis bull became more closely linked with Osiris, so that after the conquest of Alexander the Great, Osiris-Apis was transformed into Serapis. In this new Hellenistic form, the ancient Egyptian bull-god became a prominent deity.

In Mesopotamia, bulls were long venerated as symbols of majestic strength and potency. Savage wild bulls, called aurochs, once roamed the region, and colossal stone images of these beasts were set up to guard the entrances to the temples and palaces of Babylonia. In later years, the Assyrians adopted the bull-god as their guardian

The Syrian storm-god riding on a bull.

icon, often adding wings and a human face.

The deities represented as bulls were usually protective and benign, but legend also described bulls that ravaged and destroyed, and often were slain by great heroes. In the ancient Babylonian legend of Gilgamesh, the god Anu sent a bull from heaven to demolish the land with earthquakes. But the hero Gilgamesh was able to kill the bull. Similarly, the Greek hero Theseus slew the Minotaur, a fabled monster of Crete—half bull, half man—who fed on human sacrifices. In an ancient Cretan ritual, acrobatic young men and women would leap over the horns of a charging bull. In Middle Eastern mythology, there are many stories of celestial bulls bringing gales and deluges. Hadad, the storm god of the Syrians and the Hittites, rode across the sky on a bull, wielding his three-pronged lightning bolt.

When the Israelites reached the Promised Land in the 13th century B.C., the bull cult was already ancient there. Canaanite temples were sometimes built with images of bronze bulls in their foundations.

It was perhaps for this reason that the Israelites in moments of doubt were tempted by bull cults. Young bulls were favored sacrificial animals, and bovine images appeared in shrines. Before the entrance to Solomon's Temple, "twelve bronze bulls" (Jeremiah 52:20) supported a huge basin called the "molten sea." Many scholars also think that the cherubim on the Ark of the Covenant were in the form of winged bulls. Later, Israel's King Jeroboam erected golden bulls in two sanctuaries. Many believe that he intended these images as pedestals on which Yahweh stood invisibly—as perhaps had Aaron in making the golden calf.

"God's law inscribed in stone"

A covenant for a holy nation

Enraged at the sight *of the golden calf, Moses destroyed the tablets.*

THE STIRRING EVENTS that followed the march out of Egypt came to a climax when the Israelites encamped at Sinai, the "mountain of God." There, on the sacred mountain, God offered to make a covenant with Israel. The Lord said, "You have seen what I did to the Egyptians, and how I bore you on eagles' wings and brought you to myself. Now therefore, if you will obey my voice and keep my covenant, you shall be my own possession among all peoples; for all the earth is mine, and you shall be to me a kingdom of priests and a holy nation" (Exodus 19:4–6).

The covenants that God had established with the Patriarchs (Abraham, Isaac, and Jacob) were to be broadened to encompass the entire people. God had liberated them, and now pledged to maintain a special relationship with this "holy nation" if they would abide by his laws.

The Lord told Moses that he would present himself before the nation "in a thick cloud, that the people may hear when I speak with you, and may also believe you for ever." The Israelites were to prepare for the event by washing their garments, avoiding sexual relations, and staying clear of the mountain. "On the morning of the third day there were thunders and lightnings, and a thick cloud upon the mountain, and a very loud trumpet blast, so that all the people who were in the camp trembled."

From the summit of Mount Sinai, God announced, "I am the LORD your God, who brought you out of the land of Egypt, out of the house of bondage." He insisted upon absolute devotion, "You shall have no other gods before me." The Israelites were not to construct or worship any graven image. If they did, they would be punished up to the fourth generation; if they refrained from idolatry, they would benefit from his steadfast love. Furthermore, God forbade them to use his name, Yahweh, in vain.

Next, God commanded observance of the Sabbath. Resting on the seventh day was already an established Israelite tradition; now they were to "remember" it and "keep it holy." "Six days you shall labor, and do all your work; but the seventh day is a sabbath to the LORD your God; in it you shall not do any work."

The first four commandments were concerned with devotion to God. With the fifth commandment, which demanded respect for one's parents, Yahweh began setting the standard for human relationships and civil law. Murder, adultery, and theft were outlawed by the next three commandments, thus indicating the sacredness of life, marriage, and property. Israelites were not to offer false evidence in law courts, and by this commandment the Lord set forth the sacredness of justice.

The final commandment demanded that one's heart and mind be as true as one's deeds: "You shall not covet your neighbor's house; you shall not covet your neighbor's wife, or his manservant, or his maidservant, or his ox, or his ass, or anything that is your neighbor's."

The people were terrified by the power of God's presence manifested in thunder, lightning, and smoke. "They stood afar off, and said to Moses, 'You speak to us, and we will hear; but let not God speak to us, lest we die' " (20:19). Moses approached "the thick darkness where God was" and received a more extended body of law that he called the "book of the covenant."

When he read it to the people, they pledged, "All that the LORD has spoken we will do." Moses sealed the covenant with a sacrifice and "took the blood and threw it upon the people, and said, 'Behold the blood of the covenant which the LORD has made with you' "(Exodus 24:3–8). With these words he expressed the mysterious importance of blood in making a covenant between God and man. Then Yahweh summoned Moses to the top of the mountain to receive tablets of stone engraved with the Ten Commandments.

Moses stayed on the mountain for 40 days and received from the Lord all the laws that were to govern the religious and secu-lar life of the Israelites. But the Israelites felt abandoned by Moses during his absence. They went to Aaron and said to him, "Up, make us gods, who shall go before us; as for this Moses, the man who brought us up out of the land of Egypt, we do not know what has become of him" (Exodus 32:1).

How is it that, although they had just heard the majestic words of God uttered from the mountaintop, they would revert to idolatry so quickly? Commentators have struggled with this problem for centuries. Some assert that having grown up in the pagan society of Egypt, the Israelites were predisposed to idolatry. Without Moses, the people reverted to their former ways.

Modern scholars have suggested that ancient people often used "idols" not as gods, but as "pedestals" on which they imagined an invisible god to be standing or riding. The Israelites who clamored for "gods" may not have perceived any contradiction between creating images for such use and God's prohibition against idolatry.

Whatever lay behind the request for "gods," Aaron acceded to it. He collected gold from the people, melted it down, and constructed the image of a calf or young bull, a common symbol of the divine in

In Moses' absence, the Israelites turned to worship of a golden calf.

81

ancient Near Eastern religions. The Israelites acknowledged the calf as their god, and Aaron announced a religious feast to take place the next day.

God ordered Moses down from the mountain. "I have seen this people," said God, "and behold, it is a stiff-necked people; now therefore let me alone, that my wrath may burn hot against them and I may consume them." He offered to create a new chosen nation with Moses as its leader (32:7–10). But in a remarkable confrontation, Moses refused to acquiesce to the destruction of Israel. He told God that such a deed would violate his promises to Abraham, Isaac, and Jacob. "And the LORD repented of the evil which he thought to do to his people" (32:14).

Moses descended the mountain holding the tablets engraved with the Ten Commandments. As soon as he saw the Israelites worshiping the calf, his "anger burned hot, and he threw the tables out of his hands and broke them at the foot of the mountain" (32:19). The people had violated their covenant with Yahweh. Moses "took the calf which they had made, and burnt it with fire, and ground it to powder, and scattered it upon the water, and made the people of Israel drink it" (32:20). On Moses' instructions, members of the tribe of Levi put to death 3,000 Israelites who had worshiped the calf.

The next morning Moses sought to restore the people in God's good graces. He audaciously declared that if Israel was not forgiven, "blot me, I pray thee, out of thy book which thou hast written" (32:32). God

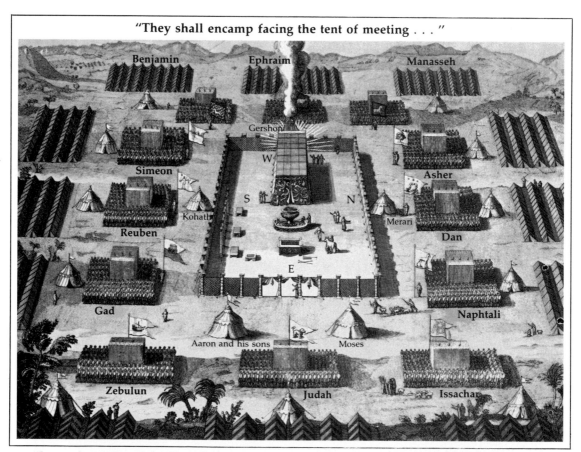

"They shall encamp facing the tent of meeting . . ."

Benjamin Ephraim Manasseh

Gershon

W

Simeon Asher

S N

Kohath Merari

Reuben Dan

E

Gad Naphtali

Aaron and his sons Moses

Zebulun Judah Issachar

The twelve tribes had prescribed positions around the tabernacle, as depicted in this 19th-century engraving. The tribes were given great significance after the conquest of Canaan.

offered a partial pardon: an angel, not God himself, would accompany the Israelites. But Moses continued to ask forgiveness for his people, and at last God forgave them.

God instructed Moses to return to the top of Mount Sinai with two stone tablets; he would again inscribe the Ten Commandments for Israel. After another 40 days in communion with God on the mountain, Moses descended with the Commandments, his face radiant with glory.

In the fourth century A.D., Jerome translated this text into Latin. However, he misread the Hebrew *qaran*, "shone," as the noun *qeren*, "horn." Thus, because of Jerome's mistranslation, Moses is often represented in Christian art with horns.

While Moses was atop Mount Sinai communing with the Lord, he received instruction for building the tabernacle. "And let them make me a sanctuary, that I may dwell in their midst. According to all that I show you concerning the pattern of the tabernacle, and of all its furniture, so you shall make it" (25:8–9).

The tabernacle was to be portable and divided into three areas: the outer court, the Holy Place, and the Holy of Holies. The outer court was open to all. In it was an altar for sacrifices and a basin for the priests to cleanse themselves.

The Holy Place was only to be entered into by the Levite priests. In it was an altar for burning incense, a table on which 12 loaves of bread were constantly on display, and a candelabrum. The Holy of Holies could only be entered by the High Priest, and only on the holiest day of the year, the Day of Atonement. Only the Ark containing the tablets inscribed with the Ten Commandments was placed in here.

"Thus did Moses; according to all that the LORD commanded him, so he did. And in the first month in the second year, on the first day of the month, the tabernacle was erected." Exodus ends on a joyous note. God is with his chosen people; his glory fills the tabernacle. The covenant had been renewed, and the Israelites were now prepared to enter the Promised Land. ✦

Aerial view of Jebel Musa.

The search for Mount Sinai

Moses received the Law of God on the peak of Mount Sinai. Yet the exact location of the sacred site remains a mystery. That the Bible itself alludes to Mount Sinai by various names— among them "the mountain," "the mountain of God," and "Mount Horeb"—complicates the search.

In fact, scholars have suggested some dozen different mountains, both in the Sinai desert and Arabia, as the place where Israel was bound to the Lord's covenant. The sites in Arabia are thought to have been volcanic in ancient times and thus may conform to the biblical description that "the whole mountain quaked greatly." To add to the confusion, the route of the Exodus has never been confirmed, so no one mountain can be identified with certainty. Nevertheless, since the fourth century A.D., the traditional location of Mount Sinai has been Jebel Musa, a jagged mountain situated on the southern end of the Sinai Peninsula. On its northwest slope sits the present-day Monastery of Saint Catherine. Although the question will probably remain unanswered forever, contemporary scholars think that this site or some nearby peak is the most likely of all.

The Ten Commandments

**"And God spoke all these words, saying,
'I am the LORD your God, who brought you
out of the land of Egypt . . . ' "** —Exodus 20:1–2

THESE MAJESTIC WORDS open the Tables of the Law, received by Moses amid thunder and lightning on Mount Sinai. In Jewish tradition the first commandment is: *"I am the LORD your God, who brought you out of the land of Egypt, out of the house of bondage."* In the Catholic and Protestant traditions the first commandment is: *"I am the LORD your God . . . you shall have no other gods before me."* The division followed here is the one generally used by Protestants. The substance is the same, and the gist is love: love of God in the first four commandments, love of man in the rest, each complementing the other, as they do throughout Bible tradition.

I. I am the LORD your God . . . you shall have no other gods before me. "To have other gods is idolatry, and that is the blanket sin. It is the term that covers all evil. Every kind of sin that man can commit boils down to idolatry because he is putting something before God. There is only one God Who is the only presence and the only power."

—Emmet Fox, *The Ten Commandments: The Master Key to Life* (1953)

II. You shall not make for yourself a graven image. "Why have you forsaken heaven to pay honour to earth? For what else is gold, or silver, or steel, or iron, or bronze, or ivory, or precious stones? Are they not earth, and made from earth? . . . Why then, vain and foolish men—once again I will ask the question—did you blaspheme highest heaven and drag down piety to the ground by fashioning for yourselves gods of earth? . . . Your statue is gold; it is wood; it is stone; or if in thought you trace it to its origin, it is earth, which has received form at the artist's hands. But my practice is to walk upon earth, not to worship it. For I hold it sin ever to entrust the hopes of the soul to soulless things." —**Clement of Alexandria (3rd century)** *Exhortation to the Greeks*

III. You shall not take the name of the LORD your God in vain. "O dear God, this commandment reminds me . . . how You have poured Your holy Name into my soul and mind. Yes, out of Your Name has it sprung, and You have given me authority to rule over all things with Your Name so that out of my mouth by Your power it is to flow forth and rule all things: Yes, I was to form and fashion holy figures and images with my mouth and expression . . . You have given Your Word with Your holy Name into my soul and mind so that I, as a form and image of Your will, am to express Your wondrous works also. What You, O great God, have formed bodily and creaturely through Your Word, I was to form spiritually for Your praise and fashion it within Your wisdom, and not to form in my mouth a strange image contrary to Your creation and order."

—Jacob Boehme
The Way to Christ 1624

IV. Remember the sabbath day, to keep it holy. "God has commanded us to abstain from work and to rest on the Sabbath for two reasons. First, by doing so we affirm the true belief in the creation of the universe. This belief leads us immediately and unequivocally to a belief in God's existence. Second, the Sabbath reminds us of God's mercies over us. After all, He freed us from the slavery and oppression of Egypt and gave us a day of rest. The Sabbath is, therefore, a double blessing for us: It implants correct notions in our minds and it promotes our physical welfare."

—Maimonides, *Guide for the Perplexed*

V. Honor your father and your mother. "Some Commandments prescribe good acts, whereas others forbid evil acts. And we should realize that it is within our power to avoid evil, but we cannot do good to everyone. So St. Augustine tells us that we should love all, although we are not obliged to do good to all. But among those to whom we are obliged to do good are those in any way united to us. . . .Now, there are no closer relatives to us than our father and mother. 'We ought to love God first,' states St. Ambrose, 'then our father and mother.' . . . Moreover, because in our childhood we receive food from our parents, in their old age we should support them. . . .For the humiliation of those who act otherwise, Cassiodorus tells how young storks whose parents have lost their feathers by the onslaught of old age and cannot find suitable food, make the parent storks comfortable with their own feathers, bringing them food for their tired bodies. 'And so by this affectionate exchange the young ones repay their parents for what they received when young.' "

—**Thomas Aquinas**
Sermon On the Ten Commandments

VI. You shall not kill. "Some scholars have translated the verb as 'you shall not murder.' That is, what is banned is not all forms of killing (such as the death penalty for certain crimes, or involvement in war), but the unnecessary taking of life out of anger or greed. . . .Jesus extended the sixth commandment to include feelings of anger, verbal abuse of another person, or derogatory namecalling (Matthew 5:21–26)."

—**Victor P. Hamilton**
Handbook on the Pentateuch **(1982)**

VII. You shall not commit adultery. "Adultery is the smashing of a rare and mystical thing, a unity, a oneness between two people who have become one because of something which God made them to be capable of having together, which had the original purpose of making two people one. . . .You are not to be unfaithful to God; and as you come together as couples you are not to be unfaithful to each other."

—**Edith Schaeffer (1982)**
Lifelines: The Ten Commandments for Today

VIII. You shall not steal. "Stealing is a double sin. It is a sin against God, for it accuses him of not giving adequately, and it is a sin against love, for it is a denial of loving one's neighbour as oneself. At the same time, it is very often a condemnation of the one stolen from, for he has not met the need of another from his abundance. We need to balance this command with, 'You shall love your neighbour as yourself' (Leviticus 19:18)."

—**H. L. Ellison**
Exodus **(1982)**

IX. You shall not bear false witness against your neighbor. "The *ninth* commandment concerns our own and our neighbour's good name . . . This forbids speaking falsely on any matter, lying, equivocating . . . slandering, back-biting, and talebearing, aggravating what is done amiss, and making it worse than it is, and any way endeavouring to raise our own reputation upon the ruin of our neighbour's. All these, however they may be called, are among the violations of this commandment. They are an abuse of our own gift of speech; abuse of the confidence of those we address; and generally, one way or another, are injurious to our neighbours, therefore are condemned in the word of God. Words cannot express how much this commandment is every day transgressed in almost all companies and amongst persons of all characters."

—**Matthew Henry and Thomas Scott**
Commentary on the Holy Bible **(1710)**

X. You shall not covet. "There is one attitude . . . that destroys the inner connection of the community even when it does not transform itself into actual action; and which indeed, precisely on account of its passive or semipassive persistence, may become a consuming disease of a special kind in the body politic. This is the attitude of envy. The prohibition of 'covetousness' . . . is to be understood as a prohibition of envy. The point here is not merely a feeling of the heart but an attitude of one man to another that leads to a decomposition of the very tissues of society."

—**Martin Buber, "The Words on the Tablets"**

Only the high priest could approach the ark of the covenant.

The might and power of the Lord's ark

A fearsome receptacle

ONE OF THE MOST mysterious objects described in the Old Testament is the ark of the covenant. Its awesome presence is captured in the ancient verse: "And whenever the ark set out, Moses said, 'Arise, O LORD, and let thy enemies be scattered; and let them that hate thee flee before thee.' And when it rested, he said, 'Return, O LORD, to the ten thousand thousands of Israel'" (Numbers 10:35–36). To the Israelites, the ark was Yahweh's throne, and thus represented his presence among them.

The Bible refers to the ark of the covenant by a variety of names. In some of the early texts it is called the "ark of the LORD" or the "ark of God." Elsewhere it is called the "ark of the covenant" and the "ark of the testimony."

Deuteronomy 10:3 indicates that the ark was rather simple: a wooden chest, built at God's command to hold the tablets of stone on which the Ten Commandments were inscribed. However, according to Exodus 25, it was far more elaborate. There, the ark is described as a wooden chest almost four feet long and over two feet wide and high. It was overlaid with gold inside and out, and it also had golden moldings. The ark was fitted with golden rings for the poles, made of acacia wood like the chest itself, that were used to carry it. Because the Israelites were a wandering people, without fixed abode, the ark had to be portable.

On top was a golden cover, called in Hebrew *kapporet,* or mercy seat. It held two golden winged creatures called cherubim. The Bible describes these mysterious creatures as having spreading wings that encircled the mercy seat. As God said to Moses, "There I will meet with you, and from above the mercy seat, from between the two cherubim that are upon the ark of the testimony, I will speak with you of all that I will give you in commandment for the people of Israel" (Exodus 25:22).

The Israelites believed that Yahweh was enthroned above the mercy seat of the ark. Thus, by his presence the ark was so holy and possessed such great power that it had to be treated with the greatest respect and care. Not to show this respect was to invite the wrath of God.

When the portable sanctuary of the Tabernacle was set up, the ark and mercy seat were alone installed in the innermost cubicle called "the most holy place" (Exodus 26:34). No one except the high priest was allowed within that inner sanctum. Even the priest could enter but once a year, on the Day of Atonement, "lest he die" (Leviticus 16:2). The ark eventually found a permanent home in the First Temple, built by Solomon in Jerusalem. ✦

A holy life defined

The rules of Leviticus

WHAT IS THE SOURCE of the inscription on the Liberty Bell? Where can one find the commandment that Jesus described as the second of the two great commandments? The answer to both questions is the same: the collection of rules and regulations in the Book of Leviticus. The Liberty Bell inscription reads, "Proclaim LIBERTY throughout all the Land unto all the Inhabitants thereof" (25:10). "You shall love your neighbor as yourself" (19:18) is Jesus' second great commandment (Mark 12:31).

The book's contents are summarized by its last verse: "These are the commandments which the LORD commanded Moses for the people of Israel on Mount Sinai" (Leviticus 27:34). Set in the period of Israel's sojourn in the wilderness of Sinai after the exodus from Egypt, these regulations were intended to govern the conduct of the Israelites. A large number of these regulations involved matters of religious ritual. Thus, the early Greek translation of the Bible called this book "the Levitical Book," after the priestly tribe of the Levites.

The book falls into six parts: laws governing sacrifices; those regarding the ordination of priests; laws distinguishing the clean and the unclean; a chapter with instructions for the annual Day of Atonement; laws governing the holy life of the chosen people; and finally, an appendix on religious vows. The book has traditionally been attributed to Moses; however, most scholars believe that Leviticus was compiled from earlier collections of laws and regulations.

One such earlier collection was called the Holiness Code (17–26). This code offered legislation for both priests and the laity. Its regulations covered sexual ethics, general morality, and ritual behavior, among others. But the general nature of the code helped to form a conception of holiness for the Israelites. Its central thrust was obedience to God's commandments. "But if you will not hearken to me, and will not do all these commandments, . . . I will appoint over you sudden terror, consumption, and fever that waste the eyes and cause life to pine away." To truly adhere to the code one had to be pure of heart as well as ritually pure. Thus, Leviticus 19:17 states, "You shall not hate your brother in your heart."

Chapters 11–15 contain a series of laws that distinguish what is "clean" from what is "unclean." This distinction was not made merely on the basis of sanitation or hygiene. Rather, unclean meant that something was

> "Granted that ritual in any realm from courtesy to worship can become formal, empty, and stiff. Nevertheless, with all its dangers it is an absolute necessity. We cannot . . . train children in the spirit of religion if the appropriate activities of worship and devotion are forgotten."
> —**Harry Emerson Fosdick**
> *World's Work*

ꙮ Scapegoat ꙮ

A scapegoat was sent into the wilderness on the Day of Atonement, as prescribed in the Book of Leviticus.

The rituals prescribed for the Day of Atonement were imbued with mystery. In particular at one point the priest cast lots over two goats: "one lot for the LORD and the other lot for Azazel" (Leviticus 16:8). One goat was slain as a sin offering for the people. Then the priest laid his hands on the second goat, confessed the people's sins over it, and sent the goat, now bearing the sins, into the wilderness. The second goat was said to be going "to Azazel."

Who or what was Azazel? One interpretation suggests that the word means "the goat that departs," or "the escaping goat," hence the English word "scapegoat." Another is that Azazel was the name of the place to which the goat was sent.

Most scholars think the word means something like "angry god." Azazel was probably a demon dwelling in the desert, an area believed to be the favorite habitat of evil spirits. It may be that the ritual of dispatching the second goat was meant to send the evil of sin back to a place of evil. Or perhaps "all their iniquities" (16:22) were being sent where they could do no harm.

ritually impure, and thus unholy. To remain holy, one had to avoid impurity, which in the case of some foods meant total avoidance. "And the LORD said to Moses and Aaron, 'Say to the people of Israel, These are the living things which you may eat among all the beasts that are on the earth. Whatever parts the hoof and is cloven-footed and chews the cud, among the animals, you may eat. . . . And the swine, because it parts the hoof and is cloven-footed but does not chew the cud, is unclean to you.' " (11:1–3; 7). To this day, many observant Jews adhere to the dietary laws as prescribed in Leviticus, and elsewhere in the Bible.

Rules for purification were prescribed when defilement could not be avoided, as in the case of childbirth or handling the dead. "The LORD said to Moses, . . . If a woman conceives, and bears a male child, then she shall be unclean seven days . . . [she shall not] come into the sanctuary, until the days of her purifying are completed" (12:1).

There were certain guidelines for determining whether or not something was unclean, as in the case of certain diseases. "When a man or woman has a disease on the head or the beard, the priest shall examine the disease." The ancient Israelites seemed to have possessed a knowledge of contagion. Their practice of washing after the handling of corpses or the sick, and the quarantine of lepers, had practical value.

The first seven chapters of Leviticus described sacrifices ordained by the Lord. The offering of sacrifices was a central part of worship, and they were a means of maintaining and repairing one's relationship with God. Through sacrifice one could remove the pollution of uncleanness and sin.

Leviticus' rules and regulations had as their goal the maintenance of a special people, living in the right relationship with their God and with each other. The sacrificial rituals, the laws of cleanliness, the Day of Atonement, the Holiness Code, and the rest of the book can all be understood as addressing what God meant by the commandment, "you shall be holy; for I the LORD your God am holy. ✦

God commanded: "You shall have just balances"

Money and measurement in the Bible

WHEN THE MODERN state of Israel changed its currency in 1980, it harked back to the biblical past for the name of its new money, choosing the shekel, an important monetary unit in the Old Testament. As a result, the world's financial press was suddenly quoting the Bible, noting that the first time the shekel is mentioned is in Genesis 23:13–20, where Abraham bought a burial site for his wife Sarah with 400 shekels of silver.

In ancient times, the shekel was not a coin but a unit of weight (approximately 8.4 grams at the time), so Abraham did not count out 400 pieces of silver, he weighed it. The word *shekel* comes from the Hebrew *to weigh*, but the Hebrews borrowed their system of weights from the Babylonians and the Egyptians.

Weighing was done on two kinds of scales: one, a balance beam that hung by a cord; the other, balances that employed weights of varying shapes and sizes. Originally the weights were grains, so that in earliest times a shekel was equal to 320 grains of barley. But even when grains were replaced with weights of cast metal or stone, the ancients were never able to achieve a uniform standard. Indeed, archaeologists have yet to find two weights that are exactly alike. It was not only a lack of precision tools—the weight of a shekel varied from city to city, from merchant to merchant, and even from use to use. There were royal weights and weights for common people; there was a commercial shekel as well as the "shekel of the sanctuary," with which the Hebrews were asked to make their religious offerings. Little wonder that some people brought their own weights along when making purchases.

The Bible is specific throughout in its numerous exhortations against dishonest weight. Leviticus 19:35, for instance, enjoins us: "You shall do no wrong in judgment, in measures of length or weight or quantity." Deuteronomy 25:13 declares: "You shall not have in your bag two kinds of weights, a large and a small," and in Proverbs 20:10 we find: "Diverse weights and diverse measures are both alike an abomination to the LORD."

Gold, being rare, was used mostly for state business, such as royal gifts and the payment of tribute. Virtually all commercial transactions in Palestine were conducted in silver. But a shekel of silver in Abraham's day did not necessarily have the same purchasing power later on. Abraham's 400 shekels bought much more than just a burial plot for Sarah; he got a cave, a field, and all the trees on and bordering the field. Jeremiah paid 17 shekels for the field at Anathoth (Jeremiah 32:9), but we have no way of knowing if this was a bargain compared to Abraham's purchase or whether it merely indicates a stronger currency.

While the shekel was the basic unit of weight in the Old Testament, it was not the only one. Principal among the others were the gerah and the beka, which were smaller than the shekel, and the mina and the talent, which were larger. Of these, the Bible gives only the beka a specified value, that of half a shekel.

Coins came into circulation around the sixth

A hoard of ancient coins was found stored in an oil lamp.

century B.C. Although the practice of weighing rather than counting money was in use at the time of Jesus, coins were increasingly prevalent, and those of Roman, Jewish, and Greek origin were available for commerce.

The standard coin in Jesus' day was the silver denarius, minted by the Romans. In the 17th century, the King James Version of the New Testament called this coin a "penny." (It would be worth more than a dollar today.) The parable of the laborers in the vineyard (Matthew 20:1–16) indicates that a denarius was equal to a day's wage. Some scholars think that 30 of these coins comprised "the thirty pieces of silver" for which Judas Iscariot betrayed Jesus. If so, all he got for the betrayal was a month's wages.

Just as the shekel was a basic unit of currency in the Old Testament, so was the cubit its principal unit of length. Measured as the length of a man's arm from his bent elbow to the tip of his middle finger, the cubit was hardly a precise gauge, but it

became standardized over time, and it is found throughout the Bible, from Genesis 6: 15–16, in God's instructions to Noah for building the ark, to John 21:8, where Jesus' disciples, fishing in the sea of Tiberias, are only 200 cubits from land. But just as there was more than one type of shekel, there was also more than one kind of cubit: a common one, which contained six handbreadths, and a royal, or sanctuary, cubit, which was equal to seven.

A handbreadth, also called a palm, was measured as the width of four fingers. It is not to be confused with the span, equal to half a common cubit, the distance between the thumb and the little finger when the hand is stretched as far as it will go.

The most accurate information we have about the length of the biblical cubit comes from an inscription found near Jerusalem in 1880, which describes the construction of a water tunnel by King Hezekiah. Mentioned in 2 Kings 20:20, the tunnel still exists, so

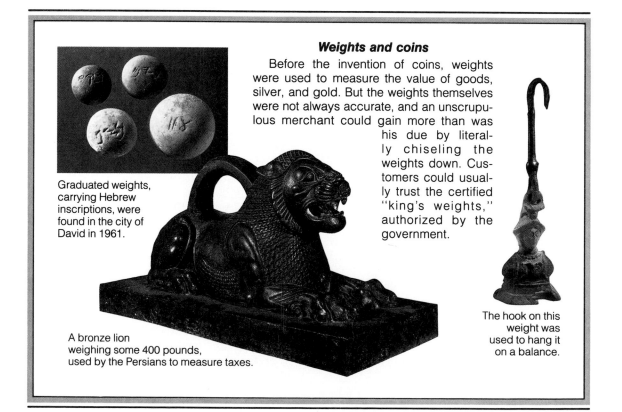

Weights and coins

Before the invention of coins, weights were used to measure the value of goods, silver, and gold. But the weights themselves were not always accurate, and an unscrupulous merchant could gain more than was his due by literally chiseling the weights down. Customers could usually trust the certified "king's weights," authorized by the government.

Graduated weights, carrying Hebrew inscriptions, were found in the city of David in 1961.

A bronze lion weighing some 400 pounds, used by the Persians to measure taxes.

The hook on this weight was used to hang it on a balance.

Measuring and recording the harvest is shown in a wall painting in the Tomb of Menena, at Thebes (18th dynasty).

when archaeologists learned from the inscription that it was 1,200 cubits long, some measurements were possible. Using the Israelite common cubit as their standard, and allowing for the fact that they did not know exactly from which point the 1,200 cubits were measured, the scholars concluded that the tunnel was 533.1 meters, or 1,749 feet, in length and that the cubit, therefore, measured 444 millimeters, or 17.49 inches.

Distances were expressed in such colorful terms as a "bowshot" or "a furrow's length," or in such vague terms as "a short distance," "a day's journey," or "a Sabbath day's journey." Land area was almost always stated in terms of a "yoke"—that is, the land a pair of oxen could plow in one day. A field was measured in terms of the amount of seed needed to sow it.

How rabbinical scholars have interpreted such inexact phrases can be seen in their reasoning that a Sabbath day's journey was equal to 2,000 cubits. This number has been arrived at in two different ways, but they both start with the section in Exodus that instructs the Jews in observance of the Sabbath, and particularly Exodus 16:29, where it says, "Let no man go out of his place on the seventh day." This certainly sounds as if everyone should stay at home.

In the first interpretation, scholars point to Numbers 35:5, where the Lord issues directions to Moses about building cities, saying that the cities should have city pastures extending 2,000 cubits outside their walls—much as today's "three-mile limit"

extends a nation's territorial waters. This was taken to mean that the "place" in Exodus 16:29 could be the city itself, which would, of course, include the 2,000 cubits outside the walls. Thus was a 2,000-cubit journey on the Sabbath justified.

In the second interpretation, scholars go from Exodus to Joshua 3:4, where the Israelites are told that when they see the priests carrying the ark of the covenant they may "go after it," but only at a distance behind it of 2,000 cubits. Since the Sabbath was a day of rest and worship, and since the ark was an object of worship, and since priests (and perhaps others) were allowed to approach it for prayer, the conclusion was that a Sabbath day's journey of no more than 2,000 cubits, or 2,916 feet, was permissible.

The New Testament has a few linear measurements that are not found in the Old. Notable among these is the fathom (Acts 27:28), which is based on the Greek word for armstretch and represents the distance between the fingertips of the outstretched arms.

A scholar who has made a study of Bible weights and measures, R.B.Y. Scott, has calculated that, by our standards, Isaiah's "acre" was only about half an acre. He estimates that Goliath stood roughly nine feet, six inches high, and the possible weight of his coat of mail was 125 pounds. Whereas some scholars, using the royal cubit, calculate Solomon's Temple to be about 140 feet long, Scott, using the common cubit, says it was about 88 feet long. ✦

Sacred numbers in the Bible

What is their inner meaning?

ECHOING MYTHIC TRADITIONS that go back before the earliest civilizations, the people of ancient Israel saw mystical and symbolic significances in certain numbers and were often given to incorporating them in their accounts of sacred events and omens. The precise symbolic intent of any of these numbers in a specific passage in the Bible can never be proved to the satisfaction of all interpreters, but some generalizations hold true in many cases.

Two is the number expressing both the duality of opposites and the unity in their pairing. Two appears in this sense in Genesis, in the persons of Adam and Eve, and in the text relating how the animals came, two by two, to Noah's Ark. Subsequently, the number two appears in the tradition of the two stone tablets on which the Ten Commandments were revealed to Moses on Mount Sinai and in the stories depicting opposites (Cain and Abel, Leah and Rachel; Martha and Mary).

Three represents the many faces of completeness—heaven, earth, and the underworld; beginning, middle, and end. Similar-ly in the Bible, many rituals are carried out in threes—daily prayers and yearly fasts, for example. Three is also associated with sacrifices—animals often had to be three years old (Genesis 15:9); fruit was not to be harvested until three years after the tree was planted (Leviticus 19:23).

Four represents cosmic order, as in the four phases of the moon, the four cardinal points of the earth, the four rivers of Paradise (Genesis 2:10), the four winds of heaven (Jeremiah 49:36), the four guardians of the throne of God, and so forth. But the number can also represent the adversaries of order—for example, the Four Horsemen who bring calamity on the earth (Revelation 6:1–8) and the four sore acts of Judgment (sword, famine, evil beasts, and pestilence) with which God threatens the idolators of Jerusalem (Ezekiel 14:21).

Seven is the most important number of all, tracing back to the cosmology of the Sumerians who recognized seven "planets"—the sun and moon, along with Mercury, Venus, Mars, Jupiter, and Saturn. As Earth was believed to be under planetary

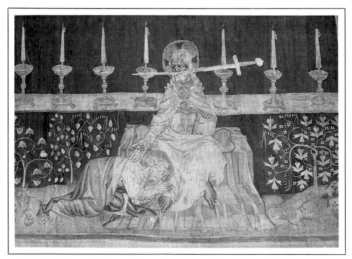

In this French tapestry, *the seven lampstands represent the seven churches of the Book of Revelation.*

influence, the number of the planets was viewed as a key to the correspondences between the changes in the heavens and those in the world of men. Seven was taken as the number of days making up a week—note that the names of the days of the week remain a living witness to the role of the planets in our lives, with the seventh day ultimately becoming sanctified in the Judaic tradition as the Sabbath, the day on which God rested after creation. The weekly pattern gave rise to the special sacredness of the Seventh Month, to the Sabbatical Year, the seventh year in which even the land itself was allowed to rest and remain fallow; and to the Jubilee Year, which came after the seventh seventh, or forty-ninth, year and marked a special time in which all Hebrew slaves were to be free, all debts resolved, and ancestral property returned to its original owner (Leviticus 25).

Seven-branched menorah on a Hasmonean coin.

Jews commemorated the number seven in the seven branches of the menorah, in the seven-day feasts of Passover and of Tabernacles, in the Seven Pillars of Wisdom (Proverbs 9:1), and in many small rituals, such as the sprinkling of bullock's blood seven times (Leviticus 4:6) and the sacrifice of seven lambs (Numbers 28:11).

Seven continues to have symbolic prominence in the New Testament, with Jesus telling Peter that it is not enough that he forgive the brother who had sinned against him seven times, but "seventy times seven" (Matthew 18:21–22). Seven is also the number of Greek-speaking Christians appointed by the Twelve Apostles in Acts 6:3.

The New Testament concludes in a great surge of sevens, with heptads, explicit and implicit, tumbling forth from many verses. Here, for example, in Revelation 1:19–20, Jesus tells John, "Now write what you see, what is and what is to take place hereafter. As for the mystery of the seven stars which you saw in my right hand, and the seven golden lampstands, the seven stars are the angels of the seven churches and the seven lampstands are the seven

churches." And later, John tells that he has beheld a lamb with seven horns and seven eyes, "which are the seven spirits of God sent out into all the earth" (Revelation 5:6). In a larger sense, then, seven denotes perfection, totality.

Twelve may have taken hold as a mystical number in the Middle East some 5,000 years ago. The ancient people recognized 12 lunar cycles corresponding loosely to 12 months in the year, and they divided the day and the night into 12-hour periods. They went on to organize the stars into the 12 signs of the Zodiac, and from their observations of the wanderings of the 7 planets through the 12 houses of heaven was born astrology.

The Bible tells that Jacob-Israel had 12 sons (Genesis 35:22–27) and that each of these became the founder of one of the Twelve Tribes of Israel, the people of God (Genesis 49:28). As if to link himself with the elective purposes of God, Jesus took Twelve Apostles (Matthew 10:2–4) to assist him in his mission. There were 24 classes of priests and Levites (1 Chronicles 24:4) and 48 Levitical cities (Numbers 35:7). And again in the Book of Revelation, the number 12 rivals 7 in importance when symbolizing the salvation of God's people. There are 24 elders around the throne of God and 144,000 of the saved (Revelation 4:4; 7:4). The perfection of the new Jerusalem is seen in its 12 gates, each "a single pearl," and 12 foundations, each adorned with jewels. Its circumference is 12,000 furlongs, and its walls are 144 cubits high (Revelation 21:10–21; Ezekiel 48:30–35).

Aside from their sacred symbolism, some of these numbers were also used to express "round'" or indefinite numbers in the following manner: 2 for a couple, 3 for a few, 7 for many, or 40 for a long period of time. And so far as larger numbers were concerned, there was never any intent to have large numbers taken at face value, but rather to express generalities—for example, the word for "thousand" in Hebrew denotes "a crowd." ✦

The spies return from Canaan.

A promise deferred

Why the Hebrews wandered for forty years

WHEN ISRAEL CAME from Sinai to Kadesh in the wilderness of Paran, they were on the doorstep of the Promised Land. Their journey had been arduous. According to the Book of Numbers, the people had complained incessantly, and God had struck them with punishments. Even Moses had cried out to God because of the burdens he carried.

When at last the end of the journey was in sight, and the Promised Land lay before the Israelites, their entry was delayed. As they neared their destination, the Lord told Moses to send a leader from each tribe to scout the land they were about to invade. For 40 days the scouts traversed Canaan. When they returned, they reported that the land was all that had been promised. "It flows with milk and honey," they said, and showed a cluster of grapes, cut near Hebron, so heavy that it had to be carried by two men (Numbers 13:23–27).

However, they also reported that the land was fully occupied and fortified. "The land, through which we have gone, to spy it out, is a land that devours its inhabitants; and all the people that we saw in it are men of great stature . . . we seemed to ourselves like grasshoppers, and so we seemed to them." One interpretation of "devours its inhabitants" is that the land did not produce enough to sustain life adequately, a

mysterious contradiction of their earlier proclamation of a land of plenty.

Only two of the 12 spies, Caleb and Joshua, recommended that the invasion proceed. The people wept at the grim news and sought a new captain to lead them back to Egypt (Numbers 14:1–4).

Yahweh responded to their lack of faith with a drastic plan. "I will strike them with the pestilence and disinherit them," he told Moses, "and I will make of you a nation greater and mightier than they." But Moses begged Yahweh to forgive them: "Pardon the iniquity of this people, I pray thee, according to the greatness of thy steadfast love, and according as thou hast forgiven this people, from Egypt until now."

The Lord responded by sparing the Israelites from death. Instead he subjected them to 40 years in the wilderness, a year for each day the spies were in Canaan. No one 20 years or older, except Caleb and Joshua, would be allowed to enter the land: "And your children shall be shepherds in the wilderness forty years, and shall suffer for your faithlessness, until the last of your dead bodies lies in the wilderness" (Numbers 14:33). "Turn tomorrow," God said, "and set out for the wilderness" (Numbers 14:25).

When the people heard the Lord's verdict, Canaan began to look much more inviting. The next day, rather than turning toward the wilderness, they immediately tried to invade the hill country of the Amalekites and Canaanites, leaving behind Moses and the Ark of the Covenant. The foolish attack failed, and Israel was left to her fate in the desert.

In later generations the image of the great company wandering in the wilderness became a powerful symbol. In Jeremiah, for example, it was portrayed as a time of Israel's purification; a time of devotion to Yahweh and loving dependence on his care.

However, in the Book of Numbers, the actual period of wandering is not described at all. Some scholars believe that the 40 years in the desert were in fact an extended sojourn at Kadesh.

In the Bible, the number 40 had deep symbolic significance. Noah's rains lasted 40 days, as did Moses' sojourn on Mount Sinai (Exodus 24:18). Forty years represented a generation, the age of full maturity (Exodus 2:11). Forty years was usually the period of a person's prime—20 to 60.

All those of the wandering generation except Caleb and Joshua had to die off before the Israelites could enter the Promised Land. This meant that those who finally entered Canaan would be young and vigorous. They had been disciplined by the desert and knew nothing of the enticements of urban life in Egypt, with its pagan cults. Nor had they been cowed by conditions of servitude. In that no-man's land of the desert, they had been molded into something that they had not been earlier, a nation that belonged to God.

Moses was also denied entry into the Promised Land. In Kadesh, God had told him, "You shall bring water out of the rock," for "there was no water for the congregation." When Moses took credit for the miracle, the Lord condemned both Moses and Aaron to die outside the land of Canaan. At the end of the Book of Numbers, the Israelites had encamped near the border of Canaan, and were preparing to attack. In Deuteronomy, Moses addressed his people three times, bidding them farewell and urging them to faithfulness. He said, "And now, O Israel, give heed to the statutes and the ordinances which I teach you, and do them; that you may live, and go in and take possession of the land which the Lord, the God of your fathers, gives you" (Deuteronomy 4:1). After explaining to them the commandments and laws, Moses gave a final blessing to the tribes. "Happy are you, O Israel! Who is like you, a people saved by the Lord, the shield of your help, and the sword of your triumph!"

Moses climbed "from the plains of Moab to Mount Nebo, to the top of Pisgah." From the height he viewed the land his people were to occupy. And there Moses died at the age of 120 years. ✦

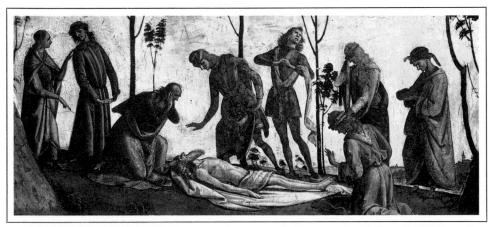

"I have let you see it with your eyes, but you shall not go over there." Moses, who had led the Israelites from bondage to freedom, died in the land of Moab.*

Numbering the people

Curious taboos in method

Leaders of the 12 tribes, *in a 14th century French miniature.*

ON THREE OCCASIONS God gave instructions to Moses on counting the Israelite nation. The basic law for conducting a census is recorded in Exodus 30:11–16. The Lord ordered the taking of the first census while the Israelites were still at Sinai, in the second month of the second year after the Exodus (Numbers 1:1–49). The Israelites were again counted 40 years after the Exodus, as they prepared to enter the Promised Land. These two censuses give the Book of Numbers its name.

Like modern governments, ancient societies used the census for two primary purposes: taxation and military recruitment. The Israelites had the same concerns. The census law in Exodus was meant to provide financial support for upkeep of the tabernacle. "Each who is numbered in the census shall give . . . half a shekel as an offering to the LORD" (Exodus 30:13).

However, the same instructions were also the source for a traditional Jewish taboo against the direct counting of people. God says, "when you take the census of the people of Israel, then each shall give a ransom for himself to the LORD when you number them, that there be no plague among them when you number them" (Exodus 30:12). Each Israelite gave half a shekel, a piece of silver of a specific weight; evidently, the money was then counted and the population was calculated by multiplying that figure by two.

The Israelites took seriously the Lord's threat to send a plague if they directly counted heads. The Bible reports that King David ordered a direct census "through all the tribes of Israel" (2 Samuel 24:2). His sin was punished with a pestilence that killed 70,000 people.

The Israelites, travelling through a desert populated by potentially hostile tribes, had to be ready for war at a moment's notice. Thus, the military purpose of the biblical censuses is also clear. Only males above the age of twenty were counted, "all in Israel who are able to go forth to war."

Moses' last census, taken immediately before his death and the invasion of the Israelites into Canaan, had yet another purpose. "To these the land shall be divided for inheritance," God told Moses, "according to the number of names. To a large tribe you shall give a large inheritance, and to a small tribe you shall give a small inheritance; every tribe shall be given its inheritance according to its numbers."

Why is direct numbering opposed in the Bible? The prohibition may be of superstitious origin, stemming from the idea that somehow an "evil eye" will do harm to a group of people if their number is known. In Jewish tradition, however, there was great stress on a moral lesson implicit in the taboo. The rabbis teach that the Jewish people are not simply a collection of individuals, rather they are part of a nation. Census-taking lays stress on the individual, whereas the contribution of a half shekel helps bind the nation. Thus each Israelite, rich or poor, gave *half* of a shekel. No one member of the community is whole without the participation of his fellows. ✦

PART II

History

The Books of Joshua, Judges, Ruth,
1 and 2 Samuel, 1 and 2 Kings, 1 and 2 Chronicles,
Ezra, Nehemiah, and Esther

*From their conquest of the Promised
Land to the dark hour of their exile, the
Israelites were tested by God. They
struggled with the temptations of
prosperity and the loss of faith in times
of adversity. Again and again they fell
from grace, but again and again God
forgave their transgressions.*

The Israelites felt that entering the Promised Land was not so much an invasion as a homecoming.

The waters part again

Crossing the Jordan on dry land

THE STORY TOLD in the Book of Joshua is one of a promise fulfilled, the promise made by the Lord to Abraham in Genesis 17:8, that his descendants would inherit "all the land of Canaan." Threaded from Genesis through the rest of the Pentateuch (the first five books of the Bible) is the account of how the children of Israel made their way to the redemption of that pledge, over long years of bondage, exodus, and wandering in the Wilderness. By the end of the Pentateuch, the Israelites were camped on the Plains of Moab, looking toward Canaan from the east bank of the Jordan River. The fifth book, Deuteronomy, ends with the death of Moses and the emergence of his successor, Joshua, as leader of the Israelites. It fell to Joshua to wage the battles that finally brought the descendants of Abraham into the Promised Land.

Picking up where Deuteronomy leaves off, the Book of Joshua describes the conquest of Canaan. In spite of the fact that the book does not name its author and indeed describes the death of Joshua, tradition has often ascribed the writing of the book to Joshua himself. Close study of the text has convinced most scholars, however, that the Book of Joshua was composed in stages over a period ranging from 300 to 700 years after the time of the conquest.

The book opens with Joshua preparing the invasion of Canaan, receiving orders and advice from the Lord himself, who plays a very active role in all the ensuing events. Biblical commentators have noted that the Lord and his works are so omnipresent in the Book of Joshua that its authors must have viewed the conquest of Canaan as a miracle rather than a series of military events. But Joshua's capability as a commander can also clearly be seen from the Bible's account of his planning and execution of the invasion.

Joshua first set his sights on the city of Jericho, whose walls and battlements seemed to represent a formidable challenge. To gauge his prospects, he sent spies into the city, where they were aided by a prostitute named Rahab. She told them the inhabitants were already afraid of the Israelites, having heard of the miraculous parting of the Red Sea and of their ferocity as warriors.

On receiving this report, Joshua moved quickly. At God's command, he instructed the priests to lead the way across the Jordan, bearing the Ark of the Covenant. Although spring floods were swelling the Jordan, when the priests' feet touched the river, "the waters coming down from above stood and rose up in a heap far off." Thus the Israelites were able to pass into Canaan on dry ground, while the priests—holding the Ark—stood in the middle of the channel. Once they reached the other side, "the waters of the Jordan returned to their place and overflowed all its banks, as before."

Seeking a naturalistic explanation for the biblical narrative, some have suggested that an earthquake may have occurred that allowed the Israelites to cross the Jordan on foot. This theory was researched by a team from Stanford University in the United States and the Weizmann Institute in Israel. Relying on historical, archaeological, and biblical documents, the scholars obtained evidence that the region has experienced earthquakes for 2,000 years. During 10 of the 30 earthquakes recorded in the documents, the Jordan did indeed stop flowing for a day or two because of mud slides.

Whatever the event that underlies the story of this extraordinary crossing, stopping the waters was the Lord's way of demonstrating his support for Joshua, for he said: "This day I will begin to exalt you in the sight of all Israel, that they may know that, as I was with Moses, so I will be with you" (Joshua 3:7). The narrative emphasizes that it was the Ark of the Covenant that was the particular instrument of this mighty miracle. The crossing of the Jordan is not described as a military invasion but as a priestly procession: the Lord opens the gate of the Promised Land to his sanctified people.

In order that the divine meaning of the crossing be handed down from generation to generation, Joshua left two mounds of rocks so that children might ask, "What do these stones mean?" One mound was in the middle of the Jordan, where the Ark had stood; the other was at Gilgal, the first Israelite camp in the Promised Land.

It was at Gilgal that Joshua carried out the Lord's command to renew the covenant with Abraham. The Lord said: "Make flint knives and circumcise the people of Israel again the second time." With this injunction, the Lord ushered in what has been described as a "new era," for God was ordering the circumcision of a later generation of Hebrews, the sons of the people who had participated in the Exodus from Egypt. Their fathers had been circumcised before leaving Egypt, but as the much later talmudic commentary suggests, newborn males were not circumcised in the Wilderness for fear of weakening them when they had hardships to endure.

Because it takes time for such wounds to heal, the Israelites were vulnerable to attack by the Canaanites. But according to Joshua 5:1, when the Canaanites "heard that the LORD had dried up the waters of the Jordan for the people of Israel until they had crossed over, their heart melted, and there was no longer any spirit in them." So the people of Israel, camped at Gilgal on the eve of the invasion of Jericho, were able to enjoy their Passover celebration in peace. ✦

"Leaders do not always realize their objectives. Nations do not always attain to what they might have attained. Individuals do not always reach their possible goals. The design and plan of God for life is so much greater than we realize. That was especially true of Israel."
—**Joseph R. Sizoo**
The Interpreter's Bible

99

Walls collapse at the trumpets' sound

Trumpet blasts that re-echo throughout history

JOSHUA IS RANKED AMONG THE GREATEST of the Old Testament's many mighty men, and his battle at Jericho was a great victory for the Hebrews. The preparation for the battle begins in Joshua 5:13, when Joshua suddenly confronts a man with a drawn sword who identifies himself as the "commander of the army of the LORD." Recognizing the man as a manifestation of the Divine, Joshua falls to the ground in worship and requests his orders. Though the meeting between Joshua and the "commander" is mysteriously inconclusive, the episode serves to reveal the presence of a supernatural army with its commander ready for battle with drawn sword.

The commander also tells Joshua that the place where he stands is holy, probably meaning that the city of Jericho, as Joshua later says, is "devoted to the LORD for destruction" (Joshua 6:17). In keeping with the concerns of a much later age, rabbinical sages explained that the angel's mission was to castigate the Israelites for neglecting their study of the Law.

Joshua did not at first know that the man with a sword was an angel, and so asked if he was friend or foe. An angel with a drawn sword also appears in the story of Balaam (Numbers 22).

At the opening of Chapter 6, the Lord himself gives the instructions that Joshua requested. The city of Jericho and its army have already been given by God to Joshua, and the Lord tells him how to receive the gift: "You shall march around the city, all the men of war going around the city once. Thus shall you do for six days. And seven priests shall bear seven trumpets of rams' horns before the Ark; and on the seventh day you shall march around the city seven times, the priests blowing the trumpets. And when they make a long blast with the ram's horn, as soon as you hear the sound of the trumpet, then all the people shall shout with a great shout; and the wall of the city will fall down flat, and the people shall go up every man straight before him."

When Jericho fell, exactly as predicted, it was totally destroyed by the Israelites. Because the narrators understand this as a holy war fought more by God than by Joshua's army, they do not wince at describing the utter destruction of "both men and women, young and old, oxen, sheep and asses with the edge of the sword." Throughout the ages the belief in holy war has increased the ferocity of armies.

It should be noted, moreover, that the fall of Jericho not only took place by God's command, but took place on the Sabbath. Spoils from this victory, consecrated as it was by "blowing the trumpets" (shofars), were thus dedicated to the Lord.

No satisfactory explanation has been put forth for the walls of Jericho collapsing when the Israelites blew their trumpets and shouted. An earthquake theory offered by an archaeologist in the mid-1930's was proved inaccurate. A British military historian, General Sir Richard Gale, thought the falling of the walls of Jericho "was in fact the crumbling of the will of the inhabitants to fight." Other commentators suggest that the story is meant to hint that Rahab be-

Blowing their trumpets, seven priests march around Jericho bearing the Ark of the Covenant.

trayed her people by opening the city gates to the Israelites when she heard a "great shout" outside. Still another theory suggests that perhaps the gates were opened by Israelites who had infiltrated the city.

The quest for the walls of Jericho, however, has been a fascinating archaeological story throughout the 20th century. Excavations at such sites as Hazor and Lachish have revealed clear destruction from the period of the conquest in the late 13th century B.C., leading one to expect the remains of Jericho's walls to be found as well.

Because of the fame of its conquest, Jericho was one of the earliest major ruins excavated in Palestine. From 1907 to 1911, a team led by E. Sellin and C. Watzinger carefully probed the site, known as Tell es-Sultan. However, what Sellin thought were the ruins of Jericho from the 9th century B.C. turned out to be from the 17th century B.C.—a difference of about eight centuries.

In the 1930's the British archaeologist John Garstang worked at Jericho and discovered that the city's remains in fact date back to the Stone Age. He, too, was unable adequately to connect Joshua's conquest to remains of the city walls.

The final stage of the quest for Jericho was led by the eminent archaeologist Kathleen Kenyon in the 1950's. She confirmed the great antiquity of Jericho, showing that it is perhaps the oldest known city in the world. She found, in contradiction to Garstang, that the last major city on the site was destroyed about 300 years before Moses (or 400 years before Joshua). Thus the long, fervent quest for the walls of Joshua's period was again unsuccessful.

Seeking an explanation for this lack of evidence, archaeologists today suggest that Jericho was probably more like a small town in Joshua's time. Hence, its walls would have been made of mud brick, a weak building material that would have eroded away over the centuries. In the absence of "rational" explanations, one thing is certain: though the mystery of Jericho's walls remains, the enduring spiritual message of the story is clear and unimpaired. ✦

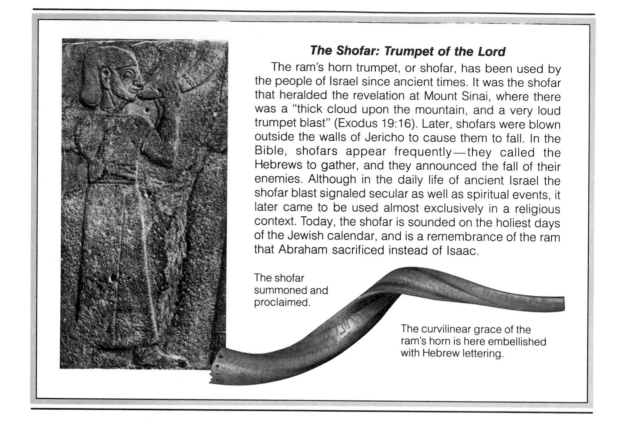

The Shofar: Trumpet of the Lord

The ram's horn trumpet, or shofar, has been used by the people of Israel since ancient times. It was the shofar that heralded the revelation at Mount Sinai, where there was a "thick cloud upon the mountain, and a very loud trumpet blast" (Exodus 19:16). Later, shofars were blown outside the walls of Jericho to cause them to fall. In the Bible, shofars appear frequently—they called the Hebrews to gather, and they announced the fall of their enemies. Although in the daily life of ancient Israel the shofar blast signaled secular as well as spiritual events, it later came to be used almost exclusively in a religious context. Today, the shofar is sounded on the holiest days of the Jewish calendar, and is a remembrance of the ram that Abraham sacrificed instead of Isaac.

The shofar summoned and proclaimed.

The curvilinear grace of the ram's horn is here embellished with Hebrew lettering.

No booty, no prisoners

A new kind of warfare—the holy war

THE FIERCE THEOLOGY OF HOLY WAR was laid out explicitly in the Book of Deuteronomy. It specified that in the cities of Canaan that were to be overthrown, "when the LORD your God gives them over to you, and you defeat them; then you must utterly destroy them; you shall make no covenant with them, and show no mercy to them." Together with all of its inhabitants, each condemned city was to be offered up, booty and all, to the Lord. Moreover, the text instructs the Israelites not to be afraid of their enemies: "for the LORD your God is he that goes with you, to fight for you against your enemies, to give you victory."

Looking back across the centuries at the bloodshed that followed, the narrators of the Book of Joshua stress that if the He-brews were successful in warfare, it was because God was leading them: they were soldiers in God's army. The conquest of Canaan is viewed, in fact, as a divine conquest—a holy war fought by Israel's God to fulfill his promise to his people—something no mortal man could alter. Indeed, the belief that "The LORD is a man of war" (Exodus 15:3), who could give victory in any situation, was to have far-reaching consequences throughout the history of Israel down to the last stand of the Zealots against overwhelming Roman forces in the first century A.D. As the Book of Joshua describes it, the Lord gave the enemy into Israel's hands: thus, they could not fail. Indeed, so terrible was Joshua's Lord of conquest that death might seem inescapable. ✦

The guile of the Gibeonites

How Joshua was tricked into an alliance

HAVING ERADICATED JERICHO and all its inhabitants, the Israelites moved on to the city of Ai. They were at first defeated at Ai because of the Lord's anger at one Israelite, Achan, who after the conquest of Jericho had tainted the holiness of their cause by stealing some of the spoils that were to be offered up to the Lord. But eventually the city of Ai and its people succumbed to the Israelites' swords. Fear of the Israelites was now widespread. The inhabitants of the Canaanite town of Gibeon devised a desperate ruse by which they hoped to save themselves.

The Israelite encampment was near Gibeon, a town that was therefore marked for destruction. The Gibeonites decided to approach Joshua as though they were people from a far-off country, coming to make a covenant of peace. They dressed themselves to look as if they had traveled a long distance, wearing worn-out clothes and carrying shabby equipage and moldy food. When the Gibeonites arrived at the Israelite camp, they were viewed with suspicion. But they were able to convince the Israelites of their peaceful intent by offering to become their servants. Joshua accepted, and gave them the covenant they sought.

It took three days for the Israelites to discover that the Gibeonites had tricked them and were really their neighbors. The Israelites were angered, but their hands were tied by the covenant, and they could not kill the Gibeonites. However, the Gibeonites did not go unpunished. "Joshua made them that day hewers of wood and drawers of water" (Joshua 9:27).

The Gibeonites' peace treaty also infuriated the rulers of five nearby kingdoms, who joined in an attack against their city. When the Gibeonites appealed to Joshua for help, he was bound to oblige them, for their treaty had made Gibeon a dependent state.

First, the narrators tell how the Lord "threw down great stones from heaven" upon the five kings. Then, when Joshua asked him to stop the sun and moon to give him a greater advantage over the foe, the Lord did that as well. Demolishing the five kings, Joshua continued his campaign through the south of Canaan, then turned to fight an alliance of cities in the north.

Eventually the warfare halted. Joshua assembled his people at Shiloh and set up the tent of meeting. According to the Bible, it was at this time that division of the conquered lands among the 12 tribes was completed. Under Joshua's command, the Israelites captured much of Canaan. But in spite of heroic campaigns and many successes, the Israelites never did consolidate their hold on the Promised Land. ✦

Joshua hung up the bodies *of the five kings as a warning to his enemies.*

Joshua demands that the sun and moon stand still

A righteous man decrees, and God fulfills his request

ONE OF THE GREAT BIBLE MIRACLES is the stopping of the sun and moon during the battle between Joshua and the five kings who attacked Gibeon. The event is the more extraordinary because the Lord stopped the sun at Joshua's request. Even narrators of the Book of Joshua look back across the centuries with wonder at the story: "The sun stayed in the midst of heaven, and did not hasten to go down for about a whole day. There has been no day like it before or since, when the LORD hearkened to the voice of a man; for the LORD fought for Israel" (Joshua 10:13–14).

All manner of explanations have been offered for this miracle, such as an eclipse, a

Israel's victory was accomplished by divine power; the Lord rained great hailstones on the enemy.

tended." The episode, he says, may reflect nothing more complicated than Joshua's wish to defeat the enemy before nightfall.

Such explanations, however, are outside the realm of the Bible itself. Accepting the accuracy of the narrative without question, scholars, both Jewish and Christian, have combed the Scriptures for parallels in order to explain its deeper meaning. Rabbinical scholars have offered numerous interpretations for Joshua's request that God make the sun and moon stand still.

One interpretation suggests that Joshua wished to finish the battle before the Sabbath and so wanted to stop the sun in an effort to gain time. The battle was fought on a Friday before sundown. And although waging war on the Sabbath was permitted for the conquest of the Promised Land, the Israelites would not be allowed to do so in this campaign because it was being fought in defense of the Gibeonites, rather than for the conquest of land. Other interpreters see this episode as a flashback to the dream in Genesis 37:9, in which Joseph saw 11 stars and the sun and moon bow down to him. This dream was considered a prophecy that the sun and moon would stop at the request of Joseph's descendant Joshua.

It is significant that the words of Joshua to the sun and moon are words of poetry. The poetry is derived from the *Book of Jashar*, an ancient anthology of poems that celebrated the exploits of the heroes of Israel. (The book is quoted at greater length in 2 Samuel 1:17–27.) Numerous interpreters have argued that the "standing still" is poetic imagery, which the authors read as a literal and remarkable miracle. However that may be, it is certainly true that the narrative in Joshua 10:13 describes a literal stopping of the sun in its course.

For the narrators, there was no ambiguity. The meaning of the miracle was quite clear. The Lord who was fighting the battles of Israel was also the creator of the universe, who could use every element of that creation as an implement of war to give his people victory. As the narrator concludes, "The LORD fought for Israel." ✦

hailstorm, the presence of the sun and moon in the sky together at dawn, and the clouding of the sky. It was the contention of Immanuel Velikovsky, author of *Worlds in Collision*, that the sun stood still because a near-collision between the earth and a comet caused a temporary halt in the earth's rotation. The biblical scholar Robert Houston Smith felt that readers of the Bible have often attributed to it "far more significance than the original storyteller probably in-

A woman warrior of Israel

Deborah, prophetess and judge

An inspired seer, *Deborah sang the recruiting song for the holy war against the Canaanites.*

THE SONG OF DEBORAH is one of the oldest pieces of Hebrew literature known. Scholars are in general agreement that this poem is the oldest text in the Bible. The accomplishments of a great woman are honored with these lines:

> The peasantry ceased in Israel, they ceased
>   until you arose, Deborah,
>   arose as a mother in Israel. . . .
> Awake, awake, Deborah!
>   Awake, awake, utter a song!
>   (Judges 5:7–12)

Ancient Hebrew society was dominated by men; hence, Deborah's rousing leadership and mighty deeds were a striking exception to the norm. She was able to rally enough of the disheartened and oppressed Israelite tribes to challenge in battle the powerful army of the Canaanite king of Hazor under his commander, Sisera. Her story

is told twice, first in a prose account and then in poetry. The poem, known as the "Song of Deborah," is an anthem of triumph celebrating Yahweh's victory over the Canaanites through this "mother in Israel." It breathes the spirit of exhilaration in victory that the Israelites experienced when the hated oppressor Sisera and his army were routed—perhaps as most scholars believe, because it was written at the very time of the battle in about 1125 B.C.

Both the prose and the poetry vividly portray the weak situation of early Israel. The northern tribes, described as "peasantry" or villagers, were in a state of near anarchy. They were unable to mount any organized resistance to Canaanite oppression enforced by "nine hundred chariots of iron." Under the Canaanite yoke, Israelite trade and communication by means of the donkey caravans that linked the tribes had become impossibly dangerous.

It was from this wretched position that Deborah, endowed with charismatic gifts, rose to the leadership of her people. She was both a prophet, who communicated the will of Yahweh to the people, and a judge, deciding legal disputes among those who came to her for judgment. As a prophet she roused Barak to command Israel's forces by telling him Yahweh's battle plan against the Canaanites (Judges 4:6–7). Barak accepted the challenge on the condition that Deborah herself accompany him in leading the army.

The two ultimately succeeded in gathering forces from the six tribes most directly hurt by the Canaanites, but these six tribes were sufficient. The battle took place in the valley of the Kishon River, southwest of the Sea of Galilee. As a combination of rain and river floods rendered the mighty chariots of the Canaanites useless on the soft ground, the Israelites saw the evidence of Yahweh's hand: "LORD, when thou didst go forth . . . yea, the clouds dropped water." ✦

Rembrandt's portrayal of the slaying of Sisera.

Killed with a tent peg

How Jael struck a blow for freedom

THE FINAL EPISODE of Deborah's campaign against the detested Canaanite general Sisera belonged to another woman. Jael was a woman of the Kenites, a Midianite clan that lived a nomadic existence in the Negeb desert south of Judah. They claimed an affinity to Israel through their descent from Hobab, the Midianite father-in-law of Moses.

Jael's husband, Heber, had separated from the main Kenite clan and "pitched his tent" in the north of Israel, where the king of Hazor held sway. As foreigners subject to the Canaanites, Heber and his wife apparently came to fear Sisera and his army of iron chariots as much as the Israelites did.

In any event, Jael's tent happened to lie in the path of Sisera as he tried to desert his own defeated army and escape from the pursuing Israelites. Jael evidently perceived Sisera as a deadly threat. Thus, she used all the guile she could muster to entrap and kill him.

The bait for the trap was the practice of hospitality, a custom of great importance to Bedouin clans such as the Kenites. To welcome a stranger into one's tent meant that one was responsible for protecting that stranger. When Sisera came asking for water, Jael welcomed him by offering him milk instead. Sisera trusted her welcome as "she brought him curds in a lordly bowl," and he rested in her tent.

Jael was no soldier, but as a nomadic woman she had set up her tent countless times—and therefore knew how to wield a mallet and tent peg. With these weapons she sprang her deadly trap. When her prey was asleep she struck and "drove the peg into his temple, till it went down into the ground" (Judges 4:21). Barak, in hot pursuit of Sisera in the hope of gaining glory for himself by killing his foe in person, found, upon arriving, that the deed had been done.

Certainly Jael's act was one of treachery, for she had betrayed both the Bedouin conventions of hospitality and the trust of Sisera. But as far as the Israelites were concerned, a far greater cause was at stake: freedom from Canaanite oppression. Thus they could sing in the "Song of Deborah":

"Most blessed of women be Jael,
 the wife of Heber the Kenite,
 of tent-dwelling women most blessed . . ."

A battle without swords

Miraculous signs of Israel's deliverance

THEMES AND IMAGES RECUR in the Bible. Faith is rewarded; idol worship is punished. So it was that when pagan altars appeared in Israelite villages, the people were brought to their knees by their enemies. In the story of Gideon, told in the Book of Judges, the enemies were the Midianites, an Arabic tribe who were distant blood relatives of Israel. Now, responding to prayers for help, an angel in human form appeared and picked an unlikely champion, a farmer named Gideon.

Without at first realizing that he was face to face with the Divine, Gideon met God's angel under an oak in Ophrah, just as Abraham had encountered three angels beneath the oaks of Mamre (Genesis 18:1–8). Like Abraham, Gideon offered his visitor food. Just as Abraham's visit from the Lord marked the birth of Israel, so Gideon's divine encounter marked a spiritual and physical deliverance of Israel. Not only did Gideon rout the desert raiders, he led a renewal of faith in Yahweh.

Like Moses before him, Gideon was skeptical when his visitor told him to go and deliver Israel. He asked for a sign. The angel drew fire from a rock with his staff, which consumed a meal of goat's meat, broth, and unleavened cakes. Then he vanished. Gideon forthwith built an altar to Yahweh.

The choice of Gideon becomes the more remarkable as the story reveals how deeply his own family and city were committed to the worship of the Canaanite god, Baal. Now, at God's command, Gideon tore down his father's altar to Baal as well as the Asherah, a totem to a pagan goddess, using a harnessed bull. The villagers were outraged at such sacrilege and wanted to kill Gideon, but his father, Joash, stopped them by saying: "If Baal is a god, let him contend for himself." Thus Gideon gained the name *Jerubbaal*, "Let Baal contend." Since Gideon had been called by God to deliver his people from the Midianites, his first act was to put an end to pagan worship among his own people. For it was not until this was done that he could hope to defeat the enemy.

In addition to being pagans, the Midianites in Gideon's time were a major military threat. Moreover, Gideon had a personal reason to hate the Midianites: they had murdered two of his brothers. There was, finally, an ancient blood feud between the Midianites and the Israelites. Stories of the Midianites in the Book of Numbers show that they were thought of as people who forsook God for Baal and enticed the Israelites to the same apostasy.

When Gideon saw that the Midianites and Amalekites had encamped in Israelite territory, "the Spirit of the LORD took possession of Gideon" (Judges 6:34), and he blew a shofar, or ram's-horn trumpet, and prepared to do battle. Gideon then asked for another sign that God would indeed fight for Israel. He was granted the sign he requested. A fleece laid down on the ground at night was soaked with dew the next morning, though the ground all around it was dry. Begging God not to be angry with him, Gideon asked to be shown the miracle in reverse. Next morning, on the dew-soaked ground, the fleece was dry. According to one of the legends that grew up around the Bible story, Gideon's mother sewed a piece of this miraculous fleece into the mantle he wore into battle.

On the deep meanings in Scripture

"How wonderful are your Scriptures! How profound! We see their surface and it attracts us like children. And yet, O my God, their depth is stupendous. We shudder to peer deep into them, for they inspire in us both the awe of reverence and the thrill of love."

—**Saint Augustine,** *Confessions*

In this stained-glass window *from a 16th-century German church,*
Gideon receives assurance of Israel's victory by the sign of the dry fleece (left, center).

In order to reinforce the meaning of these signs, God ordered Gideon to reduce the size of his army, so that Israel would not claim credit for the victory about to take place. The glory belonged to God alone.

Gideon allowed those afraid of battle to leave. More than 2 out of 3 of his soldiers departed, but l0,000 remained, and that was still far too many. God told Gideon to take his men down to the water, and to keep only those who drank from the river by putting their hands to their mouths and lapping like dogs. This seemingly arbitrary test has produced a variety of interpretations over the centuries—that God was choosing those who were least fit for battle, or most alert, or most humble. So far as the narrative of Judges is concerned, this strange test was simply a way to reduce the numbers of soldiers to a force of 300.

That same night God spoke with Gideon one more time, again commanding him to deliver Israel. If Gideon wanted more reassurance, God said, he could go visit the enemy camp. So Gideon spied on the Midianites. He listened to one soldier tell another of a dream he had had. The second sol-dier said the dream was a prophecy that the Midianites would surely lose the battle.

With this last sign from God, Gideon became invincible. He armed his men with trumpets, swords, and lighted torches concealed in jars. Under cover of night, the Israelites surrounded the enemy with three companies of soldiers. Suddenly, they blew their trumpets, smashed the jars containing the torches, and shouted, "A sword for the LORD and for Gideon." The Midianites were thrown into confusion and fled. Gideon and his army pursued them through the desert and beyond the Jordan River till at length Gideon captured two Midianite kings and threw their entire force into a panic. Thus "the day of Midian" came to stand for true Israelite victory (Isaiah 9:4).

Gideon delivered Israel from the destructive raids and achieved a peace that lasted for 40 years. He lived out his days with his harem, like a king; according to the Bible he had 70 sons. But he refused to be anointed as a king or to establish a dynastic succession for his sons, saying: "I will not rule over you, and my son will not rule over you; the LORD will rule over you." ✦

The case of the treacherous vestment

How captured treasure "became a snare for Gideon"

FTER REFUSING THE KINGSHIP, Gideon asked a favor from the men of Israel. He requested a portion of the booty of gold and jewels won by his army, and "Gideon made an ephod of it and put it in his city, in Ophrah; and all Israel played the harlot after it there, and it became a snare to Gideon and his family" (Judges 8:27). In the priestly laws of Israel there is a description of the "ephod" that the high priest was to wear—a colorful, gem-studded vestment to which an elaborate "breast piece of judgment" was attached. There is also mention of a "linen ephod" that David wore when he danced before the Ark as it was being brought to Jerusalem. But Gideon's ephod of gold does not match other mentions of ephods.

The fact that the ephod "became a snare" suggests that it was some sort of image of Yahweh, perhaps in the form of an elaborate golden garment. Although for Gideon it may have simply symbolized God's rule, Israel was seduced into idolatry by Gideon's ephod, and once more veered away from faith in Yahweh. Soon they were led astray by a son of Gideon, Abimelech. The Israelites again suffered oppression at the hands of their enemies, until Jephthah, a new judge, appeared to deliver them. ✦

110

"Jephthah came to his home . . . and behold, his daughter came out to meet him with timbrels and with dances."

The man who killed his daughter

Why Jephthah sacrificed his only child

THE MIGHTY WARRIOR JEPHTHAH of Gilead was unbeatable on the field of battle. He defeated the Ammonites, a pagan people with whom the Israelites had been feuding since the time of Moses. Jephthah also repelled the Ephraimites, a contentious tribe of Israel who challenged his rule. But Jephthah's life was marked with tragedy because he made a disastrous vow, which caused him to sacrifice his only daughter. He burned her as a votive offering to God, paying to God what he had promised for his victory over the Ammonites.

Jephthah is hardly the typical hero of Israel. Disinherited in his native Gilead as the son of a harlot and thus only half Israelite, he became an outlaw and led a band of brigands in the hills of Tob on the edge of the Arabian Desert. Still, when danger threatened Gilead, the elders of the region came to him and asked him to lead the struggle against the Ammonites, who were preparing to wage war against the Hebrews of Gilead. Jephthah agreed on the condition that he rule Gilead in peacetime as well. After sealing this pact before Yahweh at the shrine at Mizpah, Jephthah attempted to negotiate peace with the Ammonites. When their king refused, we are told, "the Spirit of the LORD came upon Jephthah," and he prepared for war (Judges 11:29). It was then that he made his vow. He promised that if God gave him victory over his foes, he would sacrifice the first person from his house to greet him on his return.

Jephthah was victorious in battle, for "the LORD gave them into his hand." But upon his homecoming, Jephthah was greeted by his daughter, his only child. She led a victory procession, singing and dancing in accordance with tradition. Rending his clothes in anguish, Jephthah revealed his vow: "I have opened my mouth to the LORD, and I cannot take back my vow."

With amazing calm the unnamed daughter acquiesced to the fulfillment of the vow. She only requested a little time. "Let me alone two months, that I may go and wander on the mountains, and bewail my virginity." This her father granted. She and the maidens of her entourage retreated to the mountains. After two months, she returned to her father and was sacrificed.

Why did Jephthah kill her? Why did he ever make such a vow? Human sacrifice was not typical of Israelite religion at the time. However, child sacrifice was not unknown. In 2 Kings 3:26–27 we are told how the king of Moab, in an act of desperation in a losing battle with Israel, had sacrificed his eldest son, and Israel had been turned back. There were even kings of Israel who sacrificed their sons (2 Kings 16:3; 21:6).

But as the narrative makes clear, Jeph-

thah does not fall into the same category as these kings. He had only one child, and he certainly never intended to sacrifice her. The narrators of the Book of Judges are very restrained in telling Jephthah's story. They do not rush to pronounce judgment against Jephthah; rather, they allow the unfolding events to reveal the character of his actions.

Jephthah had been restored from the position of an outcast to one of honor among his people. He had felt the Spirit of God. He wished to make a mighty vow—to make a bargain with God that would assure victory. Perhaps he believed that one of his many servants would come forth from his house when he arrived. In any case, the vow was open-ended—and a foolish act of bravado.

As the vow was uttered, the bargain was sealed. When Yahweh fulfilled Jephthah's wish, Jephthah had no choice; he could not take back his vow (Judges 11:37). Thus in a few brief sentences the narrators reveal at least two things. First, they show the foolhardy swaggering of this man of war. For all his military prowess and bandit cleverness, he did not have the foresight or the good sense to think ahead—through the implications of his actions. Second, they show the power of a vow. A vow was an absolutely binding obligation based on the holiness of God, to whom it was sworn (Leviticus 19:12). The narrators do not suggest that either Jephthah or his daughter thought of contravening the vow.

Jephthah's daughter is perhaps the most striking figure in this tragic story. She, like so many of the women in that world of men, was trapped. Through no fault of her own, she was caught by her father's preparations for war and his lavish gesture. Yet she appears with a calm dignity that stands in sharp contrast to her father's behavior. When he sees her coming, he wails for the "great trouble" she has brought him, even though it is she who is losing her life.

Caught in a trap, Jephthah's daughter meets her fate with dignity. She bewails her virginity, for her future in herself and her progeny has been cut off. Then she returns to her father and to her death. ✦

THE STORY BEHIND THE WORD

❧ Shibboleth ❧

The word *shibboleth* in Old Testament Hebrew means "ear of grain" and also "flowing stream." But in present-day English usage *shibboleth* refers to a word or phrase that distinguishes a speaker's native region, social background, or group affiliation. How did the definition change so drastically? This modern meaning derives from a story in Judges 12:5–6.

The Gileadites, after defeating the Ephraimites, a rival Israelite tribe, in battle, used the word *shibboleth* as a password in order to catch Ephraimite fugitives. Jephthah, leader of the Gileadites, posted sentries at the fords of the Jordan River to make sure that no Ephraimites got across.

Each man who approached to cross was asked, "Are you an Ephraimite?" Each Ephraimite, aware of the gravity of the question, would reply "no." The sentry would then ask the man to say the word *shibboleth*. Ephraimites spoke a different dialect of Hebrew and could be distinguished from the Gileadites by their inability to pronounce the *sh* in *shibboleth*—they pronounced it *sibboleth*. Thus, any man who replied *sibboleth* was revealed as an Ephraimite, and was seized and slain on the spot.

Hair as a status symbol

Beards and hair were natural ornaments and badges of dignity

IT IS RECORDED in the Second Book of Samuel (10:1–5) that when King David learned of the death of Nahash, king of the Ammonites, he sent a delegation to the dead man's son, conveying his condolences. But the mission was viewed with suspicion and David's men were taken for spies. They were seized and their clothes were cut in half so that they were left bare from the hips down; each man had half his beard shaved off; and they were sent home, "greatly ashamed." David was soon at war with the Ammonites, but to spare his ambassadors further disgrace, he ordered them: "Remain at Jericho until your beards have grown, and then return."

The Ammonites knew what they were doing when they mutilated the Hebrews'

beards. The cutting of a man's beard was a deadly insult among the ancient Hebrews, a people to whom a full set of whiskers represented masculine dignity and honor, and bountiful hair was a mark of male as well as female beauty: "the beauty of old men is their gray hair" (Proverbs 20:29).

In the Hebrew Scriptures, the man most famous for his unblemished beauty, made glorious by long, thick hair, was Absalom, a son of David. He had his hair trimmed once every year because it grew so heavy. The lavishness of his locks is indicated by 2 Samuel 14:26, which recounts that Absalom's hair, when cut, weighed 200 royal shekels, or about five pounds.

In their reverence for human hair, many peoples of antiquity endowed it with mystical properties. Hair, like fingernails, can be cut off without pain or bodily impairment; not only does it renew itself during a lifetime, but the shrinking of the skin makes it appear that hair continues to grow after death. The ancients believed that hair re-

Rich Egyptians customarily wore elaborate wigs like this.

Because Israelites *were prohibited from making graven images, few representations of them exist. In this Egyptian bas-relief, Hebrew prisoners are at left.*

tained some sort of mystical connection with the body even after being shorn from the head and that the clippings could be used to work magic on the person to whom they belonged. The view of hair as a life-force and a source of a man's vitality is found in several cultures; its significance for the Hebrews can be seen in the story of Samson, whose uncut hair was both a sign of his being dedicated to God and the source of his immense strength.

Although razors, shaving, and cutting the hair are mentioned on numerous occasions in the Bible, only a single passage in the Old Testament, Ezekiel 5:1, makes reference to barbers. And although barbers are not even mentioned in the New Testament, there is outside evidence of their existence. In the time of Herod the Great, there was a staff of barbers at the royal court, as indicated by the Jewish historian Josephus. In all probability, there were also Temple barbers,

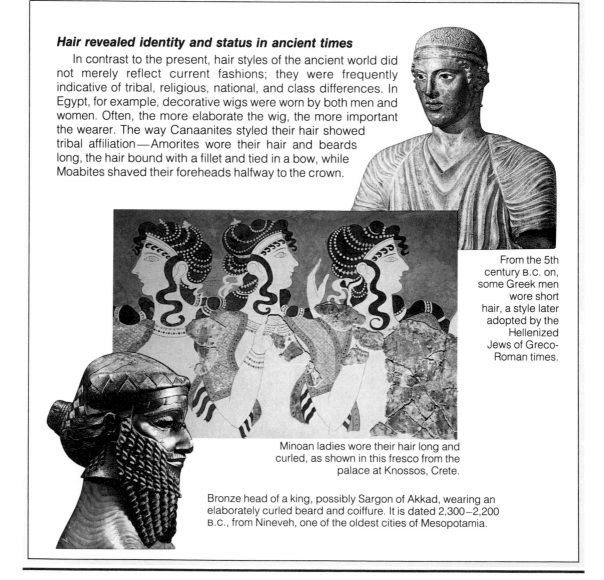

Hair revealed identity and status in ancient times

In contrast to the present, hair styles of the ancient world did not merely reflect current fashions; they were frequently indicative of tribal, religious, national, and class differences. In Egypt, for example, decorative wigs were worn by both men and women. Often, the more elaborate the wig, the more important the wearer. The way Canaanites styled their hair showed tribal affiliation—Amorites wore their hair and beards long, the hair bound with a fillet and tied in a bow, while Moabites shaved their foreheads halfway to the crown.

From the 5th century B.C. on, some Greek men wore short hair, a style later adopted by the Hellenized Jews of Greco-Roman times.

Minoan ladies wore their hair long and curled, as shown in this fresco from the palace at Knossos, Crete.

Bronze head of a king, possibly Sargon of Akkad, wearing an elaborately curled beard and coiffure. It is dated 2,300–2,200 B.C., from Nineveh, one of the oldest cities of Mesopotamia.

114

who administered the ritual shavings of Nazirites and Levite initiates.

Throughout the history of ancient Israel the shaving of all the hair either from the head or the face was a radical act that marked a time of great grief or suffering (Job 1:20 and Jeremiah 48:37). This practice, however, was associated with pagan mourning customs and was forbidden in Deuteronomy 14:1, "You shall not cut yourselves or make any baldness on your foreheads for the dead."

In Leviticus 19:27, the Lord ordered Moses to tell the children of Israel: "You shall not round off the hair on your temples or mar the edges of your beard." The reason for these strictures is unknown; possibly it was to distinguish the Israelites from neighboring peoples. Thus, shaving the head and beard was not ordinarily permitted. The exceptions were ritual shavings performed during certain purification ceremonies.

The Nazirite who had become impure through contact with a corpse or who had fulfilled his vow was required to shave his head (Numbers 6:9,18). Some purification rituals called for shaving the entire body. As part of their ritual cleansing, Levite initiates were to "go with a razor over all their body." Similarly, one of the rites of purification for persons cured of "leprosy" (the traditional Bible translation for several skin diseases) entailed shaving all the hair of the body before the "leper" reentered society.

One of the rituals affecting women's hair is in Deuteronomy 21:10–13, where it states that if a man wishes to marry a woman captured in war, she must first shave her head, pare her nails, take off her captive's clothing, and then mourn her parents for a month. The shaving of her head marks the great rift in her life as she loses ties to her parents and clan and is forcibly incorporated into an enemy nation. The hair of women in Israel was not necessarily covered, but maidens were expected to follow the example of Rebekah in Genesis 24:65 and veil their faces in the presence of potential husbands. The ornamental veil is referred to in the Song of Solomon (4:1), which makes it clear that a woman's hair was definitely an asset honored with these lines:

> Behold, you are beautiful, my love,
>   behold, you are beautiful!
> Your eyes are doves
>   behind your veil.
> Your hair is like a flock of goats,
>   moving down the slopes of Gilead.

In New Testament times, long hair was still approved for women, but for men, perhaps influenced by the short hair styles of the Greeks and Romans, long hair was no longer the ideal. The Apostle Paul argues, "Does not nature itself teach you that for a man to wear long hair is degrading to him, but if a woman has long hair, it is her pride?" (1 Corinthians 11:14–15). ✦

IN MODERN TIMES

Pe'ot

In Me'ah She'arim, the neighborhood just north of the Old City of Jerusalem, men and boys commonly wear *pe'ot*, or side locks, grown in accordance with the biblical prohibition: "You shall not round off the hair on your temples." Me'ah She'arim, like some neighborhoods in Brooklyn, New York, has a high concentration of Orthodox and Hasidic families. It is, in fact, a common practice among many Orthodox and Hasidic Jews all over the world to wear *pe'ot*—a style that instantly identifies the wearer as Jewish. Yet there is no evidence that the ancient Hebrews wore *pe'ot*. The wearing of side curls did not become the custom until the 16th century, when it was started by the disciples of the philosopher Isaac Luria. It later became popular in central and eastern Europe.

Young Jewish boy wearing *pe'ot*.

The three strange vows of the Nazirites

Why did people take them?

NAZIRITES WERE MEN AND WOMEN who were "separated unto the LORD." They were sanctified—either through divine endowment or because they chose to dedicate themselves to God. But they were neither cloistered nor celibate, their consecration did not bind them to a lifetime of religious service, and they wore the same clothes as everyone else. What distinguished them was that they expressed their loyalty to God by taking three vows for a stated period of time: first, to abstain from any product of the vine, whether alcoholic or not; second, to avoid contact with any dead body, even that of a parent or close relative; and third, to leave their hair totally uncut. When the period of the vows was completed, the Nazirite was not released from them until he or she had shaved the head and offered the hair to be burnt as a part of a series of sacrifices to God.

Nazirites were lay people who lived in the everyday world. But the effect of their vows, which are spelled out in Numbers 6, was to elevate the Nazirites to a level of sanctity comparable to that of high priests. Ordinary priests were not barred from handling the dead bodies of close relatives, though they had to undergo ritual purification before returning to priestly duties. Both ordinary priests and high priests were allowed to drink wine outside the sanctuary; in addition, as stated in Ezekiel 44:20, they could trim, but not shave off, their hair. So these vows, which to us do not seem all that onerous, were highly significant in Bible times, distinguishing Nazirites from others.

The earliest Nazirites were those who were endowed by God with charismatic gifts or bound by vows made by their mothers before they were born. Samson and Samuel were the two most prominent men who became Nazirites at birth. Samuel adhered all his life to the vows made for him by his mother. Samson was also vowed by

his mother, but he was so badly behaved that many scholars question his commitment to the Nazirite vows, although the Bible describes him as a Nazirite. The example of Samson shows that the "sanctity" of the Nazirite was not necessarily a matter of piety; rather, it had to do with ritual purity and responsibility to a vow.

Samuel's mother chose to take the vow that resulted in his consecration. This marks the first appearance of the idea of choosing to take a vow, which was to become a characteristic feature of the cult. Once such a vow became voluntary, a person could decide how long he wished to be bound. According to the Talmud, there was a minimum service of 30 days. Women and slaves, as well as men, could become Nazirites, but under certain circumstances a father or husband could void a woman's vow.

The Talmud suggests that Nazirite vows were often taken for purely practical reasons. In some cases, as when a barren woman wanted a child, the vows were taken to make the wish come true. In addition, men who discovered that their wives were unfaithful to them were encouraged to take Nazirite vows. Talmudic scholars may have made this connection because Numbers 5, in which adulterous women are discussed, immediately precedes the chapter that outlines Nazirite laws. ✦

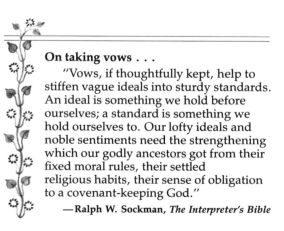

On taking vows . . .

"Vows, if thoughtfully kept, help to stiffen vague ideals into sturdy standards. An ideal is something we hold before ourselves; a standard is something we hold ourselves to. Our lofty ideals and noble sentiments need the strengthening which our godly ancestors got from their fixed moral rules, their settled religious habits, their sense of obligation to a covenant-keeping God."

—**Ralph W. Sockman,** *The Interpreter's Bible*

In this woodcut by an unknown artist, Samson slays
1,000 Philistines with the jawbone of an ass.

The tragedy of the strongest man in the Bible

Samson's fatal flaw

FOUR CHAPTERS totaling 96 verses (Judges 13:1–16:31) give us Samson's story, which starts with his miraculous birth into a family of Israelites living under Philistine domination. Like the patriarchs Isaac and Jacob before him and like Samuel and (much later) like John the Baptist after him, Samson was described as a son born as a special gift of God to a woman who was barren. His mother had been visited by the angel of the Lord who warned her to begin living according to the Nazirite vows because she would bear a son who was to be "a Nazirite to God from birth," and she was never to cut the child's hair. The child would have a mission, the angel said—"he shall begin to deliver Israel from the hand of the Philistines."

We meet Samson as a passionate young man, in love with a Philistine girl. In the comings and goings before his wedding,

Samson was menaced by a lion, which he killed with his bare hands. Later, he came upon the lion's carcass and saw that bees had made a comb in it. Scraping out the honey, he ate it as he walked.

At his wedding feast Samson asked a riddle about the lion and the honey, with a wager of 60 garments riding on the ability of a certain 30 guests to answer within seven days. His Philistine bride wheedled the answer out of him and gave it away. When he was thus betrayed, the narrative says, "the Spirit of the LORD came mightily upon him," and he went out and killed 30 Philistines and took their garments to pay the wager. When his new wife was then taken from him and given to another man, he retaliated by burning the Philistines' crops. He caught 300 foxes and tied their tails in pairs "and put a torch between each pair of tails. And when he had set fire to the torches, he let the foxes go into the standing grain of the Philistines, and burned up the shocks and the standing grain, as well as the olive orchards." To Samson it was a simple matter of revenge, "As they did to me, so have I done to them." But to those who told Samson's story it was the beginning of deliverance from the Philistines.

On another occasion, when Samson allowed the men of Judah, who had been intimidated by the Philistines, to tie him up and bring him to the Philistine camp, he easily broke his bonds and, seizing the jawbone of an ass, used it to kill 1,000 Philistines. Thirsty after this feat, he asked God for water and God opened a "hollow place," from which water flowed.

Samson then went to Gaza, where word went around that he was in town, visiting a harlot. The Philistines planned to kill him, but he anticipated them by ripping out the doors of the city's gate, which he carried on his shoulders to a hill near Hebron—which was some 40 miles away.

We next find Samson in the valley of Sorek, in love with Delilah. The climax of the story was not slow in coming. The Philistine lords had promised Delilah 1,100 pieces of silver if she could help them capture Samson. Worming the secret of his strength out of him by nagging him until "his soul was vexed to death," she called a man while Samson slept, and had him shave off Samson's seven locks of hair. Samson was seized, his eyes were gouged out, and he was fettered and set to turning the grindstone in the prison mill.

Thrice Delilah teased him to tell the secret of his strength, and thrice he put her off with a lie—each of which she relayed to the Philistines. But, when on the fourth time he told the truth, she betrayed him once again: the hair was cut. Did Samson trust Delilah to keep his secret? Was he a simpleton? No, but he was deeply human, and, throughout, he repeats his mistakes.

The story ends at the Temple of Dagon in Gaza, where some 3,000 Philistines came to make sport of their blind captive. But during his imprisonment Samson's hair had grown back, so when he was led into the temple he asked to feel its supporting pillars. Calling on the Lord for the strength to avenge the loss of his eyesight, he pressed against the pillars and brought the building down, killing himself and everyone else. His family then came and took his body away for burial. In the end he had not been just a great hero or a subject of tall tales, but a recognizably human figure who perished in the chaos that he spread about himself. For the narrator, the epitaph for all his mighty power is that "the dead whom he slew at his death were more than those whom he had slain during his life."

Samson escapes *from Gaza, taking the city gates with him.*

Many have retold the tale of Samson. Rembrandt, Milton, Handel, and Voltaire are among the masters lured by the tragedy of his love for Delilah. But the fascination is not limited to the biblical narrative itself; it lies as much in what the Bible does not say, the explanations that are not forthcoming, and the questions for which there may never be conclusive answers.

THE BOOK OF JUDGES says that Samson "judged Israel twenty years." Israel's judges were not solely legal authorities as we know them today. They were primarily military leaders. Samson, however, unlike the other principal judges, never led his people into battle, and he operated alone. Moreover, the narrative never attributes to him a religious motive for any of his actions, nor even a patriotic or nationalistic motive. Romantic love or lust, a delight in trickery, anger at injured pride, and revenge were the driving forces of Samson's life.

The fascination of these adventures of an earthy hero with superhuman strength among the judges of Israel has led to a wide range of interpretation of these stories. Many have noted, for example, that the name *Samson* in Hebrew is *Shimshon*, closely related to the Hebrew word *shemesh*, meaning "sun." This, in turn, has led scholars to compare him to other supernaturally strong heroes of ancient myth and legend who were also associated with the sun, figures such as the Greek Hercules, the Phoenician Melkart, or the Babylonian Gilgamesh. His seven locks have been compared to representations of the sun's rays, and it is perhaps significant that the name of his nemesis, Delilah, may be a pun on the Hebrew word *laylah*, meaning "night."

As the stories of Samson were retold in Jewish legends, he became a folk hero with superhuman powers. Sometimes he was described as gigantic in size, more than 200 feet across the shoulders. The onset of his superpowers, which the Book of Judges describes with the words, "the Spirit of the LORD began to stir him in Mahanehdan, between Zorah and Eshtaol," was expanded. In these legends, Samson manifested

Though the Bible says *that it was a man who cut off Samson's "seven locks," folk tradition has it that Delilah did the cutting while the Philistines stood by and watched.*

the stirring of God's power by lifting two mountains and rubbing them against each other, and, in one stride, covering a distance equal to that between the towns of Zorah and Eshtaol. But it's not only Samson's strength that increases in later versions of the story. The particular "props" of his strength grow in dimension, too. The jawbone of an ass, with which he slew Philistines, became the jawbone of the very ass on which Abraham had ridden when he traveled to Moriah to sacrifice Isaac.

Though the tradition delighted in describing Samson's physical strength, it also emphasized that he was morally weak, yielding impulsively to attractive women. "He who went astray after his eyes, lost his eyes." The one virtue with which he could be credited was unselfishness toward his people; though he did them great service, he never asked them for the smallest thing. Thus in Jewish tradition, the stories of Samson combined the delights of a tall tale with a moral purpose that was brought into focus by the tragic end of the story. ✦

The Philistines, who had put Samson in bronze fetters, must have been confident that he lacked the strength to get free. "But the hair of his head began to grow again"(Judges 16:22).

Thus it was that when Samson was brought to the temple of Dagon as an object of ridicule, he pulled the pillars down, killing himself and his enemies in a final act of vengeance.

120

The enduring mysteries of Samson

Hidden meanings behind bees, foxes, jawbone, and hair

IN THE BOOK OF JUDGES itself, numerous puzzles remain. There has never been a satisfactory explanation of how bees came to be producing honey in the carcass of a lion. Bees have never been known to swarm in rotting flesh. Some scholars have noted that the difficulty of capturing alive 300 foxes to use as torches would be so unbelievably great that the narrator must be referring to some other animal, one that runs in packs, such as the jackal. (Samson's torching of the fields at harvest time antedates by hundreds of years the Roman custom of chasing foxes with burning torches attached to their tails during rites for Ceres, the Roman goddess of agriculture.)

Others have suggested that the "jawbone" of the story was probably some more adequate weapon such as a curved sickle or scimitar resembling a large jawbone. The place where the slaughter took place was Ramath-lehi, "hill of the jawbone," which has led others to suggest that the place-name gave rise to the jawbone story.

Underlying the whole narrative is the question of whether Samson can be considered a Nazirite from birth. There is no doubt that he is described as such. Still the question arises because the regulations for a Nazirite given in the Book of Numbers fit so ill with the figure of Samson. The Nazirite was to avoid strong drink and indeed every product of the grape, to leave his or her hair uncut, and to avoid all contact with a dead body. All three of these restrictions appear in some form in the angel's conversation with Samson's mother, though the avoidance of any corpse is replaced by the command to eat nothing unclean.

As for Samson himself, the narrative shows him often in contact with corpses—creatures that he himself killed—and he eats such clearly "unclean" food as honey taken from the carcass of a lion. Samson's unconcern for these vows of purity has led some scholars to argue that the description of him as a Nazirite is an attempt by the narrators to make him seem respectable.

The only Nazirite vow he may be said with certainty to have maintained was to keep his hair uncut. This he did until Delilah discovered his secret. But it is precisely the power of his hair that has mystified generations of readers. For other Nazirites, however, long hair provided no supernatural powers, and indeed the narrative strongly implies that his superhuman strength was not always with Samson but only when "the Spirit of the LORD came mightily upon him." When his hair was shaved, "the LORD had left him," perhaps because the last of his lifelong vows had been broken. At his death, the story suggests that Samson's hair had begun to grow again, but it was by his prayer for revenge that he was empowered to bring down the Temple of Dagon.

It was in the tragedy of Samson's life that the narrative of the Book of Judges finds a lesson. Samson received a great gift but squandered it in lust, vengeance, and practical jokes. Finally he did not have the inner strength to stand against his weaker but more devious enemies. ✦

"In some ways the Judges seem to be presented as persons from whom deliverance is not to be expected in virtue of their personal qualities. This is certainly true of Deborah, a woman; Gideon is the youngest son of his father's house; Jephthah is a bastard and a bandit chieftain; and Samson is scarcely a man of elevated moral character and spiritual endowments. They become saviors not by choice or by election or by office but simply by the mysterious movement of the spirit. The charisma comes to equip them for their mission of deliverance and then leaves them."

—**John L. McKenzie, S.J.**
The World of the Judges

The conflict between Yahweh and Dagon

WHEN THE PHILISTINES invaded Canaan in the early 12th century B.C., not only did they take over a portion of the Canaanites' land and cities but several of their chief gods as well. One of these was Dagon, a god whose worship goes back to Mesopotamia in the third millennium B.C. In the pantheon of the Canaanites, Dagon ranked very high as the father of Baal, and his temples often rivaled those of Baal.

The name *Dagon* is closely related to the Hebrew word *dagan*, meaning "grain." He was a deity who, among other things, governed the important cycle of the grain crops. Dagon was the principal god worshiped in Ashdod and Gaza, two of the five cities of the Philistine Pentapolis. As a god of the Philistines, he was seen as a rival to Yahweh, the Lord of the Israelites. The story of their conflict covers the centuries of Israel's conflict with the Philistines.

Statues of the pagan god Dagon are depicted as half-man, half-fish. These representations reflect an early mistranslation of Dagon from the Hebrew word *dag*, meaning "fish."

A confrontation surfaces when Samson was captured and blinded by the Philistines. The lords of the five cities of the Philistines brought Samson into Dagon's temple in Gaza and made sport of him. Although Yahweh had forsaken Samson when he broke his Nazirite vows, the Lord now answered him, empowering him to destroy both the Temple of Dagon and its worshipers.

The next episode of the conflict came some decades later when the misguided Israelites attempted to use the Ark of the Covenant as a magical talisman in battle to give them victory against the Philistines. The Philistines understood the significance of the Ark and expected the worst, crying in terror, "A god has come into the camp."

Neither side understood Yahweh, the Lord of hosts, however. It was Yahweh who allowed the Ark to be captured by the Philistines, like any other war booty, and then to be taken to Dagon's temple in Ashdod. The first night in the temple the image of Dagon fell down before the Ark; the second night it fell again and broke in pieces with the head and hands lying on the threshold of the temple. This was taken as an evil omen by the Philistines: the First Book of Samuel reports that "the priests of Dagon and all who enter the house of Dagon do not tread on the threshold of Dagon in Ashdod to this day."

When David rose to power, the episode of the capture of the Ark was repeated in reverse. The Philistines carried the images of their gods into battle. When Yahweh helped David's forces to break through the enemy lines "like a bursting flood," then "the Philistines left their idols there, and David and his men carried them away" (2 Samuel 5:20–21).

Dagon was a god who was hard to destroy, however, and his worship continued for centuries in his temple in Ashdod. In the time of the Maccabees, almost exactly a thousand years after the arrival of the Philistines in Canaan, the house of Dagon in Ashdod was still an active temple.

122

The military might of the Philistines

Where did these "Sea Peoples" come from?

THE SEAFARING PHILISTINES are known to history almost entirely through the eyes of their enemies, the Hebrews and the Egyptians. No decipherable Philistine literature has survived. Our only direct link to the Philistines is their pottery and their clay coffins, unearthed in a variety of sites from Egypt to the coastal region of present-day Israel, the Canaan of biblical times. But their impact on the Mediterranean was such that their name remains there as "Palestine," which is derived from a Hebrew word meaning the "land of the Philistines."

The Old Testament provides the chief source of information about the Philistines. In the historical writings and the prophets, they play a key role in the history of the Hebrews. The Philistines were part of a group of Sea Peoples, who invaded Egypt in 1188 B.C. They were defeated by the forces of Ramses III, an event commemorated in vivid reliefs and in inscriptions on Ramses' temple walls in Medinet Habu, Egypt. But where had these Sea Peoples come from?

In the eighth century B.C. the prophet Amos cited a word of the Lord, "Did I not bring up Israel from the land of Egypt and the Philistines from Caphtor?" *Caphtor* is the Hebrew name for Crete, and in biblical tradition the Philistines are closely associated with the "Cherethites," or Cretans. The prophet Zephaniah cries, "Woe to you inhabitants of the seacoast, you nation of the Cherethites! The word of the LORD is against you, O Canaan, land of the Philistines." Based on this tradition, archaeologists have attempted to find a direct link between the Philistines and Cretan civilization, but no archaeological evidence for such a link has been discovered. The writing on Philistine tablets and the remains of Philistine pottery both show a possible—but not definitive—influence of the two great civilizations that reigned on Crete and the Greek mainland.

By the time of the invasion of the Sea Peoples into Egypt and the surrounding regions, the great Minoan civilization of Crete had passed, and the invasions seem to be associated with a period of unrest and upheaval that beset Asia Minor and Syria in the late 13th century B.C. Peoples who had been influenced by the powerful Minoan and Mycenaean Greek civilizations began to force their way southward until they ran into the strong armies of the Egyptians. One of these groups was the people who became the Philistines.

We are given a vivid view of these tall, slender, clean-shaven warriors in the victory reliefs of Ramses III at Medinet Habu. They came in ships powered only by sails—without the oars and lion-headed ramming prows of the Egyptian ships. They carried straight swords and round shields; they wore kilts fastened by a broad belt and on their torsos what is apparently a breastplate or armored shirt. Others of the Sea Peoples were similarly outfitted except that some of them wore horned helmets instead of the feather headdresses of the Philistines.

The Philistines were very adaptable; within a short time after settling in Canaan, they adopted the religion and language of

A Philistine sarcophagus with modeled lid.

123

their Canaanite neighbors and worshiped Dagon, Ashtoreth, and Baal. They organized themselves as a confederation of five cities—Ashkelon, Ashdod, Gath, Gaza, and Ekron—each headed by a *seren*, or lord. The five lords functioned as a council for common affairs and together were able to maintain a united and powerful army.

Both Ashkelon and Ashdod were major cities of the day. Eventually, the town of Ashkelon covered about 160 acres. It prospered as a seaport on the Philistine section of the "Way of the Sea"—the main coastal trading artery connecting Egypt and the land of Canaan. Just inland, Ashdod spread out over some 70 acres, and had an acropolis of about 20 acres.

The Philistines entered the Iron Age while the Israelites were still in the Bronze Age. In that technological advantage, carefully guarded by the Philistines, lay much of their military superiority and fearsomeness. The sharp irony of such power standing against the holy war of the Israelites is revealed when the Book of Judges says, "The LORD was with Judah, and he took possession of the hill country, but he could not

The Philistines wore *a headdress set with what appear to be flaring feathers all around, secured by a chinstrap.*

drive out the inhabitants of the plain, because they had chariots of iron" (Judges 1:19). In periods of Philistine dominance, they prevented the Israelites from obtaining and using iron and charged them for sharpening whatever implements they had.

The Philistine invasion of Canaan came perhaps 50 years after the main thrust of Israelite conquest, and from that point on the two expansionist forces, one moving west from the desert, the other east from the sea, pressed against each other in persistent conflict. Shamgar, the third of the judges in the Book of Judges, is credited with killing 600 Philistines with an oxgoad (Judges 3:31). Samson killed thousands but ultimately could do little more than harass the Philistines with his prowess. In the time of Eli and the young Samuel, the Philistines were able even to capture the most important religious object of Israel, the Ark.

It may well have been the pressure of a united Philistine army that caused the Israelites, divided in their various tribes, to wish to be united under a king. Saul, the first of their kings, however, did not fare well against the Philistines; they defeated him in battle and displayed his severed head in the Temple of Dagon in Beth-shan as a warning to the Israelites.

The tide of Philistine expansion was turned back only by David, the successor of Saul. He was able to break the unity of the Philistines and reduce their individual cities to vassalage. Still, the Philistine cities were never assimilated into Israel. More than two centuries after David, King Uzziah was warring against the same cities of the Philistines (2 Chronicles 26:6). The last vestiges of Philistine independence were quelled in 604 B.C. by the forces of the Babylonian king Nebuchadnezzar II. In the face of the Babylonian invasion, the Philistines allied with the Egyptians, but Nebuchadnezzar subdued the revolt and exiled both the rulers and citizens from the cities of Gaza, Ashdod, and Ashkelon. Later the Philistine cities were characterized by highly mixed populations, and only the name *Palestine* connects them with their Philistine past. ✦

Pissarro captures the anguish of Orpah, Ruth, and Naomi as Naomi prepares to return to Israel.

The wife who would not leave her mother-in-law

Ruth's story sheds light on a mysterious custom

THE BOOK OF RUTH, one of the most beloved stories of the Old Testament, can be viewed on many levels. Admired as a literary work, this engaging tale skillfully carries the reader to a satisfying conclusion. Ruth is read, too, for what it says about the warm relationship between two women, a mother-in-law and a daughter-in-law. It is a story of unusual scope, one that shows how a pagan foreigner could be a model of human kindness and devotion. And the story claims our attention for the light it sheds on a remarkable institution in ancient Israel, the levirate marriage.

The story of Ruth begins in the land of Moab, often hostile to Israel, where an Israelite family—Elimelech, his wife, Naomi, and their two sons—had gone to escape a famine in the land of Judah. After Elimelech died, the two sons married Moabite girls, Ruth and Orpah. But the sons also died and the three childless women were alone. When the famine ended, Naomi decided to

return to Judah. Ruth and Orpah insisted on going with her, but Naomi urged the girls to remain in Moab. Orpah stayed, but Ruth courageously went with the impoverished Naomi, though it meant forsaking her own people and the traditions she knew. She told Naomi, "Entreat me not to leave you or to return from following you; for where you go I will go, and where you lodge I will lodge; your people shall be my people, and your God my God" (Ruth 1:16).

Returning to Judah and the city of Bethlehem, Ruth and Naomi arrived at the time of the barley harvest. Ruth joined the other poor people, who were allowed to glean the fields after the reapers passed, and she caught the eye of Boaz, a landowner and "a man of wealth." Inquiring about her, Boaz was impressed by what he learned of her goodness and of her loyalty to Naomi. When Naomi heard of Boaz' interest in Ruth, she was delighted, for Boaz was a relative of her late husband, "one of our

The wealthy landowner Boaz was won by ties of kinship, and by perception of Ruth's virtue.

ing the winnowing of the grain. She lay at his feet until he awoke, startled by her presence. She stated her claim forthrightly: "I am Ruth, your maidservant; spread your skirt over your maidservant, for you are next of kin" (Ruth 3:9).

Boaz was much taken with Ruth but recognized that within the complexities of the levirate tradition there was another kinsman, "a kinsman nearer than I," who had the first responsibility to marry the widow, and in so doing to function as her redeemer. We learn also that the land formerly owned by Elimelech was in danger of being sold outside the clan.

The next day, at the gates of Bethlehem where the city elders met, Boaz approached the other kinsman, telling him of his opportunity to redeem both the land and the widow Ruth. When the kinsman was unable to fulfill his responsibility, he asked Boaz to take it on, and he sealed the bargain by the curious custom of giving Boaz one of his sandals. Thus Boaz kept the entire estate within the clan, both the land and the widow Ruth, in order to "perpetuate the name of the dead in his inheritance."

In due course, Ruth gave birth to a boy, and the women of the neighborhood celebrated the preservation of the family line by saying, "A son has been born to Naomi." The boy was named Obed, and Naomi became his nurse. Obed grew up to be the father of Jesse and the grandfather of David, one of the greatest of the Hebrew kings. ✦

nearest kin," and might marry Ruth within the tradition of levirate marriage.

The term *levirate* derives from the Latin word *levir* meaning "husband's brother" (Hebrew, *yabam*). As the institution was described in Deuteronomy 25:5–6, it applied to the rather limited case of brothers living together. If a married brother died without a son—a male heir—his widow was to be kept within the family by marriage to another of the brothers.

Remarkably, the first son born to this union was to be reared as the son of the dead brother. Thereby the dead brother's name would be perpetuated through a "first-born son," who could rightfully inherit his estate. The case of Ruth shows that this desire to maintain the "name" and inheritance within the extended family caused levirate marriage to reach considerably beyond the actual brothers of the deceased to include other kinsmen.

Seizing the opportunity, Naomi devised a bold plan for Ruth. Ruth went to Boaz as he slept on the threshing floor after celebrat-

On Ruth's lineage . . .

"The sparks of goodness are scattered throughout creation. One was in Lot and remained glimmering even in the moral filth of Sodom. To salvage that spark, God sent the angel Rafael, who, after healing Abraham, went to Sodom to save Lot, bearer of the spark that would become the soul of David. It went down the generations until the time came for it to leave the impurity of Moab and enter the Jewish nation through Ruth."

—**Rabbi Nosson Scherman**
The Book of Ruth

Marriage contract, *or* ketubbah, *from Trieste, 1774.*

When husbands were lords and masters

Wives still had a strong influence

IN THE BOOK OF GENESIS, when the time came for Abraham's son Isaac to marry, Abraham summoned a trusted household servant and sent him on a journey back to the region where the clan of Abraham's father still dwelt. The servant took a caravan of men, camels, and choice gifts and was commissioned to find and negotiate for a wife for Isaac.

When with God's help the servant found Rebekah, who was the daughter of Abraham's nephew Bethuel, he gave her two gold bracelets and a ring that was to be worn through the side of her nose. Then he negotiated with both her father and her brother Laban, telling them of Abraham's

wealth, of Isaac's inheritance, and of God's guidance in finding Rebekah.

When Bethuel and Laban agreed to the marriage, the servant gave gifts of gold, silver, clothes, and ornaments to Rebekah, Laban, and their mother. Soon the servant and Rebekah returned to Abraham's home with Laban's blessing: "Our sister, be the mother of thousands of ten thousands; and may your descendants possess the gate of those who hate them!" (Genesis 24:60). When Rebekah first saw Isaac from afar, she veiled herself. Isaac then received her into his tent, "and she became his wife; and he loved her" (Genesis 24:67).

Few institutions illustrate so well the cultural distance of the modern Western world from ancient Hebrew society as the institution of marriage. In Western society, the decision to marry usually follows a period of growing romantic attraction between a young man and woman that reaches an intensity that we call "falling in love." Parental involvement in this process is often minor or absent. This modern notion of individual choice was virtually unknown among the Israelites. They of course knew about passionate sexual attraction, but generally they did not base marriage and family on that foundation. Neither Isaac nor Rebekah made any decisions in the process, but affirmed the decisions of their families.

In all societies, marriage is part of a web of social relationships by which a people express and perpetuate themselves. In ancient Israel, kinship was central to society. The entire nation perceived itself as the "children of Israel." The whole was broken down into tribes, each of which was thought of as children of a single patriarch. Within those tribes there were smaller clans and extended families until, at least theoret-

Jacob worked for seven years to win the hand of Rachel, but because Leah was older, Laban tricked him into marrying her instead. Jacob then worked another seven years for Rachel. This 1495 French manuscript shows Jacob with both wives.

ically, every single individual could be accounted for within the great family.

In some societies, ours among them, ties of kinship are distributed through both parents. In Israel's patriarchal society, kinship was defined through the father only. (This practice contrasts with Jewish law in more recent centuries in which one's status as a Jew is established through the mother.) Children were part of their father's clan and had no special ties to the ancestors of their mother unless she was of the same clan. This was how kinship groups were defined, which functioned powerfully as political and economic units as well as social ones. Children had a single line of ancestry through their father and father's father, rather than a family tree spreading back from both parents.

So powerful was the patrilineal pattern that Jesus' descent is considered only in these terms. The genealogies of Jesus given in the Gospels of Matthew and Luke tell how Jesus was born of the Virgin Mary without any involvement of Joseph, her betrothed husband. Still, when each Gospel comes to present Jesus' extended genealogy, it is listed through Joseph rather than Mary. Jesus was considered to be a descendent of David because Joseph descended from David; no mention is ever made of Mary's ancestors. The tradition of kinship being defined through the male simply could not be overturned.

In ancient Israel, marriage often took place relatively soon after a child reached puberty. The idea of waiting until after adolescence was practically unknown. The father of a boy took the lead in finding an appropriate match, though he might well take the boy's feelings into consideration, especially if they were passionate. There was no question about it; a boy would get married. At a later date the rabbis would intone, "He who has no wife is not a proper man." It was unlikely that the idea of his son remaining a bachelor ever entered an Israelite father's head.

Marriages between first cousins were common. Thus, it seems that in seeking a

Even though Abraham's wife, Sarah, was barren, he did not take a second wife. Instead, in accordance with custom, Sarah gave her husband a handmaiden, Hagar, to bear a child for him. But when Sarah herself bore a son, she demanded that Abraham send Hagar and her son, Ishmael, away.

This cuneiform tablet reveals that the Hebrews' neighbors had similar customs, allowing a handmaiden to bear children if a wife could not.

daughter-in-law, the father was guided by a desire to preserve the distinctiveness of his clan, or tribe, so his search usually focused on his own community and its environs. In Genesis we find Rebekah marrying her first cousin, Isaac. Later, we find Isaac telling his son Jacob, "Arise, go to Paddan-aram to the house of Bethuel your mother's father; and take as wife from there one of the daughters of Laban your mother's brother."

There were strict rules to prevent incest. Though the bride and groom could be first cousins without violating Leviticus' rule on consanguinity, other marriages between those who were "near of kin" were banned, including marriages between mothers and sons, grandfathers and granddaughters, sisters and brothers, aunts and nephews. Ties of affinity also were regulated, barring such unions as those between a son and his stepmother, a man and his paternal uncle's wife, and a brother-in-law and sister-in-law.

After the conquest of Canaan, there were warnings against intermarriage with the non-Israelites of the land. Such marriages were seen as a snare designed to entice Israel to follow other gods.

In spite of this prohibition, however, mixed marriages were apparently not uncommon. For example, Samson married a Philistine woman, and Naomi's sons married Moabite women—one of whom was Ruth, the great-grandmother of King David. Bathsheba, the woman with whom David fell in love, was already married to a Hittite. Even the strictures of the law provided an exception that allowed a man to marry a woman captured in war, after she had ceremonially mourned the loss of her family and country (Deuteronomy 21:10–13).

It was only after the Babylonian exile that serious attempts were made to enforce a ban on intermarriage. During the religious

A household of 1,000 women—*wives and concubines*—*which seems outlandish today, was expensive to maintain even in Solomon's day. Harems were an expression of wealth and power.*

more than one wife. The ideal of happiness was indeed the image of a prosperous man with his wife and many children. The prophets also joined in urging faithfulness to a single spouse.

Polygamy was never outlawed in ancient Israel, however. Quite the contrary, many of the greatest heroes of Israel's history were polygamous. The form of polygamy in Israel is more accurately described as polygyny—one husband married to more than one wife—never the reverse, polyandry. Polygyny was known and practiced from earliest recorded history, but usually only by a relative few. The expense of maintaining more than one wife as well as the rivalry and even hatred that often developed between wives militated against the practice. It is primarily among the wealthy or in the special situation when a first wife could bear no heirs that examples of polygyny are described in the Scriptures.

revival and purification of Israel under Ezra, the leaders believed the problem was so urgent that a large number of men divorced their non-Israelite wives and disowned the children of those marriages. The Book of Ezra provides a list of men with foreign wives who submitted to this rigorous reform, but it does not tell how many refused to go along with it or ignored it altogether.

Throughout the history of Israel, monogamy was the rule for most ordinary folk. When the story of creation was told, the ideal pair of one man and one woman was set: "a man leaves his father and his mother and cleaves to his wife, and they become one flesh" (Genesis 2:24). Perhaps significantly, it was to the progeny of Cain that the Scriptures attributed the first marriage to

The kings of Israel were polygamists on a grand scale. David had at least 20 wives and concubines, but that seems practically ascetic compared to the lavish harem of his son Solomon, who reportedly had "seven hundred wives, princesses, and three hundred concubines" (1 Kings 11:3). By contrast, Solomon's son Rehoboam lived on a more modest scale, with 18 wives and 60 concubines, who bore him a total of 88 children. Such practices among kings are condemned in Deuteronomy 17:17, but regulations regarding polygamy are limited. In Deuteronomy 21:15–17 the concern is to control the almost inevitable effects of favoritism and rivalry in inheritance rights.

A standard part of the marriage negotiations was the matter of the *mohar*. This was not a dowry, but a gift (usually in the form of money) that was negotiated between the two families and that the bridegroom or his father had to pay to the bride's father. There are many different theories on the significance of the *mohar*. Some scholars believe that it was probably intended to compensate the father of the bride for the loss of a daughter and all the progeny she represented, as she now became part of another family. In any event, the giving and receiving of the *mohar* sealed the validity of the marriage. The Bible does not specify how large the *mohar* had to be. Although it could vary, it was probably less than the punitive 50 shekels of silver that the law says a man who has seduced an unbetrothed virgin must pay to her father. In addition to the *mohar*, the bridegroom would also give gifts to the bride and her family that were in keeping with his financial status.

The time of betrothal was an intermediate period between the transfer of the *mohar*, which accompanied the formal commitment of the bride's father to the marriage, and the time when the bride actually moved to the house of the bridegroom. Betrothal was far more binding than a modern engagement. While the couple did not yet cohabit, they were essentially married. So binding was this commitment that if a betrothed girl was raped, the crime was treated as adultery with a married woman. Finally, a betrothed man was exempted from military service until after the marriage.

The Bible most often refers to marriage

Wedding symbols of antiquity

Wedding rings are not mentioned in the Bible, but ring ceremonies were in use by talmudic times. Most likely, the wedding ring was derived from the Egyptian marriage bracelet. In the seventh or eighth century A.D., Jewish grooms gave a ring upon betrothal to signify a pledge—replacing a coin as symbol of future obligations. In the next century, the ring ceremony became an official part of Christian marriage rites.

Wedding rings of wealthy women in the 17th and 18th centuries often bore the inscription *mazzal tov* and were topped with a symbol of the new home.

An Italian Jewish marriage of the 15th century, conducted in splendor: under the huppah, or bridal canopy, the bridegroom places the ring on the bride's finger.

in terms of a man "taking" a woman. Indeed, the heart of the "wedding" was the transfer of the bride's residence; no particular ceremonies, either religious or civil, were required. The joy and festivity of the event, however, led to great celebration.

On the wedding day, the groom put on a crown and went to the bride's house accompanied by his friends, who sang and played musical instruments. On the return trip the veiled bride, adorned with jewels, was also escorted by her exuberant friends.

The next 7 to 14 days were spent in celebration and feasting, with guests coming and going. The entire book of the Song of Solomon provides us with examples of the beautiful and sensuous love poetry that could be sung on such occasions. It was a time for food, laughter, and free-flowing wine. According to a practice that is known from the Jews of Egypt, the bridegroom would at some point solemnly announce, "She is my wife, I am her husband, from this day forever." Later, it became customary for the bridegroom to recite the following words: "Behold, you are consecrated unto me with this ring according to the laws of Moses and Israel."

Social and economic status largely determined the quality of life in the marriage. While society included the spectrum from slaves to royalty, the life of most men and women was one of unremitting toil. A woman's life centered around a multitude of household tasks: preparing food, including cooking and small farming, making cloth and clothing. She reared the children. And she made her own household equipment from baskets to oil lamps. In wealthy households, she supervised the servants. It is no wonder that when the ideal wife is described, we are told that "She rises while it is yet night and provides food for her household and tasks for her maidens."

Honor could accrue to such a woman, but very few rights were ever hers. This is clear in the matter of divorce. In keeping with Deuteronomy 24:1, a man could divorce his wife for practically any cause, "if then she finds no favor in his eyes because he has found some indecency in her." The wife, however, could not seek a divorce at all and had very few safeguards against her husband seeking one. The blood-stained sheet from the night the marriage was consummated was kept by the bride's family against the possibility of a husband charging that she had not been a virgin at the time of the marriage.

The many taboos and legal hedges that surrounded the institution of marriage show its importance for a society that was as family-centered as Israel. The Bible is in a sense a book of generations—generations of marriages and the love that grew within them, the children that they produced, and the struggles that they survived. ✦

THE STORY BEHIND THE WORD

✑ Concubine ✑

Few institutions seem as foreign to the modern age as that of concubinage. The concubine was a part of the household. She cohabited with the man of the house or with his son, but her status was that of a secondary wife, a captive, or a slave. She was subservient to the wife, who was her mistress; nevertheless, it was dishonorable to sell a concubine, especially if she had children. The Deuteronomic Law allowed both polygamy and slavery, but having more than one wife was an economic burden. Concubines, however, served two purposes: bearing children—who were regarded as legitimate— and providing labor.

Over time, possessing a large number of concubines, or a harem, became a status symbol. David had 10, Solomon had 300, and Rehoboam 60. The harem was usually overseen by a eunuch. To lie with a royal concubine was tantamount to usurpation of the throne. Thus, when Solomon's brother Adonijah asked for their father David's concubine, Abishag the Shunamite, Solomon had him put to death.

"Therefore a man leaves his father and his mother and cleaves to his wife, and they become one flesh." —Genesis 2:24

MARRIAGE IN BIBLE TIMES was a very different institution from what it is nowadays. The extended family was the basic social unit in the ancient Middle East; the "nuclear family" is the rule in today's world. Nevertheless, the teachings of Scripture have continued to provide a framework for marriage and family life in both Jewish and Christian traditions down to the present.

"Love thy wife as thyself, and honor her more than thyself. Be careful not to cause woman to weep, for God counts her tears. Israel was redeemed from Egypt on account of the virtue of its women. He who weds a good woman is as if he had fulfilled all the precepts of the Torah."   —*Talmud*

"When God at the first institution of marriage had . . . in his contemplation that it should be a remedy against burning, God gave man the remedy before he had the disease; for marriage was instituted in the state of innocency, when there was no inordinateness in the affections of man, and no burning. But as God created rhubarb in the world, whose quality is to purge choler, before there was any choler to purge, so God according to his abundant forwardness to do us good, created a remedy before the disease, which he foresaw coming, was come upon us. . . .

"The second use of marriage was . . . for children . . . and here also may another shower of his benedictions fall upon them whom he hath prepared and presented here. 'Let the wife be as a fruitful vine, and their children like olive plants.' . . .

"The third and last use in this institution of secular marriage was . . . for mutual help. . . . Every body needs the help of others; and every good body does give some kind of help to others. Even into the Ark itself, where God blessed them all with a powerful and immediate protection, God admitted only such as were fitted to help one another, couples. In the Ark, which was the type of our best condition in life, there was not a single person. . . .Christ . . . saved none but married persons, to show that he eases himself in making them helpers to one another."
—**John Donne,**
Sermon Preached at a Marriage **(1621)**

"God has laid upon marriage both a blessing and a burden. The blessing is the promise of children. God allows man to cooperate with him in the work of creation and preservation. But it is always God himself who blesses marriage with children. 'Children are a gift that cometh of the LORD' (Psalm 127), and they should be acknowledged as such. It is from God that parents receive their children, and it is to him that they should lead them. Hence parents exercise an authority over their children which is derived from God. . . .

"God intends you to found your marriage on Christ. . . .live together in the forgiveness of your sins, for without it no human fellowship, least of all a marriage, can survive. Don't insist on your rights, don't blame each other, don't judge or condemn each other, don't find fault with each other, but take one another as you are, and forgive each other every day from the bottom of your hearts.

"From the first day of your marriage until the last your rule must be: 'Receive one another . . . to the praise of God.'

"Such is the word of God for your marriage. Thank him for it, thank him for bringing you thus far. Ask him to establish your marriage, to confirm and hallow it and preserve it to the end. With this your marriage will be 'to the praise of his glory.' Amen."
—**Dietrich Bonhoeffer,**
A Wedding Sermon from a Prison Cell

The reluctant king-maker

How a man of God gave in to the people

SAMUEL COMBINED THREE ROLES— those of prophet, priest, and political leader—at a turning point in the history of his people. He was the last of the judges and the one who inaugurated the monarchy by anointing Israel's first two kings. His name provides the title for two books of the Old Testament.

One way in which the Scriptures mark the importance of Samuel is by describing his miraculous birth. Samuel was born to a woman named Hannah, who was barren "because the LORD had closed her womb." She was one of the two wives of Elkanah, whose other wife had numerous children. During a visit to the sanctuary of Yahweh at Shiloh, Hannah vowed that if the Lord would give her a son, "I will give him to the LORD all the days of his life, and no razor shall touch his head." Thus like Samson, who was also born to a barren woman, this child was to be a Nazirite from birth.

When Yahweh granted her petition and the child was born, Hannah brought Samuel to Eli, the priest and judge at Shiloh, and told him, "I have lent him to the LORD; as long as he lives, he is lent to the LORD." Her soaring prayer of exultation on this occasion became the model for the "Magnificat" of Mary, the mother of Jesus.

While yet a child—at the age of 12, according to a later tradition—Samuel began his career as a prophet. Yahweh repeatedly called him by name during the night. At first the child did not understand what was happening, but as Eli had instructed him, he finally answered: "Speak, LORD, for thy servant hears." Hearing the divine message was painful, however, for the first task for Samuel was to pronounce punishment on the house of his mentor, Eli. That household, a line of priests that harked back to Aaron, was destined for oblivion because of the corruption and immorality of Eli's sons and the fact that Eli did not restrain them.

Samuel's first prophecy came true during the ongoing wars with the Philistines. Eli's sons foolishly used the Ark of the Covenant to try to force Yahweh to protect their armies in battle. Instead, they were both killed by the Philistines, the Ark was captured, and Eli, when he heard the news, fell backward, broke his neck, and died.

Inheriting Eli's position, Samuel struggled to bring about a religious renewal in Israel and a rejection of idolatry. He established a circuit of towns, which he visited as judge and "administered justice to Israel" (1 Samuel 7:17). Though he was not a military leader, he was credited with leading Israel to victory against the Philistines through his prayer and sacrifices.

It is characteristic of the biblical narrative, however, that no matter how heroic a person may be, human beings cannot be perfect; no one is without flaws. In Samuel's case, as with Eli, the flaw was in his sons, whom Samuel appointed as judges. But they "took bribes and perverted justice." It

---

On Hebrew government . . .

"Some nations place the sovereignty of their land in the hands of a single ruler (monarchy), some in the hands of a small number of rulers (oligarchy), and some in the hands of the people (democracy). Moses our Teacher taught us to place our faith in none of these forms of government. He taught us to obey the rule of God, for to God alone did he accord kingship and power. He commanded the people always to raise their eyes to God, for He is the source of all good for mankind in general and for each person in particular and in Him will people find help when they pray to Him in their time of suffering, for no act is hidden from His understanding and no hidden thought of man's heart is hidden from Him."
—**Josephus Flavius,**
Contra Apion, Volume One

Pledged to the service of the Lord at the shrine at Shiloh, Samuel was in the care of Eli, to whom he reported that he had heard the divine voice.

was the prospect that his sons might succeed their father in office, and Israel's wish to be like other nations, that precipitated the greatest crisis of Samuel's life. The elders of Israel asked Samuel to anoint a king, but Samuel was reluctant to do this.

On one hand, there was a clear need for a stronger, more unified government. The Book of Judges notes that in earlier times a state of near anarchy existed in Israel: "In those days there was no king in Israel; every man did what was right in his own eyes." The nation, continually harassed by enemies around it, had no government capable of maintaining an army to defend itself.

On the other hand, great dangers were inherent in the institution of monarchy. The First Book of Samuel emphasizes that no mere man should be king over Israel, because only Yahweh is king. When the elders petitioned Samuel at Ramah, their request for a king was regarded by some as a rejection of the Lord, and worse, a kind of idolatry. The people, in asking for a king, were denying their distinctiveness in order to be like other nations. They had to be solemnly

warned that such a king would ultimately become their slave master.

Ultimately, Yahweh tells Samuel to anoint the young man Saul as a prince and a deliverer: "He shall save my people from the hand of the Philistines." Saul is described as a man of admirable humility. He is anointed both with oil and with the spirit of the Lord, becoming king and prophet.

How, then, did Saul come to be accepted by Israel as their first king? It was through the test of battle. When a force of Ammonites threatened Israel, "the spirit of God came mightily upon Saul." By threatening any who did not join the fight, he forced all the tribes of Israel to unite against the common foe. After the battle "all the people went to Gilgal, and there they made Saul king before the LORD."

The fateful step had been taken, it would never be reversed. Both the good and evil effects of monarchy would be played out in history. Samuel retired from his position as leader of the people, but he lived to regret the choice of Saul. ✦

135

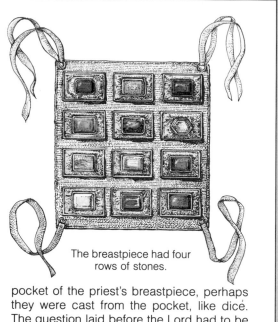
Provoking divine wrath

When Israel's holiest object fell into pagan hands

THE ARK OF THE COVENANT, Israel's holiest object, was the visible symbol of God's presence. It was a rectangular box made of acacia wood, overlaid with gold inside and out, in which the tablets of the Ten Commandments were placed: "And in the Ark you shall put the testimony that I shall give you." Thus the Ark was the repository of the law and was also a constant reminder of God's covenant.

By the time of Samuel, the Ark had become established in the shrine at Shiloh, where a yearly festival dedicated to the Lord took place. At Shiloh, the Ark was in the care of the priest Eli and his sons, Hophni and Phineas. These sons had displayed their disrespect for the Lord by treating the

sacrificial offerings with contempt. In his first revelation to Samuel, the Lord had thus vowed to punish the house of Eli for the sins of his sons.

When the army of Israel was defeated by the Philistines, Eli's sons, along with the elders of Israel, thought that they could force God to give them victory by bringing the powerful presence of the Ark into battle. Yahweh would not be forced: the Ark was captured and Eli's sons were slain.

The capture of the Ark in no way diminished its power. Indeed, it wreaked havoc among the Philistines. It was brought into the house of the Philistine god Dagon, and was set up next to Dagon's image. Twice the image of Dagon fell to the ground before the

Ark. Next, a plague of tumors beset the Philistines: "The hand of the LORD was heavy upon the people of Ashdod, and he terrified and afflicted them with tumors." The plague did not end until they returned the Ark to Beth-shemesh, along with an offering of "golden mice and tumors" to appease the Lord. By sending the golden images of the tumors and the mice that had ravaged their land, the Philistines hoped to rid their cities of these troubles.

The Ark went into a period of obscurity when it was kept for some 20 years in the house of Abinadab in Kiriath-Jearim. Finally, King David made preparations to bring it to Jerusalem. It was mounted onto a cart and brought forth with dancing and song. A mysterious incident occurred while the Ark was being transported. Uzzah, a son of Abinadab, who was driving the cart, "put out his hand to the ark of God and took hold of it, for the oxen stumbled." Though the gesture was not disrespectful, he was instantly killed. Three months later, the Ark was at last restored to its rightful position in Jerusalem, where it was greeted with great rejoicing. Its establishment there was a political coup for David, for it marked the centralization of the national religion in the nation's new capital. ✦

Not with sword and spear

How David killed Goliath

SAUL, THE FIRST KING OF ISRAEL, governed a still-loose confederacy of tribes. David, his successor, was the builder of a nation. The rise of David and the establishment of the Davidic dynasty in Israel was a crucial event in the nation's history. David's circuitous path to the throne is recounted, in abundant detail, in the two books of Samuel.

The stories of David, beginning in the 16th chapter of 1 Samuel, contain the seeds of the different traditions that developed around this hero. There are in fact three apparently independent stories about David, each of which introduces him to the reader in a different way.

In the first of the stories (1 Samuel 16:1–13), Samuel anoints David. This shapes the next 20 chapters of the narrative. For though David would not become king of Israel until many years later, when he was anointed by the elders of Israel, this first gesture by Samuel makes David's kingship inevitable. Indeed, it was God who looked into the heart of the boy David and chose him as king in the place of Saul, whom he had rejected. With such an introduction to David's story, we read all that follows not so much with a sense of suspense as with a sense of wonder at how God brought him through his adventures and battles, to the fulfillment of his original anointing.

The next two stories give an account of how David became known to Saul and prominent in the royal court. The first of these (1 Samuel 16:14–23) is a continuation of the story that begins with God's rejection of Saul. Now "an evil spirit from the LORD" tormented the king. Saul's courtiers suggested hiring a musician to play the lyre to soothe him, and it was David who was recommended. When David entered Saul's service, the king loved him and made him both his armor bearer in war and his personal musician at home.

The second story is one of the best known in all the Bible—that of David and Goliath. Although it is placed after David has already been introduced as Saul's musician, the narratives themselves demonstrate that events are not being recounted in sequence. Whereas at the end of the first story Saul has appointed David as his personal attendant, at the end of the second story, Saul doesn't even recognize him. Yet there is an explanation for this apparent contradiction: the narrators of 1 Samuel knew of two distinct traditions about how David became known to Saul, and they included them both. Not only did they make no attempt to smooth out all the differences between the two, but also they included yet another version, attributing the killing of Goliath not to David but to another man entirely, a Bethlehemite by the name of Elhanan (2 Samuel 21:19).

The story of David defeating Goliath throws light on David's essential nature, highlighting those characteristics that made him an ideal king. David is a mere youth—the youngest of many brothers—who manifests great personal bravery and valor in the face of overwhelming odds. His bravery, however, is based entirely on trust not in himself and his weapons but in Yahweh, "God of the armies of Israel," who "saves not with sword and spear."

In contrast to David, Goliath is an archetypical villian. He embodies the vaulting

David played the lyre *for King Saul, in accordance with the ancient tradition of having musicians appear at court.*

self-trust and bravado of the warrior. Encased in his 150 pounds of bronze armor, carrying a massive spear, "with a javelin of bronze slung between his shoulders" (1 Samuel 17:6), Goliath defies the entire army of Israel and disdains the sticks and stones that David brings against him.

As for Goliath's famous height, two traditions exist. One, represented by the ancient Greek translation of the Bible and by the Jewish historian Josephus, makes Goliath merely a very tall warrior, 4 cubits and a span—about 6 feet 8 inches. The other, older tradition, found in the Hebrew Scriptures, makes Goliath truly superhuman. He was 6 cubits and a span, nearly 10 feet tall.

No matter what his exact height, Goliath was such a remarkable figure that numerous legends developed around him. One of them makes an interesting connection back to Naomi and her two Moabite daughters-in-law, Ruth and Orpah. Ruth, though from the land of Moab, stayed faithfully with Naomi and chose to worship the God of Israel. She became the great-grandmother of David. But what of Orpah who went back to Moab? Legend had it that God rewarded her tears at parting from Naomi by granting that she should be the mother of four giant sons, one of whom was Goliath (2 Samuel 21:15–22). When she returned to Moab, however, she became such a harlot that her son was jeered at as "the son of a hundred fathers and one mother." Thus when David met Goliath, the offspring of the two daughters-in-law stood face to face.

The confrontation is narrated with great dramatic power. Goliath, champion of the Philistines, demanded single combat against a champion of Israel. The enslavement of thousands of Israelites hung in the balance. And David was not even old enough for military service, as emphasized by the fact that he was the youngest of eight brothers, of whom only the three eldest were fighting in the army of Saul. Neither they nor any soldier of Israel dared to meet the challenge, but instead, quaked with fear when they heard Goliath's taunting roar.

David's victory over Goliath in the Valley of Elah was the beginning of a famous military career. Goliath, who was equipped with heavy armor, was felled by a stone.

For 40 days the armies remained immobile while the shame of Israel before these unmet challenges grew, until at last the shepherd David, bringing bread and cheese to his brothers in the ranks of Israel, volunteered to meet the giant.

The physical contrast between David and Goliath is as complete and dramatic as possible—a gigantic, armored, professional warrior against a shepherd youth armed with nothing but a sling and five smooth stones. But it is the words that the two exchange before the climactic moment that reveal the meaning of the whole story. While Goliath ridiculed David, with powerful solemnity David proclaimed that the triumph of the God of Israel would arise from David's triumph, "that all the earth may know that there is a God in Israel, and that all this assembly may know that the LORD saves not with sword and spear; for the battle is the LORD's and he will give you into our hand" (1 Samuel 17:46–47).

Moments later, David was the victor. His smooth stone was embedded in Goliath's forehead, and he used Goliath's own sword to behead the villain. ✦

139

Alone, frightened, and desperate, Saul consulted a medium. She summoned the ghost of Samuel, who told Saul, "Tomorrow you and your sons will be with me."

A death foretold

The witch of Endor summons Samuel from the grave

WHEN SAUL CONSULTED THE MEDIUM at Endor, he was in despair. He faced a major attack by the Philistines in the Valley of Jezreel. Realizing that his own children had turned against him, that God had forsaken him, and that David would ultimately triumph over him, he was afraid. He wished to know God's will.

That desire to know the future—especially when the stakes were high—ran deep in the peoples of the ancient world. Every nation had its preferred methods for discerning the future or seeking divine guidance. The many methods included astrology, casting lots, examining the entrails of sacrificial animals, interpreting dreams, understanding various natural omens, prophecy under inspiration, and necromancy, or consulting the dead.

Saul regularly sought help from those means of divination that were acceptable in Israel. He had first met Samuel when he wanted Samuel to use his powers as a clairvoyant to find some lost donkeys. As king, Saul used the Urim and Thummim, two objects that were used in a sacred form of casting lots. These were kept by the priest in the "breastpiece of judgment," which was worn over the priest's ephod. Exactly what they were and how they were used has been lost, but they evidently answered yes or no to an inquiry. A third response—a refusal to answer—is another possibility.

Discovering the future through the interpretation of dreams was another practice permitted in Israel. For example, the Patriarch Joseph was both a dreamer and an interpreter of dreams. It is important to note that before he visited the medium of Endor, Saul had attempted to divine the future by all the legitimate Israelite methods—dreams, the Urim, and inspired prophets—but from these he had learned nothing.

Then, in his despair, Saul stepped over the line. He decided to consult the dead

Samuel through a medium. Saul himself had banned necromancers from Israel, not because he believed they did not work but because Yahweh commanded: "If a person turns to mediums and wizards, . . . I will set my face against that person, and will cut him off from among his people."

Although the medium Saul consulted has traditionally been described as "the witch of Endor," she was not a "witch" in any modern sense. Moreover, among the non-Israelites, her profession was considered an honorable art. In some periods, mediums were openly patronized by Israel's royalty (2 Kings 21:6).

The witch of Endor knew of Saul's ban and was reluctant to risk arrest for practicing her art for a stranger. Still, neither she nor Saul questioned her abilities. When she finally recognized Saul, and the king promised not to harm her, she proceeded.

Samuel rose from the underworld like "a god coming up out of the earth" (1 Samuel 28:13). But he devastated Saul by letting him know that the future held no hope: "tomorrow you and your sons shall be with me."

Given the condemnation of necromancy in the Scriptures, it is remarkable that this narrative reports a successful seance in such a matter-of-fact manner. It is no less remarkable that the text describes the medium of Endor as a kindly woman who cared for the human needs of the distraught king by urging him to eat and then preparing a large meal for him. Through this gesture she conveyed sympathy for the tragedy of the man whose career had begun with promise and ended with hopeless terror. ✦

On consulting the dead

"It is to be feared that, so long as the world lasts, there will always be an ample supply of knavery to meet the demand of folly."
—**Sir James George Frazer**
Folklore and the Old Testament, Volume 2

Saul's suicide

"How are the mighty fallen"

THE FIRST BOOK OF SAMUEL ends with the death of Saul, Israel's first monarch, in a sad scene of complete physical and spiritual defeat. Although Saul had been chosen by God and had been filled with the Spirit of the Lord, he had failed to recognize that in Israel even the king must always submit to divine rule. He lost his mandate through disobedience.

After his mysterious meeting with the spirit of the dead Samuel, Saul knew that he would die during the next day's battle with the Philistines. But he met his fate with dignity. True to Samuel's prediction, Israel's army was put to flight from the Jezreel Valley and fled up the slopes of Mount Gilboa. Saul saw his hopes fade as one by one, three of his sons, including the beloved Jonathan, were killed. When the king himself was wounded by enemy archers, he realized that his end had come.

Even more than he feared death, Saul feared life as a captive of the Philistines. When, despite Saul's urgings, his armor bearer could not bring himself to strike and kill the king, Saul committed suicide. The next moment, his armor bearer did the same. Suicide, even in hopeless battle, was rare in ancient Israel. That the king died in such a fashion was the ultimate defeat. Later, David lamented:

> Thy glory, O Israel, is slain upon thy high places!
> How are the mighty fallen! . . .
> Saul and Jonathan, beloved and lovely!

The next day the Philistines came upon Saul's corpse and exulted. They sent messengers to bear the good news of victory back to their gods and their people. Then they hung the beheaded body of Saul from the walls of the captured city of Beth-shan.

The Second Book of Samuel begins with a somewhat different story of Saul's death. This version is told by a young Amalekite. Bringing Saul's crown and armlet to David, the young man reported how, in defeat, Saul had attempted suicide unsuccessfully: "So I stood beside him, and slew him."

The narrators understood this as a false report intended to gain David's gratitude for killing his enemy—but it backfired. David believed that the person of the king was inviolable. Twice he had refused to kill Saul when he had the chance. The Amalekite's report sentenced him to death. David said: "Your blood be upon your head; for your own mouth has testified against you, saying, 'I have slain the LORD's anointed.' " ✦

When his armor bearer *refused to slay him, Saul killed himself, falling on his weapon.*

❧ David's psalm of thanksgiving ❧

GOD HAS RESCUED DAVID from a sea of troubles, the poet exclaims, as a reward for David's continuing loyalty to God and to his commandments. This beautiful poem is the only chapter of Scripture to appear in two different parts of the Bible—as 2 Samuel 22 and as Psalm 18. According to a much later rabbinical tradition, the psalm is number 18 because David fought 18 wars in his lifetime. Some scholars say he wrote the poem in his youth, after Saul's death; others say he wrote it in old age, after his men vowed not to allow him to go onto the field of battle with them any longer.

I love thee, O LORD, my strength.
The LORD is my rock, and my fortress,
   and my deliverer,
     my God, my rock, in whom I take refuge,
     my shield, and the horn of my salvation,
     my stronghold.
I call upon the LORD, who is worthy
   to be praised,
   and I am saved from my enemies.

The cords of death encompassed me,
   the torrents of perdition assailed me;
the cords of Sheol entangled me,
   the snares of death confronted me.

In my distress I called upon the LORD;
   to my God I cried for help.
From his temple he heard my voice,
   and my cry to him reached his ears.

Then the earth reeled and rocked;
   the foundations also of the mountains
     trembled
   and quaked, because he was angry.
Smoke went up from his nostrils,
   and devouring fire from his mouth;
   glowing coals flamed forth from him.
He bowed the heavens, and came down;
   thick darkness was under his feet.
He rode on a cherub, and flew;
   he came swiftly upon the wings of the wind.
He made darkness his covering around him.
   his canopy thick clouds dark with water.
Out of the brightness before him
   there broke through his clouds
   hailstones and coals of fire.
The LORD also thundered in the heavens,
   and the Most High uttered his voice,
   hailstones and coals of fire.

And he sent out his arrows, and
   scattered them;
   he flashed forth lightnings, and
   routed them.
Then the channels of the sea were seen,
   and the foundations of the world
     were laid bare,
at thy rebuke, O LORD,
   at the blast of the breath of thy nostrils.

He reached from on high, he took me,
   he drew me out of many waters.
He delivered me from my strong enemy,
   and from those who hated me;
   for they were too mighty for me.
They came upon me in the day of
    my calamity;
   but the LORD was my stay.
He brought me forth into a broad place;
   he delivered me, because he
    delighted in me.
❧ ❧ ❧ ❧ ❧ ❧   *Psalm 18: 1–19*

The LORD lives; and blessed be my rock,
   and exalted be the God of my salvation,
the God who gave me vengeance
   and subdued peoples under me;
who delivered me from my enemies;
   yea, thou didst exalt me above my
    adversaries;
   thou didst deliver me from men of violence.

For this I will extol thee, O LORD,
   among the nations,
   and sing praises to thy name.
Great triumphs he gives to his king,
   and shows steadfast love to his anointed,
   to David and his descendants for ever.
❧ ❧ ❧ ❧ ❧ ❧   *Psalm 18: 46–50*

Crossroads of destiny

Where Solomon prayed for wisdom

THE TOWN OF GIBEON, about six miles northwest of Jerusalem, appears repeatedly in the history and legends of Israel. Its story reflects both the violence and the piety of ancient days, and in modern times it has become the site of remarkable archaeological discoveries. First occupied about 2800 B.C., biblical Gibeon's site is located in an Arab village in whose name— El Jib—Gibeon's first syllable survives. (The name *Gibeon* means "hill.")

When the Israelites, under Joshua, first entered Canaan (about 1200 B.C.) the site of Gibeon already had a millennium and a half of human history. Its inhabitants were prosperous vintners and wine merchants. It was a far more important settlement than the town to its south—the town that was to become the capital, Jerusalem.

The Gibeonites had a special relationship with Israel from the time of the conquest. Through an elaborate ruse they convinced Joshua that they were "from a very far country" and thus were able to make a treaty with Israel and escape the destruction that befell the other cities in the area.

When local Amorite armies attacked Gibeon for breaking the united defense against the invading Israelites, Joshua came to their aid. It was during that decisive battle that the Lord threw great stones down from heaven and Joshua commanded the sun to stand still (Joshua 10:11–14).

Gibeon next appeared on the stage of Israelite history in the stormy aftermath of the death of King Saul. David had been anointed as king of Judah, in the south. Saul's son Ishbosheth, meanwhile, had been installed as king of Israel, in the north. Gibeon, now a city belonging to the tribe of Benjamin, was near the border between the northern and the southern regions.

In a mysterious incident that began as some sort of duel or tournament—but soon

The ancient pool of Gibeon, where the bloody "game" between Joab and Abner took place, was uncovered in 1956. A spiral staircase leads to a tunnel, which, in turn, leads to a cistern outside the city walls.

144

erupted into a full-scale battle—the opposing sides confronted each other around the great rock-cut pool of Gibeon (2 Samuel 2:12–17). David's commander, Joab, sat on one side; the dead Saul's former commander, Abner, was on the other. Abner proposed the duel by saying, "Let the young men arise and play before us." Then Joab said, "Let them arise."

Twelve soldiers on each side stepped forward and paired off for their bloody "play." In the duel, "each caught his opponent by the head, and thrust his sword in his opponent's side; so they fell down together" (2 Samuel 2:16). The death of the 24 initiated a fierce battle in which David's side clearly had the advantage but the other camp was not totally defeated. Thus at Gibeon began "a long war between the house of Saul and the house of David" (2 Samuel 3:1), in which David ultimately triumphed.

After David's victory, the Gibeonites again took part in another remarkably bloody incident. When a famine ravaged the land, David was told that it was caused by a "bloodguilt on Saul and on his house, because he put the Gibeonites to death"—an event that is not previously recorded in the Bible (2 Samuel 21:1). The Gibeonites demanded the death of seven sons of Saul to expiate this guilt. But by this time, many of Saul's sons had already died. David satisfied the Gibeonites by giving them two of Saul's sons and five of his grandsons, "and they hanged them on the mountain before the LORD, and the seven of them perished together" (2 Samuel 21:9).

Their bodies were left out to be devoured by birds and animals, but they were spared this indignity through the remarkable perseverance of Rizpah, the mother of two of Saul's sons. Day and night, from April to late autumn, she guarded the hanging bodies. Finally David, hearing of Rizpah's vigil, had the bones buried with Saul's near Saul's home in the land of Benjamin.

During the reign of Solomon, David's successor, Gibeon was a great high place, where Solomon sacrificed a thousand burnt offerings to the Lord. Moreover, it was at Gibeon that Solomon had his famous dream, in which he asked the Lord for the wisdom to rule justly. Not only was he granted unsurpassed wisdom, but he was also given great riches and honor.

Biblical references to Gibeon are often in connection with a "pool," or "great pool." But it was not until 1956 that the "great pool" was located. In that year, an archaeological expedition led by J. B. Pritchard discovered the pool of Gibeon. It was a cylindrical water shaft—37 feet wide and 82 feet deep—that had been cut into the rock. Seventy-nine rock-cut steps spiral down the inner wall of the shaft. This enormous excavation is estimated to have required the removal of approximately 3,000 tons of limestone, a work that in those days would probably have been done by hand. The giant well together with two extensive water tunnels, also hewn from the rock, formed a water system that—until relatively recently—continued to supply water to the modern town of El Jib. ✦

"Acquaint yourself with the needs and fears, the moods and manners, of the broken array of peoples and civilizations that appeared at intervals along the horizon of time and, in a general way, you will know in advance where to look for the clues they left behind in the course of their passage. . . . And above all, read the Bible, morning, noon and night, with a positive attitude, reading to accept its historical references. . . . And then go forth into the wilderness of the Negev and discover, trite as it may sound, that everything you touch turns into the gold of history, and that it is almost impossible not to stumble across the treasures of a robust past, whose existence becomes as real and as full of content and color and sound and fury and the thrill of progress and the pity of failure as the transient present, which is always ticking away so furiously to join the throng of those that need no longer hurry."
—Nelson Glueck, "Exploring Southern Palestine (The Negev)" (1959) *The Biblical Archaeologist Reader*

The House of David

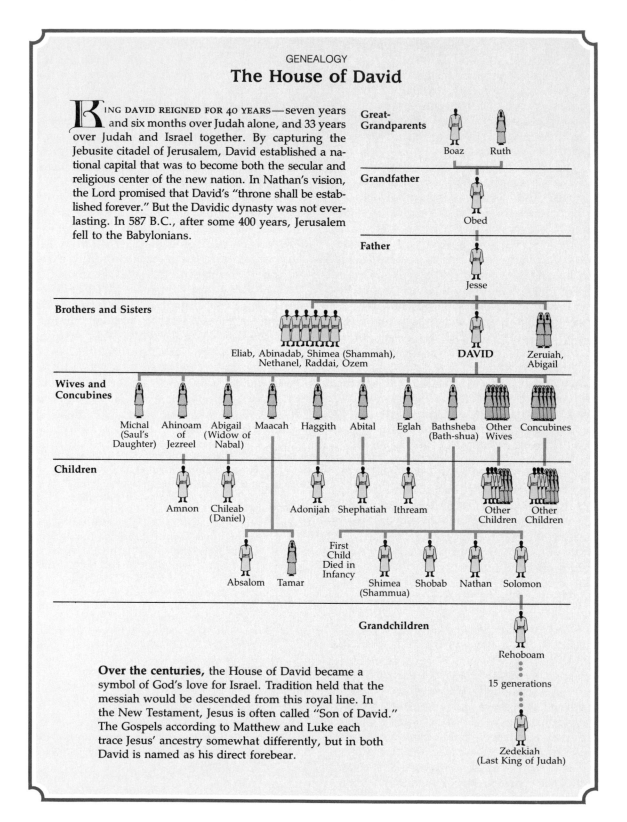

KING DAVID REIGNED FOR 40 YEARS—seven years and six months over Judah alone, and 33 years over Judah and Israel together. By capturing the Jebusite citadel of Jerusalem, David established a national capital that was to become both the secular and religious center of the new nation. In Nathan's vision, the Lord promised that David's "throne shall be established forever." But the Davidic dynasty was not everlasting. In 587 B.C., after some 400 years, Jerusalem fell to the Babylonians.

Great-Grandparents
Boaz Ruth

Grandfather
Obed

Father
Jesse

Brothers and Sisters
Eliab, Abinadab, Shimea (Shammah), Nethanel, Raddai, Ozem

DAVID

Zeruiah, Abigail

Wives and Concubines
Michal (Saul's Daughter) Ahinoam of Jezreel Abigail (Widow of Nabal) Maacah Haggith Abital Eglah Bathsheba (Bath-shua) Other Wives Concubines

Children
Amnon Chileab (Daniel) Adonijah Shephatiah Ithream Other Children Other Children

Absalom Tamar First Child Died in Infancy Shimea (Shammua) Shobab Nathan Solomon

Grandchildren
Rehoboam
15 generations
Zedekiah (Last King of Judah)

Over the centuries, the House of David became a symbol of God's love for Israel. Tradition held that the messiah would be descended from this royal line. In the New Testament, Jesus is often called "Son of David." The Gospels according to Matthew and Luke each trace Jesus' ancestry somewhat differently, but in both David is named as his direct forebear.

A great king's lust

David's transgression and repentance

THE BIBLICAL NARRATIVE of David's rise to power is filled with vivid detail. From the start, when Samuel prophetically anointed David, the narrative follows him through the dangerous rivalries of Saul's court, and through his years as an outlaw. After Saul's death, we witness David's struggle to consolidate his position. Finally, David was anointed as king by all the tribes of Israel. He brought unity to the nation, defeated its enemies in battle, and captured Jerusalem—making it his capital and moving the Ark of the Lord there. Success attended him as he built his empire.

But it is just at this point that the biblical narrative takes a strange turn. David's public success is followed by the dark narrative of his private sins and their dire consequences for himself and his family. The negative side of even so great a hero as David must also be told so that the reader will be reminded that it is God, and not a human being, who is the focus of the story.

The tragedy begins with David's adultery with Bathsheba. There are hints, planted in the story's introduction, that David had forsaken his heroic role. It was spring, "the time when kings go forth to battle," but David sent a subordinate to do his kingly duty while he "remained at Jerusalem."

While his troops besieged the Ammonites, David took a walk on the roof of his palace. Gazing down, he spied a beautiful woman bathing nearby. He found out that she was Bathsheba, the wife of a Hittite named Uriah, a man who was not an Israelite but was fighting in David's army. In a raw exercise of power, "David sent messengers and took her." He committed adultery with her, and she became pregnant.

The king sought a way to hide his crime. He had Uriah summoned back from the front, and, over the course of three days, tried to get the man to visit his wife so as to make plausible Uriah's paternity of the child. To David's chagrin, Uriah the foreigner remained true to the Israelite tradition of continence during a time of battle—a tradition that David himself had formerly observed. Uriah refused to go to his wife so long as his comrades were in combat.

David resorted to a more desperate stratagem. He sent Uriah back to the war with a sealed message to his commander instructing that Uriah be placed in the front line of battle. The order was followed, and, as David had hoped, Uriah was killed. David quickly married the widowed Bathsheba, and when their son was born, they assumed that they were beyond the reach of any who could call them to account.

"But the thing that David had done displeased the LORD." The prophet Nathan came to the king and asked him to judge the case of a wealthy man with many flocks of sheep who stole the one little lamb that belonged to his poor neighbor. Not realizing that Nathan was offering a parable of his own crime, the king angrily declared that the rich man deserved death. The prophet replied, "You are the man."

David confessed and was repentant, but his remorse could not release him from the consequences of his sin. "And Nathan said to David, 'The LORD also has put away your sin; you shall not die. Nevertheless, because by this deed you have utterly scorned the LORD, the child that is born to you shall die.' " One of the most beautiful prayers of the Hebrew Scriptures, Psalm 51, was later attributed to this moment in David's life.

Nathan also predicted further strife and turmoil for David as punishment for adultery and murder: "the sword shall never depart from your house." Indeed, the remainder of David's reign was a sorry spectacle of jealousy, rape, murder, and rebellion within his own family.

The manner in which this story unfolds

Gazing down on Bathsheba, *David lost his heart—and endangered his righteousness.*

allows the reader to see the moral purposes of the narrators. The initial sin of David and Bathsheba is told with almost austere brevity, but the consequences of their sin are narrated with pathos and great detail.

The inclusion of such a story about this otherwise heroic king reveals much about the understanding of human beings in Israelite tradition. There are heroes and villains throughout the Scriptures, but none of them is a paragon of virtue—not the Patriarchs, not Moses, and certainly not King David. David was chosen by God to rule over Israel; he was blessed with victories; he was the progenitor of a monarchical dynasty; he was the prototype of the Messiah destined to come and redeem the world. Nevertheless, he committed a heinous sin.

When David neglected his responsibilities and began to exceed his prerogatives as an anointed monarch, his actions led to disaster. Even though divinely anointed, David was bound by the same rules of morality and justice that governed the lives of his subjects. The prophet Nathan did not hesitate to enter the palace and confront the king with his crime. David, for his part, felt obliged to acknowledge the truth and repent. Until he laid eyes on Bathsheba, David is portrayed as one immune to sinful temptations—in fact, he seems to be almost too good to be true. But some later Jewish commentators felt that David was overly confident and wished to be tested by God so that he could prove that he compared favorably with the Patriarchs. He complained to God; he wished to be put through a trial so as to attain the spiritual greatness of Abraham and the other Patriarchs. Sure enough, when temptation was placed before his eyes, the great king succumbed. David overestimated his own strength of character and was punished for his pride.

Thus the view of David that emerges from this moving story is of a man like other men. David's public success could not mask his private vice. At the same time, David is not perceived to be a villain—his reputation is merely tarnished. Repentance restored him in the eyes of the Lord, the Israelites, and posterity. ✦

148

Plots and counterplots

David's deathbed choice of a successor

ROYAL SUCCESSION DURING the early years of the Israelite monarchy was fraught with great peril. The monarchy was a relatively new institution, and a pattern of peaceful transfer of power from one king to another had not yet been established. Moreover, the practice of royal polygamy added to the complexity of succession, since the son of one wife might be vying for power with the son of another. In the case of King David, just such a crisis clouded his final days.

First, his health declined. Afflicted with chills, he could get no relief in spite of being covered with clothing. Abishag the Shunammite, a beautiful young woman, was brought to the king to lie beside him and give him warmth. She "became the king's nurse and ministered to him; but the king knew her not" (1 Kings 1:4).

Adonijah, King David's handsome oldest surviving son, seized the initiative and began to act as the king designate. He gathered a large entourage and offered lavish public sacrifices. Evidently, David had made no public declaration of a successor. So Adonijah, acting in concert with two of David's long-time associates, Joab, the commander of the army, and Abiathar, the priest, declared himself king.

The actions of Adonijah, who was the son of David's wife Haggith, stirred up a counterplot, however, among those at David's court who supported another of his wives, Bathsheba, and her son, Solomon. The prophet Nathan, who years before had condemned David for his marriage to Bathsheba,

had now become her counselor. He urged Bathsheba to go to the ailing king, tell him that Adonijah had usurped the throne, and remind David of his promise that their son Solomon would rule after him. When Bathsheba aroused the old man's interest, Nathan went to the king, corroborated her story, and added further details of Adonijah's treachery.

Determined to thwart the coup, David instructed his ministers to anoint Solomon as king. When this was done, a trumpet was blown, and "all the people said, 'Long live King Solomon!' " (1 Kings 1:39).

David's support of Solomon's succession dashed Adonijah's hopes; when the latter's erstwhile supporters heard about it, they "trembled, and rose, and each went his own way" (1 Kings 1:49). Adonijah himself, fearing for his life, took refuge at the sacred altar, involving ancient claims to sanctuary. He seized the "horns" that projected from the top of the altar and would not let go until he secured a promise from Solomon that he would not be harmed so long as he, Adonijah, transgressed no more.

When David was on his deathbed, he gave his final testament to his son Solomon. David urged him to use his wisdom to destroy two powerful men who had done great wrongs in the past. He also warned his son that his kingship would succeed and the dynasty would continue only if Solomon and his successors faithfully followed the Lord's commands. "Then David slept with his fathers, and . . . Solomon sat upon the throne of David his father; and his kingdom was firmly established." ✦

King David *is lowered into a tomb, while his son Solomon watches.*

149

Death and burial in the Bible

"When your days are fulfilled and you lie down with your fathers"

THE PSALMIST TELLS US that "the years of our life are threescore and ten," meaning that a person may expect a lifetime of 70 years (Psalm 90:10). But in all likelihood, few people in ancient times lived so long. War, famine, and disease put them at hazard. Medicine was primitive; people died of injuries and infections that today are considered minor and that we are able to treat effectively with simple antiseptics. Anything as serious as a wound received in battle, or a mangled limb, would most likely prove fatal. And, not understanding how disease spread, people in ancient times could not guard against plague.

A set of burial rituals evolved among the ancient Israelites in accordance with the cir-

The modern *figure of mourning by sculptor Augustus Saint-Gaudens captures the pall of death on the spirit.*

cumstances of the times. None was more important than to bury the dead as quickly as possible. The hot Middle Eastern climate made a speedy burial essential; more pressing, however, was the age-old fear, pervasive throughout the Mesopotamian region, of lying unburied after death. It was believed that after death the soul continued to feel what was done to the body.

Archaeological evidence has revealed that the Israelites did not develop their own burial practices but instead adopted the customs of Mesopotamia. "May the earth not receive your corpses" is a curse frequently cited in Mesopotamian texts. Its echo can be found in Deuteronomy 28:26, where the litany of curses for those who disobey the Lord's rule includes: "And your dead body shall be food for all the birds of the air, and for the beasts of the earth; and there shall be no one to frighten them away."

The urgent need to provide the dead with a proper grave is the focus of the poignant story of Rizpah, one of King Saul's concubines, told in 2 Samuel 21. When famine struck the Israelites after Saul died, it was blamed on Saul's breach of a treaty with the Gibeonites, entered into years before by Joshua (Joshua 9:3–27). Seeking to ease the famine and placate the Gibeonites, Saul's successor, King David, agreed to let the Gibeonites execute two of Saul's sons together with five of his grandsons. The two sons were Rizpah's children.

The seven were hanged and their bodies were left unburied as a way of expiating the bloodguilt of Israel. Rizpah kept faithful watch at the execution site for a period of several months, guarding them against birds and animals. When David heard of her vigil, he journeyed to Jabesh-gilead to retrieve the bones of Saul and Jonathan, which had been buried there after the father and son died in battle against the Philistines (1 Samuel 31). Then he buried their bones with those of the seven hanged men, laying them all to rest in one grave.

For the ordinary Israelite family, the rituals of death began when, following a precedent set in Genesis 46:4, a close relative closed the eyes of the deceased. The body was then bathed, fully dressed, and carried on a wooden bier to the grave site. Coffins were not in common use. Ideally the deceased would be buried in a family tomb, but most Israelites could not afford such a luxury, so the dead were interred in pits, trench graves, or caves.

Embalming was not practiced by the Israelites, nor was cremation, since it would have run counter to the precept given in Genesis 3:19, "You are dust and to dust you shall return."

Leviticus and Deuteronomy are very clear in their bans against excessive rites of mourning, such as cutting one's hair or mutilating one's own flesh, but there is evidence that the Israelites engaged in these immemorial customs all the same. For instance, in mourning the destruction of Moab, the prophet Jeremiah writes that "every head is shaved and every beard cut off; upon all the hands are gashes." Expressions of grief that were not forbidden included fasting, the wearing of sackcloth, the tearing of one's clothes, and, of course, weeping and wailing.

Professional mourners, usually women, played a prominent role, and assured an orderly and ritually proper ceremony. More than that, they orchestrated the grief, making sure that the cries of woe were rendered at the appropriate times. The professional mourners often wrote their own songs or poems for the dead; the more distinguished the deceased, the longer the dirge.

Egyptian woman in an *eloquent gesture of mourning.*

It is remarkable that many of the lamentations preserved in the Bible lack specific religious content. This may be because the Old Testament itself prescribes no special veneration of the dead, nor does it set any rules for honoring them. On the contrary, it apparently takes the view that the remains of the dead are unclean.

Did the Israelites believe in an afterlife? In Genesis 37:35 is the first of many references to Sheol, a dismal underworld inhabited by the shades of the deceased where there is no memory or possibility of action. Psalm 139:8 is one of several passages in the Old Testament expressing the belief that the dead are subject to the rule of God, although in Sheol they are not aware of his presence.

The Christian concept of resurrection is believed to have developed from two other important themes in the Old Testament—death as a form of sleep and death as a condition that the Lord can ultimately conquer. In Job 14:10–12, for example, we find death viewed as a sleep from which there is no awakening; later, in Isaiah 25:8, we come upon the prophecy that "the Lord will swallow up death forever." These two passages are taken by scholars as the major building blocks leading to the concept of resurrection, introduced in the Bible in Daniel 12:2: "And many of those who sleep in the dust of the earth shall awake, some to everlasting life, and some to shame and everlasting contempt."

For the ordinary person of the ancient Middle East, however, the most one could hope for in the way of immortality was to be remembered by one's family; remembered, especially, by sons who would bear one's name into the future. ✦

"He will swallow up death for ever, and the Lord GOD will wipe away tears from all faces"

—Isaiah 25:8

THE OLDER BOOKS of the Bible present death as a terminal event of desolate finality. Then—starting with the Psalms and continuing with the utterances of the prophets—there is an unfolding of hope and comfort, a promise of eternal life. It is a long way from the bleak image of Sheol in the Book of Proverbs to Paul's exultant cry in 1 Corinthians 15:55: "O death, where is thy sting? O grave, where is thy victory?" In subsequent tradition there is a steady emphasis on personal hope, reflecting an ever increasing awareness that each individual believer counts.

"Tears shed at the demise of a good man are counted by the Holy One and deposited in His treasury."
    —**Bar Kappara**
    Talmud: Sabbath

In the verse "Weeping may tarry for the night, but joy comes with the morning" (Psalm 30:5), "This world is compared to the darkness, the next world is the bright dawn. Similarly, this world is but a brief moment of anger compared to the future eternal bliss."
    —**David Kimhi,**
    13th-century Jewish theologian,
    traditionally called "Radak"

"How is it possible, you ask, that a bereaved person, being a man, should not grieve? On the contrary, I ask, how is it that being a man he should grieve, since he is honored with reason and with hopes of future good? Who is there, you ask again, that has not been subdued by this weakness? Many, I reply, and in many places, both among us and among those who have died before us. Job, for instance, the whole circle of his children being taken away, hear what he says—'The LORD gave; the LORD hath taken away; blessed be the name of the LORD.' A wonderful saying, even when merely heard; but if you examine it closely, your wonder will greatly increase."
    —**Chrysostom (c. 347–407 A.D.),**
    "Excessive Grief at the Death of Friends"

"Death be not proud, though some have
        called thee
Mighty and dreadful, for thou art not so,
For those whom thou thinkst thou dost
        overthrow
Die not, poor death, nor yet canst thou
        kill me.
From rest and sleep, which but thy
        pictures be,
Much pleasure, then, from thee much more
        must flow;
And soonest our best men with thee do go,
Rest of their bones and soul's delivery.
Thou'rt slave to fate, chance, kings and
        desperate men,
And dost with poison, war, and sickness
        dwell;
And poppy or charms can make us sleep
        as well
And better than thy stroke. Why swell'st
        thou then?
One short sleep past, we wake eternally
And death shall be no more; death thou
        shalt die."

    —**John Donne,** *Holy Sonnets*

"Everything that grows begins little and becomes big, except grief; it starts big and becomes little, till it disappears."
    —**Ibn Gabirol,** *Ethics*

One baby, two mothers: *Solomon's judgment earned him fame for wisdom.*

The golden age of empire

King Solomon's fabled reign

KING SOLOMON'S REIGN (961-922 B.C.) marked the high point of prosperity for the Israelite monarchy. Building upon the success of his father, David, who had unified the nation and expanded Israelite control over neighboring territories, Solomon made Israel into a great power. Yet, only a few of Solomon's achievements lasted beyond his own lifetime.

Soon after his coronation, Solomon had an experience that set the course of his reign. God appeared to him in a dream and asked what special gift he would like to have. The king responded: "an understanding mind to govern thy people, that I may discern between good and evil." Pleased with this request, God promised him not only wisdom, but long life, riches, and honor as well, provided that Solomon "walk in my ways, keeping my statutes and my commandments" (1 Kings 3:14).

Solomon soon had occasion to demonstrate his exceptional wisdom. Two harlots came before the king with a seemingly insoluble dispute. The two, each with her own baby, had been living in the same house. One of the babies had been found dead—but which one? Each woman claimed that the surviving infant was hers. Since they were without family or friends who might have identified the babies, there was no one else who could testify.

The king ruled that the surviving child should be cut in two and divided between the women. As the king had foreseen, the woman who was not the real mother accepted this verdict, while the true mother offered the child to her rival rather than let it be cut in half. Thus the king awarded it to her: "And all Israel. . .stood in awe of the king, because they perceived that the wisdom of God was in him, to render justice."

Solomon's wisdom was not confined to the judicial sphere. According to the First Book of Kings, he was "wiser than all other men," and he composed 3,000 proverbs and more than 1,000 songs—hence the attribution to him of 3 biblical books: Proverbs, Ecclesiastes, and the Song of Solomon, as

153

well as that part of the Apocrypha called the *Wisdom of Solomon*. The king knew the lore of nature: "He spoke of trees, from the cedar that is in Lebanon to the hyssop that grows out of the wall; he spoke also of beasts, and of birds, and of reptiles, and of fish." So great was his reputation as a wise man that folklore would elaborate on the biblical account and transform Solomon into a magician. For example, *The Testament of Solomon* relates how Solomon was given a special ring from the Lord, which gave him the power to "confine all the demons both female and male, and, through their agency, build Jerusalem."

King Solomon was also a great builder. Eager to centralize a monarchy that had only recently replaced a loose confederation of semiautonomous tribes, he oversaw the construction of a magnificent temple dedicated to God in his capital city of Jerusalem. The Temple would house the Ark of the Covenant, containing the tablets of the law that Moses received on Mount Sinai. This Temple became the national sanctuary of the Israelites. Solomon built his royal palace beside it, linking his own high office to the prestige of the Temple. Solomon also con-

structed several fortified cities in strategic parts of the country—including Hazor, Megiddo, and Gezer—which have been unearthed and identified by archaeologists.

The narrators of the First Book of Kings, who in a time of national crisis looked back across the centuries to Solomon, saw his reign as a golden age. "Judah and Israel were as many as the sand by the sea; they ate and drank and were happy." "Judah and Israel dwelt in safety . . . every man under his vine and under his fig tree, all the days of Solomon." The kingdom's prosperity was enhanced because it controlled the trade routes running between Mesopotamia to the northeast and Egypt and the Red Sea in the south and west.

Solomon's merchant fleet was built and manned by the Phoenicians of Tyre. For centuries, Tyre was a great port and commercial center in what is now Lebanon. The fleet, a monopoly of the crown, was based in the port city of Ezion-Geber, which was on the northern tip of the Gulf of Aqaba (Gulf of Elath). The ships are said to have sailed as far as "Ophir, and brought from there gold" (1 Kings 9:28). The mysterious "Ophir" has been variously identified, but was probably present-day Somalia on the

Folklore transformed King Solomon into a wonder-working wizard who contracted demons to build the Temple.

horn of Africa. The ships brought back diverse cargoes—gold, silver, jewels, rare woods, ivory, and other commodities. Thus Solomon's kingdom appears to have been a bustling crossroads of commerce. Presumably Solomon's fortunes were amplified by the work of subordinates who acted as middlemen or agents. In any case, trade brought handsome profits to the kingdom.

But in time, serious problems arose. Two captive territories, Edom in the south and Syria in the northeast, rebelled, weakening Solomon's hold on the empire. More dangerous still, Jeroboam, the son of Nebat, a young man of the tribe of Ephraim who held a high position in the king's service, "lifted up his hand against the king." Forced to flee into exile in Egypt by Solomon, Jeroboam bided his time until the moment would come for a full-scale civil war.

After his brilliant beginning, marked by wisdom and prosperity, why was King Solomon beset by challenges from without and from within? From a political perspective, Solomon's drive for centralization—while strengthening and enriching the country as a whole—antagonized a good many people. Undoubtedly, there were Israelites who still looked back with nostalgia to the old days before the monarchy when tribes ran their own affairs, and government rarely, if ever, interfered in the lives of individuals. Solomon, in contrast, tried to weaken local clan loyalties by dividing the kingdom into administrative districts that did not coincide with tribal boundaries.

The king's ambitious policies had serious practical consequences as well. Heavy taxes were exacted from the people to pay for the splendor of Solomon's court. His building projects were carried out by the forced labor of Israelite and non-Israelite subjects. His heavy-handed rule ultimately provoked opposition. When Solomon died, the common people did not mourn the passing of a golden age; rather they hoped for an improvement in their lot. The assembly of Israel petitioned Solomon's successor for relief from the "hard service" and

---

IN MODERN TIMES

Star of David
Seal of Solomon

Symbols of the 12 tribes of Israel appear on this modern Star of David pendant.

The origin of the Star of David, now widely recognized as the emblem of Judaism, is obscure. One legend is that King David bore a hexagram-shaped shield when he fought Goliath. Originally a pagan ornament, the hexagram was later named both the Star of David, or *Magen David*, and the Seal of Solomon. By the Middle Ages, the symbols were used as talismans against evil; the terms *Seal of Solomon* and *Magan David* were used interchangeably in magical texts. By the 19th century, the Star of David had gained ascendancy, and appeared in Jewish ritual and on synagogues. The Seal of Solomon, often depicted as two interlacing triangles, retained its magical associations. One interpretation is that its cojoining light and dark triangles represent the unity of body and soul.

In 1897 the Star of David was adopted by the Zionist Congress. But it was not until World War II, when the Nazis forced European Jews to wear a yellow star as a badge of shame and, ulti-

Solomon's seal

mately, death, that it took on a powerful resonance of triumph over despair. In 1948 it was chosen as the central design in the flag of the State of Israel.

"heavy yoke" that Solomon had imposed.

At the same time, the Bible attributes Solomon's difficulties to religious apostasy. God's gift of wisdom, granted at the outset of his reign, had been conditional on Solomon's obedience to God's will. By contracting marriages with foreign noblewomen, Solomon came under alien influences. His harem, which included the daughter of the Egyptian Pharaoh, grew until he had seven hundred wives and three hundred concubines. These "turned away his heart after other gods" (1 Kings 11:4).

Solomon's many marriages probably do not indicate any special weakness for the opposite sex. Many of these were dynastic marriages; each time he married a foreign princess, Solomon created or strengthened an alliance with another state. But so careful

was he to attend to the religious needs of his wives that he built "high places" for foreign gods—to Ashtoreth, the goddess of the Sidonians; Chemosh, the god of Moab; Milcom, the god of Ammon—evidence that Solomon himself "did not wholly follow the LORD" (1 Kings 11:6).

The Bible depicts Jeroboam's abortive revolt not simply in political terms but as the result of divine guidance. Ahijah the prophet, clad in a new garment, met Jeroboam in a field. The prophet tore his garment into 12 pieces, giving 10 to Jeroboam, "for thus says the LORD, the God of Israel, 'Behold, I am about to tear the kingdom from the hand of Solomon, and will give you ten tribes." This prophecy would be fulfilled soon after Solomon's death, when the great kingdom of David split in two. ✦

Solomon's Temple

"The glory of the Lord filled the house of the Lord"

SO GREAT WAS THE FAME OF Solomon's Temple that it lives on in the world's imagination more than 2,500 years after its destruction by the Babylonians in 587 B.C. Begun within four years after Solomon's rise to power, the Temple was completed in the remarkable short period of seven years. Later legend told that none of the workmen fell sick or died during the construction, nor did any tool wear out.

Solomon's Temple was the first permanent sanctuary built as a "house of Yah-

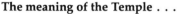

The meaning of the Temple . . .

"It was the heart of the nation's life, beating rapidly and joyfully, or slowly and erratically, but beating nevertheless throughout her life. That was the basic concern of the Chronicler, whose portrait is not merely that of a symbol or lifeless formality; the temple was the life center of the people of God, the hub of the Lord's kingdom on earth."

—Jacob M. Myers
The Anchor Bible, 1 Chronicles

weh." It was intended as a sanctuary for the Ark of the Covenant, and it provided a focus of worship for all Israelites.

The Temple was built on a site that harked back to the reign of King David. According to 2 Samuel 24, he had seen a vision of an angel of the Lord "by the threshing floor of Araunah the Jebusite." David was instructed by a seer named Gad to build an altar on this spot as a means of averting a plague on Israel. David purchased the site and raised the altar. It was here, then, that Solomon built the Temple. Perhaps equally significant, the location was traditionally identified as the mysterious place where, centuries earlier, Abraham had taken his son Isaac to be sacrificed in accordance with God's command.

This site is now the location of one of the most sacred shrines in Islam. It is from this place that Muhammed is said to have ascended to heaven. A mosque, known as Dome of the Rock, was built over the site in the seventh century A.D.

*"**Now therefore command** that cedars of Lebanon be cut for me." Hiram, king of Tyre, provided timber for the Temple.*

Because of its continuing religious significance, the site is not open to archaeological excavations. Some scholars believe that even if it were, few remains from the First Temple could have survived on that stony hilltop. Hence, our knowledge of Solomon's Temple comes principally from the descriptions in 1 Kings 6–8 and 2 Chronicles 2–4.

The interior of the Temple was rectangular, about 35 feet wide and 140 feet long. It was divided into three parts. It seems that a priest would have ascended a flight of ten steps at the eastern end of the structure and passed between two massive bronze columns nearly 21 feet in circumference. The columns were named Jachin and Boaz.

Some 40 feet high, they were topped with elaborate capitals. The priest would have entered into a vestibule, or porch, which was about 17 feet deep. He would then have passed through gilded cypress doors decorated with flowers, palm trees, and cherubim, and entered the main room of the Temple—often called the "holy place."

Beyond a set of gilded olive wood doors lay a room that no ordinary priest would ever see. This was the Holy of Holies. It was a perfect cube, with each side measuring nearly 35 feet, the darkness of which was penetrated only once a year, when the high priest on the Day of Atonement made expiation for the people. In it was the Ark, containing the "two tables of stone" of the Ten

Commandments. The room, in Hebrew, was called the *debir*, possibly from the verb meaning "to speak." From this chamber Yahweh would speak to his people.

The outside of the Temple, except for the vestibule, was surrounded by side chambers, which were probably used for storing the treasures of the Temple. These rooms were arranged in three stories around the exterior wall and may have been reached through a door from the main room.

No expense was spared in the decoration of the Temple. The interior was lined with rare woods—the floor with cypress,

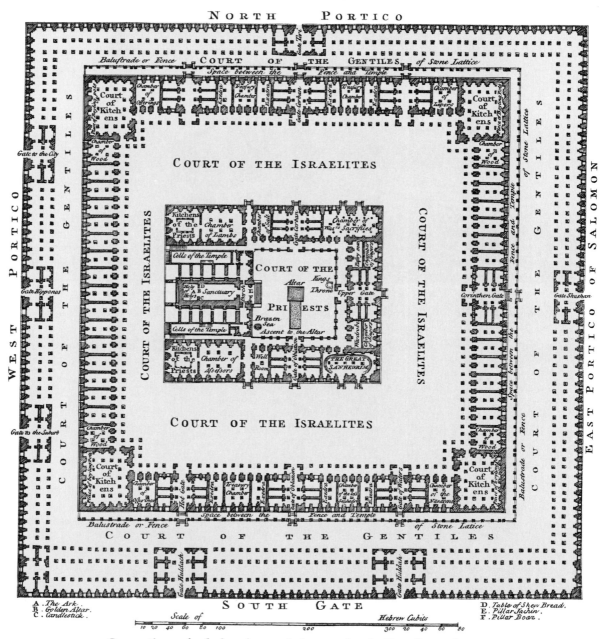

Generations of scholars *have tried to render the Temple. In this 1777 architectural plan, it is depicted as an elaborate series of chambers.*

the walls with cedar. All was lavishly carved and overlaid with gold. There were altars, tables, and other furniture of gold, bronze, or gold-covered wood. Finally, the Temple was illuminated by 10 golden lamp stands.

In the court was a bronze altar for burnt offerings and "the molten sea" or "the bronze sea." This was a bronze basin measuring about 17 feet in diameter and weighing nearly 30 tons. It rested on 12 bronze oxen (grouped in four triads, each facing a cardinal point of the compass). It could hold over 10,000 gallons of water, which may have been used for ritual cleansing.

The dedication ceremonies for the Temple were part of a great celebration attended by elders, tribal heads, leaders of clans, and "all the assembly of Israel." Two events dominated the proceedings—the installation of the Ark in the Holy of Holies and Solomon's long, impassioned prayer, in which he besought continuance of God's covenant with Israel. When the priests had deposited the Ark in the sanctuary, a cloud—"the glory of the LORD" (1 Kings 8:11)—filled the chamber and the Temple, preventing the priests from ministering further. The cloud marks the presence of Yahweh in his house. It is interpreted in the narrative by contrasting the sun, which Yahweh set in the heavens as a light for humanity, and his choice for himself "that he would dwell in thick darkness." ✦

Ancient mine found near Elath.

King Solomon's mines
Based on explorations in the 1930's, some archaeologists believed that King Solomon's copper mines—reputed to have provided the metal to cast the bronze portions of the Temple and its vessels—were located in the Timnah Valley near the Gulf of Aqaba (Elath). Archaeologists working in the region had found slag heaps that showed evidence of very ancient copper-smelting activities. But further excavations revealed no evidence of mining at these sites during King Solomon's reign. Hieroglyphic inscriptions from the ruins of a nearby temple suggest that the mines belonged to the ancient Egyptians, several centuries before the time of Solomon.

Who was the Queen of Sheba?

Why the legend lives

THE QUEEN OF SHEBA EXISTS in history and legend almost entirely in relation to King Solomon. Through the centuries, their story has been celebrated. In 1919 the poet William Butler Yeats wrote:

Sang Solomon to Sheba,
And kissed her Arab eyes,
"There's not a man or woman
Born under the skies
Dare match in learning with us two . . .

Yeats was honoring a long artistic tradition. The composer Handel had invoked the queen's mystery in his oratorio *Solomon*. Sculptures of the queen of Sheba are found in some of the great Gothic cathedrals of Europe. Indeed, the story was elaborately revised, expanded, and transformed in numerous accounts over the centuries. But what really happened between Solomon and the queen of Sheba? Scholars are divid-

Splendidly ornamented with gold, *King Solomon's court dazzled all comers.*

ed on the subject. While some hold that the story is a later legend, written to glorify the period of the united monarchy, others believe in the historical accuracy of the story as it stands in the biblical texts.

According to the biblical account, the queen of Sheba came, after hearing of Solo-mon's great wisdom, "to test him with hard questions." The geographical location of Sheba, the homeland of the Sabean people, was probably in southwestern Arabia, in the region of present-day Yemen. Thus, the queen's journey to Jerusalem would have covered some 1,300 miles. Others, howev-

large part by a brisk trade in frankincense and myrrh. It was situated at an intersection of trade routes that linked East Africa and southern Arabia to the markets of Palestine and Mesopotamia. Solomon controlled the northern legs—and in some cases the terminus—of many of these routes. Moreover, in conjunction with their Phoenician allies, the Israelites under Solomon had built an impressive fleet of ships at the port city of Ezion-Geber (near present-day Elath) that made regular trade voyages enriching the kingdom—and the king—with "gold, silver, ivory, apes, and peacocks." Thus, it is not unlikely that the queen's visit was in fact nothing more romantic than a trade mission. She may have traveled overland by caravan or perhaps made most of the journey on one of the vessels in Solomon's fleet, which normally negotiated the Red Sea.

The Bible account describes how the queen tested Solomon's wisdom with questions and riddles. She witnessed the manifestations of his great wealth, and was profoundly impressed by all she saw—"there was no more spirit in her."

Sheba gave Solomon lavish gifts— spices, gold, precious stones—and Solomon gave her in return "all that she desired." This phrase has given rise to many romantic interpretations of the Sheba-Solomon relationship. "All that she desired" has been interpreted as meaning that the queen wanted a child by Solomon.

The belief that the queen of Sheba had a child by Solomon may be the basis of one of the most durable of the tales to emerge from the original story. According to Ethiopian tradition, the son of Solomon and Sheba was Menelik I—or Ibn al-Hakim, "son of the wise man." As a young man, he visited Solomon, studied the Israelite religion, and returned to his own land to found a dynasty. This version of the tradition was certified by the authority of the revised Ethiopian constitution as recently as 1955. It stated that the royal line "descends without interruption from the dynasty of Menelik I, son of the Queen of Ethiopia, the Queen of Sheba, and King Solomon of Jerusalem." ✦

er, located Sheba elsewhere. The ancient Jewish historian Josephus, for example, described Ethiopia and Egypt as the realm of this mysterious queen.

Although Sheba was not a large nation, archaeological findings have shown that it enjoyed a sophisticated culture, financed in

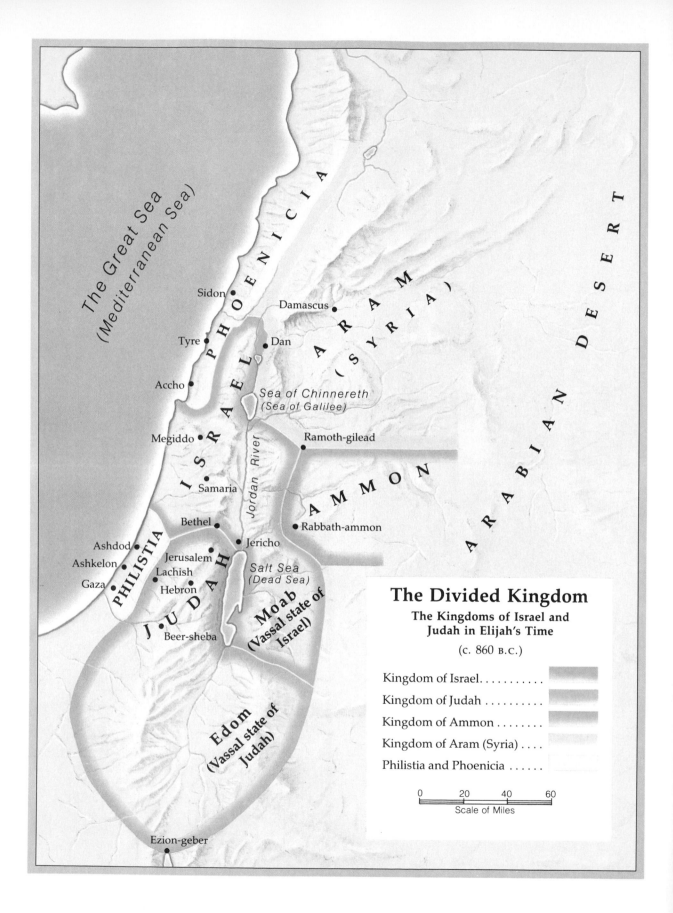

The Great Sea
(Mediterranean Sea)

PHOENICIA

Sidon

Damascus

ARAM
(SYRIA)

Tyre

Dan

Accho

Sea of Chinnereth
(Sea of Galilee)

ISRAEL

Megiddo

Ramoth-gilead

Jordan River

Samaria

AMMON

Bethel

Rabbath-ammon

Jericho

Ashdod

Jerusalem

Ashkelon

Lachish

Gaza

Hebron

Salt Sea
(Dead Sea)

JUDAH

Moab
(Vassal state of
Israel)

Beer-sheba

Edom
(Vassal state of
Judah)

Ezion-geber

PHILISTIA

ARABIAN DESERT

The Divided Kingdom

The Kingdoms of Israel and Judah in Elijah's Time

(c. 860 B.C.)

Kingdom of Israel . . . .

Kingdom of Judah . . . .

Kingdom of Ammon . . . .

Kingdom of Aram (Syria) . . . .

Philistia and Phoenicia . . . . . .

0   20   40   60
Scale of Miles

The split of Israel and Judah

How oppression destroyed a kingdom

W HEN SOLOMON DIED, his son Rehoboam was readily acclaimed as king in Judah, but met with opposition when he faced the leaders of the northern tribes in Shechem.

The old inter-tribal rivalries that had been covered over by the Davidic kingdom reemerged around the issue of forced labor. The northern tribes offered loyalty to Rehoboam if he would "lighten the hard service" that Solomon had imposed on them. Rehoboam's elder advisors counseled accommodation, but his younger advisors urged him not to capitulate. When Rehoboam threatened to add to their burden, the northern tribes abandoned all loyalty to the crown.

Jeroboam, who had returned from exile in Egypt, was then acclaimed as king over the northern ten tribes. Realizing how much Solomon had focused the unity of his kingdom on the Temple in Jerusalem, Jeroboam countered by building new sanctuaries to God in Bethel and Dan, complete with golden images of calves. From the viewpoint of the leaders of Judah, the golden calves were proof of idolatry, and they stamped Jeroboam forever after as the apostate who led Israel into sin. ✦

Warlords and dynasties

Who's who in the ancient world

A FTER THE DIVISION of the united kingdom, the power and prosperity of Israel and Judah depended to a large degree on the military might of their Near Eastern neighbors. Fewer than 350 years after Solomon's death, both kingdoms would perish under foreign oppression.

The ancient empire of Egypt had collapsed into a period of long decline, but Pharaoh Shishak had hopes of regaining past glory as he founded Egypt's twenty-second dynasty in 935 B.C. Hoping to weaken Solomon's kingdom, Shishak interfered in its affairs. After Jeroboam's unsuccessful revolt against Solomon, Shishak gave Jeroboam asylum until he returned to lead the northern Israelite tribes in their revolt against Solomon's successor. Five years after the united kingdom split in two, Shishak invaded Judah, plundering the Temple and palace. The invasion swept over the northern tribes as well, and in an inscription carved on the walls of an Egyptian temple, Shishak claimed to have subjugated more than 150 towns. His plans of rebuilding the Egyptian empire failed, however, and more than two centuries of Egyptian weakness followed. During this period, Egypt ceased to be a major threat to Israel and Judah, but other Near Eastern powers, such as Assyria, moved to dominate the two kingdoms.

The first direct military contact between Assyria and Israel took place in 853 B.C. The Assyrian king, Shalmaneser III, was intent on expanding to the west. This posed a threat to Israel and Syria, which were long-time enemies, but joined forces against Shalmaneser and temporarily stopped the Assyrian advance. Several years later, however, King Jehu of Israel was forced to pay tribute to Shalmaneser.

But early in the 8th century, Assyria retreated during a period of weakness, and the kingdoms of Israel and Judah had room to flourish. By the second half of the century, however, Assyria was back in full force, conquering most of the Near East. Both Israel and Judah were reduced to vassalage.

Under Tiglath-pileser III, the Assyrians adopted a policy intended to suppress the nationalism of its captives. A defeated people might not simply be reduced to vassalage and the payment of tribute; it might instead be completely disintegrated by having its population scattered throughout the reaches of the Assyrian empire. A nation fighting the Assyrians was thus fighting for both freedom—and its very existence. Indeed, the final days of the northern kingdom of Israel came when King Hoshea tried to throw off the Assyrian yoke by refusing to pay the required tribute. In response, Israel's capital, Samaria, was placed under siege, and three years later (722 or 721 B.C.), it was destroyed. The northern kingdom disappeared as Sargon II, then king of Assyria, deported tens of thousands of Israelites. Judah under King Ahaz, having earlier submitted to Assyria, managed to survive, but was destined to face a similar fate within little more than a century.

In spite of repeated revolts among its vassals, the Assyrian empire continued to expand. In the 7th century B.C., even Egypt was—for a time—under Assyrian domination. But as a result of internal problems, Assyria's hold on her empire weakened. The decisive blow came when two subservient peoples—the Babylonians led by Nabopolassar and the Medes led by Cyaxeres—joined forces. They were able to drive into the heart of Assyria and conquered the capital of Nineveh in 612 B.C. What had for centuries been the greatest empire of the known world ceased to be.

The Neo-Babylonian empire that succeeded the Assyrians continued their imperialist policies. Nabopolassar was followed by Nebuchadnezzar, who barely left his campaigns of conquest long enough to be crowned. Thus for Judah, though the politics of the region as a whole had changed, the fact remained that a great outside conquering army posed a constant danger to the internal integrity of the state. It was eventually the Babylonian Nebuchadnezzar who accomplished what the Assyrians had threatened—he destroyed Jerusalem. ✦

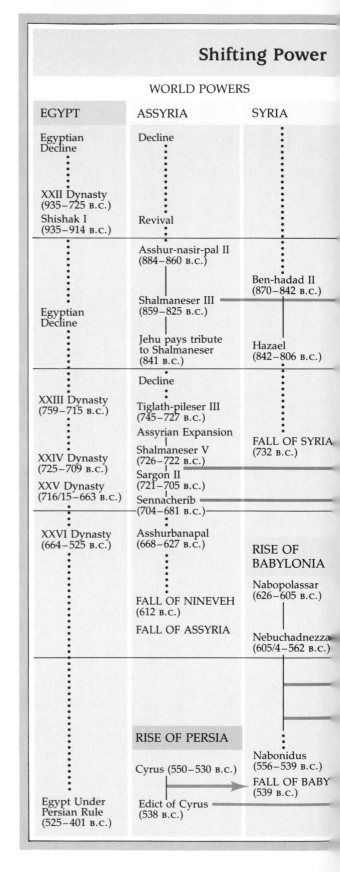

Shifting Power

WORLD POWERS

EGYPT	ASSYRIA	SYRIA
Egyptian Decline	Decline	
XXII Dynasty (935–725 B.C.) Shishak I (935–914 B.C.)	Revival	
	Asshur-nasir-pal II (884–860 B.C.)	Ben-hadad II (870–842 B.C.)
Egyptian Decline	Shalmaneser III (859–825 B.C.) Jehu pays tribute to Shalmaneser (841 B.C.)	Hazael (842–806 B.C.)
XXIII Dynasty (759–715 B.C.)	Decline Tiglath-pileser III (745–727 B.C.) Assyrian Expansion Shalmaneser V (726–722 B.C.)	FALL OF SYRIA (732 B.C.)
XXIV Dynasty (725–709 B.C.) XXV Dynasty (716/15–663 B.C.)	Sargon II (721–705 B.C.) Sennacherib (704–681 B.C.)	
XXVI Dynasty (664–525 B.C.)	Asshurbanapal (668–627 B.C.)	RISE OF BABYLONIA Nabopolassar (626–605 B.C.)
	FALL OF NINEVEH (612 B.C.) FALL OF ASSYRIA	Nebuchadnezzar (605/4–562 B.C.)
RISE OF PERSIA		Nabonidus (556–539 B.C.)
	Cyrus (550–530 B.C.)	FALL OF BABY (539 B.C.)
Egypt Under Persian Rule (525–401 B.C.)	Edict of Cyrus (538 B.C.)	

in the Ancient World: 1000 B.C.– 500 B.C.*

THE UNITED KINGDOM

1000 B.C.

David (1000–961 B.C.)

Solomon (961–922 B.C.)

THE DIVIDED KINGDOM

JUDAH (Southern Kingdom) (922–587 B.C.)	ISRAEL (Northern Kingdom) (922–722/1 B.C.)

– 900 B.C.

Rehoboam (922–915 B.C.)

Jeroboam I (922–901 B.C.)

Omri (876–869 B.C.)

Jehoshaphat (873–849 B.C.)

Ahab (869–850 B.C.)   *Elijah*
Ahaziah (850–849 B.C.)
Jehoram (Joram) (849–843/2 B.C.)   *Elisha*
Jehu (843/2–815 B.C.)

– 800 B.C.

Ahaziah (843/2 B.C.)

Jehoash (Joash) (802–786 B.C.)

Jotham (co-regent: 750 B.C.–742 B.C.)

Jeroboam II (786–746 B.C.)   *Amos*   *Hosea*
                             (750 B.C.)   (745 B.C.)

Jotham (King)   *Isaiah*
(742–735 B.C.) (742–700 B.C.)   *Micah*

Pekahiah (737–736 B.C.)

Jehoahaz (Ahaz)
(735–715 B.C.)

Hoshea (732–724 B.C.)

Hezekiah
(715–687/6 B.C.)

FALL OF SAMARIA
(722/1 B.C.)

(Judah invaded by Sennacherib, 701 B.C.)

700 B.C.

Josiah (640–609 B.C.)

Zephaniah   *Jeremiah*
(628–622 B.C.)   (626–587 B.C.)

Discovery of Book of the Law   *Nahum*
Josiah's Reform (621 B.C.)   (626–612 B.C.)

Jehoiakim (609–598 B.C.)   *Habakkuk*
                               (605 B.C.)

600 B.C.

Jehoiachin (598-597 B.C.)

FIRST DEPORTATION TO BABYLONIA (597 B.C.)

Zedekiah (597–587 B.C.)   *Ezekiel*
FALL OF JERUSALEM (587 B.C.)   (593–573 B.C.)

THE EXILE

Second Isaiah
(540 B.C.)

RETURN OF EXILES   *Haggai*   *Zechariah*

Rebuilding of Temple (520–515 B.C.)

500 B.C.

*Note:

- All dates on this chart are approximate
- Kings are shown in Roman type
- Prophets are shown in Italics
- Solid lines between kings, prophets, and others indicate direct succession
- Dotted lines between entries indicate that names have been omitted
- Horizontal arrows emphasize when one power particularly influenced another

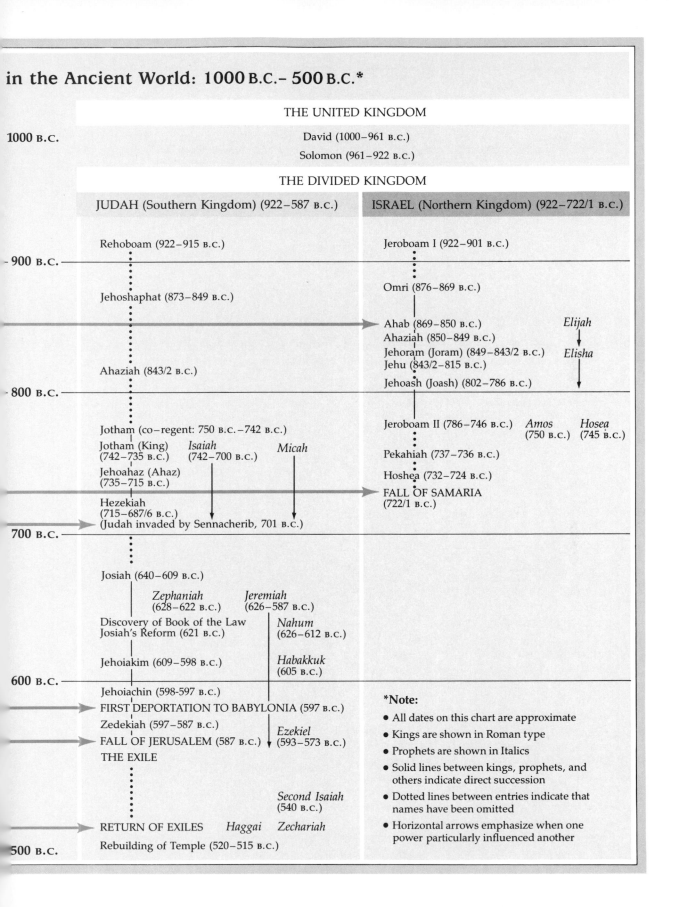

To burn incense unto Baal

As long as the israelites lived among a large Canaanite population, Baal, the principal god of the native peoples, loomed large in Israel's religious life. The name *Baal* means "Lord" and may imply any sort of lordship. For the Canaanites it indicated Baal's lordship over the land.

Baal, unlike Yahweh, was part of a family of gods. The high god and creator was called El, a name that means simply "god." Baal was the son of the grain god, Dagon, and came to be the principal god through his mighty works, related in the mythology of the Canaanites. His exploits are known to us principally through a series of inscribed clay tablets that were discovered in the Canaanite city of Ugarit, also known as Ras Shamra. The stories make Baal a heroic deity intimately linked to the stability of life and the fertility of the land. In a society in which the great majority of the people were farmers and herders, their lives dependent upon agriculture, it is not difficult to understand the attraction of a god such as Baal.

One story told how Baal came to be king among the gods by standing against the threat of chaos in the world, as symbol-

Canaanite chief god, Baal, was often depicted with one arm raised, grasping a thunderbolt or brandishing a club, indicating his mastery of the universe.

ized by the waters of Sea and River. Even the gods in the Council of El were intimidated by the threatening waters, but Baal in a titanic battle overcame Sea and River, confined them to their proper place, and restored order to the world. Thus Baal gained an "eternal kingship" and "dominion forever." Through the gods' struggles, the Canaanites expressed the mystery of the life cycle.

Myths such as this one, together with the attendant celebrations and sacrifices, held a fascination for many Israelites. The Book of Judges repeatedly indicts the people because they "served the Baals; and they forsook the Lord, the God of their fathers." In periods such as the reign of Ahab and his wife Jezebel, the worship of Baal was the state-supported religion of Israel.

But it was the attractiveness of the Canaanite religion that threatened the worship of Yahweh and made the prophets of Yahweh implacable enemies of Baal and his related deities. Elijah stood against Baal on Mount Carmel. Jeremiah, shortly before the Babylonian exile, warned that "as many as the streets of Jerusalem are the altars you have set up to shame, altars to burn incense to Baal." The prophets warned against the immorality of the fertility cult. They warned against the materialism and corruption of Canaanite religion, as well as its lack of concern for the welfare of the needy. But most of all they warned that Israel was being untrue to her covenant with Yahweh to "have no other gods before me."

The very competition between the two faiths, however, led Yahweh's worshipers to praise him with descriptions that adapted and challenged those long attributed to Baal. Thus Yahweh is described in Psalm 68 as he "who rides upon the cloud," a designation usually reserved for Baal. Psalm 82 even goes so far as to make a confrontation of the gods explicit. The threat of Baal to the worship of Yahweh continued until the fires of the Babylonian exile finally purged the Canaanite deity from the heart of Israel.

The infamous Jezebel

A Phoenician princess who defied the God of Israel

IN MODERN TIMES, the name of Jezebel is practically synonymous with sin. What did Jezebel, the Phoenician wife of the Samarian king Ahab, do to earn such a reputation? First and foremost, she conducted a campaign to displace Yahwism, the religion of Israel, with the worship of Baal (1 Kings 16:31–33). In this light, it is interesting to note that the root of her name, related to the Phoenician word for "exalted one," appears in Canaanite writings as an epithet for the god Baal.

Jezebel was the daughter of Ethbaal, the King of Sidon, himself successor to Hiram, the Phoenician king who supplied Solomon with the materials and craftsmen to build the Temple. She married Ahab, who succeeded Omri, his father, as king of Israel. As a matter of course, when Jezebel arrived, she brought the faith of her own people with her. Once she had exerted sufficient influence on her husband, the queen moved swiftly to impose the Baal cult upon all Israel. A temple to Baal was erected in the capital, Samaria, and the worship of Baal received further official sanction through her support for a large college of prophets of Baal, who could function as religious and political advisors at the Israelite court. It seems clear that few in Israel saw any great danger in this development. It is even likely that many identified Baal, whose name means "Lord," with the Lord Yahweh and worshiped them as the same god.

However, the zeal of Jezebel for her religion made it clear that Baal was to be the dominant deity. She killed or drove into hiding scores of prophets of Yahweh who had surrounded the court. She then appointed 450 prophets of Baal and 400 prophets of the goddess Asherah. Evidently she also tore down the altars to Yahweh on Mount Carmel, a site traditionally given over to the worship of Baal.

Along with her religion, Jezebel also brought the principle of royal prerogative and priority, especially in matters of property rights, from her homeland to Israel. Whereas the biblical ideal asserts that the monarch, like everyone else, is subject to the Law of God, and thus is obliged to deal fairly with the people, Jezebel arrogated to

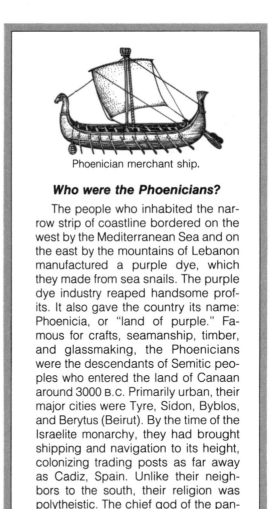

Phoenician merchant ship.

Who were the Phoenicians?

The people who inhabited the narrow strip of coastline bordered on the west by the Mediterranean Sea and on the east by the mountains of Lebanon manufactured a purple dye, which they made from sea snails. The purple dye industry reaped handsome profits. It also gave the country its name: Phoenicia, or "land of purple." Famous for crafts, seamanship, timber, and glassmaking, the Phoenicians were the descendants of Semitic peoples who entered the land of Canaan around 3000 B.C. Primarily urban, their major cities were Tyre, Sidon, Byblos, and Berytus (Beirut). By the time of the Israelite monarchy, they had brought shipping and navigation to its height, colonizing trading posts as far away as Cadiz, Spain. Unlike their neighbors to the south, their religion was polytheistic. The chief god of the pantheon was El, but Baal was worshipped in most cities. Jezebel, the daughter of the king of Tyre, brought Baal worship to its zenith in Israel.

In a fury inspired by the love of the Lord, *Elijah denounced King Ahab and the haughty Queen Jezebel for their faithlessness and immorality.*

herself and her husband unlimited royal powers. When Naboth turned down Ahab's offer to buy his vineyard or exchange it for another, Ahab returned to the palace in distress. When he reported the incident to Jezebel, the queen replied, "Do you now govern Israel?" The statement shows her astonishment that the king tried to bargain with Naboth rather than simply taking over the property he desired. Jezebel subsequently ordered Naboth's arrest and execution on a trumped-up charge of treason. Naboth was stoned and his land was appropriated by the king. This horrific incident prompted the prophet Elijah to prophesy, "The dogs shall eat Jezebel."

Despite the turbulence surrounding her time, she and Ahab lived in great luxury. Archaeological excavations have unearthed proof that the "ivory house" of Ahab and Jezebel, recorded in 1 Kings, was no metaphor. More than 500 fragments of ivory, most from ivory-inlaid wooden wall panels and furniture, attest to the magnificent splendor of the palace.

Jezebel survived beyond the death of Ahab and lived during the reigns of her two sons, Ahaziah and Jehoram. She at last met her death during the massacre of Ahab's family by Jehu, the commander of the army who had been chosen for this action by the prophets Elijah and Elisha. She was thrown out of an upper-story window. Even in the face of death, however, she was defiant. Jehu, her implacable foe, observed that she was a "king's daughter" and gave orders to bury her. But when the burial party went out to pick up Jezebel's body, "they found no more of her than the skull and the feet and the palms of her hands." Elijah's prophecy had been fulfilled. ✦

The Omride dynasty

Israel's best and worst times

OMRI: HIS NAME EVIDENTLY means "worshipper of Yahweh," but he was, ironically, founder of the Israelite dynasty most notorious for its support of the pagan god Baal. The biblical text views him entirely through the lens of its religious indictment: "in the sight of the LORD" Omri "did more evil than all who were before him." His governmental accomplishments, however, have caused some historians to consider him one of the greatest kings of Israel.

Omri may not have been an Israelite at all: the Bible never mentions his father or family. His rise to prominence was accomplished by his prowess as a commander in the royal army. He at last became king through the storm of a civil war that broke after King Elah was assassinated in 876 B.C. After several years of anarchy, Omri reunited the kingdom of Israel under his rule.

Omri established his rule on strong international alliances and stability at home. He ended the nearly fifty years of war with the kingdom of Judah and regained Israel's domination over Moab. He sealed an alliance with the powerful Phoenicians by marrying his son Ahab to Jezebel, the daughter of the king of Tyre. He founded the city of Samaria as his new capital and improved the economy through building and trade.

The Omride dynasty bore the stamp of its founder to the end. During the long and stable reign of Ahab the kingdom remained cosmopolitan. A tide of foreign culture flowed in through Jezebel, who as queen brought her way of life and her gods, especially Baal, with her to Samaria. Jezebel continued her power during the reigns of her sons Ahaziah and Jehoram. She even extended her reach southward when the king of Judah married her daughter Athaliah. Jezebel became the lightning rod for the stern reaction against Baalism led by the prophets Elijah and Elisha.

The dynasty ended in 842 B.C. when Jezebel and Jehoram were assassinated by an army officer named Jehu, who then assumed the throne. The outside world so associated the kingdom of Israel with the Omride dynasty that, long after Omri's descendants had ceased to rule, Assyrian records still referred to Israel as "the land of the house of Omri." ✦

Samaria: Ahab's city of ivory

A key to the record of early Israel

THE CITY OF SAMARIA stood on a hill about 42 miles north of Jerusalem and 25 miles east of the Mediterranean Sea. Omri, king of the northern kingdom of Israel, bought the hill from a man named Shemer, built the city and its surrounding fortifications, and then made this newly founded city his capital. Samaria remained Israel's capital until its capture by the Assyrians in 722 B.C., at which time the northern kingdom ceased to exist as a political entity.

Archaeological excavations were conducted at Samaria from 1908 to 1910 and again from 1931 to 1935. Among numerous finds from the Old Testament period were the remains of a two-story palace of the dynasty founded by King Omri, a large adjacent pool, and the three walls of the defensive system that helped the city withstand sieges until the Assyrian conquest. The more spectacular finds included more than 500 fragments of ivory and about 70 ostraca, or inscribed potsherds.

The ivory fragments were inlays from

wooden wall panels, furniture, and small boxes and toiletries. Beautiful in design, they are thought to have been made by Phoenician artisans for the Omride imperial family including Ahab, king of Israel and son of Omri, and Ahab's notorious wife Jezebel. She was a Phoenician princess and a strong supporter of her ancestral religion and culture. Although ivory utensils and inlays are not unusual in the ancient Near East—ivory gaming pieces and spoons, and inlaid ivory beds, couches, and boxes have been found in quantity, for example—the finds at Samaria attest both to the powerful Phoenician cultural influence on the northern kingdom and to the accuracy of the biblical record. In 1 Kings 22:39, King Ahab is said to have built an "ivory house." Moreover, the prophet Amos, whose ministry was in the northern kingdom of Israel, refers to ivory beds and couches as examples of the excesses of the Samarian elite.

The ostraca date to the eighth century B.C., many

Miniature ivory sphinx from Samaria is slightly over three inches high.

Ahab's house of ivory was filled with beautifully carved ornaments such as this decorative palm leaf panel.

specifically from the years 778 to 770 B.C., during the reign of Jeroboam II (786–746 B.C.). These inscribed potsherds are invoices for the delivery of oil and wine to the royal treasury, another excess of which Amos speaks: "Woe to those who lie upon beds of ivory/ . . . who drink wine in bowls/ and anoint themselves with the finest oils." In addition to providing historical records from a period of peace and prosperity, these ostraca have provided scholars with data and information on the dialect of Hebrew then spoken in the northern kingdom, on religion (from personal names incorporating the names of Phoenician deities), and on state administrative procedures.

The fall of the city is recorded not only in the biblical material (2 Kings 17:5–6), but also in the annals of Sargon, the Assyrian king who was on the throne when the city fell. The strategic placement of the city and its strong fortifications made it important to any state wanting to control the region, and thus the city was rebuilt after the Assyrian destruction and continued to survive into the seventh century A.D.

The excavations uncovered fragments of an Assyrian stele and a cylinder inscription, clay cuneiform tablets, and shards of pottery from the period of Assyrian domination. During the period of Babylonian rule, Samaria was the administrative center for the province, as was also the case during the subsequent Persian period.

The city and district of Samaria figure prominently in the New Testament, especially in the work of Luke (Gospel and Acts) and John. Memorable personalities are mentioned and described in these books— the Samaritan woman in the Gospel of John, for example, and the hero of the parable of the Good Samaritan (Luke 10: 29–37).

The importance of Samaria lies both in the fact that it was the capital of the northern kingdom, and in its religious, cultural, and civic wealth. It has given us an understanding of the architecture, art and craft, language, religion, and administration of early Israel and subsequent periods. Samaria has indeed been a gold mine. ✦

Elijah's offering is consumed by holy flame, as the prophets of Baal and the people fall back in awe.

Trial by fire

Elijah challenges the prophets of Baal

ELIJAH BURSTS ACROSS the pages of Scripture like a lightning flash. In the midst of the description of the reign of Ahab, king of Israel, without a word of introduction or explanation, the reader is suddenly confronted with a prophet who in the name of Yahweh turns off the fountains of heaven and proclaims a drought: "Now Elijah the Tishbite, of Tishbe in Gilead, said to Ahab, 'As the LORD the God of Israel lives, before whom I stand, there shall be neither dew nor rain these years, except by my word' " (1 Kings 17:1).

The sheer brashness of that last phrase, "except by my word," marks out for us the character of this man. We learn nothing of his childhood, of his ancestry, of his religious experiences, of how he came to be a prophet of the Lord. Still, with his first words he is shown to be a man of conflict and confidence, one who speaks for a God intent on renewing the vitality of his covenant with his people—and intent on punishing their betrayal.

Elijah's name means "Yahweh is God," and his life was a continual struggle to strengthen the worship of Yahweh in Israel against the encroaching presence of the Canaanite god Baal. Elijah came from Tishbe in Gilead, an area east of Jordan where the Canaanite culture had never been strong. The worship of Yahweh evidently maintained an exclusive, uncompromising character there. But when Elijah crossed into the northern kingdom of Israel, west of the Jordan, he came into a very different world.

In Israel, King Ahab ruled as the second in a powerful dynasty established by his

171

father, Omri. Ahab was at least a nominal worshiper of Yahweh and gave names to three of his children incorporating the divine name (Ahaziah, Jehoram, and Athaliah). But his commitment to Yahweh was by no means exclusive. In order to cement his ties with the powerful Phoenicians to the north, Ahab married Jezebel, the daughter of Ethbaal, king of Sidon and a worshiper of Baal. In many ways the marriage mirrored the mixed character of the people under Ahab's rule, a people that included dominant Israelites and many Canaanites.

To the extent of her powers, Jezebel fostered the worship of Baal, the lord of rain and giver of fertility. So great was her devotion to this pagan god, that she killed the prophets of Yahweh and replaced them with the prophets of Baal. Because of this transgression of faith on the part of Israel, Yahweh sent drought upon the land.

When Elijah came proclaiming the drought, he was attacking Baal on his home ground and asserting that it was Yahweh, and not Baal, who was lord of the life-giving rains. During the drought, Elijah hid by the Brook of Cherith. The length of this drought is not known. In the first century A.D. the Jewish historian Josephus cited a source that gave its length as one year. An alternative version, mentioned twice in the New Testament, describes the drought as lasting a full three and a half years.

Throughout the drought Elijah was a wanted man as Ahab spared no effort to seize this "troubler of Israel." The search ended only when Elijah summoned Ahab to meet him. Elijah charged that it was Ahab and his worship of Baal that had troubled Israel, and he challenged Ahab to set up a contest between the prophets of the two gods before all Israel on Mount Carmel.

The purpose of Elijah's life was brought to its zenith in the confrontation that the First Book of Kings describes between the lone prophet of Yahweh and the 450 prophets of Baal and the 400 prophets of the goddess Asherah. With uncompromising clarity Elijah asserted the total incompatibility of the worship of Baal and of Yahweh.

" 'How long will you go limping with two different opinions? If the LORD is God, follow him; but if Baal, then follow him.' And the people did not answer him a word." The silence of the people probably indicates that in their mixed society they were not accustomed to think in terms of such an exclusive choice. But they agreed to the dramatic contest by fire that Elijah set before them. Two sacrifices were to be prepared, one for Baal, one for Yahweh. The prophets of each were to pray, "and the God who answers by fire, he is God."

Finally a clear demonstration of the divine would be available. They could choose not on the basis of ancient myth or stories of past generations but by an obvious and present verification of divinity.

The drama that ensued is laid before the reader in arresting detail. With confident generosity Elijah allowed his opponents to choose their sacrificial offering and go first. He did not hurry them but allowed hour after hour for them to raise their chorus of voices to Baal. The prophets in desperation cried, "O Baal, answer us!" and waited for a response: "But there was no voice, and no one answered" (1 Kings 18:26).

After a morning of such cries, Elijah mockingly suggested that perhaps their god was lost in thought, or on a journey, or asleep. As the afternoon passed, the scene became even more frenzied as Baal's prophets lacerated themselves with knives in the entranced fervor of their prayers. Still, the narrators emphasize, "no one answered, no one heeded" (1 Kings 18:26).

As evening drew near, Yahweh's prophet finally summoned the people to him, and the scene shifts from frenzy to a sense of calm and absolute confidence. Elijah re-

---

On moral courage

"It showed the courage of Elijah, that he, lately a poor, starving exile, durst stand alone in the cause of God against such powers and numbers; and the issue encourages all God's witnesses and advocates never to fear the face of man."

—**Mathew Henry and Thomas Scott**
Commentary on the Holy Bible

stored tradition by rebuilding an old altar, using twelve stones to symbolize the twelve tribes. The wood was laid in order, and the sacrificial bull properly butchered. Then, in his confidence, Elijah made it impossible for any ordinary altar fire to burn the sacrifice. The offering, the wood, and the altar were thrice drenched in water.

The moment of truth had arrived. At the time for the sacrifice, the prophet offered a brief prayer. No raving and self-mutilation were needed. He called on Yahweh, God of Abraham, Isaac, and Israel, to answer, "that this people may know that thou, O LORD, art God, and that thou hast turned their hearts back" (1 Kings 18:37).

Instantly Carmel was illuminated with consuming fire. The offering was gone; the wood was burnt up; even the stones and the water had been consumed. Perhaps the people had thought that they were going to choose between deities, but the narrators want to show that in fact it was God alone who chose. He turned their hearts back, and they could only respond, "The LORD, he is God; the LORD, he is God" (1 Kings 18:39).

For the prophets of Baal, the day was far more than an embarrassment. Elijah immediately sentenced the false prophets to death, as the law prescribed in the Book of Exodus. With the help of the people and evidently without interference from Ahab, hundreds were summarily executed.

With this complete victory in the battle against Baal, the god of storms, Elijah immediately predicted the end of the drought. Yahweh would now give the rain, and the crisis that had brought on this contest of gods would be at an end.

So total and glorious was Elijah's triumph that one might think that the narrators intended to portray the complete extinction of the worship of Baal. The succeeding events in Elijah's life, however, show that for all its drama, the contest on Mount Carmel had little effect in restoring the devotion of the entire people to Yahweh. Paradoxically, the mighty miracle of Carmel, far from settling all theological questions, only intensified the conflict. ✦

The slaughter of the prophets of Baal: "And Elijah said to them, 'Seize the prophets of Baal; let not one of them escape.' And they seized them; and Elijah brought them down to the brook Kishon, and killed them there."

Elijah is miraculously fed by a raven.

The sound of silence

Elijah meets God on the mountain

THE TASTE OF VICTORY that Elijah had experienced after the confrontation on Mount Carmel turned to ashes in his mouth. There was one person who was wholly unimpressed and unconvinced by the demonstration of power on the mountain, and that was Ahab's Phoenician queen, Jezebel. She was as zealous for Baal as Elijah was for Yahweh. The slaughter of Baal's prophets did not diminish Jezebel's commitment to Baal; it only fired her wrath toward the prophet of Yahweh. As soon as she heard what had happened, she swore the punishment of death for Elijah because of the murder of the prophets.

The mighty Elijah shrank into suicidal despair. He fled south through the land of Judah toward the Negev desert. In his distress, he cried: "Oh LORD, take away my life; for I am no better than my fathers." He had apparently expected to gain immediate and total victory for Yahweh after his successful campaign on Mount Carmel. But now, he anticipated utter defeat.

Yet the narrative emphasizes God's con-tinuing care for his prophet. As Elijah slept under a tree far out in the wilderness, an angelic messenger from God brought him freshly cooked food. Refreshed, he was able to endure a 40-day fast as he traveled into the wilderness to "Horeb the mount of God." Indeed, the narrative describes "the word of the LORD" as Elijah's constant guide; and in his anguish, hunger, and defeat it encountered him once more: "What are you doing here, Elijah?"

The long march through the wilderness had done nothing to quench the fire of anger, hopelessness, and self-concern that Elijah had felt. The narrator lets his complaint pour forth twice in exactly the same words.

The situation pictured in Elijah's complaint is dark. Although Elijah had been "very jealous for the LORD, the God of hosts," still the worship of Yahweh seemed to be practically at an end. The people had forsaken the covenant with Yahweh. They had destroyed the altars to the Lord. And they had killed the prophets who spoke the word of Yahweh. Thus, Elijah felt that he was the only faithful individual left, and he was under threat of death.

Thus, the story that unfolds emphasizes similarities between Elijah and Moses, who also experienced the revelation of God on Mount Horeb. Moses too had fasted 40 days and nights when he encountered God. As Moses was sheltered in a rocky cleft, so Elijah stayed in a cave on the mountain. As the people in Elijah's time had defected to Baal, so in Moses' day they had worshipped the golden calf. As the revelation to Moses had served to form the people of Israel in their covenant with God, now the revelation to Elijah served to restore Israel to its abandoned allegiance to Yahweh. Elijah moreover felt that he was the only faithful person left—and he was under threat of death. The implication was that by escaping to the wilderness, Elijah believed he was preserving God's only hope against the complete extinction of his worship.

But Elijah was to perceive that God is both more profound and more mysteriously powerful than even he imagined. As Yahweh passed before Elijah on the mountain, there came the stupendous but not unexpected manifestations of the powers of nature in God's control—wind strong enough to tear apart mountains, earthquake shaking the foundations of the mountains, consuming fire. The narrator specifies that Yahweh was not in the wind, the earthquake, or the fire. These were traditional signs of divine power, signs ascribed likewise to Baal, the Canaanite god of storm winds and lightning whose voice shook the earth.

But after the fire had passed and still Yahweh had not become manifest, there came another sign, "a still small voice," literally "a sound of thin silence." Elijah was prophet enough to know that this was the true spiritual event, the epiphany; wrapping his mantle about his face he went forth to stand before Yahweh.

The mystery of this unique manifestation of God as "a sound of silence" has fascinated interpreters. It is a paradoxical revelation of the awesomeness of God, and some have thought that it pointed to a particularly ethical or gentle and compassionate understanding of the divine, including perhaps a pointed rebuke to the zeal of Elijah and his accusations against Israel. Such an interpretation, however, is not fully supported by the rest of the story.

The striking contrast between the wind, earthquake, and fire and the sound of silence seems to have had its message for Elijah along somewhat different lines. The struggle between Yahweh and Baal was in no sense a struggle between equals. When

THE STORY BEHIND THE WORD

Prophetic mantle

Elijah's mantle served not only to clothe him, but it played a role in his prophetic duties as well. He used it to part the waters of the Jordan River, just as Moses had used his staff. And later, after Elijah had been borne to heaven in the fiery chariot, his mantle was left behind for Elisha—indicating that, by donning the traditional robe, Elisha had acquired Elijah's prophetic gifts.

The prophet's mantle was simply a loose robe or cloak. It was made of animal hair, perhaps goat or camel. The garment's rough, simple quality was a reflection of the prophet's essential character—humility in the face of God. While Elijah is portrayed as being fierce and brash in his challenge of the Baal worshipers, when confronted by the Lord on Mount Horeb, he "wrapped his face in his mantle and went out and stood at the entrance of the cave" to await the word of God.

Just as Moses' rod was a symbol of his divine office, so too was Elijah's mantle—and both were a sign of God's presence. Elijah's mantle, though of no material value, was taken up by Elisha as if it were made of the most precious materials. He took it up not as a sacred talisman, but as a symbol of divine duty.

Elijah: the perennial hope

During Seder, the ceremonial meal that marks the beginning of the Jewish festival Passover, four cups of wine are consumed. Then a fifth cup of wine is poured—but this one is not drunk. Instead, it is placed on the table for the prophet Elijah. According to a centuries-old blend of tradition, legend, and revelation, Elijah will arrive on the eve of Passover to herald the redemptive age. After Elijah's cup has been filled, the door to the house is flung open to let him in. Scholars agree that Elijah's Passover appearance is a later addition to the Seder ceremony that evolved out of the belief that Elijah had not died, and would reappear as a precursor to the Messiah. As Passover celebrates the *continual* deliverance of Israel from Egyptian bondage, it was natural that Elijah would visit every Jewish home during the "season of redemption."

Elijah's cup (late l9th century, Bohemia).

Jews the world over celebrate Passover with great rejoicing. In this modern painting, Elijah, always present in spirit, actually appears.

Yahweh had manifested all those mighty powers that were typically attributed to Baal, he had still not manifested himself. The presence of Yahweh and his power and divinity were on quite a different plane from that of a nature god. The struggle in which Elijah was engaged was not one that could be measured in victories and defeats for the prophet; thus Elijah's fears and despair for the religion of Yahweh were unfounded. The God who is heard in the sound of silence did not depend on even so zealous a defender as the prophet for his well-being.

That sense of God's control was directly spelled out in the commission Yahweh gave to Elijah. Elijah was to anoint three men as instruments of judgment on Israel. But like the quiet voice that followed the destructive force of nature, a remnant of those faithful to Yahweh would remain after the punishments inflicted by these three: "I will leave seven thousand in Israel, all the knees that have not bowed to Baal, and every mouth that has not kissed him." ✦

176

Arrogance punished

Ahab's bloody end

THROUGH THE CENTURIES, the concept of Satan has changed. In Hebrew, the language of the Old Testament, *satan* simply means "adversary." Satan, as an independent manifestation of otherworldly evil, does not enter the biblical canon until the New Testament, but a precursor to this development occurs in the Book of Kings during the reign of Ahab. It was a "lying spirit" who fulfilled the prophetic pronouncement of Ahab's doom.

The event that sealed Ahab's doom at the instigation of the "lying spirit" occurred three years earlier, during a time of relative peace. In spite of Ahab's notorious idolatry, the crucial event that damned his dynasty did not involve foreign gods, but an abuse of royal power against the traditional rights of an Israelite citizen. Naboth was a citizen of Jezreel and owned a vineyard next to royal land where Ahab had a residence. Ahab desired to expand his holding and offered to purchase the land outright or to barter a royal vineyard for it.

The king was unprepared for Naboth's abrupt refusal, as he called God to witness that he would not sell his ancestral property. Naboth evidently invoked the ancient law that the land belonged to God, and each family had been given a portion to maintain as a patrimony in accordance with the divine command, "The land shall not be sold in perpetuity, for the land is mine."

In spite of his chagrin, Ahab recognized Naboth's right. Jezebel, however, did not. She sent letters under Ahab's seal to the elders of Jezreel brazenly commanding them to cause false witnesses to say that Naboth had cursed God and the king. Then they were to take him out and to stone him to death. The elders obeyed and the dirty work was done. Jezebel sent Ahab to collect his prize. In the vineyard, Ahab met Elijah and his word of doom: Ahab's descendants, Elijah said, would be utterly swept away.

When Ahab decided to invade Ramothgilead, a city on the shifting border between Israel and Syria, he was, unknowingly, courting his own death. Now was the time that the Lord, through his agents, would punish Ahab.

The invasion was endorsed by the prophets of his own retinue, but Ahab decided to consult another prophet in the land, one who had traditionally been hostile to him. The prophet Micaiah was called in and asked whether it would be wise for the king to proceed with the planned invasion.

In Micaiah's reply, he reveals a mysterious vision of the Lord: "I saw the LORD sitting on his throne, and all the host of heaven standing beside him on his right hand and on his left; and the LORD said, 'Who will entice Ahab, that he may go up and fall at Ramoth-gilead?' . . . Then a spirit came forward and stood before the LORD, saying, 'I will entice him.' And the LORD said, 'By what means?' And he said, 'I will go forth, and will be a lying spirit in the mouth of all his prophets.' And he said, 'You are to entice him, and you shall succeed; go forth and do so.' "

The "lying spirit" has been described by scholars as being an aspect of the prophetic spirit of Yahweh. The spirit has no moral character of its own; the Lord himself is responsible for whatever is done to Ahab. Unlike the idea of Satan that would develop later, this lying spirit is still under the control of Yahweh, and, in fact, is sent directly from the Lord. Thus, he is not the adversary of God, but the adversary of man.

As a result of his oracle, Micaiah was thrown in jail, and King Ahab proceeded into a battle that he was preordained to lose. The Syrians at Ramoth-gilead not only triumphed over the combined forces of Israel and Judah, but they also slew Ahab. "And they washed the chariot by the pool of Samaria, and the dogs licked up his blood . . . " (1 Kings 22:38). ✦

Mysterious demons of the Near East

OR THE PEOPLES of ancient Mesopotamia the universe was full of spirits. It is difficult for a modern Westerner, reared in a monotheistic and secular society, to imagine how the world seemed to ancient Babylonians or Assyrians. These peoples shared beliefs that had grown from prehistoric roots among the early Sumerians and remained largely untouched by the world outside Mesopotamia. They saw an almost endless variety of supernatural life in every portion of the world. Human life was just one part of a living, breathing, active universe.

At the top of the divine scale were the gods of official religion known from priests' records on clay tablets unearthed by archaeologists—Anu, the remote god of heaven; Enlil, the sometimes stormy lord of wind; and Ea, the beneficent god of water and wisdom. These presided over a complicated pantheon that included literally thousands of named deities. Especially important were astral deities of sun and moon and the planet Venus, along with national gods like Marduk of Babylon or Asshur of Assyria.

Ideas that in a monotheistic religion appear as superstition formed the core of ordinary religious life in Mesopotamia. Deities truly inhabited their images. The images produced in temple workshops were consecrated to give them life and open their eyes to see the world.

Demons were a continual danger, to be warded off. Often, they lurked about graves and in deserts, and caused sleepers to have nightmares. They were a hazard to a woman in childbirth, ready to kill the newborn or the mother or both.

For example, one particularly vivid demon linked closely to the geography of Mesopotamia was Pazuzu, demon of the hot west wind that blew in sandstorms from the desert. He is known from statues and other pieces of art that have been discovered. One representation of Pazuzu included a monstrous head, hands and feet ending in eagle talons, a thunderbolt in one hand, a curled tail, and four wings. The back of the statue or amulet often carried an incantation to ward off the desert wind. It began by allowing the demon to identify himself: "I am the god Pazuzu, son of the god Hanbi, king of the evil wind-demons. It is I who rage mightily in the Mountain. . . ." The incantation ended with what was probably a simple magical formula to destroy the power of the demon: "The winds, their wings are broken."

Similar rituals protected one from Lilitu, probably the same as Lilith, the "night hag" of Isaiah 34:14; Namtar, the plague demon; and Lamashtu, the dread female spirit that threatened childbirth. The universe was full of spirits, not all of them good.

Mesopotamian demon

Pazuzu

7th or 6th century B.C. demon

The chariot of fire

The prophet's mantle falls to Elisha

THE STORY OF ELIJAH is filled with the miraculous from beginning to end. His first act was to cause a lengthy drought; his last was to ascend into heaven in a whirlwind and chariot of fire.

Careful study of the Hebrew texts has led most scholars to assert that the Elijah stories were written down in the form in which we read them only 200 or more years after the prophet's lifetime, which is assigned to a period shortly before 850 B.C. However, the time lag does not necessarily prove that the stories did not originate during Elijah's lifetime. Rather, it implies that the reports were selected and shaped by generations of retelling in Israel and Judah. By the time the two books of Kings were written down, Elijah was already a figure of the distant past. The whole northern kingdom of Israel where he prophesied had been lost forever to Assyrian conquest. The authors of the books of Kings attributed that fact to the very idolatry and faithlessness to Yahweh against which Elijah struggled. They emphasized that Yahweh had warned Israel of its sins "by every prophet and every seer" (2 Kings 17:13). Elijah is thus seen as one part of a larger story in which Yahweh struggled in vain to save the kingdom of Israel from its own idolatry and apostasy. Elijah's story fulfills the meaning of his name, "Yahweh is God." The final miraculous episode of the life of Elijah, his ascension to the heavens in a chariot of fire, is also the first episode in a new cycle of traditions that center around Elisha.

The mysterious story of Elijah's ascension is told in a highly stylized manner in 2 Kings 2. Thrice Elijah instructed Elisha—who was chosen by the Lord to carry on Elijah's struggles—to "tarry here" while he traveled on toward the Jordan. Thrice Elisha with identical words refused. Thrice the "sons of the prophets" marked their journey, twice with prophecies of what was about to happen. When they reached the Jordan, Elijah struck the waters with the mantle he had cast over Elisha when he called him to be a prophet. As waters had parted beneath Moses' rod, and again before the Ark, in the time of Joshua, so also the prophet's mantle divided the waters and they crossed on dry ground.

When Elijah asked whether Elisha had any final request of his master, Elisha asked to "inherit a double share of your spirit"—the share that a first-born son would inherit from his father. Elijah responded that such a difficult request could be realized only if Elisha was granted the vision to see Elijah as he ascended to the heavens.

They walked on conversing, when suddenly "a chariot of fire and horses of fire separated the two of them. And Elijah went up by a whirlwind into heaven. And Elisha saw it and he cried, 'My father, my father! the chariots of Israel and its horsemen!' " (2 Kings 2:11–12). Only the mantle of Elijah was left behind—and Elisha took it up.

This remarkable scene transformed the figure of Elijah for the future. Its significance is amplified by two incidents later on in the cycle of Elisha stories. The first occurred when the Syrian army surrounded the city where Elisha lived, and the prophet's youthful servant fell into despair. But Elisha, assuring him, made a request. And "the LORD opened the eyes of the young man, and he saw; and behold, the mountain was full of horses and chariots of fire round about Elisha." Thus the supernatural vision of the chariot of fire represented the mighty

> "Elijah was a whirlwind, and his spirit the incarnation of fire. Everywhere fire accompanies him and illustrates him. This is the final lesson taught by this majestic prophet."
> —Raymond Calkins, *The Interpreter's Bible*

179

Elisha falls on his knees *at the sight of Elijah ascending to heaven in the chariot of fire.*

forces of God that surrounded and protected both his prophet and his people.

The second incident occurred at the deathbed of Elisha himself. The narrative describes Joash, the king of Israel, as he wept beside the dying prophet and cried out to him the very same words that Elisha had cried to Elijah: "My father, my father! the chariots of Israel and its horsemen!" These mysterious words pointed to the prophet as God's choice as protector and defender of his people. It emphasizes that God is still with the people of Israel. Hence, in the final moments of Elijah's life, Elisha's

company, alongside only Enoch (Genesis 5:24), as one who escaped the universal experience of death. Already in the fifth century B.C., less than a hundred years after the writing of the Book of Kings, the prophecies of Malachi promised that Elijah would return as a reconciler and restorer in Israel "before the great and terrible day of the LORD comes." About 200 B.C. the teacher Ben Sira also celebrated Elijah as ready at the appointed time "to calm the wrath of God" and "restore the tribes of Jacob."

As the traditions about Elijah developed in Judaism, he was seen as one who would in the end bring peace to the world, as one who would be precursor and partner of the Messiah, and as one who would interpret the mysteries of the Torah. Also, he was seen as a spiritual companion to the pious; some rabbis were said to have a spiritual communion with him, and to be guided by him in their studies. The Elijah of fable continued to be intensely concerned with the suffering of his people. In the time of Esther he was said to have intervened to save Jews from the extermination of Haman. Numerous stories were also told of how he helped save individual pious Jews from suffering or death. An extensive folklore grew up around the figure of Elijah as an emissary from Heaven sent to earth to overcome injustice by rewarding the poor and punishing their rich oppressors. He was sometimes described as traveling the earth in disguise as a beggar or even as a poor gentile discovering who possessed true righteousness and generosity.

The New Testament also made much of the coming of Elijah. During his life Jesus was thought by some to have been the returning Elijah or, more commonly, the New Testament identified John the Baptist with the ancient prophet (Matthew 17:10–13). When the first three Gospels described Jesus' "transfiguration," they portrayed Moses and Elijah appearing in glory with Jesus and conversing with him. Moses and Elijah represent the link between God's covenant with his people in the past and Jesus, the future of Christianity. ✦

eyes were opened to see powers of God beyond human sight and the prophet himself as God's defender of his people.

That indelible image of fire and wind lifting Elijah into heaven beyond the reach of death opened up Elijah's importance to later generations. Elijah stood in very select

"Is anything too hard for the LORD?"
—Genesis 18:14

FROM EARLIEST TIMES believers have experienced apparently supernatural interventions in their lives and have taken them as signs from God, to be pondered deeply and declared in tones of awe and praise. It was a prophet's role both to predict miracles and to explain what they meant: "Ah Lord GOD! . . . Nothing is too hard for thee . . . who hast shown signs and wonders in the land of Egypt, and to this day in Israel and among all mankind" (Jeremiah 32:17–20).

"We . . . believe that the Divine Will ordained everything at creation and that all things, at all times, are regulated by the laws of nature and run their natural course in accordance with what Solomon said, 'As it was so it will ever be, as it was made so it continues, and there is nothing new under the sun.' (Ecclesiastes 1:9). This occasioned the sages to say that all miracles which deviate from the natural course of events, whether they have already occurred or, according to promise, are to take place in the future, were foreordained by the Divine Will during the six days of creation."
—Maimonides
Commentary on the Mishnah, Avot

"[Belief in] hidden miracles is the basis for the entire Torah. A man has no share in the Torah, unless he believes that all things and all events in the life of the individual as well as in the life of society are miracles. There is no such thing as the natural course of events." **—Nahmanides**
Commentary on Exodus 13:16

"Miracles are not wrought outside of nature, but above nature." **—Martin Luther**

"I say that the miracles and the extraordinary interventions of God have this peculiarity that they cannot be foreseen by any created mind however enlightened."
—G. W. Leibniz
The Discourse on Metaphysics

"I know not, brethren, if you are likeminded—I at least believe, cherish, reverence and follow the teaching of Jesus Christ not because of the miracles which were done in the service of that teaching, but because of its inner truth and excellence."
—C. F. Bahrdt, *Letters on the Bible*

"Miracles happen at all times. However, since they come to us not because we deserve to be saved but because of His great mercy and grace, they remain unnoticed. Only a generation that serves Him wholeheartedly is worthy of knowing the miracles that happen to it." **—Rabbi Eliezer of Tarnegrod,**
Amaroth Tehorot, **on Psalm 136:4**

"A miracle is an event with which human comprehension has not yet caught up. It is not an interruption of law, but the working of a law which human reason has not yet charted." **—Ralph W. Sockman**
The Interpreter's Bible

"Miracle and prophecy belong together. . . .What would be sorcery in the hands of the magician, becomes portent in the mouth of the prophet. And by pronouncing the portent, the prophet proves the dominion of providence which the magician denies. . . .This explains the delight in miracle. The more miracle, the more providence."
—Franz Rosenzweig, *"On the Possibility of Experiencing Miracles"*

Elisha's miracle of the oil vessel.

Elisha: the wonder-worker

A people's prophet and maker of kings

LATE IN THE NINTH century B.C., the Israelite monarchy reached its two hundredth anniversary. Standing astride this century are two great prophets, Elijah and Elisha. The first half of the century was dominated by the image of the lone Elijah against the massed prophets of Baal. The second half of the century was dominated by his successor, Elisha.

Elisha was a farmer, the son of a man named Shaphat, from the ancient town of Abel-meholah near the Jordan River. In the midst of Elisha's plowing, Elijah came and cast his prophetic mantle over him. At the touch of the prophet's mantle, Elisha recognized what it meant: his days of plowing the fields were behind him. He was to continue Elijah's work as a prophet of judgment on Israel. Elisha asked only to be allowed to kiss his father and mother goodbye before leaving. He marked his break with the past by butchering the oxen he was driving, using the wood of their yokes to cook them, and serving the meat to the people around.

As soon as Elijah departed in the whirlwind and chariot of fire, the miraculous works of Elisha, as heir to both his mantle and his spirit, began. Indeed, Elisha's works are packed with miracles—moments that indicated the inexhaustible power of God. Throughout the accounts of Elisha, the marvels multiply. Furthermore, the tapestry of miracles reveals the variety of roles that a great prophet could play in ancient Israel. These ranged from meeting the basic needs of ordinary individuals to changing the course of wars and destiny of nations.

Elisha's first miracle was the parting of the Jordan River. Just as Elijah had parted the Jordan by striking it with his mantle, so in the same way "the LORD, the God of

183

In a perplexing incident, *Elisha looks on while a group of boys are killed by bears after jeering at the prophet.*

Elijah" parted the Jordan for his successor.

Once across the Jordan, Elisha met a band of "the sons of the prophets," who recognized that "The spirit of Elijah rests on Elisha" (2 Kings 2:15). "The sons of the prophets" were prophetic guilds that had appeared as early as the time of Samuel and Saul and would continue for nearly five centuries. In Elisha's time they seem to have been organized in communities within various cities. And while Elijah had been a lonely figure whom the sons of the prophets had revered at a distance, Elisha was to live closely among them. It was among such communities that the stories of Elisha were told and retold over the decades until the time came to write them down.

The first such community that Elisha stayed with was in Jericho, and there his first miracle of service took place. The water from the town spring was causing sickness,

death, and miscarriages. When the city fathers asked the prophet for help, he took a new bowl that had been filled with salt, went to the spring, threw salt in it, and proclaimed that Yahweh had made the water wholesome. And so it was.

Following this useful miracle, another is described that is troubling and apparently useless. While Elisha was traveling from Jericho to Bethel, some boys mocked his baldness—possibly not natural baldness but a tonsure, which, along with his mantle, marked him as a prophet. The prophet cursed the boys in the name of Yahweh, and two bears "came out of the woods and tore forty-two of the boys" (2 Kings 2:24).

Why would the prophetic circles have repeated such a seemingly unflattering story about Elisha? They probably did so because, flattering or not, the story demonstrated the aura of power that surrounded the holiness of the prophet. No one could treat the holiness of the prophet with contempt without dire consequences.

It is fitting that several of the biblical stories about Elisha preserve vignettes of life among the "sons of the prophets." In one of these, the widow and two children of a member of the prophetic guild were left destitute and at the mercy of a creditor who threatened to take the children as his slaves to settle the father's debts. Elisha saved the children by causing the family's last possession, a jar of oil, to pour out its valuable liquid until it filled every available container in the community. The oil was then sold and the debts paid (2 Kings 4:1–7).

In a time of famine, the sons of the prophets in Gilgal shared Elisha's pot of stewed vegetables made with wild herbs. When poisonous wild gourds were mistakenly added to the stock, the results could have been disastrous. But the wonder-working prophet had a ready solution. Just as he had earlier poured salt into a spring and had made it wholesome, so now by simply adding ground meal to the poisoned food, Elisha removed the danger and preserved the valuable food (2 Kings 4:38–41).

Again when a gift of 20 loaves of barley and some fresh ears of grain was brought to Elisha, representing a farmer's first fruits of harvest, Elisha miraculously made it possible for a hundred of the men to eat their fill and have leftovers. Centuries later similar miracles would be reported of another wonder-worker, Jesus of Nazareth.

Ready though he was for private needs, the narrative of 2 Kings also shows Elisha to be a man of great national power. Elisha's first miracle on behalf of the state came early in his career when Jehoram, the king of Israel and son of the infamous Ahab, went to war. He was trying to subdue a rebellion by Mesha, king of Moab, whom Ahab's father, Omri, had conquered, and to force him to renew his payments of tribute. For this attempt to quell independence, Jehoram made an alliance with the kings of Judah and Edom and marched toward the south. At first the campaign bogged down,

and the kings feared for their armies in the vast stretches of the waterless wilderness.

Jehoshaphat, the king of Judah, suggested that they consult a prophet of Yahweh. This suggestion brought to light how far the kings of Israel had pushed the prophets of Yahweh from the centers of power. Jehoram, who apparently had numerous prophets of Baal around him, knew of no such prophet of Yahweh: he indeed had to be informed about Elisha.

At first Elisha refused to have anything to do with Jehoram, but for the sake of the king of Judah, who was more faithful to the worship of Yahweh, he consulted the Lord. Here the narrative describes one of the techniques of inspiration used among the prophets. Elisha asked a minstrel to play, and with the flow of the music, evidently, the ecstasy of inspiration was reached: "the power of the LORD came upon him."

The oracle that Elisha gave promised miraculous water in the desert, the conquest of the Moabites, and the destruction of their land. And sure enough, the next day water flowed in the desert and the needs of the armies were met. The early battles went in favor of the Israelites, and the spoiling of

On the power of example

Elisha's "is the type of ministry which may be ours. No one of us may be an Elijah, but every one of us may be an Elisha. If possessed by God's Holy Spirit, we may perform deeds of mercy which will seem like miracles in other men's eyes. It is a high calling to move among men and bring courage and happiness into disheartened and bewildered souls. The character and career of Elisha are often disparaged in comparison with the more heroic figure of Elijah. Yet his beneficent life, less spectacular and more humane, is the inspired symbol of a ministry which lies within the reach of us all. Small kindnesses, small courtesies, small considerations, habitually practiced, give a greater charm to the character and often do more good in the world than great accomplishments."
—**Raymond Calkins,** *The Interpreter's Bible*

185

the land proceeded apace. But then, as the campaign neared its end, the fortunes of war took a remarkable turn.

When Mesha saw his hopeless situation against the combined forces of Israel, Judah, and Edom, he was driven to desperate measures. The book of 2 Kings narrates it concisely. "Then he took his eldest son who was to reign in his stead, and offered him for a burnt offering upon the wall. And there came great wrath upon Israel; and they withdrew from him and returned to their own land." Among the Moabites, evidently, what Mesha did was considered a noble, though extreme, act of devotion to their god Chemosh. Jehoram's campaign ended in utter failure.

Remarkably, two accounts of this war survive—the Hebrew *and* the Moabite. The latter is from a black basalt stele set up by Mesha to commemorate his victory over the Israelites. The stone was discovered intact in 1868, but was later broken by Bedouins. Eventually the surviving pieces were reassembled in the Louvre. In the inscription, Mesha attributes his victory to Chemosh, who "saved me from all the kings and caused me to triumph over all my adversaries."

The stele of Mesha *describes the Moabite victory over Israel.*

From the Moabites' point of view, it was the displeasure of their god, Chemosh, that had allowed Omri and the armies of Israel to conquer Moab in the first place, "for Chemosh was angry at his land." But, in victory, Mesha exulted with considerable exaggeration that in his time and under his leadership "Israel hath perished for ever!"

Mesha did not mention the sacrifice of his own son, but did describe his slaughter of the population of whole towns during the war. As an outgrowth of the war, he boasted that he reigned peacefully over the hundred towns which he added to his land. Rarely have the destructive forces of the

passage of time allowed us to have a view of both sides of an ancient battle.

Elisha's involvement in matters of state extended beyond the war with Moab. Once when Syria was warring against Israel, Elisha became a kind of Israelite spy against Syria. By using clairvoyance, he was able to forewarn the king of Israel about the enemy's moves. When the Syrian king learned that Elisha was frustrating his plans, he massed his army with its chariots and horses against the town where Elisha was staying. The prophet's young servant was distraught, but Elisha was unafraid. The servant learned the reason for that fearlessness when Elisha prayed that God would open the young man's eyes. To his amazement the servant saw the supernatural forces that protected Israel focused on Elisha: "the mountain was full of horses and chariots of fire round about Elisha."

Carrying out a commission that God had originally given to Elijah on Mount Horeb, Elisha instigated two political revolutions, one in Syria and one in Israel. The Syrian revolution began when Elisha was in Damascus. King Ben-hadad, who lay seriously ill, took the opportunity to send his minister Hazael to ask the prophet whether he would recover. Elisha recognized that this Hazael was the one whom God had chosen to punish Israel for its apostasy. He urged Hazael to tell Ben-hadad that he would recover even though "the LORD has shown me that he shall certainly die." As he stared at Hazael, Elisha's miraculous foresight struck him with pain and he began to weep. He foresaw the horrible carnage that this man would wreak upon Israel. Hazael returned to Ben-hadad and told him that he would certainly recover. But the next day, he murdered the king and usurped the throne.

The second revolution took place after Hazael had begun his attacks on Israel. The king of Israel at that time was Joram, one of the sons of Ahab. After a battle in which Joram was wounded and had to withdraw to recover, Elisha sent one of the sons of the prophets on a secret mission to the council of Israelite commanders. There, he was to find Jehu, the son of Jehoshaphat. In private, he would then pour a flask of oil over his head with the words, "Thus says the LORD, I anoint you king over Israel."

The young prophet carried out his task as commanded. He also urged Jehu to destroy the house of Ahab and Jezebel for their crimes against the prophets of Yahweh. When what the young prophet had done became known, the commanders unanimously acclaimed Jehu as king: the coup d'etat was under way. Jehu moved quickly against Joram. Joram was assassinated, Jezebel was thrown from a window and her body eaten by dogs, and 70 other sons or grandsons of Ahab were killed.

As Elijah had executed the prophets of Baal after the contest on Mount Carmel, so Jehu instituted a deadly purge of all Baal worshippers in the land. Once he tricked a large number of people devoted to Baal into assembling in the temple of Baal. He surrounded the building with armed men and slaughtered everyone inside. He then destroyed the building and turned the house of Baal into a latrine: "Thus Jehu wiped out Baal from Israel." Thus did Yahweh punish the apostasy of the house of Ahab.

Many of the wonder stories of Elisha are relatively brief episodes. In several cases, however, the tradition handed down longer narratives that resembled miniature dramas with several characters and scenes.

One of these is the account of Elisha's dealings with a wealthy Shunammite woman. Along with her husband, she decided to support the prophet's ministry by providing him food and a room to use on his regular travels across the land.

In response, Elisha determined to reward the woman's generosity. He learned that the couple had no son and heir and that the husband was too old to beget children. Nevertheless, the prophet promised the Shunammite woman that she would bear a son within the year. And so she did.

Years later, when the boy was old enough to go into the fields to his father, he unfortunately suffered an apparent sunstroke. The boy was carried to his mother and died on her lap. In great distress the

Elisha's miraculous breath woke the child from the slumber of the grave.

187

mother laid him out on Elisha's bed and hastened to find the prophet. She found him at Mount Carmel.

After returning with the woman to her home in Shunem, Elisha prayed to Yahweh. He stretched his body out over the dead child, "putting his mouth upon his mouth, his eyes upon his eyes, and his hands upon his hands" and the child's flesh became warm (2 Kings 4:34). Then Elisha got up, walked back and forth, and again stretched out over the boy. This time the child sneezed seven times and opened his eyes. Mother and son were reunited.

Through this small drama the power of God in Elisha is shown as life-giving, life-restoring, and life-preserving. The prophet is never depicted as performing his astounding feats in public so as to impress the crowds. The manifestations of God's power met deep personal needs and are as private as the problems they remedy. Only long after the fact do others—including the king of Israel—learn of these mighty deeds.

Elisha did not escape the fate of mortality as his predecessor Elijah had, but even on his death bed his powers are said to have been in full force. As he lay near death, Elisha laid out for King Joash the future course of his conflict with Syria.

Elisha's last reported miracle was perhaps the most astounding of all—since it was performed after he was dead. A funeral procession passing near his grave was attacked by marauders. In panic, the mourners cast the corpse into a nearby grave: it was Elisha's. When the corpse touched the bones of Elisha, the man revived and stood up. Even death could not limit the life-giving power of the prophet. ✦

The prophet's bones restored life to a dead man.

188

"Unclean! Unclean!"

The surprising facts about leprosy in ancient times

NAAMAN, THE COMMANDER of the Syrian army, was a "mighty man of valor." But power and prestige do not bring immunity from disease: Naaman had leprosy. A maiden from the land of Israel told Naaman's wife of a prophet who could give him the cure that the gods of mighty Syria could not provide.

Naaman was to go to the prophet in Israel. His visit was arranged through royal channels and backed by a letter from the king of Syria. Naaman was a man used to wielding authority: he expected that the prophet would meet him personally and would directly carry out the healing. Furthermore, he expected to pay royally for everything he received. Laden with gifts, he set off to visit the king of Israel.

When Naaman arrived at the prophet's dwelling, Elisha would not so much as come to the door. He did not even look at the commander's condition, much less personally speak magical words of healing over his disease. Instead, he sent a lowly messenger out with unexplained instructions. "Go and wash in the Jordan seven times, and your flesh shall be restored, and you shall be clean" (2 Kings 5:10).

Naaman was outraged. But eventually, his slaves convinced him to do what the prophet had said. And, when he emerged from the Jordan, "his flesh was restored like the flesh of a little child" (2 Kings 5:14). Naaman was a changed man: he was now convinced that "there is no God in all the earth but in Israel" (2 Kings 5:15). When the prophet refused his offer of lavish gifts, he accepted the rebuff but in turn requested a curious gift from the prophet. He wanted to carry back to Syria two mule-loads of earth from the land of Israel so that he could set up an altar to sacrifice to Yahweh. Elisha gave him no long instructions about the requirements of his new faith, but sent him on his way in peace.

When Elisha's servant Gehazi saw Naaman departing with the lavish gifts that he had brought, he ran after Naaman and pretended that Elisha had changed his mind and now wanted some of the gifts. Naaman was happy to give more than he requested. But when Gehazi tried to hide his deed from Elisha, the story comes full circle. The prophet had the power to judge and punish as well as to heal and restore. Indeed, Elisha knew all that had happened, and condemned Gehazi to suffer the very leprosy that he had removed from Naaman. The drama closes as the servant departed from the scene, his skin white with the disease.

But with what disease was Gehazi now inflicted? Leviticus 13–14 describes the diagnosis and treatment of various symptoms of a disease that the Bible calls "leprosy." Modern scholarship has determined that these symptoms describe a variety of skin diseases, among which may be Hansen's disease, the medical name for what is now known as leprosy. But leprosy as we know it was rare in the ancient Near East until around 350 B.C., when the armies of Alexander the Great may have carried it back with them on their return from India. Furthermore, the Hebrew word *zara'at*, which is translated as "leprosy," is a general term for a litany of skin afflictions; in the original Greek translation of the Hebrew, the Greeks applied their term *lepra* indiscriminately whenever the word *zara'at* appeared in the

> "According to Jewish tradition, sneezing during prayer is considered to be a special pleasure sent from God. For Jacob, sneezing was a sign that his soul was about to leave his body, but when Elisha revived the dead son of the Shunammite woman, the Bible says: 'the child sneezed seven times, and the child opened his eyes.' "
> —**Dr. James Le Fanu**, *Medical News, England*

Naaman was miraculously cured *of leprosy by bathing in the Jordan River. In antiquity, lepers were social outcasts.*

text. The Greek term *lepra* (leprosy) referred in general to noncontagious, scaly skin afflictions, the types most commonly alluded to in Leviticus. These skin conditions produced white patches (or scales) on the skin. If the scaling spread to the head, its presence would resemble ringworm. Psoriasis and eczema have symptoms similar to those described in Leviticus 13–14, and have been suggested as possible candidates for biblical "leprosy." Curiously, the Hebrew word *zar-a'at* was also used to describe the blemishes on the walls of houses as the result of dry rot in the woodwork or precipitates on the masonry.

Priests were responsible for diagnosing "leprosy," and the depth of the skin lesions helped the priest determine his diagnosis according to the laws of Leviticus. When a priest had certified that a member of the community had "leprosy," the carrier had to rend his clothes, dishevel his hair, veil his mouth, and cry, "Unclean, unclean," as a warning to those around him. And at this point he had to isolate himself from the populace. These purification rituals were similar to those imposed upon an individual who had touched a corpse, reflecting the belief that contamination could occur through contact. They clearly represented ritual as well as medical precautions.

The biblical literature suggests that moral failings were one reason for these afflictions. Thus, in the Old Testament, Miriam was stricken with "leprosy" for defaming Moses (Numbers 12:1–10), Gehazi for greed (2 Kings 5:20–27), and Uzziah was stricken as divine punishment for sacrilege.

As the disease was probably a noncontagious but ritually impure affliction, measures were prescribed to insure that no contact take place between the affected person and the sacred. The carrier was barred from the sanctuary and from eating sacred food. In this context, the veiling of the mouth probably stemmed from the folk belief that the scaly skin disease could be transmitted through the air. Thus, because ritual contamination of others could occur simply by being under the same roof, the affected person was isolated. It was not in fact the disease that caused ritual impurity but the appearance of outward symptoms. When those symptoms faded, the person was declared pure by the priest, who was acting not as a doctor but as an interpreter of the Law.

The quarantine of the afflicted lasted for a period of seven days, after which time the priest examined the victim to determine if the disease had healed and the person could resume a normal routine. If the afflicted was declared pure, a series of cleansing rituals were performed before the "leper" was declared fit to rejoin society. ✦

From Rehoboam to Hezekiah

The continuing covenant of the Davidic dynasty

WHEN THE NORTHERN kingdom of Israel rejected Rehoboam's rule, it also repudiated the claims of the Davidic house to a special covenant with God. In that covenant God promised David: "your kingdom shall be made sure for ever before me; your throne shall be established for ever." These claims provided stability for Judah throughout its history.

In the beginning, the prospects of the southern kingdom of Judah looked dim. Rehoboam presided over the loss of Jerusalem's empire, continual skirmishes with the north, and invasion from Egypt. Both royal and Temple treasures were lost. His son Abijam (also called Abijah), who reigned about three years, tolerated the worship of foreign gods that began under Solomon.

Judah found a more successful ruler in Abijam's son Asa (913–873 B.C.). Though Asa was hard-pressed when Israel tried to impose a blockade of Jerusalem, he made a successful alliance with Syria and forced the north to withdraw. He also carried out religious reforms against foreign cults, and even removed his own mother, a worshipper of Asherah, from her office as queen mother. His policies were continued through the long and prosperous reign of his son Jehoshaphat (873–849 B.C.). But Jehoshaphat sealed an alliance with Israel by the marriage of his son Jehoram to Athaliah, daughter of Ahab and Jezebel. This move, though well-intentioned, nearly brought down the Davidic dynasty.

When Jehoram succeeded to the throne (849–843 B.C.), he undid his father's religious reforms, and formed an even closer alliance with the north, which his son Ahaziah continued. Thus it was that Ahaziah was present when the king of Israel was assassinated by Jehu, and he, Ahaziah, was killed as well (843 or 842 B.C.). That left his mother Athaliah, the daughter of Ahab, as ruling queen of Judah. She attempted to kill all members of the royal family. After six years of rule, however, she was overthrown when the chief priest revealed that an infant son of Ahaziah, Joash, had been saved from the purge and hidden in the Temple.

Under a succession of kings, Judah suffered the vicissitudes of a small power. By the time of Ahaz (735–715 B.C.), the combined forces of Syria and Israel threatened. Ahaz sought help from the Assyrian king, whose armies repelled the invasion. This alliance with the Assyrians, which was undertaken against the advice of the prophet Isaiah, led Ahaz to give bronze ornaments of the Temple as tribute. Ahaz's idolatrous practices—including sacrificing his own son as a burnt offering—wiped out the religious policy of decades. ✦

The wisdom of a foolish king

Hezekiah surrenders but triumphs

THE SOUND OF ASSYRIAN chariots was practically within earshot of Jerusalem when the 25-year-old Hezekiah succeeded Ahaz to the throne of Judah in 715 B.C. It was a time of great danger for all the smaller kingdoms of the region. The power of Assyria was at full strength under Sargon II, the king who had led thousands of Israelites, a very few miles to the north, into permanent exile only six years earlier.

Ahaz had bought the survival of Judah at the price of subservience to Assyria. He had allied himself with Assyria against the attacking forces of Israel and Damascus, had willingly paid tribute, and had "reformed" worship in Jerusalem to be more like Syrian and Assyrian patterns, even burning one of his own sons as an offering.

Hezekiah evidently wanted to reassert the distinctiveness of Judah's religious traditions as well as its political independence. He began a radical religious reformation and sought allies to withstand Assyria. He seized an opportunity to free Judah following the death of Sargon II in 705 B.C. Many of the vassal states in the Assyrian empire were looking for an opportunity to regain independence, and the most effective leader was Babylon's leader Marduk-apaliddina, known in the biblical text as Merodach-baladan. He tried not only to effect a rebellion in his own region but also to stir up revolts in other parts of the empire.

Hezekiah was in about the tenth year of his reign when Merodach-baladan sent an embassy to visit him in Jerusalem. Hezekiah was eager to establish a link with Babylon, and he gave his visitors a full tour of his treasure house and showed them all the gold and silver and everything of value in his palace. When the prophet Isaiah heard about this, he confronted the king and asked what Merodach-baladan had seen. When Hezekiah said he had shown his guest everything, the prophet pronounced

an oracle of judgment: Babylon would one day come and take it all away and some of Hezekiah's sons would be deported to Babylon. Rather than expressing dismay, Hezekiah stated that the word of the prophet was good, for he thought, "There will be peace and security in my days."

Isaiah's proclamation was intended to warn the king against the dangers of invasion. Because it was not the fledgling Babylonia, but the mighty Assyria, that threatened conquest of Judah, Hezekiah probably believed that his kingdom was secure.

Assyria posed a great military challenge to Israel and Judah at the end of the 8th century B.C. The progressive conquest of Palestine by Assyria is recorded both in the Bible and in Assyrian wall reliefs and cuneiform texts on clay tablets. The kingdom of Israel had come to its end at the hands of Sargon II, who vanquished Samaria, its capital, in 722 B.C. His death in 705 B.C. set off a chain of rebellion throughout the empire. Sargon's son, Sennacherib, swept down the western coast and onto the plain of Palestine, conquering Lachish (less than 30 miles from Jerusalem) in 701 B.C.

Hezekiah's response was to ally himself with Egypt and several smaller kingdoms against Assyria, and to prepare Jerusalem for the coming siege. He strengthened the walls of the city, and he secured the water supply of Jerusalem by diverting its main water source to within the city walls.

Scholars have noted that the biblical account of the campaign waged against Hezekiah by Sennacherib is somewhat ambiguous. In 2 Kings, Hezekiah surrendered to Sennacherib, even going so far as to strip the Temple doors of their gold so as to pay the Assyrians a massive tribute. Following this passage, however, is a lengthy description of Sennacherib's demands for the city's capitulation. Perhaps Sennacherib was not satisfied with the initial agreement worked

In fulfillment of God's promise, the invading Assyrian king, Sennacherib, and all his host are cut down outside the walls of Jerusalem. As depicted by the Flemish painter Rubens, angels swoop down from a stormy sky, while King Sennacherib, whose warriors had conquered much of Judah, falls screaming from his horse. As told in Isaiah, a single angel of the Lord slaughtered the troops at night; when morning came, the camp was filled with corpses.

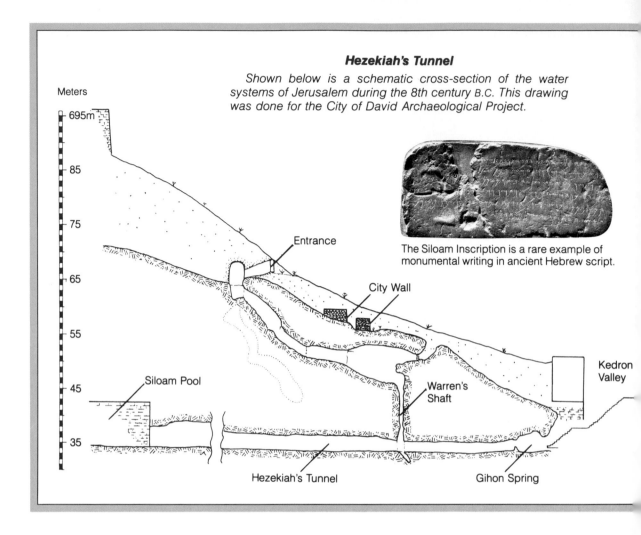

Hezekiah's Tunnel

Shown below is a schematic cross-section of the water systems of Jerusalem during the 8th century B.C. This drawing was done for the City of David Archaeological Project.

Meters

695m
85
75
65
55
45
35

Entrance

City Wall

Siloam Pool

Warren's Shaft

Kedron Valley

Hezekiah's Tunnel

Gihon Spring

The Siloam Inscription is a rare example of monumental writing in ancient Hebrew script.

out in 701 B.C., when Hezekiah showed his willingness to pay tribute to his adversary so as to have the city spared. Apparently, the Assyrian king then demanded complete surrender, which Hezekiah refused. The prophet Isaiah was opposed to Hezekiah's initial decision to join forces with Egypt against Assyria. But later Isaiah gave assurances that the Lord would not allow Sennacherib to enter Jerusalem.

According to the biblical story, "that night the angel of the Lord went forth, and slew a hundred and eighty-five thousand in the camp of the Assyrians; and when men arose early in the morning, behold, these were all dead bodies" (2 Kings 19:35). Sen-

nacherib now departed for home, where he was eventually assassinated by his sons.

What could have killed so many men so quickly? Writing almost three centuries later, the Greek historian Herodotus describes an incident in which Sennacherib's army, encamped along the border of Egypt, was besieged by an army of mice, which ate the Assyrians' quivers and bowstrings, causing "great multitudes" to die for lack of arms. It is not altogether clear that Herodotus was referring to the same incident, but the reference to mice could be an allusion to plague, which is often carried by rodents, and which could explain the massive loss suffered by Sennacherib's army in 701 B.C., an explanation already advanced by the Jewish

In ancient Israel, many cities were built high on hills and enclosed by walls for defense. Nature, however, usually places fresh water on low ground. In the event of a prolonged siege, such a city, cut off from its water supply, could literally die of thirst.

King Hezekiah overcame one of the dangers of living within closed walls when he diverted Jerusalem's main fresh water supply and thwarted the forces of the invading King Sennacherib. "They stopped all the springs and the brook that flowed through the land, saying, 'Why should the kings of Assyria come and find much water?' " (2 Chronicles 32:2–4).

Today, visitors can wade through King Hezekiah's achievement: Hezekiah's tunnel carried fresh water almost one third of a mile under the city walls from a spring outside Jerusalem to the Siloam pool, inside. The tunnel was carved through 1,749 feet of solid bedrock, which represents a staggering feat of engineering. The construction of the tunnel was accomplished by two sets of miners boring toward each other from opposite ends of the tunnel.

A plaque, written in classical Hebrew, describes the digging of the tunnel. It was found adjacent to the pool: "Behold the tunnel. This is the story of its cutting. While the miners swung their picks, one towards the other, and when there remained only 3 cubits to cut, the voice of one calling his fellow was heard—for there was a resonance in the rock coming from both north and south. . . . and the water flowed from the spring towards the pool, 1200 cubits. The height of the rock above the head of the miners was 100 cubits." The plaque, removed in 1880, now hangs in a museum in Istanbul.

Visitors wade through the low waters of the Gihon Spring in Hezekiah's Tunnel.

historian Josephus in the first century A.D.

While Hezekiah's military victory was important, the Bible speaks approvingly of Hezekiah mainly because of his religious reform. Hezekiah had his priests purify and reconsecrate the Temple in Jerusalem, and then he urged all of the citizens of Judah and the recently conquered northern kingdom, Israel, to come to Jerusalem to celebrate the Passover feast at the newly dedicated Temple. In this he hoped to establish the status of the Temple as the only legitimate cult place. Centralizing the worship of Yahweh in Jerusalem was a step toward political unity, and unity would be useful in confronting the common enemy, Assyria.

In efforts to purify the religion, in particular to cleanse it of its Assyrian elements, Hezekiah "removed the high places," and destroyed the pillars, the Asherim (wooden poles used in pagan worship), and the bronze serpent in the Temple.

The high places were sites of worship and sacrifice, initially Canaanite, later Israelite, that were spread throughout the biblical territory. The pillars and Asherim were used in the pagan worship of the Canaanite fertility goddess Asherah. The bronze serpent had been cast by Moses himself on an order from God. Incense was burned to it in the Temple of Jerusalem. By Hezekiah's time, the bronze serpent was a relic whose original meaning had been forgotten. ✦

King Hezekiah was at the point of death *when he prayed to the Lord. The miracle of the sun dial was the sign that his life would be extended.*

When the sun's shadow retreated

Hezekiah's prayers were answered

PRAYER IN THE BIBLE renders both personal and national deliverance. Ordinary human beings, sometimes through prophets or other holy men, called upon this personal God of the Old Testament to perform even the most particular wonders. Hezekiah prayed to God to save Jerusalem from the wrath of Sennacherib, and the Lord sent his assurances through the prophet Isaiah.

The story of Hezekiah is full of mystery and wonder. For not only was Jerusalem divinely spared during his reign, but also, Hezekiah himself was restored, by the hand of God, from death. Indeed, he is said to have been brought near to death by an illness whose only symptom was a boil. Isaiah came to the ailing king and told him to prepare for the end. The finality of the prophecy caused Hezekiah great grief, and

he besought God for help. The prayer was answered. Before Isaiah had even left the middle court of the palace, he was told by God to return to Hezekiah with the news that 15 years would be added to his life.

Isaiah then called for a poultice of figs to be laid upon the king's boil. Such a therapy was commonly used in ancient times to open up hard boils and ulcers. Hezekiah asked for evidence that God intended to heal him, and, given a choice of signs by Isaiah, called for the progress of the sun to be reversed. "Rather let the shadow go back ten steps." The miracle occurred—revealed by the retreat of the shadow on a sun dial. Afterward, Hezekiah recovered. The king's recovery is attributed both to prayer and to medical intervention, but it is ultimately through prayer that he was delivered. ✦

"**Then you shall call, and the** L**ORD**
will answer;
you shall cry, and he will say,
Here I am." —Isaiah 58:9

PRAYER IS an intensely personal dialogue with God. Many have written eloquently on the subject. Some emphasize thanksgiving, others beseeching. Some urge composure, others recommend strong emotion. But all agree, that prayer should be a believer's total involvement with the source of eternal life.

"Any prayer uttered without mental concentration is not prayer. If a service has been recited without such concentration, it must be recited again devoutly....What is to be understood by concentration of the mind? The mind should be freed from all extraneous thoughts and the one who prays should realize that he is standing before the Divine Presence. He should therefore sit awhile before beginning his prayers, so as to concentrate his mind, and then pray in gentle tones, beseechingly, and not regard the service as a burden which he is carrying."

—**Maimonides,** *Mishneh Torah* **(c.1178)**

"Prayer hath raised dead men to life, hath stopped the violence of fire, shut the mouths of wild beasts, hath altered the course of nature, caused rain in Egypt, and drought in the sea. It cures diseases without physic, and makes physic to do the work of nature, and nature to do the work of grace, and grace to do the work of God; and it does miracles of accident and event. Yet prayer, that does all this, is, of itself, nothing but an ascent of the mind to God, a desiring things fit to be desired, and an expression of this desire to God as we can, and as becomes us...to do our duty, to glorify God, to do good works, to live a good life, to die in the fear and favour of God. These things God delights to give, and commands that we shall ask, and we may with confidence expect to be answered graciously . . . . Our prayers must be fervent, intense, earnest, and importunate."

—**Jeremy Taylor**
The Rule and Exercises of Holy Living

"[Prayer] is the humble correspondence of the human spirit with the Sum of all Perfection, the Fountain of Life. No narrower definition than this is truly satisfactory, or covers all the ground."

—**Evelyn Underhill**
The Spiritual Life **(1937)**

"Prayer is *our* humble *answer* to the inconceivable surprise of living. It is all we can offer in return for the mystery by which we live. Who is worthy to be present at the constant unfolding of time? Amidst the meditation of mountains, the humility of flowers—wiser than all alphabets—clouds that die constantly for the sake of His glory, *we* are hating, hunting, hurting. Suddenly we feel ashamed of our clashes and complaints in the face of the tacit glory in nature. It is so embarrassing to live! How strange we are in the world, and how presumptuous our doings! Only one response can maintain us: gratefulness for witnessing the wonder. . . .

"As a tree torn from the soil, as a river separated from its source, the human soul wanes when detached from what is greater than itself. Without the holy, the good turns chaotic. . . . Unless we aspire to the utmost, we shrink to inferiority. . . . Prayer is our attachment to the utmost. Without God in sight, we are like the scattered rungs of a broken ladder. To pray is to become a ladder on which thoughts mount to God to join the movement toward Him which surges unnoticed throughout the entire universe."

—**A.J. Heschel**
Quest for God **(1954)**

The fabled Hanging Gardens of Babylon appear behind this reconstruction of the massive Ishtar Gate, originally built by Nebuchadnezzar.

The death throes of the kingdom of Judah

Exile to Babylon

IN 701 B.C., when Sennacherib, the king of Assyria, withdrew his forces from Judah, he left in his wake a devastated land, but Jerusalem remained intact. The city had been spared through the payment of tribute by King Hezekiah of Judah. In the next 100 years, from the death of Hezekiah (687 or 686 B.C.) to the final destruction of Judah by the Babylonians (587 B.C.), Judah experienced many ups and downs of independence and subjection.

With the payment of tribute by Hezekiah, Judah came under Assyrian domination. The kingdom remained a vassal of

Assyria throughout the reign of Manasseh (687–642 B.C.), Hezekiah's son. His reign was long and, although marred by atrocities that were connected with a revival of Canaanite religion, Manasseh's policies broke with those of his father. He had altars dedicated to the Assyrian astral deities placed in the Temple of Yahweh, tolerated a revival of the worship of Baal and of Asherah and its cult of sacred prostitution, and practiced human sacrifice. Although the biblical writers lay much of the blame for the destruction of Judah on the outrageous sins of Manasseh, it is recorded in 2 Chronicles that, later in his life, he prayed to Yahweh for forgiveness. His prayer was recreated by an unknown author in the Greco-Roman period and is preserved in the apocryphal book, The Prayer of Manasseh.

Manasseh was succeeded on the throne by his son, Amon, who reigned only two years before he was assassinated by his own servants. They, in turn, were executed by the gentry of the land, who placed Amon's young son, Josiah, on the throne. Josiah's reign lasted about 31 years. It was one of the most turbulent periods in ancient Middle Eastern history.

The Assyrian Empire, which had dominated the entire region for almost a century, was both weakened by internal political conflict and hard-pressed to defend its overextended borders. The empire's preoccupation with revolts in the north and the east allowed Judah to stop paying tribute and become independent. It is likely that Josiah broke from Assyrian domination around 630 B.C. and extended Judah's territory to include some northern regions, approximating the borders of the United Kingdom of David and Solomon. During this part of his reign the kingdom, thus expanded and restored, enjoyed a renewed nationalism.

In the 18th year of his reign, about 621 B.C., Josiah ordered the repair of the Temple in Jerusalem. In the course of those repairs, the "Book of the Law" (probably some form of the book of Deuteronomy) was found. "When the king heard the words of the law he rent his clothes . . . 'great is the wrath of the LORD that is poured out on us, because our fathers have not kept the word of the LORD, to do according to all that is written in this book' " (2 Chronicles 34:19–21). Its stringent commands concerning the exclusive worship and service of Yahweh, the Lord of Israel, as well as the centralization of rituals in the Jerusalem Temple became the order of the day. The Temple was cleansed of pagan altars and rededicated to the worship of Yahweh. All foreign cults and places of worship were purged from Judah, and the priestly personnel of those cults were deposed. Josiah moreover eliminated the practice of divination and magic. Piety and patriotism went hand in hand.

The reforms were advanced by the prophets Zephaniah and Jeremiah. Zephaniah proclaimed the imminent coming of the Day of the Lord, a day of wrath and ruin. (This message has become familiar in the Latin rendering of the prophecy: *Dies Irae*.) Zephaniah urged repentance, predicting that only a remnant of the people, "humble and lowly," would remain. Jeremiah, whose ministry began about 626 B.C., during the initial phases of Josiah's political and religious moves, also prophesied impending disaster. At first he seems to have supported the reforms; ultimately he became disillusioned and critical of the behavior of both leaders and the people.

In 626 B.C., Babylon, led by the Chaldean prince Nabopolassar, won its independence from Assyria. Efforts to reclaim this crucial province of the empire proved futile, and eventually the tables were turned. In 612 B.C., the Babylonians joined forces with the Medes and captured and destroyed Nineveh, the Assyrian capital. (The Book of Nahum had prophesied the fall of Nineveh.) A few years later, despite desperate efforts by the remaining Assyrian forces and the uncertain help of the Egyptians, the empire collapsed. Into the power vacuum rushed the Babylonians, led by Nabopolassar and his son Nebuchadnezzar.

By 610 B.C., Assyria had been fully conquered by the Babylonians and the Medes. The Medes were content to remain in con-

Hebrew, Israelite, Jew

In 2 Corinthians, Paul uses the terms *Hebrew*, *Israelite*, and *Jew* interchangeably. All three are names for the people who were the authors of the Bible and the principal actors in it. *Israelite* is probably the most accurate of the three terms to use as a name for these people, since they were members of a confederation of 12 tribes which called itself Israel and which believed itself to be descended from the patriarch Jacob—also called "Israel."

The word *Jew* comes from the tribe of Judah, which eventually gave its name to all those who followed the Israelite religion. After the fortunes of war had sent most of the northern tribes into exile, the name of the surviving tribe of Judah became applied to both all the Israelites who remained living in their ancestral homeland and those living abroad. Since this happened only in late biblical times (Jerusalem fell to Nebuchadnezzar in 587 B.C.) most of the Bible's references to Jews come from the New Testament.

The origin of the name *Hebrew* is considerably less certain. The Bible derives it from that of Eber, one of Abraham's ancestors. Israelites in the Bible often use the term *Hebrew* to refer to themselves in front of foreigners. "I am a Hebrew," Jonah said when he was asked to identify himself. Foreigners also used the term when referring to Israelites.

But *Hebrew* is a word that remains mysterious. Some think the word is related to Habiru, the name of a group of people who migrated throughout the Middle East hiring themselves out as soldiers or laborers. Others disagree. Finally, *Hebrew* is the name for the language in which most of the Old Testament was written. It's a Semitic tongue spoken by the ancient Israelites, on which modern Hebrew, the language of present-day Israel, is based.

trol of the lands they had in the east, whereas Syria-Palestine became a pawn in the power struggle between Babylon and Egypt. In 609 B.C. Josiah was killed in battle against the Egyptians at Megiddo, a town frequently mentioned in the Bible. His son Jehoahaz was made king, but reigned only three months before the king of Egypt took him captive and replaced him with Jehoahaz' brother Jehoiakim (Eliakim).

During Jehoiakim's reign, many of the same evils previously associated with Manasseh were revived. Judah remained under Egyptian domination until a Babylonian army under Nebuchadnezzar defeated Egyptian forces at Carchemish, and Jehoiakim had switched his allegiance to Babylon by 603 B.C. However, Jehoiakim rebelled in 600 B.C., and although the Babylonian king could not immediately respond, he did so about three years later, capturing the city of Jerusalem and deporting a number of high officials and the royal family in 597 B.C.

The Babylonians placed Zedekiah (Mattaniah), the third of Josiah's sons to reign, on the throne, and he ruled during the last years of the kingdom.

Zedekiah looked for an opportunity to break from Babylonian domination. In about 594 B.C., a conference was held with neighboring countries, all of which had grievances against the central authorities.

Jeremiah intervened at this crucial moment, denouncing the conspiracy against the Babylonians. He said that Babylon's ascendency had been ordained by God. Rebellion was not part of God's plan and indeed would be punished. Nevertheless, around 589 B.C., Zedekiah rebelled along with Egypt, Ammon, and Tyre. The rebellion was crushed, and in 587 B.C. Jerusalem—and the Temple of Solomon—were destroyed, and much of the population was led away to exile. Thus ended the Kingdom of Judah. Just as the northern Kingdom of Israel had been destroyed by the Assyrians 135 years earlier, so now the southern kingdom of Judah had been laid to waste by the Babylonians. The people of Yahweh ceased to exist as a nation. ✦

Return to the Promised Land

King Cyrus paves the way to a new Jerusalem

WITH THE DESTRUCTION of Jerusalem in 587 B.C. and the deportation of its people to Babylon, the dynasty of David and the nation of Judah came to an end. However, many of the exiles in Babylon never gave up hope that one day they would return to the land Yahweh had given them, to restore the kingdom and the Davidic dynasty—a hope that was encouraged by the prophetic conviction of a new day for the people of Yahweh.

But when would this new Jerusalem be a reality? The prophet Jeremiah had predicted that the exile would last 70 years—which was commonly regarded as a full life span and conformed to his belief that few if any-

one then alive would survive until the return. The actual period from the destruction of Jerusalem until the edict of Cyrus permitting the return was just under 50 years. The Babylonian Empire collapsed rapidly under pressure from the Persians and their triumphant king, Cyrus the Great.

Coincident with the rise of Cyrus as world conqueror were the oracles and proclamations of the anonymous prophet of the Exile, whose words are part of the Book of Isaiah and who is often called Second Isaiah. His message to the people was one of hope and encouragement, of renewal and restoration. Yahweh was now prepared to bring them back across the wilderness to the Holy Land as he had done long years before in the days of Moses and the Exodus. Yahweh's instrument in this plan was to be Cyrus, his "shepherd" and "anointed." The return would represent a new age, with the bonding of the people to Yahweh based on a renewal of the ancient covenant made through Moses on Mount Sinai.

The initial hopes came to fruition in 539 B.C., when Cyrus made a triumphant entry into Babylon. The following year, in line with his policy toward other nations, the new king issued a decree that allowed the exiles to return to Palestine, rebuild the Temple, and restore their religion.

Little is known of the initial phase of the return, except that the rebuilding of the Temple was begun in an atmosphere of excitement. However, there was intense opposition to this project from the Samaritans and others. They considered the establishment of a new Judah as a threat to the political stability of the region and were angry when their offer to help rebuild the Temple was rejected, probably on the grounds that they were not authentic Israelites but a mixed group. Due to their opposition, work on the Temple stopped until the second year of Darius.

The Persians: commerce and trade

Late in the second millennium B.C., a nomadic people from Russia migrated south and settled on the Iranian plateau. In 539 B.C., when the armies of Cyrus II took Babylon, the Persians entered the world political scene. They would remain a major power for centuries. The state religion of ancient Persia was Zoroastrianism, which declares the universe to be governed by the dualism of good and evil. But the Persians did not impose their religion on the Israelites. Judaism flourished; (a thousand years later, the Babylonian Talmud was compiled). A standardized monetary system, empire-wide mail service, and uniform taxes resulted in the rapid growth of commerce.

When the prophets Haggai and Zechariah chastised the new community for its failure to finish the Temple, a renewed effort was undertaken by Zerubbabel, who was in the direct line from David, and was probably the nephew of Sheshbazzar, the governor of Judah. Opposition was overcome when a search produced a copy of the decree of Cyrus. The rebuilding of the second Temple was resumed—and completed in 515 B.C. (Ezra 6:13–15).

While some, unwilling to forsake their new homes and occupations, had stayed on in Babylon, others returned, hoping for a renewal of the glorious days of David. The governor, Zerubbabel, was called the "signet ring" of Yahweh and the "Branch"— terms suggesting the dynastic promise embodied in a number of prophetic utterances.

The historical reality, however, did not entirely fulfill these hopes and expectations. The province of Judah was administered by Joshua, a high priest of the house of Zadok, and by Zerubbabel, the new governor, who was of Davidic descent. He reported to the Persian regional governor, or satrap, and through him to the king. Although Zerubbabel served as governor of the province of Judah, he never became king. Any connection of the governorship with the House of David had evidently ended by the time Nehemiah, a man with no royal claims or pretensions, took the post in 445 B.C. There was little room for even a puppet king in the Persian scheme of administering rule by satrap, so the hopes for the reestablishment of the monarchy were dashed.

The covenant with Yahweh assumed central importance instead. When Ezra, a priest and scribe of Yahweh, led another wave of exiles to Jerusalem, he brought with him a copy of the book of the law of Moses. This he presented to the people as the basis of their faith and daily lives. Thus the Jews' focus changed from the House of David to Yahweh's covenant, received by Moses on Mount Sinai, and expressed in the laws of the Pentateuch. This is how the Jews in the province of Judah would live, retain their identity, and serve their God. ✦

202

The mysterious and beautiful Esther

A Jewish Queen who saved her people

THE STORY RECOUNTED in the Book of Esther differs markedly in content and tone from the rest of the Bible. God's name does not appear even once in the entire book. Depicting the triumph of the Persian Jews over their enemies some time during the 5th or 4th century B.C., it is an account of hatred and revenge, murderous plots and court intrigues, impending catastrophe and last-minute salvation.

The drunken King Ahasuerus (possibly Xerxes I, who reigned from 486 to 465 B.C., or Artaxerxes II, who ruled from 404 to 358 B.C.) capped a half-year of banqueting by calling his queen to appear before the assembled guests. Enraged by her refusal to come and advised by his counselors that her disobedience might damage the authority of husbands throughout Persia and Media, Ahasuerus had her deposed.

When the king's anger had abated, he took steps to find a new queen. After an empire-wide search among all the beautiful virgins, Esther, a Jewish woman, was chosen queen. Following the advice of her cousin, Mordecai, an official at court, Esther did not tell anyone of her Jewish identity—not even her husband the king.

The scene shifts to a struggle at court. When Ahasuerus elevated Haman the Agagite to be grand vizier, "all the king's servants who were at the king's gate bowed down and did obeisance to Haman"—except for Mordecai the Jew. Enraged at this insult, Haman sought to punish not only Mordecai, but all Persian Jews. He convinced the king that the Jews were actually a foreign minority who did not keep the king's laws, and he obtained royal approval for their extermination. Government officials were informed of the decision and advised to carry it out on the 13th day of the month of Adar, a date Haman chose by lot.

Mordecai enlisted the aid of his cousin, Queen Esther, in averting the anti-Jewish

The enigmatic Esther feasts with her husband, king of Persia, and the evil courtier Haman.

decree. At first she was fearful to intercede because of a rule at the palace that no one was to appear before the king unless specifically summoned. Finally, though, she plucked up her courage, went to the king, and invited him to a banquet—which Haman was also asked to attend. There, Esther requested that both men come back the next night for another banquet.

The very night of the first banquet, however, fate began to turn against Haman. Ahasuerus, suffering from insomnia, had the chronicles of his reign read to him: he learned that Mordecai had never been properly rewarded for uncovering an assassination plot against the king. In the morning, the king asked Haman how to treat a man worthy of royal honor. Thinking that he, himself, was the person to be honored, Haman suggested that the honoree be dressed in the king's robes, mounted on the king's horse, and paraded through the city's open square of the city in splendor. Ahasuerus accepted this advice, and, to Haman's chagrin, ordered him to prepare this magnificent treatment for his enemy—Mordecai.

Stung by disappointment, Haman went off to Esther's second banquet, where an even worse fate awaited him. As they were drinking wine, Esther asked the king to spare her life and that of her people. Ahasuerus, who seemed to have forgotten the whole matter, wanted to know who was responsible for the impending destruction of her people. Learning that Haman was the villain, the fickle king sentenced him to the very gallows that Haman had prepared for Mordecai. And, making the reversal of fortunes complete, Mordecai was appointed grand vizier in Haman's place.

Haman's downfall, however, did not yet ensure the salvation of the Jews. Since Persian law stated that official documents, carrying the seal of the king, could not be revoked, there was no way to avert the attacks on the Jews scheduled for the 13th of Adar. So Mordecai got royal permission to do the next best thing: a new edict, written in the name of the king and sealed with the king's ring, was sent to all government officials, allowing the Jews to fight back against their enemies.

On the 13th of Adar, the Jews of Persia defeated those who were bent on their destruction. And "on the fourteenth day they rested and made that a day of feasting and gladness." In the capital city of Susa, however, the Jews were allowed to inflict further losses on their opponents for an additional day. The Jews in Susa "rested on the fifteenth day, making that a day of feasting and gladness."

According to the Book of Esther, to commemorate this deliverance, the feast of Purim was instituted as an annual two-day festival on the authority of letters sent out by Mordecai and Esther. To this day, Jews celebrate Purim with the public reading of the Scroll of Esther.

The Book of Esther has several puzzling aspects. For example, there is as yet no extra-biblical evidence, either literary or archaeological, to corroborate the events it describes. And while the author does demonstrate knowledge of Persian society and manners known to us from other sources, certain elements of the account—the possibility, for instance, that a Persian king would marry a woman of unknown lineage—contradict historical evidence.

Subsequent Jewish tradition nevertheless canonized the Scroll of Esther and made Purim a central event in the Jewish calendar. This is because the story of Mordecai and Esther reflects the realities of Jewish life after the exile. ✦

Esther as a story of salvation

"It was natural for this story of salvation, which parallels the wonder of the Exodus, to be celebrated by the Jews. Simeon ben Lakish (c. 300) declared that . . . the Scroll of Esther would not pass away after the coming of the Messiah, and Maimonides reiterated this view. Probably both felt . . . that, alas, the time of miracles ended with Esther. The Church, which considered itself the new and true Israel, valued no less the wonderful event that had saved the people of the LORD. Beginning with Clement of Rome (c. 100), ecclesiastical writers glorified the perfect faith of Esther and her beauty which brought about the deliverance of Israel. She was viewed as the prototype of the Church and, later, of the Virgin Mary."
—Elias Bickerman,
Four Strange Books of the Bible

***Nehemiah returned from exile** to a devastated Jerusalem, vowing to rebuild the city walls.*

Ezra and Nehemiah

Prophets of the return

THE EDICT OF KING CYRUS of Persia in 538 B.C. allowing the Jews to return to Judah did not guarantee the success of the new community there. It took more than 20 years for the Jews to complete rebuilding their Temple in Jerusalem, and even then, economic troubles, internal squabbles, and the ambitions of neighboring peoples kept the Jewish community small and insignificant.

Ezra and Nehemiah were two Persian Jews who came to Judah in the 5th century B.C. and breathed new life into the fledgling colony. Their mission was to ensure that Judah would neither fade away nor lose its Jewish character. As a priest and a "scribe of the Law," Ezra had practical experience in matters of ritual, along with knowledge of the Mosaic traditions. The Persian King gave him authority to enforce "the Law of the God of Heaven" in Judah along with the right to punish transgressors.

Upon his arrival in Judah, Ezra was appalled at the degree to which the Jewish returnees from Persia had intermingled with other nations. Of special concern was a group that came to be known as Samaritans. They claimed descent from the ten northern tribes of Israel which had been defeated by the Assyrians more than two centuries earlier. Since the Samaritans worshipped the God of Israel and claimed equal rights with the Jews in the Temple worship of Yahweh, many of the Jews returning from Persia viewed them as coreligionists and probably intermarried with them. Ezra, however, suspected that their religion was a mix of idolatry and Israelite modes of worship—

205

Who were the Samaritans?

In 539 B.C., when the Jews were permitted to leave Babylon for their home in the west, they did not return to a deserted land. Though large numbers of the native peoples of Israel and Judah had been deported by the conquering Assyrians and Babylonians, other peoples from the far reaches of the Assyrian empire had also been displaced. The two groups lived side by side, colonists intermarrying with native Israelites. The offspring of these marriages became known as Samaritans.

However, Samaritans worshipped the God of Israel, understood Moses to be the true prophet of God, and held the Torah (the Pentateuch) to be the only divine law. This ancient sect exists to the present day. Primarily a religious community, they live near Mount Gerizim, which they believe is the chosen place of God; there they celebrate the Passover. Among their sacred objects is a Pentateuch scroll that they believe dates from the time of Joshua, in the early years of the conquest of Canaan.

The Abisha Scroll from the Samaritan Pentateuch, c. 12th century A.D.

them from danger in the past, and yet how far Jews had strayed from God's laws. The destruction of the First Temple, he stressed, was a punishment for sin, as was the fact that even now, with its Second Temple functioning, Judah remained under Persian rule. As a direct consequence of Ezra's preaching, the Bible tells us, the people solemnly swore "to follow the Teaching of God, given through Moses the servant of God, and to observe carefully all the commandments of the LORD."

Nehemiah was a Persian Jew, a courtier who rose to the important position of cupbearer to King Artaxerxes I. He was deeply grieved to hear about the troubles of his fellow Jews in Judah, and was especially concerned about the fact that Jerusalem's walls were in disrepair, exposing the city to attack at any time. Nehemiah convinced the king to appoint him governor of Judah with specific authority to rebuild Jerusalem's walls. Soon after arriving in Judah, Nehemiah succeeded in getting the walls up, despite the opposition of Samaritan, Ammonite, and Arab chieftains who tried to sabotage the effort with the claim that the walls were part of a plan for Jewish revolt against their Persian overlords.

As governor, Nehemiah had to deal with other pressing matters as well. Poor Jews complained that inability to repay their debts had enabled the wealthy to seize their land and even to take their children as slaves. Alert to the danger of increasing social polarization, Nehemiah told the rich, "What you are doing is not right." At the same time, he forced a return of all assets taken from the debtors.

Nehemiah issued several regulations to strengthen the community. Ten percent of all Judeans were required to live in Jerusalem so that the capital would not become depopulated. All citizens had to pay a tithe for the upkeep of the Temple. And, to safeguard the Jewish Sabbath, Nehemiah had the gates of Jerusalem shut from sundown on Friday to sundown on Saturday, ensuring that no business would be transacted on the biblical day of rest. ✦

precisely the kind of practice that had brought the downfall of the first Judean state. He took drastic measures to preserve spiritual purity. He compiled lists of all the men who had married alien wives (from Ashdod, Ammon, and Moab), announced that they had transgressed, and issued the drastic order that these wives be sent away.

Ezra read the Torah (the five books of Moses) to the entire community. Through this process of education, he impressed upon the people how often God had saved

PART III

Poetry and Wisdom

The Books of Job, Psalms, Proverbs,
Ecclesiastes, and Song of Solomon

*The Temple in Jerusalem rang with the
poetry of the Psalms; the faithful sang
hymns of praise, thanksgiving, and
lament. These passages grapple with the
dark enigma of suffering, yet they
speak with even greater eloquence of love
and the search for divine wisdom.*

A righteous sufferer

How Job's patience became proverbial

WHY DO PEOPLE SUFFER? Does God reward good and punish evil? Is God responsible for evil? Is there finally any justice in the world? Such are the questions probed by the poet of Job. The book of Job is remarkable not only in the Bible but in all literature for the intensity and depth with which it struggles with these questions, questions that embody perennial mysteries of human existence.

Job is a book of elevated poetry, of scorching human drama, and of penetrating theological debate. It dares to challenge piety and faith, to ridicule accepted explanations of God's ways, and even to raise an open and absolutely serious challenge to divine justice. It resolutely refuses to accept easy answers to the profound problems of human existence and prefers to leave mysteries mysterious rather than resolve them with conventional clichés.

As a work of literature, the book confronts the reader with two basic parts. There is a prologue and epilogue written in prose, which provide the basic story of Job and his suffering. Between these prose sections lies the poetic heart of the book, a dramatic dialogue written in Hebrew verse. Scholars have long debated the relation of the prose and poetic sections to each other, the relation of the story to historical events, and other questions of literary development. Still, it is the book of Job as a whole that has lived for centuries in the human mind and heart. The prose and poetry are equally vital: together they form a powerful story.

"We are allowed to cry out against God, the Bible is full of such cries, and belief can deepen as persons are encouraged and allowed to cry out and to doubt and question."

—**Archbishop Ted Scott,
Anglican Church of Canada**

The prologue is especially important because it establishes some of the "givens" of the whole drama. For example, in its first sentence it informs the reader simply and absolutely that the man Job "was blameless and upright, one who feared God, and turned away from evil." He also is portrayed as a man of great wealth, large family, and concern for the uprightness of his children as well as himself. Thus, Job's righteousness is established for the entire story.

In a series of scenes that switch back and forth between heaven and earth, some of the other givens that the prologue reveals are more startling. The first of these scenes is set in the heavenly court. Yahweh is conversing with Satan, whose name means "adversary" or "accuser." He is presented not as an enemy of God but as a member of the divine court with the special function to accuse human beings before God. When Yahweh praises Job, Satan raises a question that is both cynical and serious: "Does Job fear God for nought?" Job's righteousness had paid off in wealth, healthy family, every happiness. No wonder he was upright.

Satan puts the problem in a sarcastic and contemptuous manner, but the basic question regarding whether righteousness brings prosperity while sinfulness brings suffering continues through the book. Satan had asserted that Job's righteousness is not for itself, but in exchange for prosperity.

The belief that righteousness is rewarded with blessings while sin is punished is very common in the traditions of Israel. A well-known example comes in the blessings and curses near the end of Deuteronomy:

"And if you obey the voice of the LORD your God, being careful to do all his commandments. . . .Blessed shall you be in the city, and blessed shall you be in the field. Blessed shall be the fruit of your body, and the fruit of your ground, and the fruit of your beasts, and the increase of your cattle,

Though all he loved had been destroyed, *Job, in his torment, would not curse God.*

and the young of your flock. Blessed shall be your basket and your kneading-trough. Blessed shall you be when you come in, and blessed shall you be when you go out.

But if you will not obey the voice of the LORD your God. . . .Cursed shall you be in the city, and cursed shall you be in the field.

Cursed shall be the fruit of your body, and the fruit of your ground. . . .The LORD will make the pestilence cleave to you until he has consumed you. . . .The LORD will smite you with the boils of Egypt. . . ."

Satan asserted, in effect, that if Job experienced curses rather than blessings, he in turn would lose faith: he would curse God. As a test of Satan's cynical interpretation of Job's piety, God grants Satan the power to destroy all that Job possesses.

During this heavenly scene, several more significant "givens" are revealed. First, God is in complete control; Satan must have permission before he attacks Job. Second, Job's suffering will be absolutely unjust. He has done nothing whatever to deserve it; in fact, it is precisely his blameless righteousness that has brought it about. Third, at least in this particular instance, the traditional formula—that obedience brings blessings and sin brings curses—does not hold up. In short order, traditional theology has been turned on its head.

The scene switches to earth and we watch the inexorable application of the curses to Job. Oxen, sheep, camels, servants, children—all are killed. The description of these calamitous events is carefully

stylized. After each disaster, a single servant is left to tell the tale. Because this is a story, rather than a historical record, the focus is on Job: the morality of slaughtering Job's servants and children is not at issue.

Job's response to the disasters that befall him is mourning and worship: "the LORD gave, and the LORD has taken away; blessed be the name of the LORD" (Job 1:21).

In the heavenly court, the original conversation of Yahweh and Satan is repeated, and Yahweh's confidence in Job renewed. But Satan is convinced that if Job's own life and physical well-being are threatened, his faith will collapse: "Skin for skin! All that a man has he will give for his life. But put forth thy hand now, and touch his flesh, and he will curse thee to thy face." This time, God permits the curses of physical affliction to be visited on Job.

When we return to earth, we see Job collapsed on an ash-heap scraping his loathsome sores with a potsherd. He has lost all but his wife. His wife has drawn the conclusion that seemed so obvious to Satan: "Curse God, and die." Though Job recognizes that he has indeed received evil from the hand of God, he refuses to curse him.

At this point the theme of the Book of Job has been established. The author has given us, the readers, a privileged view both in heaven and on earth and has shown us that this is a case of unmitigated suffering, caused by God, that seems completely unjust. But why? This is the question that permeates the entirety of the Book of Job. Thus, the author leads us into the dramatic dialogue that will attempt to penetrate the meaning of Job's suffering.

Eliphaz, Bildad, and Zophar, three of Job's friends, come to comfort him. They sit faithfully with him in agonized silence for seven days and seven nights. Finally, Job breaks the silence, but neither his friends nor we as readers are prepared for his blazing outburst. No, Job does not curse God, but he curses his suffering, his human plight: he curses the day he was born. Job's famed patience is gone.

Job sits *on an ash-heap while his wife pours water on his sores.*

210

*"**Behold, Behemoth,** which I made as I made you; he eats grass like an ox. Behold, his strength in his loins . . . Can you draw out Leviathan with a fishhook, or press down his tongue with a cord? . . . Whatever is under the whole heaven is mine."*

Gone too from the drama is Satan, never to reappear. Throughout the remaining narrative, there is no attempt to blame Satan for evil. Nor are there further visions of the divine court. Instead, we, the readers, are trapped with Job on earth under a silent heaven with the impenetrable mystery of why God has visited these disasters upon this good man. "Why is light given to a man whose way is hid, whom God has hedged in? For the thing that I fear comes upon me, and what I dread befalls me."

Job's cry prompts a round of responses from his friends, to whom he in turn also responds. Job's friends are by no means evil. They fear God, know the promises of reward and punishment, and piously believe that God's world is just and ordered. "Think now," Eliphaz says, "who that was innocent ever perished?" (Job 4:7). Quite reasonably, they draw on these theological resources to help Job understand his suffering. The evidence of Job's plight shows that his confidence in his integrity is misplaced. "Can mortal man be righteous before God?" Eliphaz asks rhetorically. "Despise not the chastening of the Almighty" (Job 5:17). Such arguments appear to be perfectly sound. However, Job is, in fact, righteous; his suffering is utterly undeserved. Thus, the logical application of traditional theology becomes distorted and false.

What is more, Job himself knows that he is innocent. He is not willing to surrender that truth for any amount of piety. Though he is not recalcitrant, he asks that Eliphaz and the others point out specific errors, rather than ask rhetorical questions about sinfulness. "Teach me, and I will be silent; make me understand how I have erred.

211

How forceful are honest words! But what does reproof from you reprove?"

Back and forth the dialogue goes as the friends, with increasing certitude, defend the justice of God's treatment of Job: "Does God pervert justice?" Bildad asks, "or does the Almighty pervert the right? If you are pure and upright, surely then he will rouse himself for you." Job shares their basic point of view and has no other answer for his plight. His certainty of his innocence, however, calls into question God's justice in the workings of the entire world. He cries out for a fair hearing from God and accuses his friends of lying in order to defend God.

"How long will you torment me, and break me in pieces with words? These ten times you have cast reproach upon me; are you not ashamed to wrong me? . . . know then that God has put me in the wrong, and closed his net about me. Behold, I cry out, 'Violence!' but I am not answered; I call aloud, but there is not justice. He has walled up my way, so that I cannot pass, and he has set darkness upon my paths."

After three cycles of dialogue with his three "friends," Job is beset by a fourth and younger accuser named Elihu, who attempts to sharpen and redirect the earlier arguments for God's justice, posed by the friends. Ultimately, however, Job's debate is not with any of these men, but with God. For the pain of physical suffering has been surpassed by the horrible vision of chaotic injustice in the world. Knowing God's power and his own weakness, confident in his own integrity, Job believes that there must be light for his darkness. He cries out to the heavens: "Oh, that I had one to hear me!"

Amazingly, Job's challenge is heard. In a whirlwind of power and mystery, God answers! Even more remarkable is the character of God's response. Job longs for a clear explanation, the solution to the puzzle of injustice and human suffering in the world. The perennial power of God's response lies precisely in the fact that he gives no all-encompassing explanation. He does not refer to his conversations with Satan, nor does he explain how everything is just and right after all. Rather, with a barrage of ironical questions, he challenges Job to recognize the mystery that bounds all human knowledge and indeed all human existence. The questions range from the origin of the universe to the birthing patterns of mountain goats to battles with mythical monsters.

The questions have no answers, but they have an effect. They show Job that both he and his friends shared a theology that had clarity but lacked understanding and mystery. They thought that they could engage in objective calculations of rewards and punishments and thus understand the ways of God. Job had been outraged with the results of such calculations in his own life and thus driven to cry out against God. But in the final words of the drama, he realizes that such a distant and calculating stance must ultimately dissolve in the face of the vision of God's mystery.:

> I had heard of thee by the hearing of the ear, but now my eye sees thee; therefore I despise myself and repent in dust and ashes (Job 42:5–6).

In the epilogue, after the long struggle, all Job's fortunes are restored. The effect of the epilogue is perhaps to show that not even the insight that Job achieved can stand for long in the face of the human desire for an ordered and rational existence. Still, at least for a moment, the author helped us, through Job, not to destroy but to see the mystery of human life. The power of that vision lives across the centuries. ✦

On the ending of Job . . .

"God has not justified Job, but he has come to him personally; the upholder of the universe cares for a lonely man so deeply that he offers him the fullness of his communion. Job is not vindicated but he has obtained far more than a recognition of his innocence: he has been accepted by the ever-present master-worker, and intimacy with the Creator makes vindication superfluous."

—Herbert G. May and Bruce M. Metzger, *The New Oxford Annotated Bible*

"What is my strength, that I should wait?
And what is my end, that I should be patient?"
—Job 6:11

WHY GOD ALLOWS PEOPLE to suffer is one of the Bible's greatest mysteries. There are no obvious answers. Our own suffering, or that of someone we love, is unbearable only in those dark days when—as the Bible puts it—God hides his face. At such times we cry out, "How much longer?" We may even exclaim, "Why me?" The Bible says that we will overcome suffering if God answers us. It also says that he *does* hear us and that if we are patient and wait for him, he will reveal to each of us a way to understand and transcend our suffering.

"In stormy times, when the foundation of existence is shaken, when the moment trembles in fearful expectation of what may happen, when every explanation is silent at the sight of the wild uproar, when a man's heart groans in despair, and 'in bitterness of soul' he cries to heaven, then Job still walks at the side of the race and guarantees that there is a victory, guarantees that even if the individual loses in the strife, there is still a God, who, as with every human temptation, even if a man fails to endure it, will still make its outcome such that we may be able to bear it; yea, more glorious than any human expectation."

—S. Kierkegaard, *Edifying Discourses* (1843)

"Affliction makes God appear to be absent . . .During this absence there is nothing to love. What is terrible is that if, in this darkness where there is nothing to love, the soul ceases to love, God's absence becomes final. The soul has to go on loving in the emptiness, or at least to go on wanting to love, though it may only be with an infinitesimal part of itself. Then, one day, God will come to show himself to this soul and to reveal the beauty of the world to it, as in the case of Job. But if the soul stops loving it falls, even in this life, into something almost equivalent to hell."

—Simone Weil, *Waiting for God* (1951)

"The justification of the injustice of the universe is not our blind acceptance of God's inexplicable will, nor our trust in God's

love—His dark and incomprehensible love—for us, but our human love, notwithstanding anything, for Him. Acceptance—even Dante's acceptance—of God's will is not enough. Love—love of life, love of the world, love of God, love in spite of everything—is the answer, the only possible answer, to our ancient human cry against injustice. . . .Our labor always, like Job's labor, is to learn through suffering to love . . . to love even that which lets us suffer."

—**Archibald MacLeish**
"God Has Need of Man" (1955)

"One cannot use his individual sufferings to deny the manifold evidence in God's world of his goodness. Without the goodness of God in creating and sustaining the world, man indeed could have no hope. Finally, the very fact that God chose to appear before Job is an act of grace. Job is comforted, not because he has an intellectual understanding of a problem which is hidden in the mystery of God, but because his own eyes have seen God and he can trust even where he cannot understand."

—**G. Ernest Wright**
The Book of the Acts of God **(1957)**

"The inequalities of life belong to man's outer lot; but this is immaterial to his spiritual life."

—**H. H. Rowley**
From Moses to Qumran **(1963)**

Singing the Lord's praises

Psalms: hymnbook of ancient Israel

WHAT ARE THE ORIGINS of the Psalms? The 150 separate poems that in Hebrew were called "The Book of Praises" were the hymnbook of ancient Israel. As in much of the Old Testament, the authorship of specific Psalms is unknown. However, the Bible itself attributes 73 of them to David; and later Jewish tradition held that David had in fact composed them all. Generations have found spiritual renewal in their great beauty.

In reading the Psalms it is important to remember that they were all originally set to music. In Israel, as in much of the rest of the ancient world, poetry and music were sister arts. And whether or not the historical David was the author of those psalms ascribed to him, there can be little doubt that he was famous not only as a poet but as a musician. His skill at playing the lyre brought him to the service of Saul. Likewise, he is called the "sweet psalmist of Israel" (2 Samuel 23:1). But other than the names of instruments, the musical accompaniment has been almost entirely lost. However, the texts make occasional reference to actions performed as the hymns were sung—such as processions, ritual gestures, and responsive singing. Psalm 68, for example, tells of processions with "the singers in front, the minstrels last, between them maidens playing timbrels." Together with the descriptions of liturgical occasions related elsewhere in the Bible, these brief notices give a vivid idea of the color and ceremony of Israelite worship.

Like the five books of Moses (or the Pentateuch), the book was divided into five parts. The final psalm of each of the first four "books" concludes with blessings; however, Psalm 150 may have been intended as a conclusion to the entire Psalter, rather than of the fifth book. Modern scholars have analyzed the psalms into various forms. The most frequent form is that of the "individual lament," in which a person asks God for help in a particular situation.

Be gracious to me, O LORD, for I am
    languishing;
  O LORD, heal me, for my bones
    are troubled.
My soul also is sorely troubled.
  But thou, O LORD—how long?
                  (Psalm 6:2–3)

On the opposite side of the coin are "individual thanksgivings," in which gratitude for help received is expressed:

O LORD my God, I cried to thee for help,
  and thou hast healed me.
                  (Psalm 30:2)

A related type is the "individual song of trust," which expands the expression of confidence forming a central part of an individual lament—a famous example is the Twenty-third Psalm. "Community laments" are petitions for help in national calamity, such as military threat, or defeat:

O God, why dost thou cast us off
  for ever?
Why does thy anger smoke against
  the sheep of thy pasture?
                  (Psalm 74:1)

The corresponding "community thanksgiving" may express gratitude for military victory or a plentiful harvest:

Thou crownest the year with thy
  bounty;
the tracks of thy chariot drip with
  fatness . . .
                  (Psalm 65:11)

A less precise category is that of the hymns, in which God is praised for various actions and qualities, such as the Creation:

O LORD, how manifold are thy works!
  In wisdom hast thou made them all;
  the earth is full of thy creatures.
Yonder is the sea, great and wide,
  which teems with things
    innumerable . . . .
                (Psalm 104:24–26)

Miniature from the Stuttgart Psalter, *about 820 A.D., illustrating Psalm 43. "I will praise thee with the lyre, oh God, my God."*

A small but important minority is formed by the "royal psalms." These are prayers for a coronation, a royal wedding, a victory for the king's army, or the like. The language of these psalms is often highly mythological. Here, perhaps more than anywhere else in the Bible, language and figures of speech freely echo the literature of Israel's Canaanite neighbors. Like the storm god Baal, the Lord of the royal psalms is praised in the divine assembly for his defeat of the sea, and it is he who delegates his task of keeping the forces of chaos in check to the king of Israel: "I will set his hand on the sea and his right hand on the rivers."

This connection between the literary languages of Israel and Canaan may indicate that other types of psalms as well may have echoed non-Israelite counterparts. From ancient Mesopotamia and Egypt also, we have a number of personal and communal prayers not unlike those found in the Psalter. For example, Psalm 104 is remarkably close to the Egyptian Hymn to the Sun-disc (Aten) in its praise of the creator. While no direct links need be assumed, these parallels remind us that Israel existed not in a vacuum but in close relationship with many neighboring peoples.

This continuity is most apparent in the Psalms' very style and language. Like most poetry in the Bible, the Psalms' leading characteristic is use of parallelism. In this technique, common to both Canaanite and Mesopotamian literature, an idea is developed by the use of parallel structure. Thus, in Psalm 27, the first verse expresses essentially the same idea twice:

> The LORD is my light and my
>   salvation;
>   whom shall I fear?
> The LORD is the stronghold of my
>   life;
>   of whom shall I be afraid?

It is at the very least a happy coincidence that the Psalms, which have been used by Jews and Christians for millennia for prayers, should have as their basic formula a principle of balance that may well be the most accurate possible rendering of the actual rhythms of human thought. Perhaps this explains their lasting appeal. For the Psalms are concerned with the fundamental aspects of living and of the human condition, with individuals and communities that are in turn frightened, sick, persecuted, or happy, grateful, and trusting. ✦

"Let us make a joyful noise . . ."

The rich musical legacy of the Bible

NO SINGLE BOOK has had more influence on the music of the Western world than the Bible. Its songs have been sung continuously by Jews and Christians ever since ancient times. They shaped the liturgy in both the early church and synagogue. Their modes have been much altered by passing time, to be sure, but they live on in the chanting of Roman Catholic and Eastern Orthodox churches and in the cantillations of cantors in the synagogue. Their words and style are found in the gospel singing of today. Thus the tradition of King David of Israel has been alive for more than 3,000 years, and we are part of it.

Israel's sacred instrumental music was lost after the destruction of the Second Temple in A.D. 70—the sages banned such music in the synagogues as a gesture of national mourning. However, archaeological discoveries and the study of the instruments and traditions of Israel's neighbors are giving scholars a plausible handle on what music was like in the ancient Holy Land.

Old Testament people lived in extended families, clans, and tribes, and their originally nomadic way of life lent itself to the group singing of work songs, battle cries, songs to a water hole in the desert, songs of blood vengeance and of farewell. The early books of the Bible abound in these, starting with the mention in Genesis 4:21 of the progenitor of all professional musicians, Jubal, "father of all those who play the lyre and pipe." Songs celebrated major events in the life of an individual or family as well. For instance, in Genesis 31:27, Laban complains that Jacob's hasty departure has prevented the customary send-off, "with mirth and songs, with tambourine and lyre."

The prophets made use of music frequently. First Samuel 10:5 lists four instruments—the lyre (a stringed instrument), the tambourine (a hand drum), the flute, and the harp—as equipment used by them to achieve that trance in which the Lord would speak through their mouths. According to 2 Kings 3:15, Elisha called for a minstrel in the presence of the king. "And when the minstrel played, the power of the LORD came upon him. And he said, 'Thus says the LORD, "I will make this dry streambed full of pools." ' "

Music was in fact a regular part of the prophetic message; one among many examples is bold denunciation of Judah that Isaiah sang, in a bitter parody of a vintage festival tune: "My beloved had a vineyard on a very fertile hill" (Isaiah 5:1).

Throughout the ancient world, *joyous dance was an integral part of public ceremony, celebration, and worship.*

216

Assyrian musicians playing for Ashurbanipal at a feast. This relief is from the North Palace at Nineveh, c. 653 B.C.

In a similarly satirical vein, Ezekiel was to inveigh against Egypt and Tyre in mock-dirge style (Ezekiel 32, 27). Most poems in the Bible, whether long or short, are actually songs—including the textured love lyrics of the Song of Songs, and the victory hymns attributed to the prophetesses Miriam (Exodus 15:21) and Deborah (Judges 5). Women were often not just participants but leaders in music-making. The victories of Saul and David were celebrated by the women of Israel in song and dance (1 Samuel 18:6–7).

The most important musician of the Bible was David, singer of Israel. The Psalms, many attributed to David, have been the premier hymnbook of Jewry and Christendom for 3,000 years. They are full of references to music and dance. "Sing to the Lord!" and similar phrases recur in the Psalter. Amos 6:5 credits David with inventing new musical instruments, as well.

Instruments mentioned in the Bible fall into three main groups, strings, winds, and percussion. The latter included tambourines, cymbals, and bells; the strings included lyre, harp, and lute; and the wind instruments included the ram's horn shofar as well as a metal trumpet of more modern type, and several kinds of pipes and flutes. The precise translation of the names of some 20 instruments mentioned in the Bible is often a guess based on related words in other languages, various interpretations and translations, surviving pictures of various instruments in ancient Near Eastern art, as well as the occasional archaeological find.

The New Testament often quotes from or alludes to the Psalms. Psalm-singing was a regular part of services in the early Christian church (as it was in the synagogues of the same period.) From start to finish the Bible is a musical book for music-oriented people, whose lives seem to have been punctuated with alleluias and amens. ✦

The 23rd Psalm

The LORD is my shepherd, I shall not want;
    he makes me lie down in green pastures.
He leads me beside still waters;
    he restores my soul.
He leads me in paths of righteousness
    for his name's sake.

Even though I walk through the valley of
    the shadow of death, I fear no evil;
for thou art with me;
    thy rod and thy staff, they comfort me.

Thou preparest a table before me
    in the presence of my enemies;
thou anointest my head with oil,
    my cup overflows.
Surely goodness and mercy shall follow me
    all the days of my life;
and I shall dwell in the house of the LORD
    for ever.

ACCORDING TO JEWISH TRADITION, David composed Psalm 23 while hiding from King Saul and his army in a barren forest. God did not abandon the psalmist but "soaked this dry forest with a moisture which had the flavor of the World to Come, making even the grass and leaves of the forest succulent and edible." These words describe the boundless generosity of God's love—Psalm 23 embodies the grace of God so vividly that one can almost taste it.

The LORD is my shepherd. "David was the shepherd of Israel, as God says, 'You will be the shepherd of my nation Israel' (1 Chronicles 11:2). Who was David's shepherd? The LORD himself!"

    —*Midrash*

I shall not want. "David dedicated this Psalm to those servants of God who forsake all worldly desires and rejoice in their own lot, whatever it may be. They appreciate their simple bread and water more than all of the delicacies of this world, for their attention is focused on the spiritual pleasures of the World to Come."

    —Ibn Ezra (poet, philosopher, and Bible commentator, 1089–1164)

He makes me lie down. . . . He leads me. "Sometimes, a person yearns to move on, to travel, to change. But his attempts are frustrated and he is tied down to one place. 'You must realize that this is God's will,' says David. 'You must feel as if this is the very best place on earth for you!' Thus, if *'He lays me down'* I must feel that this place is as wonderful as if I were *'in green pastures.'* Conversely, sometimes a person yearns to sink down roots in one place, to establish himself securely. But circumstances force him to move on, to flee, and he never realizes his desire to rest. 'This too is for the best!' says David. 'Accept it gladly!' Thus, if *'He leads me'*, forcing me to move on, I must feel as if I am in calm repose, *'beside still waters.'* "

    —Rabbi Chaim of Volozhin (1749–1821)

The valley of the shadow of death. "Between the part of the flock on earth, and that which is gone to heaven, death lies like a dark valley that must be passed in going from one to the other. But even in this delineation of the deepest distress, there are words which lessen the terror. . . .It is the *valley* of the shadow, deep indeed, and dark, and miry; but valleys are often fruitful, and so is death itself fruitful of comforts to God's people . . . . they shall not be lost in this valley, but get safe to the mountain on the other side."
—**Matthew Henry and Thomas Scott**
Commentary on the Holy Bible

I fear no evil. "A devout person was once found sleeping alone in the middle of a barren and forbidding wilderness. When he was asked, 'Are you not afraid of the many wild beasts?' he replied, 'I am too ashamed before God to be afraid of anything in the world except for Him!' Similarly, David's heart was so filled with the fear of God that there was no room left for the fear of anything else."
—**Yalkut Eliezer**
(Anthology of rabbinical sayings)

For thou art with me. "While we live our life here on earth, so long as we live it 'with' him, and allow him to live it 'with' us, then we experience the deep joy, satisfaction and security that the sheep knows in the presence of its good shepherd. . . .We can be deeply and gratefully aware of God's continuing presence with us in days when all goes well. It is just because of that, however, David declares, that we can be sure of him when all does *not* go well, even when the light fades and we find ourselves in darkness. The phrase he uses is literally 'Valley of Deep Darkness'. So the idea is that God's comfort and strength are 'with' us in all kinds of darkness, in times of depression, serious illness, rejection by one's friends, horror at discovering the disloyalty of one's own heart, and so on, as well as the experience of death itself. . . .But God's loving presence, declares David, will be as real and true then as it is now when all goes well. We are to remember that in biblical thinking, although God *is*

light, yet he dwells in the darkness into which we must go in our turn."
—**George A. F. Knight**
Commentary on *Psalms*

Thy rod and thy staff, they comfort me. "When the sun is sinking and the *deep* shadows fall upon the valleys and gorges bringing peril of attack from wild animals or robbers, the sheep are not afraid. There is their guardian with his 'club' (*rod*) heavily nailed at the end, and with his *staff*, with which he beats down leaves for his sheep. With such protection the sheep are made comfortable. Through such Palestinian pictures of ordinary daily life the psalmist portrays what Jehovah is to him personally in life's valleys and highlands. The imagery applies both to his physical and spiritual life. The shepherd care of God is grounded in his very nature."
—**Elmer A. Leslie**
The Abingdon Bible Commentary

My cup overflows. "Just as a cup holds a precise measure, strict justice also adheres to an exact standard of recompense, i.e. measure for measure with no leniency. However, when God's kindness overcomes strict justice, He acts generously, beyond the letter of the law. Thus it is as if the precisely measured '*cup*' of justice now '*overflows*' with mercy."
—**Isaac Ben Chaim Halberstam**
Siach Yitzchak

I shall dwell in the house of the LORD for ever. "No doubt the original writer throughout had in his mind solely the protection of God in the vicissitudes of this mortal life. . . .*The house of the LORD* figured for him the actual temple on the hill. But it is quite impossible for us to interpret the psalm in so restricted a sense. The Lord has touched it with his finger, and enlarged its horizons. Indeed part of his shepherding of us is precisely the deepening and widening of such a song as this. Wherefore let it be interpreted in the light of our knowledge of him."
—**J. R. P. Sclater**
The Interpreter's Bible

"Apples of gold in a setting of silver"

Words of wisdom that light our way through darkness

THE BOOK OF PROVERBS is an anthology of several collections of sayings, some of which may date back to the time of Solomon and perhaps even farther than that. While the Book of Proverbs is traditionally attributed to King Solomon, it is doubtful that they were composed or collected by the king. Rather, the attribution was in keeping with the custom by which famous men were honored in Israel. By the time the book was collected in the form we know it today, Solomon's wisdom was legendary; thus the attribution seems particularly apt. Scholars call the proverbs "wisdom literature," and the Book of Proverbs was intended to be used by the young men of Israel for religious and moral instruction.

Many of Israel's neighbors had their own sages and traditions of wisdom literature, a fact acknowledged in the Bible itself. Scholars believe that the Hebrews were familiar with these foreign texts, particularly those of Egypt and Babylonia. In fact, a lengthy section of the Book of Proverbs corresponds closely to an Egyptian wisdom classic, the Instruction of Amen-em-ope.

The Proverbs offer the reader practical wisdom along with moral instruction, with the intent of educating and elevating the individual. Many of the Proverbs have repeated admonitions to children.

The Fifth Commandment (Honor thy father and thy mother) is strongly reinforced in the Proverbs, and a son's regard for his parents was considered a mark of wisdom:

> If one curses his father or his
>   mother,
>   his lamp will be put out in utter
>   darkness.

Honey has often symbolized wisdom and goodness. To this day, in traditional Jewish schools, new students touch a page of the Bible with a drop of honey on it to their lips, a custom strongly reminiscent of these words from Proverbs:

> My son, eat honey, for it is good,
>   and the drippings of the honeycomb
>   are sweet to your taste.
> Know that wisdom is such to your soul;
>   if you find it, there will be a future,
>   and your hope will not be cut off.
>   (24:13–14)

There are many admonitions concerning that scourge of family and social life: words spoken in anger. A poor man living alone in peace and quiet is better off than a rich man in an unhappy home. This sentiment is conveyed in the following simple lines:

> Better a dry morsel with quiet
>   than a house full of feasting
>   with strife.   (17:1)
> A soft answer turns away wrath,
>   but a harsh word stirs up anger.
>   (15:1)

Proverbs also points out that patience and forgiveness are the marks of a wise man:

"Wine is a mocker, strong drink a brawler, and whoever is led astray by it is not wise" (Proverbs 20:1).

Good sense makes a man slow to anger,
and it is his glory to overlook an
offense.   (19:11)

Many sayings may originally have been addressed to youthful aristocrats but their applicability remains universal:

Pride goes before destruction,
and a haughty spirit before a fall.
                    (16:18)
He who oppresses a poor man
insults his Maker,
but he who is kind to the needy
honors him.   (14:31)

The Proverbs are quick to admonish fools, those people who ignore the wisdom of experience, and thus repeat past errors. They are at times brutally graphic but never vulgar. For example:

Like a dog that returns to his vomit
is a fool who laps up his folly   (26:11)

Like a lame man's legs, which
hang useless,
is a proverb in the mouth of fools. (26:7)

And many of the Proverbs contrast wise and foolish behavior. They are as sound today as they were in biblical times:

The way of a fool is right in his own
eyes,
but a wise man listens to advice. (12:15)

Likewise, the rashness of a fool is more dangerous than the wrath of a wild animal:

Let a man meet a she-bear robbed
of her cubs,
rather than a fool in his folly. (17:12)

The following observation is about a type that may be found in every social setting: no group would be complete without at least one person like this:

Do you see a man who is wise in his
own eyes?
There is more hope for a fool than
for him.   (26:12)

Another contrast running through the Proverbs is that of the wicked and the righteous:

The wicked flee when no one pursues,
but the righteous are bold as a lion. (28:1)

"Hear, my son, your father's instruction, and reject not your mother's teaching."

The Proverbs call attention to the untrustworthy and faithless, and those who make a pretense of kindness:

Like clouds and wind without rain
is a man who boasts of a gift he
does not give.   (25:14)

Of the virtues praised in Proverbs, self-control is close to the top of the list, and its opposite—self-indulgence—ranks correspondingly low:

A man without self-control
is like a city broken into and left
without walls.   (25:28)

A main concern of many Proverbs was to help people decipher the chaos of everyday experience, to make sense out of life when it seems meaningless. "Such proverbs," the German theologian Gerhard von Rad writes, "had the dignity and value of knowledge painfully garnered. That one who is sated tramples honey underfoot, while to the hungry what is bitter tastes sweet; that a gentle tongue breaks bones; that he who loves his son chastises him; that the bread of deceit tastes sweet, but the mouth is afterwards filled with gravel (20:17)—these are initially hard and perplexing facts. . . .Therefore when behind what seemed to be paradoxical events or facts a hidden order could after all be discerned, the satisfaction was all the deeper. Chaos was once again averted. So wisdom of this kind is undoubtably a quite elementary form of the mastering of life . . .The purpose which these maxims are intended to serve could be called, rather than teaching, an art for living or at least a certain technique for life . . .These maxims, saturated as they are by experience, resemble buoys set out on the sea by which one can find one's position."

Other proverbs praise the virtues of old age, with its reward of insight.:

> The glory of young men is their strength,
>   but the beauty of old men is their
>   gray hair.   (20:29)

The Proverbs point out that the way in which wisdom is imparted is crucial to getting one's point across:

> Pleasant words are like a honeycomb,
>   sweetness to the soul and health
>   to the body.   (16:24)

Religious teaching begins in the home, and if one heeds his parents' advice wisdom may be the reward:

> Hear, O sons, a father's instruction,
>   and be attentive, that you may gain
>   insight.   (4:1)

Insight is impossible without self-knowledge—awareness of self is what distinguishes human beings from animals—yet the Proverbs advise us that we can learn from these small but wise creatures:

> Four things on earth are small,
>   but they are exceedingly wise:
> the ants are a people not strong,
>   yet they provide their food in the
>   summer;
> the badgers are a people not mighty,
>   yet they make their homes in the
>   rocks;
> the locusts have no king,
>   yet all of them march in rank;
> the lizard you can take in your hands,
>   yet it is in kings' palaces.   (30:24–28)

There is yet another dimension to the Book of Proverbs, and that is the realm of deeper meaning, of mystery, that lies behind the polished surface of its sayings. The book abounds in hints of this. For example:

> A word fitly spoken
>   is like apples of gold in
>   a setting of silver.   (25:11)

On the surface, this is a gorgeous poetic way of saying that the right word at the right time is a thing of rare beauty. There may be more to it than that, however. The medieval Jewish theologian Maimonides argued convincingly that the fitly spoken language in question is none other than that of the divine, of Holy Scripture—its beautiful surface meaning is likened to a "setting of silver," but its even lovelier inner meanings are to be perceived as more precious, "like apples of gold." ✦

*"**The badgers** are a people not mighty
yet they make their homes in the rocks."*

When all is vanity

The bleak vision of Ecclesiastes

WHEN WE THINK of the Hebrew Bible we tend to conjure up images of historical narrative about the ancient Israelites, law codes mandating standards of ritual and ethical behavior, and prophetic admonitions. Ecclesiastes, though part of the Bible, is none of these.

Ecclesiastes is a collection of a wise man's sayings, and has as one of its main themes the limited nature of human understanding and human capacity. Man cannot know absolute truth, and all his efforts to achieve and build will be forgotten and rendered meaningless after his death. Power, pleasure, wealth, and wisdom are repeatedly dismissed as "vanities" ("nothingness" is perhaps a better translation of the Hebrew) when seen in the perspective of a natural order and in the light of history's broad sweep. Since events move in ways not subject to human manipulation, man must simply accept injustice, suffering, and oppression as facts of life.

For two thousand years virtually everything about the Book of Ecclesiastes has been subject to dispute. From ancient rabbis to contemporary theologians and historians, scholars—and ordinary readers, for that matter—have puzzled over this fascinating and mysterious book.

Who wrote Ecclesiastes and when? No one knows for sure. The word Ecclesiastes, which means "the Convoker," is a Greek translation of the Hebrew "Koheleth," whom the text mentions several times as the author. Since the opening verse of the work refers to him as "son of David, king in Jerusalem," tradition regarded King Solomon (10th century B.C.), David's successor known for his wisdom, as Koheleth. One view had it that Solomon wrote Ecclesiastes in his old age—looking back on a life spent in search of power, knowledge, and pleasure, recognizing the futility of this.

Modern scholarship assumes a much later date for the book, but there is little agreement on details. Some argue that the Hebrew vocabulary betrays Persian influence, while others argue that the text is a translation of an Aramaic original. The book's philosophic stance may reflect the impact of Greek thought that penetrated the Near East in the wake of Alexander the Great's conquests in the 4th century B.C., though attempts to trace Aristotelian, Stoic, Cynic, or Epicurean themes in Ecclesiastes have not been entirely successful. Furthermore, there are those who claim that the philosophic concerns in the book are broadly human problems that crop up in many cultures, so that Greek influence is not definitely proven. The closest one can come to a scholarly consensus is to say that the book was written by the 3rd century B.C. by a Jew living in Jerusalem who was probably conversant with Greek modes of thought.

While the subject matter and point of view make Ecclesiastes seem a biblical oddity, it is actually part of a literary genre known as wisdom literature. This kind of writing was popular in the ancient Near East; many examples have survived from Egypt and Mesopotamia.

Wisdom literature tried to provide practical advice on how to live the good life.

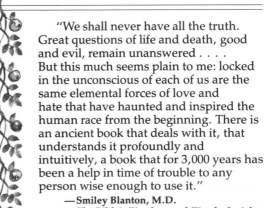

"We shall never have all the truth. Great questions of life and death, good and evil, remain unanswered . . . .
But this much seems plain to me: locked in the unconscious of each of us are the same elemental forces of love and hate that have haunted and inspired the human race from the beginning. There is an ancient book that deals with it, that understands it profoundly and intuitively, a book that for 3,000 years has been a help in time of trouble to any person wise enough to use it."
—**Smiley Blanton, M.D.**
The Bible's Timeless-and-Timely-Insights

Through polished aphorisms and clever parables, the authors treated the problems of human existence in a pragmatic way. This is why the Jewish wisdom literature that found its way into the Bible speaks to universal human concerns rather than to specifically Jewish issues.

The sanctity of Ecclesiastes, indeed its entry into the canon of sacred scripture, was by no means a foregone conclusion. Jewish sources mention conflict among the late-first-century rabbis over the book's status, and even after it was decided to include it in the Bible, some rabbis continued to argue for its exclusion, or at least the restriction of its circulation. The ascription of authorship to King Solomon could very well have been the crucial factor that secured the place of Ecclesiastes in the Bible.

Rabbinic opposition to Ecclesiastes rested primarily on two points. First, the book was riddled with blatant contradictions. Second, amid the welter of inconsistencies were opinions that could be interpreted as contrary to accepted theological beliefs. A look at some of the contradictions makes the problem clear:

Should one try to enjoy life? Ecclesiastes first answers negatively: "I said of pleasure, 'What use is it?' " (2:2). But then the author says, "I commend enjoyment" (8:15).

Which is preferable, life or death? First Ecclesiastes "thought the dead who are already dead more fortunate than the living who are still alive" (4:2), but later asserts, "a living dog is better than a dead lion" (9:4).

Is wisdom worth anything? "Wisdom excels folly as light excels darkness," we learn (2:13). But then we find the opposite: "what advantage has the wise man over the fool?" (6:8).

The author of Ecclesiastes could not make up his mind about women. He laments, "I found more bitter than death the woman whose heart is snares and nets" (7:26). And yet he advises man to "enjoy life with the wife whom you love" (9:9).

The theological ambiguities in the book are at times truly perplexing. For example:

Is everything God does good? On the one hand, "He has made everything beautiful in its time" (3:11). On the other hand we read, "who can make straight what he has made crooked?" (7:13).

What happens after death? Ecclesiastes first expresses agnosticism: "who knows whether the spirit of man goes upward?" (3:21). Yet elsewhere we are told that "the dust returns to the earth as it was, and the spirit returns to God who gave it" (12:7).

Are people rewarded and punished for their actions? Perhaps not: "there is a righteous man who perishes in his righteousness, and there is a wicked man who prolongs his life in his evil-doing" (7:15). But then we get a different view: "it will not be well with the wicked, neither will he prolong his days" (8:13).

There have been numerous efforts to make some sense out of the conflicting views found in Ecclesiastes. Throughout the ages, commentators have struggled to interpret the contradictory material in a way that is acceptable to orthodox religion, whether Jewish or Christian.

Scholars have suggested that perhaps Ecclesiastes is a composite work, parts of which were written by different people at different times. Another possibility is that Ecclesiastes, while written by one person, may portray a hypothetical dialogue representing two points of view, one that of a seeker and the other that of an instructor.

To this day traditional Jews hear the book of Ecclesiastes chanted publicly in the synagogue on the Feast of Tabernacles. This biblical holiday, which the liturgy calls "the season of our rejoicing," marks the fall harvest season, when the ancient Israelite enjoyed the produce he had worked for all year. Why read Ecclesiastes on this holiday? One rabbi explained that the book discusses joy, which is the theme of Tabernacles; another rabbi said, on the contrary, that Ecclesiastes proves the meaninglessness of joy, thus keeping the worshipper from getting carried away by the euphoria of the holiday. The meaning of this book, two millennia after its publication, remains an enigma. ✦

*"For everything there is a season . . . a time to be born, and a time to die;
a time to plant, and a time to pluck up what is planted."*

225

The beautifully sensuous Song of Songs is a rapturous celebration, expressed in nature metaphors, of human and divine love.

The nameless lovers of the Bible

The Song of Solomon

IN THE LATE FIRST CENTURY A.D., during a debate over whether to include the Song of Solomon within the biblical canon, one rabbi tried to settle the issue by asserting that all the rest of Scripture is holy, and the Song of Songs is the Holy of Holies. What he meant by this is unclear, but this short book of love poetry has fascinated and perplexed readers and exerted an enormous influence on Western culture.

The Song of Solomon is unlike any other part of the Bible. It has no mention of God's name, no theological or moral teachings, no words of prophecy, and not a hint of Jewish national consciousness. Read literally, the Song is about the love and physical passion between a man and a woman. Full of graphic imagery and arresting descriptions—though without vulgarity—the text presents love and sex from both the male and female perspectives, through the words of a young shepherd and a country girl.

Given the patriarchal nature of Israelite society in ancient times, the assertion of female sexuality in the Song of Solomon is quite startling. Indeed, the female character is so assertive that some have suggested that only a woman could have written the book. Right at the outset the girl declares: "O that you would kiss me with the kisses of your mouth! For your love is better than wine." She entices her lover:

> Awake, O north wind,
>   and come, O south wind!
> Blow upon my garden,
>   let its fragrance be wafted abroad.
> Let my beloved come to his garden,
>   and eat its choicest fruits!

The girl even describes making love:
> He brought me to the banqueting house,
>   and his banner over me was love. . . .
> O that his left hand were under my head,
>   and that his right hand embraced me!

The shepherd, for his part, extols his lover's beauty with a string of highly extravagant metaphors:

> How graceful are your feet in
>   sandals . . .
> Your rounded thighs are like jewels . . .
> Your navel is a rounded bowl . . .
> Your belly is a heap of wheat,
>   encircled with lilies.
> Your two breasts are like two fawns,
>   twins of a gazelle.
> Your neck is like an ivory tower . . .
> How fair and pleasant you are,
>   O loved one, delectable maiden!

Much of the charm of the Song of Solomon lies in the way that evocative descriptions of nature are woven into the romantic descriptions. In the following verses, for example, topographical, zoological, botanical, and seasonal images are used for their symbolic significance, as well as to invoke descriptions of the loved one:

> The voice of my beloved!
>   Behold, he comes,
> leaping upon the mountains,
>   bounding over the hills.
> My beloved is like a gazelle,
>   or a young stag. . . .
> My beloved speaks and says to me:
> "Arise, my love, my fair one,
>   and come away;
> for lo, the winter is past,
>   the rain is over and gone.
> The flowers appear on the earth,
>   the time of singing has come,
> and the voice of the turtledove
>   is heard in our land.
> The fig tree puts forth its figs,
>   and the vines are in blossom;
>   they give forth fragrance.
> Arise, my love, my fair one,
>   and come away. . . .
> Catch us the foxes,
>   the little foxes,
> that spoil the vineyards,
>   for our vineyards are in blossom."

The power and beauty of this poetry are undeniable. But what is its origin? What meaning is it meant to convey? Why is it in the Bible? There is considerable disagreement over these questions.

THE STORY BEHIND THE WORDS

ᕫ The Song of Songs ᕫ

Millions of people use a repertoire of apt and flavorful phrases in everyday speech without realizing that they are quoting directly from the Bible. The five books of Poetry and Wisdom (Job, Psalms, Proverbs, Ecclesiastes, and the Song of Songs) are especially rich in these vivid phrases: Survival is won by "the skin of my teeth" (Job 19:20). Wisdom is cited as coming "by the mouth of babes" (Psalms 8:2). A loved person is called the "apple of the eye" (Psalms 17:8) and a world of yearning is summed up in the phrase "his heart's desire" (Psalms 21:2).

But the Song of Songs (called, in the Latin Vulgate, the Canticle of Canticles) is perhaps the single most frequently quoted book in the Bible. Its inclusion in the biblical canon is due in large part to Rabbi Akiva, a father of rabbinic Judaism, who at the Council of Jabneh of 90 A.D., declared that "all the Writings are holy, but the Song of Songs is the Holy of Holies."

Some phrases of the Song have been especially inspirational. The verse "I am a rose of Sharon, a lily of the valleys" has come to be a poetic representation of the virtue of humility. Likewise, "for lo, the winter is past . . . the time of singing has come" might indicate the rejuvenation of the soul; "catch us the foxes," the importance of lowly things; and "I slept, but my heart was awake," the immortal life of the soul.

Countless works of art borrow directly from the language of the Song. The modern American composer Lukas Foss entitled his work for voice and orchestra *The Song of Songs*; both the Yiddish writer Shalom Aleichem and the English novelist Israel Zangwill gave love stories this same title. Finally, the "voice of the turtle" (King James Version, Song of Songs 2:12) is the voice of the turtledove: turtles have no voices.

The book opens with an ascription of authorship, "The Song of Songs, which is Solomon's" (1:1), and there are several other cryptic references to Solomon in later chapters. Since the book of 1 Kings 4:32 ascribes 1,005 songs to King Solomon, traditional commentators have assumed that the material in the Song is a selection of his work. Modern scholars, while noting some postbiblical word forms and possible borrowings from Persian and Greek, have come increasingly to accept the antiquity of the book, dating some of it to the period of the Judean monarchy—possibly to the age of King Solomon himself.

The lack of a central theme tying the Song of Solomon together, as well as the abrupt shifts within it between the male and female voices, have led to a number of hypotheses about the book's origin. According to one theory, the Song was intended as a dramatic composition in which the two lovers are the major actors, and minor characters, or a chorus, also have parts. Some have detected a second male figure in the book—perhaps King Solomon himself—who vies for the affection of the maiden.

Another view has it that the Song of Solomon was an ancient wedding song. Perhaps composed originally for the marriage of King Solomon to an Egyptian princess, the work caught on, and the name *Solomon* became an honorific title for all grooms on their wedding days.

The discovery of similar texts emanating from other ancient Near Eastern cultures has led to the suggestion that an early version of the Song of Solomon had a cultic function in pagan ritual, with the relationship of the two lovers describing the sexual union of a god and a goddess. Advocates of this theory argue that the Israelites made the Song their own after removing all overt signs of idolatry from it.

Twentieth-century psychoanalytic theory has also shed light on the Song of Solomon. Scholars have pointed out that the vivid but disjointed sexual images in the book bear a striking resemblance to the dream sequences that patients often recount to their analysts. What does not hang together according to conventional literary style, then, may make perfect sense as descriptions of reveries.

What the Song of Solomon meant to its authors and original audience, however, is of less importance than what it has come to represent for later generations. Both Jews and Christians looked beyond the plain meaning of the words and constructed allegorical interpretations of the book.

For some Jewish commentators, the story of the two lovers hinted at the relationship between the Jewish people and their God. Some commentators went so far as to interpret each verse as a reference to some event in this ongoing relationship, beginning with the biblical patriarchs and ending with the expected messianic age. Lest this appear to be farfetched, it should be noted that the biblical prophets made explicit use of the husband-wife bond as a metaphor for divine love.

Christianity also found allegorical meaning in the Song of Solomon. The two lovers in the Song of Solomon were interpreted to be Christ and the Church, or the individual believer. In the late Middle Ages certain Christian commentators forwarded the suggestion that Christ and the Virgin Mary were the man and woman of the Song.

Many commentators, then, use the Song of Solomon to draw explicit—indeed daring—analogies between divine and human love, and in this way illuminate both. Just as we get a hint of religious rapture when we experience mortal love—the love of another human being—so too, the physical love of a man and a woman contains within it intimations of holiness. ✦

"To love is to sing. The best songs, the most familiar songs, the songs we all love to sing are love songs. Love puts music in the heart, translates prose into poetry, and fills the mind with images and dreams and visions. That is why the world's great music and poetry and art are inspired by love."

—**Hugh Thomson Kerr**
The Interpreter's Bible

Inspired by Jewish legends, stories, and myths, the Russian-born artist Marc Chagall here renders a fanciful interpretation of the Song of Songs.

The riddle of love and death

Hidden meanings in the Song of Songs

NEAR THE END OF the Song of Solomon, the maiden pronounces: "love is strong as death."

How can love be compared with death? People have long recognized that love is a mysterious force and have even seen it as something that outlasts death. For example, the 17th-century English poet Thomas Carew wrote: "Nor shall my love die, when my body's dead." But the poet of the Song of Songs is more subtle when he compares love to death.

To understand this comparison, it is necessary to understand what death meant to the ancient Hebrews. The Hebrew view was not that love outlasts death. There was, in fact, no belief in an afterlife beyond the grave—a place where love might flourish. Rather, the deceased went to Sheol, the netherworld that was neither "heaven" nor "hell," but a land of darkness. It was a place where beings were reduced to weak and powerless shades dwelling in a world of silence. Nevertheless, the text compares love to death: "love is strong as death."

How can love be likened to the netherworld that awaits all mortals? The answer lies in the strange character of Sheol, which the ancient Israelites conceived not merely as the dreary destination of every life's journey, but in dynamic terms, as a power that pursues. But, one could in fact elude Sheol's grasp with God's help; in the end God alone was greater than death.

A compliment is paid to love when it is compared to death and the grave, or Sheol. The poet is saying that, alongside death, love is the most powerful force in human life. This celebration of the mysterious power of love serves as a climax to these poems, which often seemed impenetrably enigmatic to both ancient and modern readers.

The ancients—as far as one can go back in both Jewish and Christian traditions—interpreted the Song of Songs in a manner that contradicted its obvious meaning. "O that you would kiss me with the kisses of your mouth!" is the opening line of the poem. Taken at face value, it designates intimacy between a man and a woman. But, according to ancient interpreters, that is merely its surface meaning. Its deeper meaning refers to the love between the Lord and his chosen people. The Targum, an ancient Aramaic translation of the Hebrew Scriptures, understood the Song of Songs as a celebration of the marriage of God and Israel. The Christian Church taught that the Song was an allegory of Christ's relation to the Church.

So it happened that sexual love became a symbol of the spiritual love linking God and mankind. The idea was not a new one. The prophet Hosea, for instance, speaking of the covenant relationship between the Lord and Israel as a "marriage," had already explored the same theme. But the Song of Songs goes much further than any of the prophets in the audacity of the language it uses to describe love: "Its flashes are flashes of fire, a most vehement flame" (8:6).

Literally, the Hebrew text of this verse is describing love as "a flame of Yah," in other words, a flame of God. However, many English-language translations (including the Revised Standard Version) render the phrase, "a most vehement flame." The

*This **Yemenite bride** is dressed in the traditional finery of her people.*

"flame of Yah" can indeed be understood as a superlative ("most vehement"). But the literal rendering, relating the flame of love to Yahweh, to God, is not only valid but underscores the deepest mystery of human love—that it comes from God, who is the source of all love. Or, in the words of the Apostle John: "God is love" (1 John 4:8).

The average modern reader is often puzzled, with good reason, by the metaphors that are used in the work. The hair of the woman is compared to "a flock of goats, moving down the slopes of Gilead." Her neck is "like the tower of David, built for an arsenal, whereon hang a thousand bucklers, all of them shields of warriors." Her nose is "like a tower of Lebanon, overlooking Damascus." In our Western manner we immediately look for the point of the comparison, such as color or size. But these comparisons are not suitable in such descriptions. Color may be the point in the statement "your lips are like a scarlet thread," but other comparisons are not easy to decipher. The key to unlocking the comparisons may lie in the fact that they are more evocative than descriptive. They are intended to awaken pleasant sights and memories, such as a flock of goats streaming down the hillside, or the strength and impregnability of a tower. The extravagance and wealth of imagery of the Song are mystifying to us today.

The traditional understanding of the Song of Songs has had a glorious career in literature. The commentaries of Church Father Origen (second century A.D.), the *Sermons* of Bernard of Clairvaux, the poetry of the Spanish Carmelite mystic, John of the Cross, and many more reflect the traditional understanding of the Song—that God is love. This belief has enriched the human spirit through the centuries. ✦

PART IV

Prophecy

The Books of Isaiah, Jeremiah,
Lamentations, Ezekiel, Daniel, Hosea,
Joel, Amos, Obadiah, Jonah, Micah,
Nahum, Habakkuk, Zephaniah, Haggai,
Zechariah, and Malachi

*The prophets were the distinctive
conscience of Israel. Through their varied
voices, the mysterious power of God's
word touched the particular evils and
anguish of the people. Reckless wealth
and oppression met with the prophets'
scathing rebuke. But in the darkness of
defeat and exile, they ignited hope.*

Dreams, visions, and omens

In quest of the future

WHAT DOES THE FUTURE hold? The mystery of the future bears a perennial fascination. In the ancient world the future was almost universally believed to be the province of the divine. Only God or a supernatural being could know what lies ahead; a human being could only gain such knowledge by some sort of divine revelation or omen.

Practically every ancient society had its particular procedures—usually a wide variety—for discovering the will of its deities about coming events. Israel, like other nations, had a long history of gaining knowledge of the future through a variety of means. The distinctive religious traditions of Israel also, however, produced remarkable types of prophecy that set it apart.

The most common type of prophecy in the ancient world was through divination. The term "divination" refers to methods of discovering the direction of future events or a secret of the present either by manipulating objects or by interpreting phenomena. The diviner focused on something that is random and beyond human control and that thus might be used by divinity to give an omen. Sometimes the procedure was as simple as the casting of lots, but often it involved specialized techniques of interpretation. The location of planets and stars, the way arrows fall, the patterns of birds in flight, the shape and markings on the liver of a sacrificial animal, all might provide an omen to the one with the skill to interpret. For example, the prophet Ezekiel described the king of Babylon trying to make a decision: "he shakes the arrows, he consults the

Dreams as a form of prophecy

The prophet Daniel's ability to interpret dreams earned him a high place in the court of Nebuchadnezzar. Yet unlike the pagan sages and astrologers in the king's retinue, Daniel's skill came not from magic or wizardry, but from the Lord. The ancient Hebrews believed that, for a true prophet, dreams were a legitimate means of divine communication. An exile from Jerusalem, Daniel refused, under threat of death, to give up his religious heritage. The combination of his piety and visionary skill won him fame. Indeed, he foresaw the succession of empires—the Babylonian, Median, Persian, and Greek—culminating in the triumph of the kingdom of God. When Nebuchadnezzar dreamed of a huge tree reaching up to the heavens, and a voice telling him, "Let a beast's mind be given to him," Daniel predicted that Nebuchadnezzar would be deposed and eat grass like an ox until he recognized the glory of God.

Tenth-century Spanish illustration of Nebuchadnezzar's second dream.

teraphim, he looks at the liver." Armed with the proper omens, a person could then act so as to avoid impending evil.

The Torah in Israel banned the most commonly practiced forms of divination (Deuteronomy 18:10–12). Despite condemnation, however, divination did not disappear from Israel. Isaiah could describe the people as "full of diviners from the east and of soothsayers like the Philistines."

Besides consultation with God's prophets, the one officially sanctioned form of divination in early Israel was the use of the Urim and Thummim. These were small sacred objects of unknown form that could be cast as a lot to obtain a "yes or no" answer to an inquiry. They were carefully controlled, kept in the "breastpiece" of the high priest's sacred robe, or "ephod."

Joshua, for example, was to obtain guidance in leading the people by standing before the priest, "who shall inquire for him by the judgment of the Urim." Centuries later, King Saul used the Urim and Thummim to find the culprit who had brought a curse on the people. He unintentionally condemned his son. He prayed, "If this guilt is in me or in Jonathan my son, O LORD, God of Israel, give Urim; but if this guilt is in thy people Israel, give Thummim." When the response came up Urim, he added, "Cast the lot between me and my son Jonathan." The choice fell on Jonathan.

The Urim and Thummim evidently fell into disuse during later periods of the monarchy, but the belief in divine revelation through lots did not. A thousand years after Saul, in the time of the beginning of Christianity, for example, the casting of lots was used to make the important choice of an apostle to replace Judas Iscariot. By using the lots, the disciples wanted God to show which person he himself had chosen.

Dreams were almost universally believed to be potential divine communications in the ancient world. Throughout the Bible, dreams are repeatedly cited as a meth-

Nebuchadnezzar's insanity was foreseen by Daniel: "he was driven from among men."

od of divine revelation. Abraham learned the future of his descendants while asleep. The patriarch Jacob dreamed of a ladder reaching to heaven with the Lord speaking to him from its top (Genesis 28:16). His son Joseph was both a great dreamer and an interpreter of the dreams of others. King Solomon received the gift of wisdom from the Lord in a dream. In the New Testament, the Gospel of Matthew tells how Joseph was guided by dreams in the events surrounding Jesus' birth. The book of Acts also describes how the Apostle Paul was guided by night visions in crucial decisions.

Waking visions and ecstatic experiences of possession by the spirit were thought of as similar to dreams, though not so commonly experienced. They were sometimes brought on by the use of music and could transform the prophet "into another man." The prophet Joel looked forward to a time when God would make such gifts common: "I will pour out my spirit on all flesh; your sons and your daughters shall prophesy, your old men shall dream dreams, and your young men shall see visions."

It was in the context of the widespread practice of divination, of many claims to special dreams and visions and ecstasies that the role of the prophet developed in ancient Israel. The biblical texts make it clear that in many periods prophets were very numer-

ous in Israel. For example, in the time when Elijah functioned as a lone prophet, the text indicates that there were scores of other prophets of Yahweh, many of whom were killed by Queen Jezebel while a hundred were hidden in caves. Besides these there were hundreds of prophets of Baal and Asherah, whom Elijah confronted on Mount Carmel. Often the prophets who are mentioned with favor in the Bible (some of whom we are considering in more detail in other sections) appear to have been somewhat removed from society, exceptions in some ways to the common patterns of prophecy.

Many prophets sought to make their living as advisors at the royal court, ready to guide the king in making his plans, and often, according to the biblical texts, ready to say whatever the king wished to hear. The very nature of revelation through dreams, visions, or spirit possession may have made it difficult for an observer to distinguish true prophecy from false. Thus the biblical prophets cried out against their prophetic opponents. For example, in Jeremiah's words, God says, "I have heard what the prophets have said who prophesy lies in my name, saying, 'I have dreamed, I have dreamed!' . . . behold, I am against the prophets, says the LORD, who steal my words from one another. . . . who use their tongues and say, 'Says the LORD.'"

The conflict was real, and the power of the state was often ranged against the true prophets. In such a situation, it is important that the prophetic words that survived are usually not those of spokesmen for the royal court. The prophets whose words came to be treasured as Scripture were not simple foretellers of events, but were men who in God's name called their whole society into judgment for its injustices and faithlessness. They repeatedly sought to reform the religious practice and governmental policy of their nation. They drew on the long traditions of their people to point to hope beyond the dark days in which they lived. They were a few voices among many, but provided Israel's truest guidance for the mysterious future. ✦

Clay model of a sheep's liver inscribed in 55 sections with omens and magical formulae.

*The **ardor of conviction** tranformed Amos into a powerful speaker who prophesied to Amaziah.*

Fallen is Israel

Amos: Prophet of doom

NO ONE KNOWS exactly when or how, but in the hills around the town of Tekoa in the heart of the southern kingdom of Judah, an event occurred that led to one of the great movements of spirit in the history of humanity. The time was approximately the middle of the eighth century B.C., the location about ten miles south of Jerusalem. The event was neither public nor visible and probably went unnoticed by the people of Tekoa: the event occurred within a sheepherder named Amos.

Although he was a man with no notable education or religious background, Amos somehow came to the conviction that he had had an encounter with God. He knew that he was divinely commissioned to carry an urgent message of judgment and warning to the kingdom of Israel to the north.

"The LORD took me from following the flock, and the LORD said to me, 'Go, prophesy to my people Israel.' "

Amos was the first of those prophets that are known to us primarily through the records of their words, the oracles that they proclaimed, rather than the tradition of their deeds. The book of Amos introduces his prophecies by calling them "The words . . . which he saw concerning Israel."

Peasant though he was, the words of Amos reveal the great gifts that he possessed. Indeed, he did not approach his task as a professional prophet or a member of one of the prophetic guilds, but as an ordinary Israelite. His prophecies are expressed in Hebrew poetry that is both polished and powerful. It combines an immersion in the traditions of his people, a knowledge of the political and social situation of Israel, and a fire of indignation that makes it sparkle and burn. His poetry includes hymns and dirges, fragments of liturgy, and repeating litanies of sins.

When Amos advanced into the northern kingdom of Israel with his bleak message, he described the move as the Lord roaring from Zion, as though he were a fierce lion. But Israel had soothed itself with the song of harps, and had little use for this threatening word of God.

The king in Israel was Jeroboam II, who had already been reigning for more than thirty prosperous years. Though the pagan cult of Baal was by no means dead, the worship of Yahweh was apparently strong. Israel's military situation was secure as well. Jeroboam's father, Joash (Jehoash), had begun a period of expansion and had even reduced the southern kingdom of Judah to vassal status. During Jeroboam's long tenure the borders of Israel would be restored to the greatest extent they had ever achieved— from the heart of Lebanon to the Dead Sea. Trade flourished, and, as archaeological research has revealed, cities such as Samaria and Megiddo were rebuilt or repaired. A powerful sense of patriotism and national revival flowed in public life.

The religious establishment of Israel shared in the prosperity. At the ancient national sanctuary at Bethel a continuous round of sacrifices was performed. Feasts, solemn assemblies, and festivals punctuated the calendar. A plentiful flow of tithes and offerings expressed the devotion of the people (Amos 4:4–5; 5:21–23).

The good feelings of those times, however, masked the face of coming disaster for the northern kingdom. It was the unpleasant task of Amos to unveil the dark reality behind Israel's prosperity. Amos did not simply warn of coming political reversals, however; he probed into the touchy underside of Israel's social structure and punctured its pretense that all was well. As he spoke the word of Yahweh, he revealed a society built on profound injustice. He could and did point to the outrages committed by neighboring states, but his primary word was to Israel.

Its boasted prosperity belonged only to the apex of its social pyramid. He saw a society in which corruption had become entrenched. In the face of the thoughtless self-focused luxury of the rich, the message of Amos could be fierce indeed:

> Hear this word, you cows of Bashan,
>   who are in the mountain of Samaria,
> who oppress the poor, who crush the
>   needy . . . .
>   behold, the days are coming
>   upon you,
> when they shall take you away with
>   hooks, (Amos 4:1–2).

To Amos it was deeply ironic that in the midst of corruption and injustice, religion was so popular. Amos strongly affirmed Israel's unique covenant with God, but used it not to glorify the nation but to call it to responsibility for its actions. Thus he spoke this word of the Lord:

> You only have I known of all the
>   families of the earth;
> therefore I will punish you for all your
>   iniquities.

For the leaders of the northern kingdom, however, God was far more a comfort than a threat. Since they believed that their carefree affluence was a sign of the Lord's special favor toward them, they delighted to celebrate what they called the Day of Yahweh, or the Day of the Lord. They enjoyed the solemnities of the temple at Bethel and took pleasure in its sacrifices and hymns. Amos, however, warned them that the true "day of the LORD" would bring far blacker judgment, "darkness, and not light, and gloom with no brightness in it."

Without justice, ritual worship was not just irreverent, it was an abomination. Thus Amos spoke this word of Yahweh,

> I hate, I despise your feasts,
>   and I take no delight in your
>   solemn assemblies . . .
> But let justice roll down like waters,
>   and righteousness like an
>   ever-flowing stream.

The impact of Amos' message finally brought him into direct conflict with Amaziah, the chief priest at the royal sanctuary of Bethel. Amaziah accused Amos of treason against Jeroboam for predicting the king's death and Israel's exile. Thus, Amaziah insisted that Amos leave, go back to Judah, and "eat bread there, and prophesy there; but never again prophesy at Bethel, for it is the king's sanctuary, and it is a temple of the kingdom" (Amos 7:12–13).

Since the tide of Israel's prosperity was still high, one may well imagine that Amaziah and Jeroboam believed Amos was nothing more than a misguided voice of ill omen. It was only later generations who read the words of Amos and perceived that he had seen the situation of Israel more clearly than its leaders. They recognized the greatness of this man: they recognized that in this sheepherder from Tekoa was a truly prophetic voice. ✦

The curious life of the Prophet Hosea

A message of redeeming love

Hosea and the harlot Gomer *are depicted in this miniature from a medieval Bible.*

T HE LORD SAID TO HOSEA, " 'Go, take to yourself a wife of harlotry and have children of harlotry, for the land commits great harlotry by forsaking the LORD' " (Hosea 1:2).

What an extraordinary demand for God to lay upon his prophet! That he should make his personal family life a living parable, or rather a drama, of the faithlessness and pain and love and despair and hope of God's relationship with his people. The demand is so remarkable that to this day serious readers of the Book of Hosea are sometimes at a loss to decide whether to understand it literally or metaphorically.

Since Hosea mentions his wife and children quite specifically at points, however, many scholars have concluded that in spite of the difficulties, it is best to consider that the marriage was real. It constituted a symbolic prophetic action that encapsulated the prophet's mission and message with a force that words could not match.

In about the year 746 B.C., while Jeroboam II was still on the throne, Hosea married a woman named Gomer. She is described as "a wife of harlotry," but that phrase does not necessarily mean that she was a prostitute. More likely the description indicates that she participated in the popular fertility rituals that were so widespread in Israel. These regularly involved the sexual intercourse of temple priests, priestesses, and sacred prostitutes of both sexes. The belief was that these "rites" helped to assure fertility and growth of livestock and crops.

Thus Gomer was not necessarily a woman of exceptional immorality; rather she was apparently typical of the morality of Israel as a whole. By marrying her, however, Hosea was plunged into the heart of the idolatry and faithlessness to Yahweh that was to be the focus of his prophetic mission.

Three children of the marriage are mentioned, each of whom received a symbolic name. The firstborn was a son, who was given the name *Jezreel*. It was at Jezreel that Jehu, the ancestor of King Jeroboam II, had assassinated the former king, Joram, carried out a series of purges, and usurped the throne. Now, the Lord told Hosea, the blood of Jezreel was about to be avenged.

The other two children were given names that referred to the relationship between God and Israel. A daughter was given the name *Lo-ruhamah* meaning "Not pitied," for, God said, "I will no more have pity on the house of Israel." The youngest, a son, was called *Lo-ammi* meaning "Not my people," again because God said, "you are not my people and I am not your God."

It appears that the intense strains of the marriage led Hosea to leave Gomer, and she returned to her life of "harlotry" in the worship of Baal. The story was not left there, however. The Lord commanded Hosea to attempt to restore the love between himself and his faithless wife, " 'even as the LORD loves the people of Israel, though they turn to other gods' " (Hosea 3:1). By this time Gomer had apparently sunk to a condition of slavery, and Hosea had to purchase her for 15 shekels of silver and a few bushels of barley. Still, he completed the living drama and ultimately restored to love and acceptance the wife who had earlier been faithless and degraded.

Although there is much about the marriage between Hosea and Gomer that will remain mysterious, it is clear that its wrenching emotions provided much of the language by which Hosea expressed his prophetic message to Israel.

For unlike Amos, Hosea was a native of the northern kingdom. He was the only "writing prophet" that the kingdom of Israel produced. His ministry saw the last moments of Israel's heyday under Jeroboam II, but most of it was spent in the painful years of disintegration under pressure from the expanding power of Assyria.

Rather than seeking unity against an external threat, the upper classes were filled with conspiracy and plotting. Thus Hosea pronounced the word of Yahweh against the princes of Israel:

> All their kings have fallen;
> and none of them calls upon me.
> (Hosea 7:7)

The threat of Assyria was real and ultimately inexorable. Tiglath-pileser III had restored Assyria's former imperial power by pushing south to capture Babylon before he began a drive toward Egypt. After Menahem (745-737 B.C.), who survived by paying a massive tribute to Assyria in return for support for his rule, the rulers of Israel repeatedly refused to reconcile themselves to Assyrian domination. They hoped to get support from Egypt to break free of their vassalage. Their efforts were ultimately suicidal and brought on a full-scale attack and destruction by Tiglath-pileser's successor, Shalmaneser V. The next Assyrian king, Sargon II, recorded in his annals that he led 27,290 Israelites into exile.

It was this bleak future that Hosea so piercingly foresaw:

> The days of punishment have come . . .
> Israel shall know it.   (Hosea 9:7)

But for the prophet the coming events were not just the interplay of military and economic powers; they were the punishment and discipline of God. The life of the people had to be seen as a single tapestry with no distinction between sacred and secular, no split between politics and religion. The sufferings of the coming days were intimately interwoven with the injustice and faithlessness of the years that preceded them.

However, there is hope. It is not an easy hope, but one beyond the fires of destruction. Israel will endure a long period of disintegration and loss but ultimately will "return and seek the LORD their God" (Hosea 3:5). Then God will be like a tender lover to Israel.

> behold, I will allure her,
> and bring her into the wilderness,
> and speak tenderly to her.

The mystery of God's love surpassed even the fire of his wrath. ✦

The apocalyptic vision of Isaiah

A cry of warning

THE YEAR—742 B.C. The place—the Temple in Jerusalem. Isaiah has a vision: God is surrounded by seraphim, "And one called another and said, 'Holy, holy, holy is the LORD of hosts; the whole world is full of his glory'."

Awestruck, Isaiah senses his own inadequacy, "for," he explains, "I am a man of unclean lips, and I dwell in the midst of a people of unclean lips." A seraphim cures Isaiah's impurity with the touch of a live coal on his mouth. God then assigns him to preach a message of doom to the people of Judah, "until cities lie waste without inhabitant, and houses without men, and the land is utterly desolate." But God gives him some hope, for even if just a tenth of the people survive, they may form the basis of a national renaissance (Isaiah 6:4–13).

The contents of the Book of Isaiah bear out the dual nature of God's call. Many of the prophecies in the first 39 chapters warn that destruction is the inevitable consequence of sin. Yet interspersed with these forebodings are promises of happier days when a purified Jewish people will lead all mankind toward a better world.

Beginning with chapter 40, the tone of the book shifts. Gone are the rebukes and denunciations. Instead, consolation is the keynote, almost as if God, having punished his people beyond their just deserts, wishes to make amends: "Comfort, comfort my people, says your God" (Isaiah 40:1).

While the contrast between the two halves of the Book of Isaiah has long been evident, only in modern times did scholars infer that the prophecies of two—perhaps three—different people living at different times are collected in this book.

There is now general agreement that Isaiah's first 39 chapters reflect conditions in Judah in the eighth–seventh century B.C., while the rest of the book, with its emphasis on national rejuvenation, emerged out of the experience of the exiled Jews in Babylonia two centuries later. Indeed, in 45:1 there is even a direct reference to the Persian King Cyrus as the man who would overthrow the Babylonian forces and would allow the Jews to return to their homeland. Scholars refer to the unknown author of these later prophecies as Deutero-Isaiah or Second Isaiah. Many authorities also believe that the last 11 chapters were composed many years later by yet a third "Isaiah," perhaps one of the returnees to Judah under Persian rule.

Whatever its literary origins, there is no doubt that the Book of Isaiah has exerted an extraordinary impact down through the ages. Both its hard-hitting teachings about politics and society and its inspiring message of a better world to come continue to influence the lives of millions of people today.

The first—pre-exile—Isaiah was a royal advisor whose unconventional counsel was sometimes heeded and sometimes ignored. The mighty Assyrian Empire dominated the Near East in the eighth century B.C. Judean

The prophet *Isaiah shocked the Temple establishment.*

kings moved into and out of alliances, both with Assyria and later, in the hope of ultimately escaping from Assyrian control, with their counterparts in the other small states of the area.

Isaiah opposed such a foreign policy. Instead, he advocated the avoidance of entangling alliances, which might enhance the idolatrous influences of temporary allies and, perhaps, provoke Assyrian wrath. Isaiah felt such alliances showed a lack of faith in God's plan.

Isaiah's disdain for an activist foreign policy went hand in hand with a passionate concern for the internal condition of the Judean community. In his day, the rich and wellborn did not want to share their prosperity with other parts of the society.

Isaiah's critique of the situation was devastating. Jerusalem, he says, formerly "the faithful city," is now "a harlot." "Your princes are rebels and companions of thieves. Every one loves a bribe and runs after gifts. They do not defend the fatherless, and the widow's cause does not come to them" (Isaiah 1:21–23). Not stopping at generalities, Isaiah makes specific accusations in God's name: "The spoil of the poor is in your houses. What do you mean by crushing my people, by grinding the face of the poor?" (Isaiah 3:14–15).

What must have shocked Isaiah's listeners most was his slashing denunciation of hypocrites who meticulously observe religious ritual—especially the Temple sacrifices—while neglecting their responsibilities for their fellow human beings.

"If a man is converted and leaves self and enters into God's will, even the good that he did in self will be freed from the evil that he has done, for Isaiah said: Though your sins be blood-red, if you turn and repent, they shall be snow-white as wool (Isaiah 1:18). The evil will be swallowed in the wrath of God and the good will go forth like a plant out of the wild earth."
—**Jacob Boehme,**
On True Resignation

What to me is the multitude of your
  sacrifices?
  says the LORD.
I have had enough of burnt offerings
  of rams
  and the fat of fed beasts;
I do not delight in the blood of bulls,
  or of lambs, or of he-goats . . . .
When you spread forth your hands,
  I will hide my eyes from you;
even though you make many prayers,
  I will not listen;
  your hands are full of blood . . . .
  learn to do good;
seek justice,
  correct oppression;
defend the fatherless,
  plead for the widow.

Just as Isaiah's insistence that God demands social justice has profoundly influenced the Western monotheistic religions and, through them, much of modern culture, so too has his expectation that there will come a day when oppression and suffering will cease, and a messianic world of peace and harmony will emerge.

Isaiah declares that in the end of days all nations will accept the rule of the one God and give up violence. "They shall beat their swords into plowshares, and their spears into pruning hooks; nation shall not lift up sword against nation, neither shall they learn war any more" (Isaiah 2:4).

The prophet envisions a great leader who is both holy and wise, and will remedy the social evils we experience. "He shall judge the poor, and decide with equity for the meek of the earth" (Isaiah 11:4). Indeed, nature itself will be transformed, eliminating all conflict and suffering such that: "The wolf shall dwell with the lamb, and the leopard shall lie down with the kid. . . . They shall not hurt or destroy in all my holy mountain; for earth shall be full of the knowledge of the LORD as the waters cover the sea" (Isaiah 11:6.9).

While Isaiah's prophecies provide hope for the future, there are passages in the book that have been the subject of extensive theological inquiry. For Christians, the fol-

The call of Isaiah *in the setting of the Jerusalem Temple: "Above him stood the seraphim; each had six wings."*

lowing text foretells the birth and career of Jesus, but for Jews it may refer either to the Judean king Hezekiah, or else to a Messiah yet to appear:

> For to us a child is born,
>   to us a son is given;
> and the government will be upon
>   his shoulder . . . .
> Of the increase of his government
>   and of peace
>   there will be no end,
> upon the throne of David, and over
>   his kingdom,
>   to establish it, and to uphold it
> with justice and righteousness.

Several of the prophecies in Deutero-Isaiah speak of a "suffering servant" (in chapters 50, 52, and 53) who undergoes excruciating hardships in order to save others from sin. Once again, in Christian eyes, this is Jesus, who will suffer on the cross to atone for all mankind. Jewish commentators, however, usually identify the servant either as a metaphor for the Jewish people, or as an individual such as the prophet himself. Yet the penultimate verse in this book predicts the resolution of all divisions: "From new moon to new moon, and from sabbath to sabbath, all flesh shall come to worship before me, says the LORD." ✦

Jeremiah: Prophet of retribution

The burden of wisdom

FOR JEREMIAH THE CALL to be a prophet was a call from the first moment of his existence. There never was a time, as he viewed his life, when he was not under obligation to God's commission. The responsibility was both a privilege and a torment throughout his life. He introduces himself by saying, "Now the word of the LORD came to me saying, 'Before I formed you in the womb I knew you, and before you were born I consecrated you; I appointed you a prophet to the nations.' Then I said, 'Ah Lord GOD! Behold, I do not know how to speak, for I am only a youth.' "

The book of Jeremiah presents to us a vivid personality, visible in both his external actions and interior struggles. The book is a long and rather formless anthology of oracles from Jeremiah, memoirs, most likely from his faithful and well-educated disciple Baruch, and passages added by other editors and writers. The first half of this book is composed primarily of Jeremiah's prophecies, most written in passionate and often lyrical poetry. Most of the second half consists of biographical narratives that often overlap with the first half and show the repeated rejection of Jeremiah's words. The final chapters are a collection of oracles concerning nations outside Israel, with a concluding chapter on the fall of Jerusalem.

It was Jeremiah's lot to be caught between God and his people in a time of crisis and tragedy. He lived from the hopeful times of the reforms of Josiah through the tyranny of Jehoiakim and the pain of the first deportation under Jehoiachin to the suicidal nationalism that burned during Zedekiah's years and brought an end to the Davidic kingdom of Judah.

Jeremiah lived in jeopardy. He was never in a position of security, was often viewed as a traitor, and was a cause of conflict and discomfort to those in power. At the same time he was a man of tenderness toward the people of his nation. He felt their suffering and despair as his own agony. In himself he fought against his own prophetic vision because in it he saw the coming darkness of national destruction.

Very little detail is known of the early years of Jeremiah's work, which began about 626 B.C., but major events occurred in 609 that caused him to step forward as a public and controversial voice. King Josiah had taken advantage of the weakness of Assyria in the face of rising Babylonian power and had reasserted the independence of Judah. But when, in 609, Josiah tried to block Egypt's army from aiding Assyria against Babylon, he was killed in battle, and his son Jehoahaz became king. After three months, Egypt's Pharaoh Neco II stepped in, deposed Jehoahaz, and placed his brother Jehoiakim as a puppet on the throne. Jehoiakim imposed heavy taxes not only to pay tribute but also to support his own self-indulgent opulence. Worse, he supported the return of the pagan practices that his father had banned. He and many of the people were confident that, because God's Temple would provide protection, Judah was safe from Babylonian threats.

Into this scene stepped Jeremiah. He took his stand in the court of the Temple and denounced the false trust in the inviolability of the sanctuary that was being used to mask growing injustice and idolatry. Jeremiah predicted that unless there was repentance and change, the Temple would be destroyed as completely as the old ruined shrine at Shiloh had been; and the people would be forsaken by their God.

The reaction to such treasonous statements was swift and violent, especially from the Temple priests and their supporting prophets: "And when Jeremiah had finished speaking . . . , then the priests and the prophets and all the people laid hold of him, saying, 'You shall die!' " (Jeremiah 26:8). Jeremiah was brought to trial on capital charges because he had "prophesied against this city." But because he received some support from royal officials who opposed the priests and prophets, he was spared an early death.

It was not long before the Egyptian umbrella had fallen to the Babylonians in the battle of Carchemish in 605, and Jehoiakim found himself a Babylonian vassal. It was then that Jeremiah was commissioned by God to commit to writing all the oracles he had pronounced in the years of his work. As Jeremiah dictated, Baruch wrote these on a single scroll. The prophet himself had now been banned from entering the Temple, so he sent Baruch there to read to the people the scroll with its warnings against

Furious at the prophecies of Jeremiah, the *king cuts them from the scroll and burns them.*

nationalist dreams and its call for repentance. As before, the dark words of the prophet sent a shiver of fear through his hearers. Sympathetic officials warned Baruch that he and his troublesome master should go into hiding.

The scroll of Jeremiah's words was confiscated and taken to Jehoiakim's winter palace to be read before the king. But Jehoiakim had nothing but contempt for the prophet. As one of his men read a few columns from the scroll, Jehoiakim "would cut them off with a penknife and throw them into the fire in the brazier." The fire could not destroy the message, however; Jeremiah dictated a new scroll to Baruch and added many new prophecies. That scroll probably formed the core of the first half of his book of prophecies.

During the final years of the kingdom of Judah, Jeremiah was often considered an outlaw, an enemy of the state. It was a time of personal pain and sometimes self-doubt. "I have become a laughingstock all the day; every one mocks me. For whenever I speak, I cry out, I shout 'Violence and destruction!' For the word of the LORD has become for me a reproach and a derision all day long. If I say, 'I will not mention him, or speak any more in his name,' there is in my heart as it were a burning fire shut up in my bones, and I am weary with holding it in, and I cannot. For I hear many whispering. Terror is on every side! 'Denounce him! Let us denounce him!' say all my familiar friends, watching for my fall" (Jeremiah 20:7–10). Furthermore, the many prophets and priests who supported the king's hopeful vision of Judean independence from Babylon were Jeremiah's continual opponents. "They have healed the wound of my people lightly," he charged, "saying 'Peace, peace,' when there is no peace" (Jeremiah 8:11).

"The prophet of God is always a disturber of worldly peace. He comes to give a peace, but 'not as the world giveth' (John 14:27)."
—**Ralph W. Sockman,**
The Interpreter's Bible

Even after 597, when Nebuchadnezzar had swept through, plundered the Temple, and carried away into exile the new young king, Jehoiachin, and with him much of the nobility, there were prophets who were ready to predict that this was only a momentary setback of nationalist hopes.

Jeremiah fashioned a wooden yoke that he wore in public. Along with the symbolic yoke went God's pronouncement that he had granted world rule to Nebuchadnezzar; moreover, the people of Judah and their new king, Zedekiah, should bring their necks under his yoke—only then would they live.

That was emphatically not what people wanted to hear. A prophet named Hananiah brought forward a counter-prophecy that God had "broken the yoke of the king of Babylon" and would bring back the exiles and the plundered Temple treasure "within two years" (Jeremiah 28:2–3). With his own dramatic symbolism Hananiah took the yoke bars from Jeremiah's neck and broke them. Jeremiah's personal response to this prediction was "Amen! May the LORD do so." But he soon returned with the prophecy that on the contrary God had replaced the wooden yoke with a yoke of iron. This time of trial was to be no mere two-year ripple in the flow of Israel's history. Jeremiah, more realistically, predicted seventy years—a lifetime—of exile in Babylon.

Under the weak Zedekiah, Judah's leaders tried again to play Egypt off against Babylon and ended by bringing Jerusalem under a final devastating Babylonian siege. In that setting, Jeremiah's words seemed intolerably subversive to Jerusalem's petty princes. The prophet was arrested, cast into a muddy cistern, and left to die. Though he was rescued by an Ethiopian servant of the king, there was by this time no avoiding the tragic end of the kingdom. "My grief is beyond healing," Jeremiah wept. "The harvest is past, the summer is ended, and we are not saved. . . .O that my head were waters, and my eyes a fountain of tears, that I might weep day and night for the slain of the daughter of my people!" ✦

Rembrandt's father was the model for this oil of Jeremiah mourning the ruin of Jerusalem. Jeremiah, often identified as the pessimistic prophet of doom, foresaw the terrible years of the fall of Jerusalem, the destruction of the Temple, and the exile of the Jews. He lived out his days in Egypt, along with the "remnant of Judah." The Book of Lamentations, containing dirges for the dead city, has traditionally been ascribed to him.

Astarte and Ishtar

MAJOR THEME recurring throughout the Old Testament and especially in the Prophets is the admonition and punishment of the Israelites for worshiping false gods. The Ten Commandments warn against this, stating "I am the LORD your God . . . You shall have no other gods before me. You shall not make for yourself a graven image" (Exodus 20:2–4).

There are numerous biblical references to warnings about the worship of the gods of the Canaanites, Babylonians, and Assyrians. Canaanite religion contained a pantheon of gods and goddesses who continued to be worshiped throughout biblical times; chief among the goddesses was Astarte, or Ashtoreth. She is known from Ugaritic and ancient Egyptian texts recounting the epic deeds of Baal and his cohorts. Scholars believe that the Canaanite Astarte is identical to the ancient Assyrian and Babylonian goddess Ishtar. In ancient texts and art, Astarte and Ishtar are identified, and have as their symbols the planet Venus.

Astarte is closely associated with Baal, Baal's sister and consort, Anath, and his mother, Asherah. Within the Canaanite mythology, Baal and the three female goddesses were the centerpieces of a fertility cult. The goddesses appear variously as sexual cult objects, as sacred courtesans, or as the mother goddess, depicted as a nude pregnant woman. Figurines of this sort have been found by archaeologists excavating Canaanite sites.

Ishtar is known from various Babylonian and Assyrian texts, inscriptions, hymns, and artifacts. Like Astarte, she was worshiped as the goddess of fertility, and had as her symbol Venus, the evening star. In one Assyrian hymn, Ishtar is quoted as saying, "Ishtar, the goddess of the morning, and Ishtar, the goddess of the evening, am I."

Temples were built to Ishtar in all the major cities of Babylonia and Assyria. Slaves were often dedicated to her temples, and ancient kings frequently offered her gifts. Sargon is known to have presented her with cedar and cypress wood, and Nebuchadnezzar gave her offerings of animals, birds, fish, and wine. Although child sacrifice has been associated with the cult of Astarte, there is no evidence to suggest that this terrible custom was practiced among Ishtar's devotees.

The goddess Ishtar, Old Babylonian period, early 2nd millennium.

A fertility goddess, Ishtar was also thought to bestow life, health, and innumerable other blessings upon mankind. On account of this belief, she was frequently beseeched in prayers. Ashurbanipal prayed to her for long life, as did Nebuchadnezzar. In fact, Ashurbanipal's library was found to contain a number of prayers and psalms dedicated to the goddess. In one, the poet writes: "Her song is sweeter than honey and wine, sweeter than sprouts and herbs, superior indeed to pure cream."

Despite the prohibition against the worship of false gods, and the prophets' constantly inveighing against idolatry, a cult to Ishtar was thought to have flourished in Israel during the time of the prophet Jeremiah. The cult was especially popular among women, who possessed very little status in the formal worship of Yahweh. Jeremiah speaks out against those who "make cakes for the queen of heaven." These cakes were thought to have been shaped in the goddess' image, or perhaps in the shape of her symbol, the evening star Venus.

Ezekiel's vision of four wheels *bearing the faces of a man, a lion, an ox, and an eagle.*

Prophet or madman?

Ezekiel's frightening visions

SOME 20TH-CENTURY WRITERS, perhaps influenced by modern theories of psychology, have not been kind to the prophet Ezekiel. They tend to attribute his strange visions and erratic activities to personality disorders or medical problems. Among their diagnoses are paranoid schizophrenia, including delusions of grandeur and persecution, and cataleptic fits.

According to religious tradition, however, Ezekiel was a holy man whose revelations penetrated mysteries of the cosmos. Thus, the very grotesqueness of his visions testify to extraordinary prophetic gifts. Ezekiel's uniqueness as a prophet will strike the reader at the very outset of the book, which describes his consecration as a prophet. Standing by a canal in Babylonia, Ezekiel sensed "the hand of the LORD" upon him and saw "a great cloud, with brightness round it, and fire flashing forth continually, and in the midst of the fire, as it were gleaming bronze" (1:3–4).

Then there appeared to him four creatures, each of which had four faces and four wings. There were hands under the wings, and, of the four faces, one was human, another that of a lion, the third that of an ox, and the fourth that of an eagle. Hovering above these strange forms was "the appearance of the likeness of the glory of the LORD" (1:28). Since the meaning of Ezekiel's vision is unintelligible in any literal sense, it has formed the basis for mystical speculation for centuries, with each textual detail interpreted symbolically.

Ezekiel's career and teachings are rooted in the historical context in which he lived. Since he gives specific dates for many of his prophecies, it is not difficult to trace the general connection between his career and the events of his time.

In 605 B.C. Nebuchadnezzar ascended to the throne of Babylonia and eventually established control over much of the Near East. In 597 B.C. the Babylonians took Jeru-

247

salem after a long siege and deported the king and much of the aristocracy. Ezekiel, a learned member of a priestly family, was presumably among those exiled to Babylonia. Both the plain sense of the biblical text and the weight of current scholarly opinion hold that Ezekiel did not begin to prophesy until his arrival in Babylonia. His career, then, was probably confined entirely to the conditions of exile.

The first half of the Book of Ezekiel consists of pessimistic prophecies warning that the remnant still living in Judah would soon be overwhelmed and captured. Ezekiel sought to counter the assumptions of many, in the homeland and in Babylonia, that there would be a quick restoration of Judean sovereignty. And he was right: the Judean revolt against Nebuchadnezzar brought not victory but utter calamity. In 587 B.C. the Babylonian forces captured Jerusalem, destroyed the Temple, and exiled many of the residents. The Kingdom of Judah had come to an end.

The rest of the Book of Ezekiel contains post-destruction prophecies of a more optimistic sort. Despite the sins that led to this catastrophe, the prophet taught, the Jews would be restored to their homeland, and the nations guilty of aiding in their downfall punished. The last several chapters of the book relate utopian visions of a regenerated Jewish people living an idyllic spiritual life in a united kingdom blessed by the presence of a new Temple in Jerusalem.

The Book of Ezekiel also contains visionary descriptions of events happening hundreds of miles from Babylonia, which may actually have taken place only in the prophet's imagination. He relates being transported to the Jerusalem Temple, where he sees unspeakable abominations: 70 Jewish elders burn incense before pictures of "all kinds of creeping things, and loathsome beasts, and all the idols of the house of Israel," women believe in the Babylonian god Tammuz, and men worship the sun. To Ezekiel all of this indicates the utter depravity of the Judeans and presages their

imminent downfall, though other biblical accounts of this time do not record these activities. In all likelihood, Ezekiel, who was probably far away from the events he describes, was speaking about his own internal reality, rather than the actual Jerusalem.

One of Ezekiel's most important theological explanations was his challenge to the concept of inherited guilt. In his day, the exiled Jews, seeking an explanation for their bad fortune, commonly asserted that they were being punished for the accumulated sins of past generations. Ezekiel denied this: "the soul that sins shall die" (18:4). Similarly, the sinning child of righteous forebears will not be protected from punishment by the good deeds of ancestors. The prophet applied the same formula to the stages of an individual's life. A wicked person who repents has his early sins forgiven, while a good person who turns evil gets no benefit from the good deeds of his youth. Ezekiel, then, is a great prophet of repentance.

Ezekiel advanced the doctrine of individual responsibility in the development of Judaism. "If a man is righteous and does what is lawful and right . . . does not defile his neighbor's wife or approach a woman in her time of impurity, does not oppress any one, but restores to the debtor his pledge, commits no robbery, gives his bread to the hungry and covers the naked with a garment, does not lend at interest or take any increase . . . . he is righteous, he shall surely live, says the Lord GOD."

With the end of Judean sovereignty on its own land and the reality of life in exile, the idea that all members of the nation, past and present, bear a corporate responsibility for the fate of the group lost much of its meaning. Ezekiel's stress on reward and punishment on an individual basis helped shape a relevant theology for Jews living as isolated minorities in non-Jewish lands.

Among his prophecies of consolation, Ezekiel's vision of the dry bones is surely the best known. Doubtless responding to the lament of the exiled Jews that national revival is impossible—Ezekiel described himself set down in a valley full of dry

The eerie vision of the valley of dry bones: "can these bones live?"

bones. He prophesied in response to God's command: "Thus says the Lord GOD to these bones: Behold, I will cause breath to enter you, and you shall live. And I will lay sinews upon you, and will cause flesh to come upon you, and cover you with skin, put breath in you, and you shall live" (37:5–6). The prophet's message was explicit: the bones were the exiled Jews. "And I will put my spirit within you, and you shall live, and I will place you in your own land." This vivid evocation of life's triumph over death has helped generations of Jews keep faith in the ultimate regeneration of their people.

In another vision, the prophet foretold that there would come a time when the Jews, restored to their land, would be invaded from the north by a plundering army led by "Gog of the land of Magog" (38:2). After a time, however, God himself would appear in all his awesome glory and rout Gog's forces: "So I will show my greatness and my holiness," says God.

Was the man who produced such extraordinary descriptions a religious genius or an unbalanced fanatic? To a great extent the answer depends on the reader's assumptions about the reality or illusion of a world of the spirit apart from our world of the everyday. ✦

Jonah being brought up by the whale.

The reluctant prophet

Jonah's flight from the Lord

THE BOOK OF JONAH, consisting of four brief chapters that total just 48 verses, is one of the shortest books of the Bible. Nevertheless, its influence has been far out of proportion to its size because the deceptively simple story raises timeless literary and theological questions.

Although Jonah is included among the 12 so-called Minor Prophets in the Hebrew Bible, the book is unique. First, whereas the other prophetic works are anthologies of prophecies with only minimal admixtures of narrative, Jonah is a story about a prophet, containing only one line of actual prophecy. Second, while other Hebrew prophets on occasion utter oracles concerning Gentile nations, Jonah is the only one whose entire mission is directed to non-Israelites; there is no mention of Israel in the book. In this respect Jonah bears less resemblance to bib-

lical prophecy than it does to the wisdom books, which also tend to deal with issues of universal concern, outside the strictly Israelite context.

"Arise, go at once to Nineveh, that great city," God tells Jonah, son of Amittai, "and cry against it; for their wickedness has come up before me." Nineveh was the capital of the Assyrian Empire, the great power in the eighth century B.C. To the Israelites, Nineveh was a byword for evil. Famous for their ruthless cruelty in war, the Assyrians would, in 722 B.C., conquer Jonah's own homeland—the Kingdom of Israel—and exile its inhabitants. But Jonah refused to heed God's command; rather than prophesy to Nineveh, he ran away. Jonah boarded a ship at the port city of Joppa, and headed out into the Mediterranean, "away from the service of the LORD."

250

But one cannot escape from a God who rules the entire world. "The LORD hurled a great wind upon the sea, and there was a mighty tempest on the sea, so that the ship threatened to break up." After prayers to the gods worshiped by the ship's crew failed to calm the storm, it was decided that some sinner on board was responsible for the calamity. When a drawing of lots identified Jonah as the culprit, he explained that he was fleeing from the God of heaven and earth, and that the only way to stop the storm was to throw him overboard. The sailors reluctantly did so, and "the sea ceased from its raging." So awed were the sailors that they "offered sacrifice to the LORD and made vows."

Meanwhile, God sent "a great fish" to swallow Jonah, "and Jonah was in the belly of the fish three days and three nights." From inside the fish, Jonah uttered a prayer to God—a prayer that has puzzled countless generations. Instead of repenting his refusal to obey God's command, instead of begging for forgiveness and deliverance, he praises God for having saved him: "For thou didst cast me into the deep, into the heart of the seas, and the flood was around about me; all thy waves and thy billows passed over me. . . . Yet thou didst bring up my life from the Pit, O LORD my God."

Many modern critical scholars explain the difficulty by theorizing that the prayer originated independently and was later inserted into the text despite its incongruity. Traditional commentators, however, cite other biblical examples of prophets in prayer whose faith enables them to envision salvation even before it happens, and suggest that this may be the case with Jonah as well. If so, there is no need to assume any interpolation into the original text.

However we understand Jonah's prayer, God answers it. The fish cast him onto dry land, a long walk from Nineveh. God repeated his command to prophesy to the city, and this time Jonah follows orders. Arriving at Nineveh, he announced God's message—the only words of actual prophe-

cy in the book—"Yet forty days and Nineveh shall be overthrown!" (Jonah 3:4)

Almost unbelievably to the reader, if not to Jonah, these words had an immediate and drastic impact on the Ninevites. "They proclaimed a fast, and put on sackcloth from the greatest of them to the least of them." The king "sat in ashes" and broadened the scope of the public fast to include even the animals. "Let every one turn from his evil way and from the violence which is in his hands," ordered the king. "Who knows, God may yet repent and turn from his fierce anger, so that we perish not."

Even though the Ninevites did not renounce idol worship, their repentance had the desired effect: "God repented of the evil which he had said he would do to them, and did not do it." The salvation of Nineveh put Jonah into a state of despair. He prayed: "Is this not what I said when I was yet in my country? That is why I made haste to flee to Tarshish." Jonah was so upset that he asked God to take his life.

Instead, God taught him a lesson. Jonah was staying just outside of the city, shielded from the heat of the sun by a plant that God had caused to grow over him. "Jonah was exceedingly glad because of the plant." The next day, though, God "appointed a worm which attacked the plant, so that it withered." Later, "The sun beat so that he was faint; and he asked that he might die. . . ." God confronted his prophet one final time:

It is never too late to repent

"We have only to survey the generations of the past to see that in every one of them the LORD has offered the chance of repentance to any who were willing to turn to Him. When, after Jonah had proclaimed destruction to the people of Nineveh, they repented of their sins and made atonement to God with prayers and supplications, they obtained their salvation, notwithstanding that they were strangers and aliens to Him."

—Clement of Rome,
First Epistle to the Corinthians

251

"You pity the plant, for which you did not labor, nor did you make it grow, which came into being in a night and perished in a night. And should not I pity Nineveh, that great city, in which there are more than a hundred and twenty thousand persons who do not know their right hand from their left, and also much cattle?"

Who was Jonah, son of Amittai, and when was the book attributed to him produced? Linguistic evidence, and some traces of Persian influence, have led scholars to conclude that it was probably written down in its present form some time in the fourth century B.C. But elsewhere, the Bible mentions a prophet by the same name who proclaimed in the mid-eighth century B.C. that the Israelite King Jeroboam II would expand the territorial boundaries of his nation.

The central difficulty the book presents is twofold: Why was Jonah so dead set against God's forgiveness of Nineveh that he first disobeyed a divine command, and later wanted to end his life? And what lesson are we supposed to draw from the book, which satirizes Jonah's point of view?

Traditional Jewish commentaries, surely influenced by the reference to Jonah in the Book of Kings as a nationalist prophet, explain that he was motivated by loyalty to Israel. According to this line of discourse, Nineveh's repentance would constitute a serious rebuke to the Israelites, who persisted in sin despite the constant admonitions of the prophets. Jonah, then, did not disobey God out of a spirit of rebellion, but rather out of an admirable, if misguided, love for his people.

Early Christian interpreters took a similar approach, but added a new twist. Jonah was like the Jewish contemporaries of Jesus who hoped to maintain a monopoly on God's word by refusing to accept the salvation of all mankind preached by Christ. God's rebuke of Jonah, then, is a refutation of Jewish spiritual exclusivism.

The idea that tension between Jewish exclusivism and universalism is the key to this book has survived, in secular form, into modern times. Some writers perceive the book as a Jewish protest against the inward-looking tendencies of their own leadership under Persian rule. Jonah is depicted, like the historical personalities Ezra and Nehemiah, as eager to isolate the Jews from neighboring peoples. But God, in rebuking Jonah, teaches the opposite.

Another interpretation sees the book as an analysis of prophecy. Jonah thinks prophecy is an oracle: a true prophet is never wrong, and unfulfilled prophecies are ipso facto false. God, however, is not willing to be bound by any mechanistic scheme. The Book of Jonah teaches that prophecies will come true assuming that present conditions continue. A shift in the situation—repentance from sin, in this case—can avert what has been foretold. Thus humans can use their God-given free will to modify fate.

Another modern interpretation stresses the theological issue of human responsibility for actions. Jonah is convinced that, if the Ninevites are guilty of sin, they should be punished. Why should evil people escape their just deserts by a belated resort to sackcloth and fasting?

God's response, however, shows that, just as Jonah sorrowed over the loss of the plant that God sent to shade him, so too the demands of strict justice sometimes yield to divine love of his creation. Repentance can save. In the words of the late Jewish theologian Abraham Joshua Heschel, "It would be easier if God's anger became effective automatically: once wickedness had reached its full measure, punishment would destroy it. Yet, beyond justice and anger lies the mystery of compassion."

However one chooses to interpret this enigmatic story, its spiritual legacy profoundly influences Judaism and Christianity today. For Jews, who hear the entire book read in the synagogue each year on the Day of Atonement, it provides a model of man's ability to repent and God's willingness to forgive. For Christians, the deliverance of Jonah from the belly of the fish prefigures the resurrection of Jesus, and the grace shown to Nineveh foreshadows the salvation of the nations. ✦

In Jan Brueghel the Elder's portrayal, the whale appears relieved to be giving up his charge, while Jonah emerges in a posture of piety and devotion. The subject of Jonah and the whale has been a source of endless fascination down through the centuries.

253

Surviving in the belly of a whale

The ultimate fish story

OULD JONAH HAVE survived three days and three nights in the belly of a "great fish"? This mystery has puzzled generations of Bible readers.

It has long been thought that the "great fish" that swallowed Jonah was not in fact a fish, but a sperm whale. Sperm whales swallow their prey whole and have throats large enough to accommodate the body of a man. In fact, captured sperm whales have been found to contain the remains of giant squid (a staple of their diet) larger than the body of a human being. But surviving in the belly of the beast is truly miraculous.

The main stomach of a sperm whale contains glands that release acids and enzymes to aid in digestion. In addition, it also contains a crop of hard shells and bones with which to crush the swallowed food. Despite the overwhelming odds against surviving such conditions, it has been reported that in 1891 a sailor, whose whaling ship had been capsized the previous day by a sperm whale, was found alive in the stomach of the whale when the ship's crew found and captured their prey. Apparently, the only injury the man sustained was a permanent whitening of his skin from the whale's gastric juices.

Jonah is not known to have suffered any ill effects from his three days and nights within the belly. Rather the "great fish" was the object through which God's purpose was fulfilled. Upon his release from the whale, Jonah went on to preach Yahweh's message at Nineveh. ✦

The fiery furnace, the lion's den

Daniel's incredible odyssey

HE BOOK OF DANIEL'S 12 chapters tell of the career and teachings of a Jew by that name who was exiled from Judah to Babylon at the beginning of the sixth century B.C., and served as advisor to the kings of Babylon and their Persian successors. The name *Daniel* appears as the name of a wise and righteous man in numerous ancient texts. We know from the prophet Ezekiel that Noah, Daniel, and Job "would deliver but their own lives by their righteousness"—even if everyone around them deserved destruction. Elsewhere, Ezekiel refers to a prototypical man of wisdom, Daniel. In the Book of Daniel, then, Jewish writers were elaborating on an older Near Eastern motif. In recent times, scholars have come to the conclusion that the Book of Daniel as we have it today was composed quite late, and may have been the last book admitted into the Old Testament canon.

The book lacks a coherent literary structure. Chapters 1–6 are third-person accounts of how the hero and his friends fared at the courts of Babylonian and Persian kings. Chapters 7–12, however, consist of Daniel's own descriptions of his strange visions and explanations of their inner meanings. Complicating matters further, the book is written in two different languages, Hebrew and Aramaic—the vernacular Jews spoke after the Babylonian exile—and the transition between the two does not coincide with the division between the narrative and the visionary portions of the work. In all likelihood, Daniel is a composite work, parts of which were written at different times by different people.

One key theme that runs through the first half of the Book of Daniel is the exiled Jews' heroic resistance to the temptation of abandoning their faith in a land of idolators.

If the Jew remains loyal to the Jewish religion and commandments, the book teaches, God will deliver him from danger.

As the book opens, Daniel and his friends Hananiah, Mishael, and Azariah are given Babylonian names—Belteshazzar, Shadrach, Meshach, and Abednego—and enter a three-year training course to prepare them to serve as court pages. "The king assigned them a daily portion of the rich food which the king ate, and of the wine which he drank." But they would not eat food that was not permitted by Jewish dietary laws, even though the chief officer warned them that their refusal could anger the king. Despite subsisting on vegetables and water, "they were better in appearance and fatter in flesh than all the youths who ate the king's rich food." And the king esteemed them more than "all the magicians and enchanters that were in all his kingdom."

A more serious test of faith follows. King Nebuchadnezzar ordered his subjects to worship a golden statue or else be thrown into a fiery furnace. Although Daniel was elsewhere at the time, his three Jewish compatriots refused to worship the idol and were condemned. Yet they were calm. They told the king that their God had the power to save them from the furnace, and even if he chose not to, "we will not serve your gods or worship the golden image which you have set up" (Daniel 3:18).

Infuriated, Nebuchadnezzar ordered the furnace heated up seven times its usual heat, and the three Jews were bound and thrown in. So high were the flames that the soldiers carrying out the order were themselves burned to death. But Shadrach, Meshach, and Abednego walked around unsinged inside the furnace together with a fourth figure—the protecting angel.

The king was so impressed that he called the Jews out of the fire and declared, "Blessed be the God of Shadrach, Meshach, and Abednego, who has sent his angel and delivered his servants, who trusted in him, and set at nought the king's command, and yielded up their bodies rather than serve

The pious Hebrews *Shadrach, Meshach, and Abednego would not give up their religion to worship Nebuchadnezzar's golden statue, and, protected by the hand of the one and true God, they survived the fiery furnace.*

255

and worship any god except their own God" (Daniel 3:28). He then promoted them to higher government positions.

The book's best-known lesson about trust in God and its rewards is the story of Daniel in the lions' den. Despite King Darius' decree that no one may pray to any god other than the monarch for a period of 30 days, Daniel, in accordance with Jewish tradition, prayed thrice daily to his God. Government officials, jealous because the king planned to make Daniel grand vizier, reported him to the king, who in turn had him cast into the lions' den.

Found unharmed the next morning, Daniel explained that "My God sent his angel and shut the lions' mouths, and they have not hurt me." Daniel was raised from the den; but his denouncers, their children, and their wives were thrown in, and "before they reached the bottom of the den the lions overpowered them and broke all their bones in pieces." These events convinced King Darius that Daniel's God "is the living God, enduring for ever . . . and his dominion shall be to the end" (Daniel 6:26).

Daniel's fame as a wise man rests not only on his faithfulness to the one and only God, but also on his ability to interpret other people's enigmatic dreams and portents—omens that were taken quite seriously in the ancient world. Thus, we read that King Nebuchadnezzar was agitated by a dream. He insisted that his wise men tell him what he dreamed, and the meaning of the dream. Clearly, this command was nearly impossible to fulfill. However, Daniel, with the help of God, was able to reveal the hidden meaning of the dream.

The dream was of a statue with a head of gold, breast and arms of silver, belly and thighs of bronze, legs of iron, and feet of iron and clay. In the dream, a stone struck the statue and broke it to bits. The pieces were carried away by the wind "so that not a trace of them could be found." But the stone that struck the statue became a mountain and filled the earth. Daniel explained the meaning: Nebuchadnezzar's Babylonia

will be succeeded by three other empires, which will be destroyed by God, who will set up his kingdom and reign gloriously.

In a second dream, Nebuchadnezzar saw a huge tree. A heavenly "watcher" ordered that the entire tree, with the exception of the stump, should be destroyed, so "that the living may know that the Most High rules the kingdom of men, and gives it to whom he will." Daniel interpreted the tree as Nebuchadnezzar's empire, which will be

taken from him for a time, and the remaining stump as a guarantee that "your kingdom shall be sure for you from the time that you know that Heaven rules." As foreseen, the king, afflicted by madness, suffered a temporary fall from power, but regained his position after he petitioned Daniel's God.

Daniel also demonstrated an ability to decode strange written messages. In a display of blasphemous arrogance, King Belshazzar of Babylonia "commanded that the vessels of gold and of silver which Nebuchadnezzar his father had taken out of the temple in Jerusalem be brought, that the king and his lords, his wives, and his concubines might drink from them." Suddenly "the fingers of a man's hand appeared and wrote on the plaster of the wall of the king's palace, opposite the lampstand."

When no one present could decipher the words, Daniel was called. He read: "MENE, MENE, TEKEL, and PARSIN." But what could

Daniel's great faith *protected him from violence, rendering the lions harmless.*

During a drunken feast, *King Belshazzar saw a disembodied hand writing on the wall.*

these mysterious words, all of which represent weights, mean? Daniel explained: "God has numbered the days of your kingdom and brought it to an end . . . you have been weighed in the balances and found wanting . . . your kingdom is divided and given to the Medes and Persians." The sin of desecrating the Temple utensils had doomed the kingdom. That very night, Belshazzar was assassinated and his land conquered by its enemies.

The Daniel portrayed in the second half of the book is very different from the diviner of mysteries described in the first six chapters. Rather, he is a passive recipient of a dream, visions, and signs that he cannot understand without the aid of angels.

Daniel's dream and visions constitute one of the earliest examples of Jewish apoc-

alyptic literature, a genre that became quite popular in the last two centuries B.C. and the first two centuries A.D. Apocalypses purport to reveal God's secrets for the future to a small spiritual elite by means of abstruse symbols and fantastic imagery.

Daniel's first apocalyptic dream is of four great beasts that come up out of the sea—a winged lion, a bear with three ribs in its mouth, and a four-headed, winged leopard; the fourth beast is "dreadful and exceedingly strong" with iron teeth and ten horns. An 11th horn sprouts with "eyes like the eyes of a man, and a mouth speaking great things." This fourth beast is killed, and Daniel sees "one like a son of man" descend from heaven. "And to him was given dominion and glory and kingdom . . . his dominion is an everlasting dominion."

An angel explains to Daniel that the four beasts are four successive kingdoms, the last of which, under its 11th king, will rebel against God. That kingdom will be overthrown by divine intervention and power granted to "the people of the saints of the Most High" (Daniel 7:27).

In the next apocalypse Daniel experiences a vision of a ram that has its two horns broken and is thrown to the ground and trampled by a he-goat with "a conspicuous horn between his eyes." When his great horn is broken, four other horns sprout from the he-goat, and from one of them yet another horn appears which "grew great, even to the host of heaven" and interfered with the sacrificial services in the Temple and desecrated the sanctuary.

This time the symbols are explained in terms of specific nations. The two-horned ram is the Medo-Persian kingdom, which will be defeated by the Greek he-goat, whose kingdom will in turn be divided into four kingdoms. Eventually "a king of bold countenance . . . shall arise. His power shall be great, and he shall cause fearful destruction, and shall succeed in what he does, and destroy mighty men and the people of the saints." He will meet defeat, but "by no human hand" (Daniel 8:25).

Daniel's third apocalypse interprets an older prophecy by Jeremiah that the Judeans, after a 70-year desolation, will be redeemed. An angel explains to Daniel that this means 70 weeks of years, or 490 years: during this time Jerusalem will be rebuilt and "an anointed one" cut off; a hostile army will overrun Jerusalem; sacrifices will be stopped; in their place "abominations" will be set up in the Temple "until the decreed end is poured out on the desolator."

The final apocalypse in the book predicts once again Persia's downfall, the ascendancy of Greece, and its breakup into four kingdoms. It then describes a pattern of ongoing conflict between North (Syria) and South (Egypt). Israel, on the border between the two, will suffer devastation.

Yet final deliverance is inevitable. An angel tells Daniel, "your people shall be delivered . . . many of those who sleep in the dust of the earth shall awake, some to everlasting life, and some to shame and everlasting contempt." Daniel asks when the end will be. The angel replies: "for a time, two times, and half a time."

What does all this mean? Jews and Christians have traditionally understood these apocalypses as forecasts of the Messiah's coming. For example, the term "son of man," found in the New Testament in reference to Jesus, builds directly on Daniel's assumed prediction of his coming.

Modern scholarship, however, has shown that the Book of Daniel was not written during the period of Babylonian Captivity in the 6th century B.C., but rather some 400 years later, in about the middle of the 2nd century B.C., when the Seleucid Syrian Empire—the "fourth kingdom"—and its King Antiochus IV made the Jerusalem Temple into a pagan shrine and restricted the practice of Judaism. This crisis was so intense that a small circle of visionaries thought that the only hope was divine intervention. The Book of Daniel's references to events in Persian and Greek history, then, are interpretations of the past intended to provide guidelines for predicting an imminent redemption. Even after the Maccabean revolt had driven the Seleucids out of the Promised Land, the Book of Daniel continued to exert a powerful influence. ✦

"Wonderfully written as it was, the Daniel collection was always read and listened to for sheer pleasure and entertainment. . . . The readers liked the tales because the subject was so interesting: the boy who, against all odds, by sheer intelligence and moral goodness, like Joseph of old, achieves power, money, and fame. From Joseph in Genesis to Horatio Alger's heroes, this theme of success through virtue fascinated readers, perhaps for the reason that nothing like it was ever seen in real life."

—**Elias Bickerman,**
Four Strange Books of the Bible (1967)

Rampant idolatry

The Book of the Twelve

THE TERM "MINOR PROPHETS" has been used in Christian churches at least since the days of St. Augustine (354–430 A.D.). The term is not concerned with the relative importance of the prophets but with the size of the books attributed to them. It distinguishes between the shorter prophetic books and the longer (major) prophetic books contained in the Bible. An earlier title for the same collection is The Book of the Twelve. The twelve books are Hosea, Joel, Amos, Obadiah, Jonah, Micah, Nahum, Habakkuk, Zephaniah, Haggai, Zechariah, and Malachi.

The destruction resulting from a plague of locusts is the basis for the first part of the Book of Joel. A land that, before the locusts come, is luxuriant "like the garden of Eden" becomes "a desolate wilderness." Joel, whose work is usually dated 400–350 B.C., relates this locust plague to the coming of the day of judgment. The locusts become a divinely sent army whose mission is to destroy a nation that has turned away from God. Joel calls upon the people to repent: "rend your hearts and not your garments.

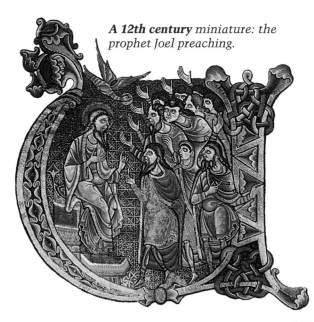

A 12th century miniature: the prophet Joel preaching.

Return to the LORD . . . " for those who worship the Lord will be delivered.

In the Book of Obadiah, the day of the Lord is the day of God's retribution against the enemies of Israel. Singled out for special attention is the kingdom of Edom, which had "rejoiced over the people of Judah in the day of their ruin." Such behavior was particularly abominable because the kingdom of Edom was related to the kingdom of Judah through descent.

Micah prophesied during the time when the mighty armies of the Assyrian Empire wiped out the Kingdom of Israel and threatened the existence of Judah. This threat lies behind Micah's proclamation of the destruction of Judah as punishment for apostasy and corruption. Micah attacks the wealthy, who have increased their wealth at others' expense, and condemns those prophets who insist that all is well, saying what those who pay them want to hear.

The Book of Micah also contains words of promise and hope. Zion, it says, will be the center of worship for all nations, and all war will halt. Over this Zion will reign one who will come forth from Bethlehem, who will establish the security of Israel. The Gospel according to Matthew understands this oracle to refer to the birth of Jesus.

In the last decades of the seventh century B.C., Nineveh, the capital of the Assyrian Empire, fell to the combined forces of the Medes and the Babylonians. In the Book of Nahum this event is celebrated as the Lord's judgment over the oppressive forces "who plotted evil against the LORD." In vivid poetry the prophet portrays the downfall of the center of the once proud empire.

The fall of Assyria meant the rise of Babylon, and once again Judah faced the threat of an expanding imperial power. This was the situation when Habakkuk came on the scene. He saw the danger posed to his land by the Babylonians (Chaldeans in the

Book of Habakkuk), and he questioned why God permitted wickedness and oppression to swallow up the righteous. The answer God gives Habakkuk is: "he whose soul is not upright in him shall fail, but the righteous shall live by his faith." According to a rabbinic tradition, this statement sets forth the principle underlying all the Law of Moses, while in the New Testament, Paul uses it as a scriptural foundation for his concept of justification by faith.

A few decades before Habakkuk, Zephaniah condemned the idolatry and corruption of Judah and warned that "The great day of the LORD is near." In words that became the inspiration for the medieval hymn *Dies Irae*, he described God's "day of wrath," when "a full, yea, sudden end he will make of all the inhabitants of the earth." However, those who seek righteousness may be spared.

Under the Persians, the Jews returned to their homeland and began to rebuild their Temple. But conflicts within the community prevented the restoration. Concerned about the neglect of the Temple, the prophets Haggai and Zechariah attempted to stir up the people. Haggai attacked the people's self-concern, arguing that their failure to rebuild the Temple was itself the reason for their present wretched state. Zechariah promised that God would strengthen Zerubbabel, the governor of Judah, that he might bring the rebuilding to a successful conclusion. The people apparently found the words of the two inspiring, for work on the Temple was resumed, and in 515 B.C. the Second Temple was completed.

Much of the material from Zechariah is presented as extended reports of what Zechariah "saw in the night." In eight reports of visions, the prophet first describes what he had seen—such things as divine horsemen patrolling the earth, or chariots emerging from between two mountains of bronze; he then tells how an angelic interpreter explained to him the significance of what he had seen. The report of such visions is more characteristic of what is referred to as apocalyptic literature (as repre-

The village-bred Micah *sympathized with the exploited.*

sented by the books of Daniel and Revelation) than it is of older prophetic literature. Zechariah seems to be a transitional figure between classical and apocalyptic prophecy.

In the Book of Zechariah, only the first eight chapters originate in the work of the prophet. Zechariah 9–11 and 12–14 are the first two of three collections of anonymous oracles that conclude the Minor Prophets.

The third collection of anonymous oracles is what we know as the Book of Malachi. The name of the book is taken from Malachi 3:1 ("Behold, I send *my messenger*" [Hebrew: *malachi*]). Malachi attacks the manner in which priests and people have corrupted the Lord's teachings.

The Book of the Twelve ends with the promise that "before the great and terrible day of the LORD comes" God will send Elijah the prophet, who will so prepare the community that the Lord's coming will not bring a curse. Thus, the Minor Prophets contain both threats against a sinful people and a hope of salvation. ✦

The descendants of the ten lost tribes *are led back to the Holy Land by Nathan of Gaza in this 17th century German engraving.*

The lost tribes of Israel

The elusive trail

DURING THE REIGN of Rehoboam (circa 928–911 B.C.), the monarchy established by David split into two—the southern kingdom, consisting of the two tribes that remained loyal to the House of David (Judah and Benjamin), which took the name of the kingdom of Judah; and the northern kingdom, comprising the seceding tribes, which became known as the Kingdom of Israel. In 722 or 721 B.C. the northern kingdom fell in final defeat to the mighty Assyrian army, and its population was led into exile in Assyria (present-day Iraq). From that time on, the exiled tribes have disappeared from history.

Many myths and legends exist regarding the fate of the ten lost tribes, as they have become known. Assyrian documents dating to the end of the 8th century B.C. and the 7th century B.C. contain several allusions to their existence in Mesopotamia. The later prophets foretold their eventual return and reunification with the descendants of the Judean exiles. However, nothing other than

legend seems to exist about the fate of the ten tribes. During the Second Temple and Talmudic periods, this was a subject of great interest and speculation. The continued existence of the ten tribes was regarded as a given. The historian Josephus states that "The ten tribes are beyond the Euphrates till now, and are an innumerable multitude and not to be estimated in numbers." Paul and James both refer to the existence of twelve tribes as fact. In rabbinic tradition the ten tribes will eventually return but are presently unable to do so because of their exile beyond the mysterious river Sambatyon, with its strong currents, rolling stones, and sand, which make crossing impossible and prevent any outside contacts.

During medieval times many scholars and travelers attempted to identify the whereabouts of the ten lost tribes. For example, in the 9th century, the Jewish traveler Eldad ha-Dani visited Jewish communities in Europe and North Africa claiming to belong to the lost tribe of Dan, which, he said, together with the tribes of Naftali, Gad, and Asher, had established an independent kingdom somewhere in Africa. The famous 12th century Jewish traveler, Benjamin of Tudela, writes in the account of his journeys to the East that he had been told that four of the tribes (Dan, Asher, Zebulun, and Naftali) resided in Persia. In the 16th century, the adventurer and messianic pretender David Reuveni claimed to be a brother of a King Joseph who ruled in Arabia over the tribes of Reuben, Gad, and half of Manasseh. Similar tales of the existence of the ten tribes turn up in the writings of travelers and scholars, Jewish and non-Jewish, throughout the Middle Ages.

Legends about the lost tribes continued to proliferate well into the modern era. Some have suggested that the native Indians of the Americas were in fact their descendants. One 17th century Jewish traveler returned home to Amsterdam from South America with tales of meeting Indians in remote areas who greeted him by reciting the *Shema*, the Hebrew prayer that devout Jews recite daily. Others claimed to have identified Jewish practices among American Indian religions. Yet another legend claims that the Jews of Ethiopia (known in Amharic as Falashas) are descended from the lost tribe of Dan; this idea in fact was used to justify their claim to be Jewish when they first began to arrive in Israel in the mid-1970's. Still others believe that the Bene Israel—an old and unique Jewish community in India—are a remnant of the ten lost tribes, who migrated east to India from their Assyrian exile. As recently as the mid-1980's, some scholars have claimed to discover "lost Jews" in remote areas of India.

There may be some kernel of truth in a few of these tales, as historical evidence of the existence of independent Jewish kingdoms in the Middle Ages—in Yemen in the 5th century A.D., and in Central Asia from the 9th to the 12th centuries A.D., for example—has been uncovered. It is also possible that the presence of crypto-Jews in some geographically remote countries, who in years past were forced underground by persecution and gradually lost all but a few vestiges of Judaism, gave rise to tales of the ten lost tribes. It is much more likely, however, that those tribes carried off into exile by the Assyrians in the 8th century B.C. were simply assimilated into the local populations and, over time, became indistinguishable from them. If so, we will never be able to trace what really happened to the ten lost tribes and their descendants. ✦

Israel among the nations

Into a new era

THE MORE THAN 400 YEARS of Israel's story from the time of Ezra and Nehemiah to the first centuries of our era are for many people largely a blank. It is a mysterious time "between"—for Jews, between the Hebrew Scriptures and the Mishnah; for Christians, between the Old Testament and the New. Portions of that "blank," however, are marked by events that in many ways transformed the western world, redirected the history of the Jews, and made possible the rise of Christianity.

The period is often referred to as "Second Temple Judaism," since it begins with the rebuilding of the Temple after the Babylonian exile and continues until the destruction of the Temple by the Romans in the first century of our era. As the ancient Jewish historian Josephus noted, it marks the time when the ancient Israelites became the Jews and their religion and culture became Judaism. Much of the first half of this long era of Jewish history is obscure, since few documents or artifacts survive to illuminate events. The province of Judah was a small backwater of the mighty Persian Empire.

In 332 B.C., however, an event occurred that radically changed the environment in which the Jews and all the peoples around them lived. Alexander, the young king of Macedon, swept through Palestine with his army of Greeks and Macedonians, already well on his way toward one of the most important conquests of all time. In a matter of a few years his lightning war had erased the supposedly invincible might of Persia, and the king of kings, Darius III, was on the run before Alexander's advancing army.

Alexander not only conquered Egypt and became successor to the ancient pharaohs, but also, he founded a new city at the western edge of the Nile delta. That new Greek city, Alexandria, was to become the cultural capital of the new era—the "Hellenistic era"—and preeminent among many such new cities. Alexander envisioned not only military conquest, but also cultural conquest—bringing to the non-Greek world the Greek way of life that he had been taught by the philosopher Aristotle and others.

New cities dotted Alexander's empire, which reached all the way to the borders of India. The cities were marked by Greek style, thus beginning the spread of Greek culture and the establishment of Greek as the new common language of the empire.

Alexander the Great died in 323 at the age of 32 or 33, and the next two decades were marked by wars among his subordinates over the pieces of his empire. When the dust settled, two powerful empires struggled against each other for control of Palestine. In Alexandria, a Macedonian named Ptolemy, one of Alexander's close associates, had begun the Ptolemaic dynasty, which was to rule Egypt for 300 years. In Syria, Seleucus, another of Alexander's subordinates, established the Seleucid kingdom, which covered the vast eastern stretches of Alexander's empire and Asia Minor.

Bust of Alexander *the Great.*

For a century Israel was under Ptolemaic rule. It was apparently granted a high degree of self-government under its ancestral law and thus developed as a kind of theocracy, governed by the high priest in Jerusalem. Many of the ordinary people in Israel were hardly touched by Alexander's revolution, but others, especially those in the upper classes, felt a growing attraction toward a Greek way of life and the doors that it opened to the outside world.

The Seleucids in the north repeatedly pressed the borders of the Ptolemies till at last in about 198 B.C. Antiochus III of Syria wrested control of Palestine from Egypt. The simmering struggle over Hellenistic culture among the Jews soon came to a boil, as the story is recounted in the books of First and Second Maccabees in the Apocrypha.

In 175 B.C. Antiochus IV came to the throne of Syria, while Onias III was the ruling high priest in Jerusalem. Onias was undoubtedly an opponent of any move to "Hellenize" Judaism, that is, to assimilate Greek patterns of religion and government. Onias' brother Jason, however, was a leader of the "Hellenizers" and was at the very center of the high-priestly aristocracy.

Jason in effect carried out a government coup by persuading King Antiochus to appoint him as high priest in place of his brother. He also arranged to establish a gymnasium based on the Greek model in Jerusalem, and to promote Greek customs at the expense of Jewish law. Thus the Jews' law was displaced from its central role in national life. Once this process was begun, Jason could not control it. He was soon replaced by another Hellenizer named Menelaus, who most likely was not part of the traditional high-priestly family.

Many Jews were outraged. They apparently began an uprising against royal appointees and their policy of Hellenization, just at a time when King Antiochus was being pressed by Rome. A frustrated Antiochus tried to suppress them and support Menelaus by putting down the revolt with considerable slaughter and by banning all observance of the Law of Moses. The Jerusalem Temple was rededicated to Olympian Zeus; circumcision and Sabbath observance were outlawed; copies of the Torah were burned; and all Jews were required to partake of pagan sacrifices.

In 167 B.C., when the Syrian King Antiochus' officers came to the small town of Modein outside Jerusalem in order to enforce publicly the requirement of pagan sacrifice, they encountered a Jewish priest named Mattathias and his five sons. Mattathias assassinated one officer who was enforcing the decree and a Jewish supporter. He then fled to the hills with his sons and summoned the people to join him in guerrilla warfare against the king. Soon after, Mattathias died, and his son Judas, nicknamed "Maccabeus," probably meaning "the hammer," brilliantly led the growing guerrilla army.

In spite of the vast resources of the Seleucid kingdom, the revolt was successful, and within three years the Temple had been retaken, and could be cleansed of its pagan elements and rededicated. On the 25th day of the month of Kislev, approximately December, exactly three years after its desecration, the new altar was consecrated and an eight-day festival was begun. Thus Judaism had survived a full-scale onslaught by the power of Syria, and the joy of that celebration was commemorated annually in the festival of Hanukkah. In later centuries the story was told that during the period of rededication, a small vial of holy oil found in the Temple had miraculously burned in the Temple lamp for eight days until more oil could be supplied. The celebration became a festival of lights, a remembrance not of the military victory but of the spiritual one, perhaps reflecting the lighting of the candelabra of the Jerusalem Temple.

Over the years that followed, Judas and

The rebel warrior *Judas Maccabeus triumphed over the forces of the Syrians.*

his brothers after him established Judea's independence. It is one of the ironies of this period, however, that their dynasty, called Hasmonean after their family name, and born in rebellion against Greek culture, eventually became highly worldly and ambitious itself. The fact that the Hasmoneans took for themselves both the office of high priest and that of ruler offended many pious Jews, who believed that the high priesthood was reserved for a single family.

The religious and political struggles of the time caused various groups with differing religious and political philosophies to emerge. The three that became especially prominent were the Pharisees, the Sadducees, and the Essenes. All three were active until the Romans brought an end to the Second Temple period, at which point only the Pharisees, the "moderates" of their day, managed to survive in a significant way.

The Pharisees developed as a group devoted to the application of the Torah to the life of all Israel. They handed down a system of oral law which expanded the written law and applied it to the needs of the people in their own time. Though somewhat involved in the power politics of the Hasmonean kingdom, they became more identified as the religious teachers of Israel.

The Sadducees were closely connected with the priestly aristocracy and the Temple with its sacrificial worship. They rejected the Pharisees' oral traditions and took a more conservative view that only the written Torah was binding. As representatives of a well-ensconced, hereditary establishment, they were able to provide a valuable continuity and base of power that both the Hasmoneans and later the Romans valued.

The most radical of the groups was the Essenes. Led by a man whom they referred to only as the "Teacher of Righteousness," they rejected the legitimacy of the entire Hasmonean government and Temple establishment. They set up as their main base a monastery at Qumran near the northern end of the Dead Sea. They devoted themselves to careful observance of the Torah and the rules of a highly structured community. Believing that the last days of the

world had drawn near, they practiced baptism, and focused their entire life on preparation for that denouement of history.

The Jews were dispersed. Indeed, during the Hellenistic and Roman periods many Jews—perhaps the majority—lived outside Palestine. Large communities were located in Babylonia, Egypt, Asia Minor, and Rome. Some of these communities had existed since at least the time of the Babylonian exile in the sixth century B.C. and had developed deep roots in the local culture. Many were quite wealthy. In the first century A.D., the Jewish community in Alexandria numbered perhaps 100,000 or more. It was here that the Jewish philosopher Philo, who was born some 20 years before Christ and lived to see Rome in 40 A.D., worked out his doctrines seeking to reconcile Greek philosophy with biblical religion.

The Hebrew Scriptures were translated into Greek in Egypt and were often interpreted by Jewish scholars who could draw on both the Scriptures and the well-known Greek philosophies for insight. It was a time of probing the limits of Jewish tradition, a time of struggle and hope. With the destruction of the Second Temple under the Romans, in 70 A.D., the synagogue became the central Jewish religious institution.

These Jews were in their own way on the front line of the conflict of cultures. They lived in a Greek-speaking world, and Philo was by no means the only one who actively took on the task of interpreting ancient tradition in the light of the cosmopolitan world. Their central local institution was not the Temple, with its rites, rituals, and priesthood, but the synagogue, a place of prayer, study, community, and education.

The scattering of the Jews outside the Holy Land that began in 587 B.C., when Jerusalem fell to Babylonia, is called the *Diaspora*—Greek for "dispersion." Today, the term refers to the voluntary dispersion of the Jewish people outside the State of Israel, in contrast to the forced exile (*galut* in Hebrew) of the Babylonian conquest. Thus, a modern Jew living in the United States is said to be living in the Diaspora. ✦

IN MODERN TIMES

❧ Menorah ❧

During Hanukkah, Jews the world over celebrate the rededication of the Temple by the lighting of an eight-branched candelabrum, or *menorah.* Often there is a ninth branch, called the *shammes* or "servant," used as a pilot light. Why eight branches? One legend states that the Maccabees had only enough oil to light the Temple menorah for one night. Miraculously, the lights burned for eight. Hence, Hanukkah is also called the "Festival of Lights."

The menorah, as described to Moses in Exodus, was of one piece of beaten gold.

PART V

The Gospels

The Books of Matthew, Mark,
Luke, and John

*The word gospel means "good news,"
and indeed the Gospels of Matthew,
Mark, Luke, and John bring to all the
good news of Jesus Christ. Through the
miracles of his birth and life, his death
and resurrection, Jesus changed the
world forever. He taught mankind how to
reach out for the great gift of God's love.*

The four Evangelists, as portrayed by Albrecht Dürer, 1526.

Matthew, Mark, Luke, and John

Four versions of the Good News of Christ

A S THERE ARE FOUR quarters of the world . . . and also four universal winds, and as the Church is scattered over the earth, and the Gospel is the pillar and bulwark of the church . . . , it is seemly that it should have four pillars." So wrote the church father Irenaeus of Lyons (140–202 A.D.), offering an explanation from nature as to why the New Testament contains its present number of books about Jesus' life and ministry. But in fact no one really knows why there are precisely four. Indeed, many more "Gospels" appeared during the first and second centuries, but by the end of the second century, the church had begun to recognize only Matthew, Mark, Luke, and John as canonical, that is, official and authoritative. Probably the decision had much to do with the church's perception that these four accounts were au-

thored by Jesus' own disciples or, in the case of Mark and Luke, by companions of the first Apostles. But such a view is based on tradition, not on the Scriptures themselves. Not one of the earliest Greek manuscripts of the Gospels contains a signature or preface indicating its author. While some contemporary scholars find eye-witness material in the Gospels, few if any believe that all four documents we have in our Bible came directly from the pens of Jesus' original followers. This means that many of the stories and sayings in our Gospels have undergone an editing process, both oral and written, as they passed from believer to believer prior to their final composition. To what extent that process involved what we now think of as historical accuracy is one of the mysteries of the Gospels. No scholarly theory has yet won the day on this issue.

The first three of our canonical Gospels are called "synoptic" (from a Greek word that means "providing an overview or synopsis") because, when placed in parallel columns, they turn out to be very similar, not only in the chronological sequence of their narratives but also in the very wording of many stories and sayings. For example, Matthew, Mark, and Luke all portray Jesus' public ministry as beginning with his baptism. When the three accounts of this event are lined up next to one another, the observer notes that all of them contain a reference to the Holy Spirit descending upon Jesus like a dove, and a voice from heaven identifying him as "my beloved Son." On the other hand, a synoptic view of the three texts also yields the surprising information that according to Mark and Luke the voice said, "Thou art my beloved Son," suggesting that Jesus alone heard it, whereas in Matthew the message appears to have come also to John the baptizer, for here the words are, "This is my beloved Son." Moreover, only in Matthew does one find a conversation between Jesus and John just prior to the baptism, and only in Luke is it recorded that Jesus was praying at the time.

How should these coexisting similarities and differences be accounted for? To resolve the paradox, scholars as far back as St. Augustine (354–430 A.D.) have proposed a literary relationship among the Synoptic Gospels. The simplest possibilities are, first, that Mark, in the shortest of the Gospels, summarized Matthew and Luke, both of which he had at his disposal; or, second, that Matthew and Luke each knew the Gospel of Mark and expanded it in his own way. Augustine favored the first option, believing Matthew to be the earliest of the three Synoptics. Today a number of scholars still take this position. Most, however, support some version of the second theory on the grounds that Mark would probably not leave out the rich material unique to Matthew (for instance the Sermon on the Mount) and to Luke (the parables of the Good Samaritan and the Prodigal Son, for example). Furthermore, Mark does not con-

tain the birth narrative, while Matthew and Luke do. Why would Mark eliminate this?

The term *gospel*, or "good news," was used at the time of Jesus' birth to describe a happy event. Historical evidence indicates that the word was used especially to announce news of royalty. This may be why Mark—if indeed he is the original Gospel writer—decided that "good news" was the appropriate term to use when speaking of Jesus as the Son of God (Mark 1:1). Indeed, this title was commonly used of Israelite and Egyptian kings, and Roman emperors.

Whether or not Mark's is the first Gospel, it is significant that originally Mark's Gospel may have ended at 16:8—without a resurrection appearance. Another theory is that the original ending has been lost. Subsequent scribes added two alternative end-

---

THE STORY BEHIND THE WORD

Old Testament New Testament

The *Old Testament* is the Christian term for the Hebrew Bible. Originally transmitted orally, some of the Hebrew Bible was written down by the time of David. For Jews, the most sacred text of the Bible is the Five Books of Moses, also called the *Torah*, the *Law*, or the *Pentateuch*. In the third century B.C., the Pentateuch was translated into Greek, the common language of the day; this translation is known as the *Septuagint* (Latin for "seventy," referring to the legend of the seventy scholars who worked on it). In the Septuagint, the word *covenant* is frequently translated as *testament*. Hence, in the 27 books of the Christian Scriptures, Christ establishes a new covenant, continuing the covenant between Abraham and God, as well as the covenant of Moses at Sinai. These books form the New Testament. Some 300 years after Christ, St. Jerome produced the definitive Latin version of Scripture, known as the *Vulgate*.

ings. The reader of the Gospel knows that Jesus is, however, going to appear after his death in Galilee.

Regardless of which Gospel one chooses as a prototype for the others, another question arises. In a number of places, Matthew and Luke provide material that is almost word for word the same but is not found in Mark. Did Matthew copy from Luke, or vice versa? Or did each of them, independently, draw upon an early list of Jesus' sayings that we no longer possess? A majority of scholars today view the third hypothesis as most probable and give the name Q (for the German word *Quelle*, meaning "source") to this lost document. But many uncertainties persist, and most contemporary interpreters of the Bible admit that the actual series of events that produced the Synoptic Gospels is more complex than we imagine.

Approaching the fourth Gospel from the Synoptics, readers may feel that they have entered a different world. Traditionally, John's book has been viewed as the most spiritual of the Gospels and is symbolized in Christian art by the high-soaring eagle. It begins not with a list of Jesus' ancestors, as in Matthew, or a description of his immediate forerunner John the Baptist, as in Mark. Nor does it begin, as Luke does, with stories of John's and Jesus' birth. Instead, it offers mystical language about the Christ in his role as God's equal and the world's creator: "In the beginning was the Word (*logos* in Greek), and the Word was with God, and the Word was God. . . . all things were made through him . . . In him was life, and the life was the light of men." This prologue, which many scholars identify as a hymn designed to be sung in Christian liturgies, proceeds to a dramatic conclusion in John 1:14: "And

the Word became flesh and dwelt among us, full of grace and truth; we have beheld his glory, glory as of the only Son from the Father." Not until the writer has completed this hymn-like prologue does he turn to earthly details of Jesus' life and ministry.

Why does John take such a lofty approach? One answer is that he wants to interpret the idea of Christ to Gentile readers steeped in the language of Greek philosophy. The word *logos* was a popular one among Stoic philosophers and stood for the controlling force in the universe. It denoted reason but also spirit, understood as a subtle form of matter. Yet this answer is probably too simple, for some of the words in John's prologue hark back to the Jewish Scriptures, especially the creation account in Genesis. And many passages in the body of the Gospel reflect a Jewish origin for John's thought and language. It is probably best to say that John combines Hebrew and Greek thinking into a unique amalgam.

But this conclusion simply raises further questions. Why is John's portrait of Jesus so different from that presented in the Synoptic Gospels? Why does the Jesus of the fourth Gospel dwell so frequently upon his relationship and union with the Father, and upon himself, stressing his identity as true light, vine, good shepherd, resurrection, life, way, truth, and bread from heaven as the key to salvation for all humanity? While a few of these notes are struck in the Synoptic Gospels, they become the entire melody for the author of the fourth Gospel. For him, Jesus' very personhood is the manifestation of God. Did something momentous happen to this writer and his co-believers to result in such an exalted picture of the prophet from Nazareth?

Interpreters have suggested a religious experience, perhaps conditioned by a traumatic tension in the relationship between John's community and its local synagogue or by contacts with various philosophical ideas. But a full explanation for the high Christology (or theological interpretation of Christ's person, life, and work) found in John has yet to appear. ✦

"The Gospels picture Jesus supremely as a Man of Joy. 'These things have I spoken unto you,' he told his disciples, 'that my joy might remain in you and that your joy might be full.' And to all he explained his mission: 'I am come that ye might have life, and have it more abundantly.' "
—**Rev. Billy Graham**
A Man Called Jesus

270

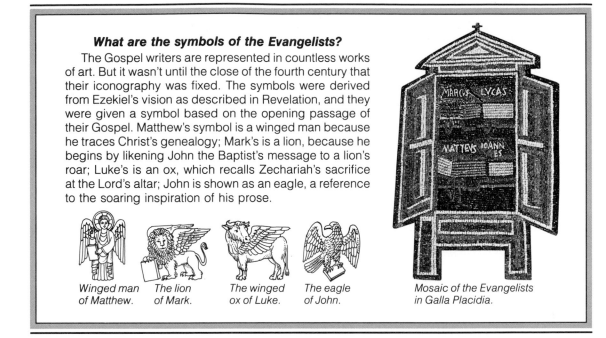

What are the symbols of the Evangelists?

The Gospel writers are represented in countless works of art. But it wasn't until the close of the fourth century that their iconography was fixed. The symbols were derived from Ezekiel's vision as described in Revelation, and they were given a symbol based on the opening passage of their Gospel. Matthew's symbol is a winged man because he traces Christ's genealogy; Mark's is a lion, because he begins by likening John the Baptist's message to a lion's roar; Luke's is an ox, which recalls Zechariah's sacrifice at the Lord's altar; John is shown as an eagle, a reference to the soaring inspiration of his prose.

Winged man of Matthew.

The lion of Mark.

The winged ox of Luke.

The eagle of John.

Mosaic of the Evangelists in Galla Placidia.

Good news for all

The Gospel according to Luke

LUKE REJOICED IN presenting Jesus as the one who "came to seek and to save the lost." Luke's identity has been much debated: some believe that, unlike other New Testament writers, Luke was neither Jewish nor from Palestine, nor was he one of the Apostles. The author of Luke's Gospel was probably "the beloved physician" whom Paul distinguished from those "of the circumcision"—that is, the Jews. It is significant, therefore, that Luke's opening address is directed to the "most excellent" Theophilus, a man of Greek name. This suggests that the readership would include Gentiles. Indeed, Luke interprets the meaning of Jesus' ministry as for those who embraced "the consolation of Israel" and saw in Jesus "a light for . . . the Gentiles."

For Luke, God's plan for salvation is all-inclusive. Divine love and mercy is for all people, and extends especially to such groups as "the lost" within Israel, the poor and lowly, women, the Samaritans, and the nations. Luke's Gospel abounds with examples of Jesus' embrace of these groups.

The lost sheep of Jesus' parable are typified by "tax collectors and sinners." Perhaps Luke's most startling story regarding such outcasts is that of the crucified criminal who practically stole heaven while dying alongside Jesus. God's outreach to the poor is visible in the Magnificat, which sings of their favored position. Women were secondary in the first century, but Luke exalts them. As a halfway stage in showing God's love for both Jew and Greek, Luke uniquely features the role of the Samaritans as candidates for true piety. In the parable of the Good Samaritan it is the Samaritan who is the exemplar of neighborliness. Finally, the Gentile mission, which becomes a dominant theme of Acts, already surfaces: thus Luke anchors his story in the Roman imperial world. Fittingly, Luke's Gospel closes with the commission to preach "in his name to all nations, beginning from Jerusalem." ✦

✍ Key to the important events in the life of Jesus ✍

THIS TABLE SHOWS the leading episodes in the story of Jesus' life as they appear in the Gospels of Matthew, Mark, Luke, and John. An old-fashioned but still useful term for a key to correspondences among the Gospels in a connected historical view is a "har-mony." Such "harmonies" have long helped Bible readers—thoughtful believers have been harmonizing the Evangelists and specu-lating on the order in which they wrote the Gospels ever since the earliest centuries of the Christian Church.

	Matthew	Mark	Luke	John
EARLY YEARS				
Birth	1:18–25		2:1–7	
Visit of the Wise Men	2:1–12			
Flight into Egypt	2:13–21			
Teaching in the Temple			2:41–51	
Jesus' baptism	3:13–17	1:9–11	3:21–22	
Changing water into wine				2:1–11
Temptation in the Wilderness	4:1–11	1:12–13	4:1–13	
JESUS' MINISTRY				
Start of the Galilean ministry	4:12–17	1:14–15	4:14–15	
Summoning the first disciples	4:18–22	1:16–20	5:1–11	1:35–51
Sermon on the Mount	5:1–7:29		6:20–49	
Naming the Apostles	10:1–42	3:13–19; 6:7–19	9:1–6	
Feeding 5,000	14:13–21	6:32–44	9:10–17	6:1–14
Walking on water	14:22–33	6:45–52		6:16–21
Peter declares Jesus to be the Christ	16:16	8:29	9:20	
Transfiguration of Jesus	17:1–13	9:2–8	9:28–36	
Raising of Lazarus				11:1–44
FINAL DAYS				
Entry into Jerusalem	21:1–11	11:1–10	19:28–44	12:12–19
Cleansing of the Temple	21:12–13	11:15–17	19:45–46	2:13–17
Judas betrays Jesus	26:14–16	14:10–11	22:3–6	
Preparations for Passover	26:17–19	14:12–16	22:7–13	
Last Supper	26:20–29	14:17–25	22:14–18	13:1–30
Arrest	26:47–56	14:43–52	22:47–53	18:2–12
Trial	26:57–27:26	14:53–15:15	22:54–23:25	18:13–19:16
Crucifixion and death	27:33–54	15:22–39	23:33–47	19:17–37
Burial	27:57–61	15:42–47	23:50–56	19:38–42
Resurrection	28:1–10	16:1–8	24:1–11	20:1–18
Appearances to disciples	28:16–20	16:12–18	24:13–49	20:19–21:23
Ascension		16:19	24:50–51	

The angel addresses Mary.

How many annunciations were there?

Angelic visitations

ONE OF THE MOST deeply moving of all
biblical stories is the announcement
to Mary by the angel Gabriel that
she would give birth to Jesus, the Messiah
and Son of the Most High. This scene has
captured the imagination of generations of
painters. Usually the angel Gabriel is depicted kneeling, exquisitely dressed and
winged, and raising a hand to bless Mary.
Gabriel's greeting, "Hail Mary, full of
grace" or "Hail, O favored one," has left its
mark on the spiritual lives of countless
Christians; and the young virgin's response
to the news of her pregnancy by the Holy
Spirit ("Behold, I am the handmaid of the
LORD; let it be to me according to your
word") has become a motto of faithful obedience for millions.

Gabriel's visit to Mary is traditionally
called the Annunciation, but in fact two
more angelic annunciations are found in the
early chapters of the Gospels. One of these,

273

delivered by Gabriel six months prior to the revelation experienced by Mary, is a message to the priest Zechariah, a kinsman of the virgin by marriage. As he served his turn at the altar of incense in the Temple, Gabriel appeared to him, astounding him with the promise that he and his wife, Elizabeth, who were old and childless, would become the parents of John—later to be referred to as "the Baptist." When Zechariah questioned the good news and asked for a sign, Gabriel informed him that he would be unable to speak until the predicted events came to pass. Immediately, the old man was mute.

Why was Zechariah punished for his initial lack of faith, while Mary, who also expressed doubt ("How shall this be, since I have no husband?") was not? After all, Zechariah was known to be "righteous before God" (Luke 1:6). Perhaps his lifelong trust in the Lord made him more accountable than Mary, a mere maiden, innocent and perplexed. Or was it that Gabriel appeared to Zechariah in considerable splendor inside the Temple ("I am Gabriel, who stand in the presence of God"), whereas to Mary he disclosed nothing of his heavenly identity and may well have greeted her in the guise of an ordinary human stranger?

The third annunciation presents yet another strange twist to the Gospel story. It occurs only in Matthew's Gospel and concerns Joseph's knowledge of the events surrounding the birth of Jesus. According to this account, when Joseph discovered that Mary was pregnant, he assumed that another man was the father, since he himself had never touched his betrothed. But because he was a just man, he did not react in anger, for he had no wish to shame Mary: instead, he resolved to divorce her quietly. Before this could happen, however, an angel of the Lord appeared to him in a dream, saying, "Joseph, son of David, do not fear to take Mary your wife, for that which is conceived in her is of the Holy Spirit" (1:20).

There is nothing in Matthew's Gospel about Gabriel's visit to Mary; Matthew's account focuses on Joseph. Luke, on the other hand, scarcely mentions Joseph, even in the birth and infancy narratives.

Luke's account contains still another annunciation, one that does not, however, involve an angelic presence. As if to confirm Gabriel's message that her aged kinswoman Elizabeth was already six months pregnant through God's intervention, Mary set out at once from Nazareth to Judah to visit.

WHEN ELIZABETH HEARD the young woman's greeting, an auspicious thing occurred. Luke records that "the babe (the unborn John the Baptist) leaped in her womb; and Elizabeth was filled with the Holy Spirit, and she exclaimed with a loud cry, 'Blessed are you among women, and blessed is the fruit of your womb! And why is this granted me, that the mother of my LORD should come to me?' " (1:41–43). Here Mary is hailed again as God's special servant, chosen to become the mother of the Lord Jesus. Because the text does not suggest any prior knowledge by Elizabeth of Gabriel's visit to Mary, both her maternal sensations and her words are best understood as prophecy. Through the Holy Spirit she feels and sees God's plan unfolding.

Here are two women, perhaps from the lower echelons of society. Elizabeth had borne the reproach of her barrenness for many years, while Mary, a very young woman, and pregnant with no husband, would be ostracized. But through God's providence, these women were about to enter the ranks of the most important human beings on the face of the earth. Mary expressed this paradox in words of praise to God:

My soul magnifies the Lord,
and my spirit rejoices in God my Savior,
for he has regarded the low estate of his
    handmaiden.
For behold, henceforth all generations
    will call me blessed;
for he who is mighty has done great
    things for me,
and holy is his name.
And his mercy is on those who fear him
from generation to generation.
He has shown strength with his arm,
he has scattered the proud in the

The aged Elizabeth *rejoicing with the young Virgin.*

imagination of their hearts,
he has put down the mighty from their
    thrones,
and exalted those of low degree;
he has filled the hungry with good things,
and the rich he has sent empty away.
He has helped his servant Israel,
in remembrance of his mercy,
as he spoke to our fathers,
to Abraham and to his posterity for ever.

In the worship of many Christian churches, this poem has come to occupy a central place as a hymn called "The Magnificat." The hymn is modeled on the Song of Hannah in 1 Samuel; Hannah, like Elizabeth, bore a son in old age. And, like Elizabeth's exclamation, Mary's prayer is also prophetic. It not only interprets the present situation of the two women but also foretells similar reversals of fortune through God's future action. In tone, it is militant. Though Mary is the very epitome of meekness and receptivity, in her exaltation she sounds fierce.

Zechariah also sang the praises of the divine. On the circumcision day of his son, the mute Zechariah wrote on a tablet that the baby should be named John. Immediately his speech was restored and he sang the Lord's praises in a hymn now called "The Benedictus," from its first line: "Blessed be the LORD God of Israel, for he has visited and redeemed his people." Like Elizabeth, Zechariah was moved by the Holy Spirit to speak his poetic words. Thus, it was revealed that God, through the Holy Spirit, directed each scene of this drama toward a redemption of his people. No split between Judaism and Christianity was envisioned. Israel in both the past and the future was viewed as God's chosen nation. ✦

The Nativity

The miraculous birth of Jesus

WHO WAS JESUS, really, and where did he come from? These are two of the questions posed by a group of Gospel stories that are usually referred to as the Nativity. But the answers to these questions come indirectly, for the most part, and in such a way that even those individuals who discover them must continue to wrestle with them.

Only the Gospels of Matthew and Luke provide specific accounts of Jesus' birth, although there is a reference to the place it occurred in John's Gospel. In it people who questioned Jesus' being the Messiah claimed that since he came from Nazareth in Galilee, he could not fulfill the scriptural forecasts concerning the rise of the Lord's Anointed from the city of David, Bethlehem in Judea (John 7:40–52). Whether or not John believed what those detractors said, he made no effort to defend the Bethlehem tradition in his Gospel. It can be surmised that for him the whole argument was beside the point, since heaven was Jesus' real home; the historical circumstances of his taking on flesh were of little consequence (1:1–14).

With Matthew and Luke, however, it was of great importance to show that the location of Jesus' physical origin was in fact Bethlehem. Luke described the place the newborn Jesus was laid. It was a manger (the original Greek word means either a feeding trough or a stall for animals) that Mary used as the baby's bed because the town inn was full (Luke 2:7). Symbolically, the manger could mean the "master's crib" of Isaiah 1:3, an analogy for Israel's misun-

derstanding of God's plan. More clearly, Luke wanted to tell his readers that even though Jesus technically fulfilled a prophecy that the Messiah would be born in Bethlehem (Micah 5:2), he also came, probably contrary to expectation, as a somewhat inconspicuous person. Both in his first moments and in his later ministry, he had no place of his own to lay his head (Luke 9:58).

Matthew also located Jesus' birth in Bethlehem, but he described the event itself in less than a sentence (Matthew 2:1). Instead, he was more interested in how people could recognize the infant as the Messiah. He accomplished this partly by studying Jesus' family tree, prefacing his account of the birth itself with a genealogy, a list of Jesus' ancestors dating back to Abraham. This not only documented Jesus' Jewish lineage but also his descent, on Joseph's side, from King David. Thus Jesus was in the royal line and was also born in David's town, Bethlehem.

Contrary to the usual biblical custom concerning genealogies, Matthew mentioned four women among Jesus' progenitors: Tamar, Rahab, Ruth, and Bathsheba. The first three were foreigners who joined themselves to God's plan for Israel. (They may be paralleled in Matthew's story of the three wise men who came from a distant land to worship the King of the Jews.) Tamar, Rahab, and Bathsheba were known to have had extramarital relations with men, although it is not clear that they were blamed for these. Bathsheba was honored as the mother of the great king Solomon, despite her adulterous union with David. In his genealogy, Matthew wanted to emphasize Jesus' identification with Israel, including its irregular heroines. While Luke also provided a genealogy, it did not serve as a part of the birth story.

Neither Matthew nor Luke neglected the divine origin of Jesus. Joseph was assured

"In the birth of Jesus in Bethlehem, and in all that the life of Jesus was afterwards to reveal, there is the message that not only is there a God, but that God comes very near."
— **Walter Russell Bowie**
The Interpreter's Bible

*"**And this will be a sign for you:** you will find a babe wrapped in swaddling cloths and lying in a manger." Jesus attended by Mary, Joseph, and the shepherds and watched over by angels, as described in the Gospel of Luke.*

277

Relief from Deir el Bahri, Egypt, shows a Boswellia tree, the source of frankincense.

The gifts of the Magi

In his "Sermon on the Epiphany of the Lord," the tenth century monk Aelfric wrote: "The astrologers went into the child's inn, and found him with his mother. Then with prostrate bodies they worshipped Christ, and opened their treasure-chests and offered him three-fold gifts: gold, and incense and myrrh. Gold befits a king; frankincense belongs to the service of God; with myrrh they treat the bodies of dead men so that they decay less rapidly. These three astrologers worshipped Christ and offered him significant gifts. The gold signified that he is a true king, the frankincense that he is the true God, the myrrh that he was then mortal; but now he remains immortal in eternity." Fragrant and resinous plants were used in ancient times for both cosmetics and medicine. Frankincense and myrrh were grown in abundance in north-east Africa and southern Arabia, and then brought to the cities along the caravan routes.

in a dream that Mary's child was "of the Holy Spirit" (Matthew 1:20), and Mary herself knew this to be true because of the message she received from Gabriel (Luke 1:35). Usually the virginal conception portrayed here is thought to be an altogether un-Jewish idea, but some scholars suggest that there was a Hellenistic-Jewish theory that the patriarchs were fathered directly by God. It was not assumed, however, that these divine men were equal to God.

Matthew devoted attention to a story that has come to be called the visit of the wise men, or Magi (Matthew 2:1–12). Who were these people? The term *magoi* in Greek refers to a wide variety of people, including fortune-tellers, priestly augurs, magicians, and astrologers. Because of their connection with the star in this story, it is safe to conclude that Matthew identified them mostly with the last group. Possibly they came from Babylonia, or Persia, where the word *magus* originated. They were almost certainly Gentiles, for if they had been Jews, they would have known better than to ask King Herod about a national ruler who would challenge his dynasty! It is not clear from the story why they wanted to pay homage to a Jewish king or what they learned about him from their observations of "his star" (Matthew 2:2).

The names given to these wise men in later Christian tradition—Gaspar, Melchior, and Balthasar—are of unknown origin. In Eastern Christianity they have different names. Regardless of what they're called, these figures clearly excited the imagination of Christian interpreters and artists from very early times. Partly this was because they were the first Gentiles to acknowledge the significance of Jesus. In Matthew, they are indeed the very first worshipers.

A central negative character in Matthew's Gospel is Herod, who appears as the personification of jealousy, insecurity, and treachery. He obviously knew only a little about Jewish expectations of a Messiah-king, as he had to inquire of his religious advisers where the legendary figure would be born (Matthew 2:3–6). But Herod did

The wise men were guided by a star *to the place where Jesus lay.*

know the significance of this mighty king; thus he pretended to be happy about the discovery of the wise men while he was secretly scheming to do away with the child. When the Magi, warned in a dream, failed to report the location of the infant to Herod, he erupted in a rage and systematically wiped out all the male children in Bethlehem two years old and younger. But he could not thwart God's plan, for Joseph too had been guided by a dream message to flee to Egypt for refuge. There is no extant record of this slaughter of babies, but Bethlehem was a small town, and everything that is known about Herod (who murdered his own sons and wife) suggests that he could have committed such an atrocity.

Matthew concluded his stories of the birth of Jesus with the return of the Holy Family from Egypt following Herod's death. They changed their residence in Palestine from Bethlehem to Nazareth; and this too was reported to be the result of instructions given to Joseph in a dream, as well as the fulfillment of an Old Testament prophecy (Matthew 2:22–23). Luke also knew that Jesus grew up in Nazareth, but he may have deduced this from information that Nazareth was already Joseph's hometown at the time of his betrothal to Mary.

279

In Luke's Gospel, the trip to Bethlehem was for a legal matter; Joseph, as a lineal descendant of David, was required to enroll for taxation in his ancestor's birthplace. Following the birth of Jesus and a short trip to nearby Jerusalem for his presentation in the Temple, the family "returned into Galilee, to their own city, Nazareth" (Matthew 2:39). While Matthew and Luke do not contradict each other, they must have drawn on different sources.

One of the most endearing of the Nativity stories is Luke's description of shepherds "keeping watch over their flock by night" in a field close to Bethlehem (Luke 2:8). Shepherds as a group were not considered to be simple, gentle people in first century Palestine. Rather, shepherds had a certain reputation for dishonesty and breaking the law, such as letting their flocks graze on land belonging to others. That they were the first to hear of Jesus' birth in Luke's

Gospel may reveal something of this evangelist's compassion for the outcast and lesser peoples of Israel. At a deeper level, however, the shepherds did form an appropriate audience for the angelic tidings granted to them. Jesus the Savior was the Shepherd and Son of David par excellence, and his great ancestor had served as a humble shepherd boy in the fields around Bethlehem.

In contrast with Luke's other stories about angelic announcements, this one contains a grand display of sound and light from "a multitude of the heavenly host." Everything else had just been a prelude; this was the birth celebration itself. The shepherds joined it by going to see the baby Jesus and telling others, who were astonished, about what had happened to them. Thus the birth of the Messiah was properly announced and recognized, but he remained an obscure figure until the time of his public ministry.

*As **Herod carried out the slaughter** of the innocents, the Holy Family fled to Egypt.*

In what year was Jesus born? Matthew indicates that his birth came during the last years of Herod (Matthew 2:1–12), who died in 4 B.C. Luke fixed the annunciation of John the Baptist's birth under the same ruler (Luke 1:5), which would mean that when Jesus came into the world, roughly six months after John the Baptist (1:36), Herod was probably still on the throne. (The Nativity of Jesus occurred in a B.C. year because of a calendrical error made in the early medieval period.)

The only difficulty with this agreement is that Luke also reported that Jesus was born in Bethlehem during a census under Quirinius, the governor of Syria (2:1–7). According to all available records, that census took place in 6 and 7 A.D., and Quirinius was not the governor during Herod's reign. Questions remain, however, such as whether a two-stage census might have been taken, the first part beginning as early as 4 B.C. Astronomers' attempts to determine a date for the star seen by the Magi have yielded interesting theories, but nothing conclusive. Thus, while the general time frame for Jesus' birth is well established, some details continue to perplex students of the Bible.

Joseph and Jesus in the carpenter's shop.

Jesus' mysterious years

Teaching in the Temple

WHAT HAPPENED DURING the 30 years between Jesus' infancy and that moment when his ministry began? How did his personality, interests, passions, and perhaps foibles develop? How did he become a person who could have such an impact on history?

Generations of would-be biographers have been frustrated by the enigma of the missing years, the puzzling fact that the Gospels record only a single story to bridge three decades of Jesus' spiritual, intellectual, emotional, and social development.

In fact, three of the four Gospels provide no specific information about Jesus' childhood at all. Both the Gospels of Mark and of John begin their stories with Jesus as an adult. The Gospel of Matthew records stories surrounding Jesus' birth but then skips directly to his adulthood. They were either uninterested in the childhood years, or they had no information concerning them.

Only the Gospel of Luke touches upon the intervening years. Between two summary statements asserting that Jesus has grown in body, in wisdom, and in God's favor, Luke relates a single incident that he hopes will reveal to the reader something of the character of the youth.

At the age of 12, Luke says, Jesus went with his parents from Nazareth on their annual pilgrimage to Jerusalem for the feast of Passover. According to the Laws of Exodus, Jewish males were expected to go to the Temple of Jerusalem three times a year to celebrate pilgrim feasts. Being 12, Jesus was now considered a "Son of the Law," and was thus expected to attend the Temple

281

feasts. This may well have been the boy's first journey to the holy city since his circumcision. When Mary and Joseph began the caravan trip home, Jesus stayed behind without telling them, while they supposed that he was among the throng of people in their caravan. After a day of travel they realized that he was missing, and returned to the city to search for the boy. After three days of searching they came upon him in the Temple listening to the teachers of the Torah, questioning them, and responding to their counter-questions with remarkable discernment.

The climax of the story occurs after Mary asks Jesus, "Son, why have you treated us so? Behold, your father and I have been looking for you anxiously." Jesus' response is mysterious: "How is it that you sought me? Did you not know that I must be in my Father's house?" (Luke 2:48–49). These are the first words that the Gospels record from Jesus, and, as with many later sayings, Luke notes that they were not understood at the time. Luke writes, "And they did not understand the saying which he spoke to them." Still, as Luke looked back and recounted the story many decades later, he found that this momentary glimpse into Jesus' youth was sufficient to illuminate the mysterious hidden years in a number of significant ways.

For Luke, Jesus' statement that "I must be in my Father's house" was crucial. It showed that Jesus' special identity as "Son of God," which Luke had already celebrated in the birth narratives, had now become part of Jesus' own mind and was a motive for his actions even against what would appear as disobedience to his parents. In addition, the entire situation demonstrated that Jesus' beginnings were firmly rooted in Jewish faith and practice. Already at the age of twelve he was absorbed in the study of the Scriptures and could knowledgeably discourse with professional teachers.

Jesus had grown up in a family faithful in its obedience to the law. Their caravan to celebrate Passover in Jerusalem is a sign of the family's piety. Other Gospel passages indicate that Jesus was one of at least seven children in his family, and that he was also a carpenter like Joseph, ready for life as a craftsman. Though he could hold his own in the environment of the Jerusalem Temple, his home was in the far less cosmopolitan setting of the villages of Galilee's hill country. All of these elements, drawn together in a single story, provided for Luke a demonstration of the depth of Jesus' roots among his own people—in spite of all the conflicts over the Torah and Jesus' teaching that were later to mark his story. ✦

Mary, Jesus, and Joseph *return home from the Temple.*

On the flight to Egypt, Jesus made wheat grow high and ripe.

Apocryphal stories about Jesus

By the second century A.D., many stories circulated among Christians about Jesus' childhood. One source for these stories was a work that scholars call the "Infancy Gospel of Thomas." According to the "Infancy Gospel," Jesus practiced a full range of miraculous powers. He could make clay sparrows by a brook, then clap his hands and make them fly. If another child quarreled with him or even bumped into him, Jesus might well strike him dead—later he might raise the child back to life. When Joseph in the carpenter's shop cut a board too short, Jesus could stretch it to the right length. When a teacher tried to begin Jesus' education by teaching him the alphabet, Jesus immediately explained to him the full mystical meaning of the letters. An anecdote that was popular in the Middle Ages related how Jesus and Mary, fleeing to Egypt, hid from Herod's men behind a field of fully grown wheat that sprang up instantly at Jesus' touch.

The hidden meaning of Jesus' name

Salvation through the anointed one

THE NAME JESUS was common in the first century of the Christian era, and a tag such as "of Nazareth" or "son of Joseph" served to distinguish one Jesus from another. The name of Jesus comes from the Greek form of the Hebrew name *Joshua*, meaning "Yahweh is salvation." As the angel predicted to Joseph, "he will save his people from their sins" (Matthew 1:21). These words confirm something highly unusual: if the name *Jesus* (*Joshua*) literally means "Yahweh is the source of salvation," then the angel is saying that Jesus himself will assume an activity hitherto assigned to God alone. Often in the Old Testament, Yahweh is said to raise up a "savior," a purely human agent who will save his people. And, as God selects the human savior, his unique, divine authority is preserved.

In this light, it is significant that the name *Christ* comes from the Greek form of the Hebrew word, *mashiah* (messiah) which means "anointed one." In the Old Testament, the ruling king of Israel was often called the "anointed one." David, for example, calls Saul "the LORD's anointed." Moreover, in later books of the Old Testament, a messianic king, descended from the House of David, is expected to lead a rejuvenation of the Jewish people. It is not until the time of the Second Temple that the Messiah was expected to oversee the end of days. The Jews of the Roman period believed that such a charismatic leader would rise up and break the yoke of foreign rule. Jesus was in fact one of many Jews of his period who was thought to be the Messiah who would bring redemption to his people.

Long before the Christian period, Jews had banned the pronunciation of the four consonants YHWH, the most sacred name of God revealed to Moses, known as the tetragrammaton. A secret pronunciation of the name may have been imparted by Jesus to his disciples which confirmed the meaning of the divine name as "He who is" or, perhaps, "He who causes to be." The Gospels tend to substitute the word *Kyrios* ("Lord") for YHWH, following the practice of the Septuagint of the third century B.C.

But perhaps the most basic confession of the early Church was "Jesus is LORD." By taking up the most sacred name of God, by pronouncing it, and by accepting it as descriptive of himself, Jesus identified himself in a most radical manner with the full mystery of God's presence in this world. So it was that in the writings of the Apostle Paul the name of Jesus became an expression of God's presence and power (1 Corinthians 1:2, 5:3, 6:11).

Christians traditionally believed that God was fully present in Jesus' words and deeds and conversely, that Christ, as depicted in the New Testament, was already present in the voice and activity of God in the Old Testament. In the opening sentences of the Gospel of John, Jesus is even identified with "the Word" that was with God before the creation of the world. Jesus acknowledges to God, "I have made known to them thy name."

New Testament writers speak of activities done "in the name of Jesus"—for example, prayer, baptism, exorcism, receiving a child (Matthew 18:5), or even giving a cup of water (Mark 9:41). What these have in common is a sense of mystical identification with the power, authority, or glory that is associated with Jesus. ✦

"The voice of one crying in the wilderness"

John the Baptist

BETWEEN THE TANGLED thickets along the Jordan River, with the rocky desert rising to east and west and the salty expanse of the Dead Sea to the south, in the days of the emperor Tiberius, a voice began to be heard crying out against sin and warning of the coming of God's judgment. It was a cry that many in Israel recognized as the voice of a prophet—in a time when the spirit of prophecy was said to be dead.

Roman prefects ruled Judea west of the Jordan while Herod Antipas, a puppet of Rome, reigned over the region of Perea to the east. Between them came John, like a voice from the past, a mysterious man of the desert, dressed in a manner that recalled the biblical descriptions of Elijah. He wore a garment of camel's hair, and a leather belt around his waist; he ate what the desert provided, locusts and wild honey.

The people, pressed on all sides by foreign power, were ready to hear a prophet. They flocked from the towns to be strength-ened by John's steely courage as he unveiled the corruption of society from king to peasant. He challenged all to prepare for the coming judgment of God, which, he said, was now like an ax laid at the root of a tree (Luke 3:9). He summoned all to be baptized by being plunged into the waters of the Jordan as a sign of their repentance and readiness for God's judgment. From this distinctive command, he received the name "the Immerser" or "the Baptist."

John was by no means a wild man. He was the son of a priestly family, and the Gospel according to Luke reports the traditions of his miraculous birth—recalling similar traditions about Isaac and Samuel—to an elderly childless woman named Elizabeth and her husband Zechariah. John gathered a considerable body of disciples and became a guide to righteous living both for them and for the people at large.

However, John was a dangerous man, at least in the eyes of Herod Antipas. Jose-

Baptism of Christ: *"he will baptize you with the Holy Spirit and with fire."*

phus, the Jewish historian, reports that the crowds that came to John were so aroused by his words that Herod became alarmed. Fearing that John would instigate a popular rebellion, Herod had John imprisoned and later put to death. The New Testament attributes the arrest to the fact that John had denounced Herod for marrying Herodias, his brother's wife.

It was to this prophet, John, whom he described as greater than anyone ever born, that Jesus went to be baptized. It was after John was arrested that Jesus took up his own ministry. ✦

The Dead Sea Scrolls

New evidence of old truths

ONE DAY EARLY in 1947 a Bedouin youth named Muhammad adh-Dhib was searching for a lost goat along the cliffs that border the Dead Sea. He threw a stone into one of the small caves there and was startled by the sound of breaking pottery. Going in to explore, he could not have known that he was probably the first human in nearly two millennia to set foot in the cave. Its last visitors had left behind several clay jars containing leather

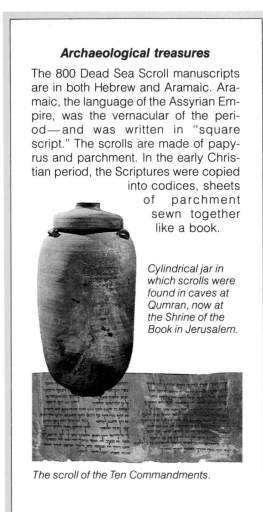

Archaeological treasures

The 800 Dead Sea Scroll manuscripts are in both Hebrew and Aramaic. Aramaic, the language of the Assyrian Empire, was the vernacular of the period—and was written in "square script." The scrolls are made of papyrus and parchment. In the early Christian period, the Scriptures were copied into codices, sheets of parchment sewn together like a book.

Cylindrical jar in which scrolls were found in caves at Qumran, now at the Shrine of the Book in Jerusalem.

The scroll of the Ten Commandments.

scrolls, some covered with linen cloth. Although dried up and decayed by the centuries, seven of the scrolls were largely intact. Thus Muhammad's stone unearthed what many now consider the greatest manuscript discovery of modern times.

The discovery eventually set off a "scroll rush" by both archaeologists and Bedouins that ultimately led to the discovery of documents in 10 other caves and to the excavation of the ruins of a monastery at Qumran about a half mile south of the original find. It became apparent that a substantial library had long been hidden. In just one cave slightly west of the ruins, perhaps as many as 40,000 fragments of scrolls were found. So far, at least 520 documents have been identified from that cave alone, but the majority of fragments remain unpublished. All told, the caves have produced scrolls and fragments from every book of the Hebrew Bible except Esther—manuscripts a thousand years older than the oldest previously known copies. In addition, hundreds of nonbiblical documents were found, including many that could be traced to the Essenes, a monastic community of Jews.

Who were the people who hid these manuscripts and why did they do it? The Essene sect—whose existence was long known through descriptions by Josephus, Philo, and Pliny—now became visible from the inside. The scrolls provided copies of, among other things, their detailed monastic rule books, their hymns and prayers, and their plans for the final battle between the "sons of light" and the "sons of darkness."

Like the Pharisees, the Essenes probably had their historic roots among the Hasideans, "the pious" Jews who fought for the Torah in the Maccabean revolt. Unlike the Pharisees, however, they completely rejected the priesthood in Jerusalem led by the Hasmonean high priests. The leader of the Essenes, a priest known in the scrolls only

The arid wilderness above the Dead Sea is the site of the Qumran caves.

by his designation as "the Teacher of Righteousness," was persecuted by "the Wicked Priest," possibly Jonathan, the Hasmonean high priest. The Teacher and his numerous followers abandoned the polluted temple and set out to establish a pure community in their desert enclave.

The Essenes considered themselves to be the true people of God living in the troubled times before the last days. They created a strict monastic community that committed each member to a life of worship that would join them as "sons of light" on earth to the angels of God in heaven.

The Essenes at Qumran were mostly celibate men who renounced all their possessions to the community and lived a life of exacting standards both in ethical practice and ritual purity. Any act of extreme disobedience brought permanent expulsion. Every aspect of life—from their white clothing to their ritual meals, from their prayers to their copying of scrolls—was organized to prepare them for the final conflict and the new age that they expected.

The movement that the Teacher of Righteousness began lasted for generations. The Qumran community continued to thrive for about 200 years until it was overrun by the Roman army during the Jewish War, between A.D. 68 and 70. Probably at that time, some of the Essenes hid their precious library in various caves around the monastery. There the scrolls remained, waiting through the centuries for the stone of a Bedouin youth. ✦

287

***Jesus countered** each of the devil's lures with the word of God.*

"You shall not tempt the LORD your God"

The devil's defeat

N O ONE WILL EVER know exactly why or how the decision was made, but sometime after his thirtieth year, Jesus, a carpenter in the hill country village of Nazareth, trekked south and east to the Jordan Valley to be baptized by John. He thereby joined with John in the expectation of the coming of the Kingdom of God.

The Gospels proclaim Jesus as God's Messiah, and they recount the beginning of Jesus' ministry, emphasizing the elements of mystery and miracle that reveal the divine character of his mission. They tell how John the Baptist subordinated himself to Jesus and even felt unworthy to baptize him (Matthew 3:14–15). The Gospel of John does not even report that John the Baptist did in fact baptize Jesus, but only that he bore witness to him as "the Son of God" and "the Lamb of God who takes away the sin of the world" (John 1:29, 34). The stress on John the Baptist as the "forerunner" of Jesus also helped to win over some of the numerous disciples of John who continued

to follow Jesus' teaching after his death (Acts 18:25; 19:1–7).

The Gospels of Matthew, Mark, and Luke describe a remarkable epiphany that accompanied Jesus' baptism. When Jesus emerged from the Jordan, "he saw the heavens opened and the Spirit descending upon him like a dove; and a voice came from heaven, 'Thou art my beloved Son; with thee I am well pleased' " (Mark 1:10–11). Thus Jesus' mission begins with the miraculous presence of God's Spirit and the emphatic assertion of Jesus' identity by God himself. As God had appeared to Moses in the wilderness, so too did Jesus begin his journey with an epiphany of God in the wilderness with John.

Another step, however, had to precede the beginning of Jesus' ministry. The Synoptic Gospels tell that the very Spirit that Jesus received at baptism "drove him out into the wilderness. And he was in the wilderness forty days, tempted by Satan" (Mark 1:12–13). Mark does not spell out what happened, but Matthew and Luke tell of a three-part encounter with "the tempter" or "the devil."

The word "devil" translates the Greek word *diabolos*, which, like the Hebrew word *satan*, means "accuser" or "slanderer." For the Gospel writers it did not conjure up images of red-suited demons or the satanic monsters of later imagination. In fact, the Gospels leave this "accuser" remarkably undefined, allowing the reader to see him only through his challenges to Jesus' identity as the Son of God.

As Israel spent 40 years being tested in the wilderness, and the prophet Elijah spent 40 days in the Sinai, where, at Mount Horeb he heard the voice of God, so now Jesus spent 40 days of fasting and trial in the barren wilds of Judea. Matthew and Luke both record the same three temptations and in both Gospels the focus is on Jesus' identity as "Son of God" and on his obedience and trust in God.

Though physically weakened by fasting, Jesus is indomitable in purpose. A story of temptation might be expected to include an account of inner struggle, of a mind divided over which way to go or what to do. The Gospel accounts, however, choose to depict only the barest hints of psychological struggle after Jesus' 40 days of fasting.

Rather, what the Gospels describe is a formal, almost stylized confrontation between Satan and the Son of God. The tempter begins without the least hint of subtlety, "If you are the Son of God. . . ." He directly challenges the identity that God himself had confirmed at Jesus' baptism. Jesus in turn responds only by quoting the Scriptures—"It is written." In each case he cites a passage from Deuteronomy concerning a lesson that Israel learned during its trials in the wilderness. Through their link to the experiences of God's people in the past, the three temptations take on a symbolic character. They are not only a new and unique experience for Jesus, but the temptations also link him with his people's often unsuccessful struggles with such temptations in the past.

Thus the Gospel according to Matthew records: "Jesus said to him, 'Again it is written, "You shall not tempt the Lord your God." ' Again, the devil took him to a very high mountain, and showed him all the kingdoms of the world and the glory of them; and he said to him, 'All these I will give you, if you will fall down and worship me.' Then Jesus said to him, 'Begone, Satan! for it is written, "You shall worship the Lord your God and him only shall you serve." ' Then the devil left him, and behold, angels came and ministered to him."

The temptation to turn stones to bread may point to the human inability to trust God in ordinary life, to pray simply, "Give us this day our daily bread," and trust God's word. Perhaps it was also a temptation for Jesus to use miraculous powers in a self-serving manner.

The temptation to receive from the devil "all the kingdoms of the world" may point to Jesus' rejection of political messiahship. It focuses on trust in God's future—"Thy kingdom come"—and a commitment to worship and serve God alone.

The temptation to leap from the pinnacle of the Temple in Jerusalem suggests that God refuses to be the object of a controlled experiment; he will not be put to such a test. God's name must be hallowed. The trials ended with Jesus, strengthened by the angels themselves, turning back to the people to begin his work. ✦

On the temptation of Jesus

"The Bible tells only two temptation stories, the temptation of the first man and the temptation of Christ, that is the temptation which led to man's fall, and the temptation which led to Satan's fall. All other temptations in human history have to do with these two stories of temptation. Either we are tempted in Adam or we are tempted in Christ. Either the Adam in me is tempted—in which case we fall. Or the Christ in us is tempted—in which case Satan is bound to fall."   —**Dietrich Bonhoeffer**
Temptation (1937)

How did Jesus reveal his mission?

The three key accounts

WHEN JESUS WAS in the wilderness of the Jordan with John the Baptist, he was not far from Qumran, where the Essenes sought to prepare for the kingdom of God by living in a rigorously structured monastic community, admitting only those who had undergone years of demanding probation. But in spite of speculations about links between Jesus and the Essenes aroused by the discovery of the Dead Sea Scrolls, there is no real evidence that Jesus ever made contact with that desert community, and neither the Essenes nor Qumran is ever mentioned in the New Testament.

It could be that Jesus had heard of the rigorist community at Qumran or had known Essenes who lived in the towns of Israel, but if he did, his ministry makes it clear that he rejected the Essene pattern for his own ministry. Jesus, as he characterized himself, was practically the opposite of the Essene ideal: "The Son of man has come eating and drinking; and you say, 'Behold, a glutton and a drunkard, a friend of tax collectors and sinners!' " (Luke 7:34). A kind of community that was withdrawn from society was clearly not what Jesus intended.

But just as Jesus did not follow the pattern of the Essenes, neither did he follow the example of John the Baptist. Though baptized by John, he did not stay with him in the desert. He did not continue John's practice of summoning the people out into the wilderness of the Jordan to renew their commitment to God; rather he went among the people, in the villages and towns of Israel, ministering to them and preaching the kingdom of God in their midst.

The beginning of Jesus' ministry is described in three distinct ways in the Gospels. Luke begins by telling of Jesus' return to his hometown of Nazareth. After his baptism and 40 days of fasting, which were followed by the temptation in the wilderness, Jesus returned home: "And he came to Nazareth, where he had been brought up; and he went to the synagogue, as his

In the early days of his ministry, *Jesus chose his first disciples from among the fishermen on the Sea of Galilee.*

custom was, on the Sabbath day" (Luke 4:16). All was as it had been before, except Jesus had been changed and now acted "in the power of the Spirit," Luke says (4:14).

In those familiar surroundings and among his acquaintances, Jesus participated in the synagogue service by reading a selection from the prophets. Jesus was handed the scroll of Isaiah, found the passage he wanted, and read to the assembly. The passage included most of Isaiah 61:1–2 combined with a phrase from Isaiah 58:6 and summarized both the mysterious power and the public work of Jesus: "The Spirit of the LORD is upon me, because he has anointed me to preach good news to the poor. He has sent me to proclaim release to the captives and recovering of sight to the blind, to set at liberty those who are oppressed, to proclaim the acceptable year of the LORD" (Luke 4:18–19).

Jesus rolled the scroll and handed it to the *hazzan*, or attendant, and sat down. Luke emphasizes a sense of expectation that filled the room as "the eyes of all in the synagogue were fixed on him," awaiting his interpretation of the Scripture. He tells how Jesus explained the text with a single remarkable and unexpected sentence: "Today this scripture has been fulfilled in your hearing" (Luke 4:21). Luke writes that those who knew him were amazed. Luke wanted his readers to see, however, that it was the Spirit that made Jesus the "anointed," the "Messiah," and set him on his ministry of proclamation, healing, and relief to the poor and the suffering. The passage becomes a keynote for Jesus' whole life.

Luke's account takes a remarkable turn at this point. One of the worshippers asks, "Is this not Joseph's son?", as if to question the validity of Jesus' divine mission by pointing to his humble origins. Rather than trying to answer the implicit criticism, Jesus began to challenge them. Jesus used two proverbs, that suggested that they would reject him as a healer and prophet, "Truly, I say to you, no prophet is acceptable in his own country." He then told two stories

---

IN MODERN TIMES

✷ Synagogue ✷

The Greek word, *synagoge*, occurs over 50 times in the New Testament. The original Greek meaning referred to the collective assembly of Israel, but the term as we know it denotes a Jewish house of worship. Thus Jesus taught in synagogues throughout Galilee, and Paul preached in synagogues in Damascus and refers to synagogues in every city he visited in Asia Minor. It is clear both from literary sources (the New Testament, Philo, Josephus, and the Talmud) and from modern archaeological finds, that the synagogue was an ancient institution by the first century A.D. Though its exact origins are unclear, most scholars agree that the development of the synagogue was organic, dating from the time of the Babylonian captivity, when the exiled Jews, forcibly removed from the Temple, gathered in groups to read the Scriptures. Throughout the Diaspora synagogues were built. The remains of a synagogue dating from the time of Ptolemy III (246–221 B.C.) has been found outside Alexandria. It is interesting that until the fall of Herod's Temple, the Temple and the synagogue existed side by side, in complementary roles. The Temple was the center of the ancestral cult; there sacrificial services were performed. After 70 A.D., the synagogue became the central institution of Judaism and prayer became the central form of worship.

The Sabbath was the day of public worship. An attendant (the *hazzan* or beadle) brought the Torah scrolls, kept in an enclosure known as the "holy ark," for reading, for the instruction of the congregation in the Law. Later, a *cantor* was added to the synagogue personnel, and still later, the preacher or rabbi. The Orthodox services themselves have changed little in some 2,000 years. To this day, the synagogue is the central religious, social, and educational institution of Judaism.

Jesus miraculously transformed *water into wine at the wedding feast of Cana.*

from Scripture that described how the great prophets Elijah and Elisha were sent to minister to people outside Israel. The people perhaps felt insulted by the implication that they would reject God's will, and that Jesus intended to take his message to the Gentiles. They quickly turned against Jesus, even to the point of trying to kill him.

This incident embodies the contradictory reception that Jesus encountered in his own ministry and in the time of the early church. From the beginning, Jesus both fulfilled and contradicted the expectations that people had of a Messiah, and thus brought forth both acceptance and rejection.

Both Matthew and Mark record this incident at Nazareth, but at a later point in their Gospels. Instead they begin the story of Jesus' ministry with another incident in which Jesus summons two pairs of brothers to be his disciples. The story is told in a spare style that adds to the mystery.

In Mark, the story appears near the beginning of the Gospel. Mark has described Jesus' returning to Galilee proclaiming, "The time is fulfilled, and the kingdom of God is at hand; repent, and believe in the gospel" (Mark 1:15). Then, as Jesus walked along the Sea of Galilee, he saw two fishermen, Simon and Andrew, casting nets into the sea. Mark's words are simple and brief: "Jesus said to them, 'Follow me and I will make you become fishers of men.' And immediately they left their nets and followed him" (Mark 1:17–18). The scene was soon repeated a little farther down the beach with James and John, the sons of Zebedee, who left not only their nets but also their father, boat, and hired servants.

There is not the slightest hint in the Gospels of Mark or Matthew that these men had ever heard of Jesus before, listened to his teaching, or seen his deeds, but some scholars believe that they may have. However, the story highlights the authority of Jesus' word. He calls; they respond; their lives are transformed. Fishermen no longer, they become "fishers of men." The reader wonders what it means to be a disciple to one who calls with such authority.

The Gospel of John begins Jesus' ministry with a different incident. When Jesus returned from the Jordan to Galilee, he and his mother were invited to a wedding in the village of Cana. The host of the wedding banquet ran out of wine for the party— hardly an incident, one would think, calling for supernatural intervention. The reader's sense of curiosity is aroused when Jesus' mother remarks to him, "They have no wine," to which Jesus answers mysteriously, "O woman, what have you to do with me? My hour has not yet come" (John 2:4). Why does he talk this way to his own mother? Does she expect something of him? What does he mean about his "hour"? The questions accumulate as the story continues. In spite of Jesus' strange response, Mary tells the servants to follow Jesus' instructions. He asks them to fill 6 stone jars, holding perhaps 120 gallons, with water, and then instructs them to draw out some and take it to the master of ceremonies. By the time the water reaches his lips, it has become wine, indeed better wine than had yet been served at the feast.

How did it happen? Why? Did anyone besides the servants know? What is this story all about? At the moment John chooses to answer very few of these questions. He wants the reader's sense of mystery to grow. The event, he says, is a "sign" that points to Jesus' "glory" that the remainder of the Gospel will reveal. ✦

"The kingdom of God is at hand"

The underlying puzzle

THE TIME IS FULFILLED, and the kingdom of God is at hand; repent, and believe in the gospel." With these words the Gospel of Mark records Jesus' first proclamation. Indeed, it can be said that the major theme of Jesus' teaching was the kingdom of God. Yet Israel acknowledged God to be Creator and Lord over the entire cosmos: what, then, did Jesus mean by "the kingdom of God is at hand"?

As a devout Jew, Jesus believed passionately in the ultimate sovereignty of God's rule. But he saw and proclaimed that sovereignty less in cosmic terms than by showing God's love of people of every degree and station. His actions and teachings in the Gospels indicate that he tried to create around him a community that could experience and share God's intimate love. That heart of his message is evident through his preaching to the outcasts of his society: God's kingship is a loving rule which, embracing the lowly and despised, frees them to respond with love and joy. In this community of love he saw and celebrated the coming of God's kingdom. According to Luke 10:18, he said: "I saw Satan fall like lightning from heaven." Thus, he believed, the forces of evil were being overcome and a new age was beginning.

Jesus mysteriously spoke of the kingdom as near, "at hand." What did he mean? When would the kingdom actually come? Did he think the end of the world was imminent? Did he expect the catastrophic demise of the physical world and its history?

Numerous passages in the Gospels indicate that Jesus believed that God's kingdom was at that very time becoming a reality through his work. For example, when Jesus said, "If it is by the finger of God that I cast out demons, then the kingdom of God has come upon you" (Luke 11:20), he was asserting that in his liberation of people possessed by the forces of evil, the power of God's rule had already become present.

John the Baptist, on the other hand, had proclaimed that God's rule was coming in the near future, and many of Jesus' words point to the future in a similar way. But whereas John's message amplified the threat of God's judgment, Jesus led his followers to hopeful expectation. When Jesus taught his disciples to pray to the Father, one of the few petitions he included was "Thy kingdom come." The image is important. The kingdom was not thought of as something toward which the disciples were to strive and struggle. Rather, God's kingdom was coming, moving, pressing into the present; indeed, as Jesus asserted, "the kingdom of God is in the midst of you."

Jesus could also speak of the kingdom of God in ways that reached into the future beyond this world and its history. Matthew reported his saying that "many will come from east and west and sit at table with Abraham, Isaac, and Jacob in the kingdom of heaven." But often Jesus identified the kingdom less by the time of its coming than by the kinds of people to whom it belonged. Jesus welcomed the children because, as he said, "To such belongs the kingdom of God." He therefore urged his disciples to "receive the kingdom of God like a child." This divine kingdom that was present and also future, that embodied the majestic sovereignty of God, that belonged to children, that created a community of inclusive love, was the reality that Jesus celebrated. ✦

Healing and exorcism

Casting out unclean spirits

MANY PEOPLE OF JESUS' time believed that the universe was divided into two competing realms, the kingdom of God and the kingdom of Satan, or the Devil. Satan was believed to seduce people into sin, which brought in its wake a loss of God's blessings of health and life. Paul said when sin came into the world, "death reigned" (Romans 5:14). But individual sinners were not always believed to be responsible for their own suffering. When evil befell them, ancient Christians and Jews suspected that someone—either Satan or a person who had sinned—was the cause. Hence Luke 13:16 speaks of a crippled woman as one "whom Satan bound for eighteen years." John 9:2 voices the common assumption that sin leads to sickness: "who sinned, this man or his parents, that he was born blind?"

Healings, then, implied that the healed person was freed from the power of Satan and brought into God's kingdom, the realm of wholeness and life. Thus Jesus' miracles were seen as aggressive actions against Satan and his kingdom, even as they served to establish the kingdom of God (Matthew 12:28; Luke 11:20).

Ancient Judaism classified certain bodily defects (as well as corpses) as causing "uncleanness," which is displeasing to the perfect and holy God (Leviticus 11:44–45; 21:18–20). Jesus' healings restored bodily wholeness: Such health was tantamount to spiritual holiness. A healed person, freed from his "unclean" defects, was now fit to be ritually purified. Thus the leper of Mark 1:44, healed by Jesus' touch, was ordered to "go, show yourself to the priest, and offer for your cleansing what Moses commanded." The demons which Jesus exorcises are fittingly described as "unclean spirits" (Mark 1:23,28; 3:11; 5:8,13; 6:7; 7:25); and so when "un-

Jesus sent the unclean spirits *into the Gadarene swine.*

294

*"**Child, arise.**" Jesus' touch restored life to Jairus' daughter.*

cleanness" is expelled from a person, he is rendered "holy."

Being possessed by a demon, however, did not necessarily result in physical disease. It was thought that some demons, while not causing illness, were the cause of what we would now call mental disorders. Demons could thus enslave a person without actually making him ill. An exorcism was the cure for this second kind of possession. Thus Jesus directly confronted and cast out the unclean spirits. The first chapter of Mark relates how one of Jesus' first public actions was an exorcism. In this role, Jesus is characterized as the chief agent of God's kingdom; he is authorized with power to attack and despoil the kingdom of Satan.

At the time of Jesus, the Essenes were also teaching the people that cleanliness could be attained through an ascetic way of life. But in the eyes of his audience, Jesus surpassed these teachers because he "taught them as one who has authority, and not as the scribes." In other words, he was empowered to effect cleanness by expelling the "unclean" spirit. Yet his actions were challenged by his rivals, who argued that he was in league with Satan and was in fact acting as an agent of Satan: "And the scribes who came down from Jerusalem said, 'He is possessed by Beelzebul, and by the prince of demons he casts out the demons.' " Jesus' reply to this charge, "How can Satan cast out Satan?" rests on the commonplace that allies do not war on each other.

Because the view of a dualistic universe was shared by many countries of the ancient world, exorcism stories are not confined to the Gospels. Similar tales occur in the other literature of the period. For example, in Book 8 of his monumental *Antiquities of the Jews*, the historian Flavius Josephus tells of an exorcist named Eleazar who cast demons out of a possessed person in the presence of the emperor Vespasian around 70 A.D., following magical procedures said to hark back to King Solomon. It is therefore not surprising that the evangelists shared with the wider culture at least some aspects of a common literary way of narrating an exorcism story. Such a narrative typically begins with an encounter between exorcist and possessed person; the severity of the disease is noted, after which the demon engages in defensive activity, such as magical use of the exorcist's name or pleas for leniency. The exorcist commands the demon to leave, demanding a visible sign that the demon is exiting; finally the crowd reacts with approval or fear. ✦

Walking on water, stilling the storm

Jesus commands the elements

FROM THE PARTING of the Red Sea by Moses, to the sun standing still at Gibeon, to Daniel being miraculously saved from hungry lions—the story of God's people is regularly punctuated with moments when nature does not follow its expected course. As they recounted Jesus' life, the writers of the Gospels included stories which demonstrated God's control over nature, and which were meant to suggest that the Lord remained in control.

The Gospel writers told the stories of Jesus' miracles with confidence, hoping to strengthen belief in Jesus. But ironically, for many modern readers, the miracles become an obstacle rather than an aid to faith. The stories become especially problematic when they seem to describe a supernatural violation of the laws of nature. This forces the reader to suspend belief in these laws and to defer to faith as a means of understanding the miracles recounted in the Gospel story. This difficulty for the modern reader, with his store of scientific and historical knowledge, would not have been so pronounced to the ancient reader; the way that people perceive their world and understand what such miracles mean has changed.

For the biblical narrators, there was never a thought of "laws of nature" that could only be violated by supernatural intervention. The entire world was both created and sustained by God and was under his direct control. God's personal care for the world was such that, as Jesus said, not one sparrow "will fall to the ground without your Father's will." The stories of nature miracles were for them truly marvels, but not because the miracle contradicted the ordinary reality of the world. Rather, it confirmed that reality. The wonder lay in the fact that the miracle gave an extraordinarily clear and marvelous demonstration of the divine control that was always present.

When the Gospel writers recount these traditions, they give not the least hint of any philosophical or scientific reticence about the events. Their focus is entirely on the meaning of such events and what the miracles contributed to the proclamation of Jesus.

Sometimes that quest for meaning is expressed very directly. When the Gospel of John, for example, describes how Jesus fed a crowd of about 5,000 people in the wilderness, using only five barley loaves and two fish, the Gospel leaves no doubt about the significance of the event. "Now there was much grass in the place; so the men sat down, in number about five thousand. Jesus then took the loaves, and when he had given thanks, he distributed them to those who were seated; so also the fish, as much as they wanted. And when they had eaten their fill, he told his disciples, 'Gather up the fragments left over, that nothing may be lost.' " The people themselves saw the sign

In Jesus' footsteps

Since the founding of the Church, Christian pilgrims have travelled to what is now the State of Israel to see the places where Jesus preached, healed, suffered—and died. In the early fourth century, the emperor Constantine and his mother, Helena, made Jerusalem one of the important cities of Christianity by building churches in and around the city. Most of the shrines were destroyed in later centuries by conquerors of Jerusalem, but restorations have been made since that time. Perhaps the most famous of these sanctuaries is the Basilica of the Holy Sepulchre. It is believed by many to be located where Jesus was buried, in addition to being the place where, according to tradition, Helena found the true Cross. It now contains a reconstruction of the tomb of Jesus. Of equally great importance is the Via Dolorosa. Along the route through the Old City, tablets indicate the 14 Stations of the Cross. Overlooking Jerusalem is the Mount of Olives.

In Bethlehem is the Church of the Nativity, built by the Byzantine emperor, Justinian, in the sixth century, on the foundations of an earlier chapel built by Constantine. In it is a grotto where, tradition holds, Christ was born.

It was in Nazareth that Jesus lived until his public ministry began; he also preached in the synagogue here. The town commemorates Jesus' family life with shrines that include the Church of St. Joseph, located on the reputed site of Joseph's carpentry shop, and the Church of the Annunciation. Nazareth was reduced to ruins by the Sultan of Egypt in the 13th century, but shrines began to be rebuilt four centuries later, under the guardianship of the Franciscans. Today the place where the annunciation is recalled is a grotto in the modern Church of the Annunciation, completed in 1966.

and recognized that "This is indeed the prophet who is to come into the world." The next day the people sought out Jesus once again. He spoke to them about the miracle's symbolism: "I am the bread of life; he who comes to me shall not hunger." The other Gospels also recount the miracle, but do not include Jesus' discourse.

Sometimes a comparison of the same miracle in two Gospels can illuminate its meaning in each. For instance, Mark, the earliest of the Gospels, recounts the story of Jesus stilling a great storm on the Sea of Galilee (Mark 4:35–41).

The Sea of Galilee is not in fact a true sea, but is more on the scale of a large lake. To this day it is known for its fierce and unpredictable winds. Signs, in four languages, warn boaters and bathers of the dangers of squalls. It was perhaps these very turbulent winds that Jesus and his dis-

ciples encountered on the Sea of Galilee.

Jesus had spent the day sitting in a boat by the shore, teaching the crowds and his disciples in parables (Mark 4:1–34). He had expressed amazement at how little of his teaching his disciples understood (Mark 4:13). Now, their perception was to be put to the test.

Jesus and the disciples had set out across the lake in the boat when a storm hit. In Greek the storm is called a *lailaps*, a "whirlwind" or "hurricane." Mark vividly describes the waves swamping the boat while Jesus serenely slept on a cushion in the stern. The disciples panicked. They roused Jesus and reproached him, "Teacher, do you not care if we perish?" Jesus simply awoke and commanded the wind and sea, "Peace! Be still!" and immediately there was calm (Mark 4:38–39).

At that point the miracle itself is com-

The painter Tintoretto's mystical conception of Jesus calling on his Apostle Peter to walk on water depicts the two under stormy skies on a dark and windswept day.

plete, but Mark wants to emphasize the crisis of fear and faith that the disciples had faced. "Why are you afraid?" Jesus asked. "Have you no faith?" Mark notes that the disciples were terrified—literally, "they feared a great fear"—and asked themselves, "Who then is this that even the wind and sea obey him?" Though they had heard Jesus' teaching and seen an epiphany of his power, the result had been terror and questioning rather than faith and serenity. Through this miracle Mark exemplified the difficulty of coming to faith and the long and difficult road to genuine discipleship.

Matthew narrates the same story (8:18–27), and his account has many similarities to Mark, of course, but also reveals Matthew's own understanding of its meaning. Several differences are obvious. The miracle is set in a new context; it does not follow the account of Jesus' teaching in parables (Matthew 13), but comes five chapters earlier. When Jesus decided to cross the lake, Matthew says that at least two men chose that moment to assert that they would follow him. Jesus warned of the rigors of discipleship, saying, "Foxes have holes, and birds of the air have nests; but the Son of man has nowhere to lay his head."

Matthew also tells a different story of danger at sea. Rather than the "whirlwind" that Mark describes, Matthew speaks of a great *seismos*, literally an "earthquake," that will bury the boat in the waves. Since earthquakes were associated with the struggles of disciples in the time before the coming of God's kingdom, this description enhances the symbolic character of the story. Faced with danger the disciples cry out to Jesus, "Save us, LORD, we are perishing." Jesus responded by first rebuking them for their lack of faith and then he stilled the winds and sea. With this, their fear and doubt was turned to wonder (Matthew 8:25–27).

Jesus' mastery over nature is again displayed in Matthew 14:22–33, and again his disciples respond with fear and doubt. At night, Jesus walked over the Sea of Galilee toward his disciples while they were struggling to sail their boat against the wind. The disciples were terrified when they saw Jesus, thinking he was a spirit. But when Jesus reassured them, Peter called to him, "LORD, if it is you, bid me to come to you on the water." Jesus replied "Come," and Peter proceeded, "but when he saw the wind, he was afraid, and beginning to sink he cried out, 'LORD, save me'" (Matthew 14:30). At that point Jesus extended his hand to Peter, saying "O man of little faith, why did you doubt?"

In both miracles the focus is on faith against doubt and fear. For Matthew and Mark, the stories of stilling the storm and walking on the sea both symbolize how in the face of tumult and chaos the disciples must maintain trust in Jesus who is present with them, and can offer them salvation. ✦

THE STORY BEHIND THE WORD

Canon

The word *canon*, as applied to the Bible, refers to those books designated as authoritative for use in the church or synagogue. By the time the word, of Sumerian origin, entered the Semitic languages, it meant "reed" or "cane." Later, it designated a measuring stick—and metaphorically evoked the idea of a supreme standard. With these various meanings the word then passed into Greek. The formation of the Jewish canon, known to Christians as the Old Testament, was hundreds of years in the making. The primary history, of which the Pentateuch forms the first part, was put together during the Exile, in the sixth century. Formal ratification of the Jewish canon finally occurred, largely in response to external pressure, some time after A.D. 100. St. Jerome produced the authoritative Latin translation of the Christian Scriptures (the *Vulgate*), in the late fourth century. The following century, it was authorized by the Church. It includes the Hebrew Bible, the 27 books of the New Testament, and the Apocrypha.

*Jesus' **most famous** discourse was the Sermon on the Mount.*

The quest for perfection

Sermon on the Mount

THE CROWDS GATHERED on a mountainside to hear Jesus and his new disciples. All awaited Jesus' words. As the Gospel of Matthew recounts, the first thing Jesus did was to pronounce God's blessings on groups of people who were often victimized or disregarded. By offering hope to these people, Jesus began to mark out values that helped his hearers to grasp what the kingdom of heaven was all about.

These "Beatitudes" or "blessings" that begin the "Sermon on the Mount," are the best known single body of Jesus' teaching. The Sermon on the Mount occurs only in the Gospel of Matthew (chapters 5–7), but a shorter version known as the "Sermon on the Plain" appears in the Gospel of Luke (6:20–49). Although close study of the Sermon suggests that it is an anthology of traditions about Jesus' teachings rather than a single sermon delivered on one occasion, still it has lived through the centuries as an arresting unity. It is the first major event of Jesus' ministry that Matthew describes in detail, and Jesus' words become a sort of "keynote" address for all that follows.

Blessed are the poor in spirit, for theirs
is the kingdom of heaven.
Blessed are those who mourn, for they
shall be comforted.
Blessed are the meek, for they shall
inherit the earth.
Blessed are those who hunger and thirst for
righteousness, for they shall be satisfied.
Blessed are the merciful, for they shall
obtain mercy.
Blessed are the pure in heart, for they
shall see God.
Blessed are the peacemakers, for they shall
be called sons of God.
Blessed are those who are persecuted for
righteousness' sake, for theirs is the kingdom of heaven. (Matthew 5:3–10)

Is there a mystery within the Sermon on the Mount? On the surface it seems quite the opposite of mysterious. Certainly it is not an esoteric or secret teaching; its setting is as public as a large crowd on a mountain-side can make it. Nor does Jesus use convo-luted or obscure language; his commands are clearly stated, and his images drawn from everyday life—salt, lamps, lilies, birds. Nor are all the sayings of Jesus unique; parallels can be found in the He-brew Scriptures.

In some ways the mystery of the Sermon emerges only when a person takes the place of one of Jesus' disciples who is committed to live according to the teachings of his master. Jesus, as it were, looks those disci-ples in the eye and with great simplicity and clarity commands the impossible. "You, therefore, must be perfect, as your heavenly Father is perfect."

Certainly there are elements of the Ser-mon on the Mount that are very down-to-earth, but again and again it seems to fly in the face of practical wisdom. Its mystery lies in the remarkable manner of Jesus' teach-ing, which combines profound trust in the intimate presence of God—the Father who is with you "in secret" and "knows what you need before you ask"—together with a radical challenge to common values and patterns of behavior.

At one point, for example, Jesus said, "You have heard that it was said to the men of old, 'You shall not kill; and whoever kills shall be liable to judgment.' But I say to you that every one who is angry with his brother shall be liable to judgment; whoever insults his brother shall be liable to the council, and whoever says, 'You fool!' shall be liable to the hell of fire" (Matthew 5:21–22).

Since Jesus uses the legal terminology of "judgment" and "council," at first glance Jesus seems simply to have made the law stricter. But in spite of its legal language, Jesus' statement is not a general law. Rather it applied to Christian communal life. One can only imagine the legal chaos that would result if every display of anger were treated as though it were murder. The casual listen-er can readily dismiss Jesus' "law" as im-practical if not ridiculous; the serious learn-er, the disciple, begins to probe his own anger, and a transformation begins.

Thus for Jesus, statements that sounded at first like legal rulings or traditional prov-erbs became a way of reaching into the hearts of those hearers, challenging their basic values and setting them on a lifelong quest for God's kingdom. At the heart of his teaching he placed love—a love that could have no boundaries: "You have heard that it was said, 'You shall love your neighbor and hate your enemy.' But I say to you, Love your enemies and pray for those who perse-cute you, so that you may be sons of your Father who is in heaven."

Characteristically for Jesus, such a quest was to be carried out not by rigorous control of one's life, but by surrender of all anxiety about life and all desire for public display of piety. The disciple must trust the care of a God who "clothes the grass of the field" and who promises, "seek, and you will find; knock, and it will be opened to you."

As Matthew recounts, Jesus did not imagine that he was minimizing the de-mands of obedience to God, but transform-ing and concentrating them so that a disci-ple could build his life on a rock that could withstand every storm. ✦

ON THE MEANING OF SCRIPTURE

The Our Father, Prayer of Prayers

Our Father who art in heaven,
Hallowed be thy name.
Thy kingdom come.
Thy will be done,
   On earth as it is in heaven.
Give us this day our daily bread;
And forgive us our debts,
   As we also have forgiven our debtors;
And lead us not into temptation,
   But deliver us from evil.
For thine is the kingdom and the power
and the glory, for ever. Amen.
   —Matthew 6:9–13 (compare Luke 11:2–4).
   Concluding lines, in italics, are an ancient addition.

THE OUR FATHER, also known as the Lord's Prayer, is the prayer Jesus taught the disciples. To many believers, it contains the essence of all possible prayer. For nearly two thousand years, millions have prayed the Our Father; it has formed a favorite topic of meditation and commentary by Church fathers, saints, theologians, clergy, and lay people. Here are some highlights from that literature.

Our Father who art in heaven. "First my mind must become detached from anything subject to flux and change, and tranquilly rest in motionless spiritual repose, so as to be rendered akin to Him who is perfectly unchangeable, and then it may address Him by this most familiar name and say: Father. What spirit a man must have to say this word—what confidence, what purity of conscience . . . to call this Being his Father!"
   —Gregory of Nyssa, (c. 335–c. 395)
   "The Lord's Prayer"

Thy kingdom come. "There is energy, drive, purpose in those words; an intensity of desire for the coming of perfection into life. Not the limp resignation that lies devoutly in the road and waits for the steam roller; but a total concentration on the total interests of God, which must be expressed in action. It is useless to utter fervent petitions for that Kingdom to be established and that Will be done, unless we are willing to do something about it ourselves."
   —Evelyn Underhill
   The Spiritual Life

"When we say: **Hallowed be thy name,** we ask that it should be made holy in us, who are in Him, and at the same time in all others, on whom the grace of God is still waiting, that we may obey this precept also, by praying for all, even for our enemies. And therefore, by curtailing our utterance and by refraining from saying 'let it be hallowed *in us*,' we mean '*in all*.' **—Tertullian (c. 160–c. 220)**
   Concerning Prayer

Thy will be done. "It is the will of God that we surrender our wills. Even though St. Paul talked much with our Lord and our Lord with him, these conversations remained fruitless until St. Paul surrendered his will and said: 'Lord, what wilt thou have me to do?' . . . The only true and perfect will is the one that has been merged with the will of God, so that the man has no will of his own.

Indeed, one step taken in surrender to God is better than a journey across the ocean without it. . . . Perfectly to will what God wills, to want what he wants, is to have joy; but if one's will is not quite in unison with God's, there is no joy. May God help us to be in tune with him! Amen."

—Meister Eckhart (c. 1260–c. 1327)
The Talks of Instruction

On earth as it is in heaven. "He commands the prayer because He wishes that everything 'on earth,' that is, the baser things and those allied with earthly things, should be made like the nobler things and those that have their commonwealth in heaven . . . with the result that there will no longer be any earth, but all will become heaven."

—Origen (c. 185–c. 254), *On Prayer*

Give us this day our daily bread. "There is a transcendent energy whose source is in heaven, and this flows into us as soon as we wish for it. It is a real energy; it performs actions through the agency of our souls and of our bodies. We should ask for this food. At the moment of asking, and by the very fact that we ask for it, we know that God will give it to us."

—Simone Weil
"Concerning the Our Father"

And forgive us our debts. "We must pray for daily pardon, as duly as we pray for daily bread. Our sins are our debts; there is a debt of duty, which, as creatures, we owe to our Creator. We run in debt continually. We receive our being and all we possess from God, to whom they all ought to be devoted in perfect love. By failure in this we contract a debt we cannot pay, but which needs continual remission. Our heart's desire and prayer to our heavenly Father every day should be, that he would forgive us our debts; that we may not come into condemnation; that we may be discharged, and have the comfort of it."

—Matthew Henry and Thomas Scott
Commentary on the Holy Bible

As we also have forgiven our debtors. "Notice that He does not say, 'As we SHALL forgive our debtors.' Consequently, we are to understand that whoever requests so great a favor, and who has previously surrendered his will entirely into the hands of God, must of necessity have forgiven his debtors. That is why our Saviour says, 'As we also have forgiven our debtors.' Hence, whoever has said sincerely, 'Thy will be done' must, of necessity, have actually forgiven his debtors, or at least have firmly resolved to do so. . . . And after all, what really have we to forgive? Not actual wrongs, but only mere trifles that amount to nothing!"

—Teresa of Avila (1515–1582)
The Pater Noster of Saint Teresa

And lead us not into temptation, But deliver us from evil. "In this life there is temptation, in this life the sailing is dangerous, in this life something is always seeping through the chinks of our frailties, which has to be bailed out. When, however, we shall be made equal to the angels, there will be no need for us to pray, no need for us to beg God to forgive our debts, since there will be none. Here on earth, then, is the place to pray for daily bread, to pray for forgiveness of our trespasses, to pray that we may not be led into temptation, for in the life to come temptation gains no entrance. Here, then, do we pray that we may be delivered from evil, for in the life to come there will be no evil, but only eternal and abiding good."

—Augustine of Hippo (354–430)
"The Lord's Prayer Explained to the Candidates for Baptism"

For thine is the kingdom and the power and the glory, for ever. Amen. "The phrase was almost certainly not in the original prayer . . . But we may be glad for the addition; it is a final peal of trumpets. . . . The word *amen* is, more deeply, trust and assurance that God can bring great things to pass: 'So let it be!' By right instinct the church added a doxology and an *amen* to the Lord's Prayer."

—George A. Buttrick
The Interpreter's Bible

Just as a poor woman would rejoice in finding one lost coin, so would heaven rejoice over the repentance of a sinner.

Daily life and the Divine Word

Why Jesus spoke in parables

JESUS WAS A STORYTELLER—his speech was filled with images. He put great emphasis on the special stories called parables. In the body of Jesus' teaching found in the Synoptic Gospels (Matthew, Mark, and Luke), some 40 separate parables appear. Certainly many other teachers in the ancient world used parables, but practically no one gave them such prominence or made them the hallmark of his work.

Jesus' parables were full of subjects easily recognizable in the everyday life of ancient Palestine—fishnets, seeds, wheat, and sheep; servants, farmers, and kings. The parables were usually brief, vivid, and, quite simply, entertaining. But they were also more. In the Gospel of Matthew, Jesus' disciples asked him why he spoke in parables. In answering, Jesus linked understanding his parables to knowing the mysteries of the kingdom of heaven.

Jesus also said that he spoke to the crowds in parables "because seeing they do not see, and hearing they do not hear, nor do they understand" (Matthew 13:10–13). Evidently, he believed that in these stories, so apparently simple and accessible, the innermost mystery of his mission was both revealed and hidden.

How was it possible for these brief stories to play such an important role? Part of the answer seems to lie in the very nature of a parable. The kernel of a parable is a comparison. In the New Testament the Greek word *parabole* ("parable") is applied to a wide range of literary forms that include some element of comparison or metaphor, from a simple simile to a long and fully developed narrative. In the Gospel of Luke, for example, Jesus used the term *parabole* for the three-word proverb "Physician, heal yourself" (4:23). It could also describe much more detailed stories like that of the "Prodigal Son" (Luke 15:11–32).

Because of the element of comparison and metaphor, there is always more than one level of meaning in a parable. The story may be very entertaining in itself, but it always points beyond itself to something else, something more mysterious that Jesus wanted his audience to perceive more clearly through the story. That something else is what Jesus called the kingdom of God. Jesus wanted the simple story to become a door that allowed access to the mystery. For most of Jesus' audience, that door remained unopened; some, however, penetrated the mystery. The parables gave them glimpses of a new world and allowed them to step across the threshold and become disciples.

How did the comparisons work? How was the story related to the mystery? Two of Jesus' briefest parables, the "Hidden treasure" and the "Pearl of great value," may help illuminate the process:

"The kingdom of heaven is like treasure hidden in a field, which a man found and covered up; then in his joy he goes and sells all that he has and buys that field" (Matthew 13:44). "Again, the kingdom of heaven is like a merchant in search of fine pearls, who, on finding one pearl of great value, went and sold all that he had and bought it" (Matthew 13:45–46).

In these stories Jesus directed the attention of his audience to two situations in which a person's everyday life was interrupted when he found something wonderful and unexpected. Realizing the value of his discovery, the person immediately broke from his past and all that he held secure by selling everything he owned in order to obtain what he had discovered and start a new life.

The very brevity of Jesus' stories leaves a lot of questions hanging. Jesus did not ask whether it was ethical or legal to buy a field knowing that it contained a treasure without letting the owner know what he was selling. Nor did he dwell on the prudence of selling all one's belongings in order to buy a single pearl. The two men's experi-

ences, Jesus said, reveal the kingdom of heaven. No exact explanation or moral application accompanies the stories. The parables "teased" the minds of the hearers into active thought and perhaps began the process of their own discovery.

Many of the other parables elaborate in some way the simple pattern of discovery, reversal, and action contained in these two parables. Several focus on the kingdom of God as something hidden, as a surprising discovery, as a joy. The parable of the "seed growing secretly," for example, compares the kingdom of God to the situation of a farmer (Mark 4:26–29). He scatters seed at the beginning and reaps a joyful harvest at the end. But in between the real work is done by the seed, mysteriously growing, "he knows not how" and by the earth which produces of itself "first the blade, then the ear, then the full grain in the ear." In this mysterious, productive interaction between farmer and seed and earth, is an insight into the kingdom of God. Again, the brief parable of the "leaven" sees the kingdom of God revealed in yeast "hid" in the flour. The yeast is unseen, but the flour is transformed into dough (Matthew 13:33).

Other parables center on the idea of a reversal of the past and its expectations (for

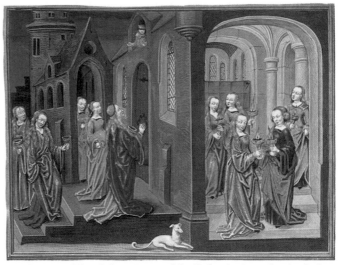

In the parable of the wise and foolish virgins, the foolish maidens missed the arrival of the bridegroom because they were unprepared, while the wise ones went on to the feast.

305

The Good Samaritan *epitomizes human compassion.*

example, the "Prodigal Son" and the "Good Samaritan"). Many emphasize decisive action (for example, the "Rich Fool"; the "Talents"; and the "Dishonest Steward"). Some use the same pattern to provide a warning. The "Unmerciful Servant," for example, was unexpectedly forgiven a massive debt by his master, and thus escaped slavery for himself and his family. He could not, however, bring himself to forgive a small debt owed by his fellow servant. When the master found out, he reversed his kindness and threw the servant into prison. The warning to "forgive your brother from your heart" is clear (Matthew 18:23–35).

Throughout the history of Christianity, the parables have been interpreted in a variety of ways. For centuries, for example, the parables were interpreted as elaborate alle-

gories that revealed the story of salvation. A favorite for this kind of interpretation was the parable of the "Good Samaritan" (Luke 10:29–37).

Jesus told the story of a man going from Jerusalem to Jericho who "fell among robbers" and was stripped, beaten, and left "half dead." By chance, both a priest and a Levite, men engaged in the service of God in the Temple, approached, but each "passed by on the other side." Then a Samaritan, a religious renegade from the point of view of Jesus' audience, happened to come along. It was he, Jesus said, who "had compassion," bandaged the victim's wounds, "pouring on oil and wine," took him to an inn, and paid the innkeeper for his care, promising to return and repay the innkeeper for what was spent on the victim.

An understanding of this parable as an allegory of humanity's fall and redemption began to develop in the Church of the second century and reached its full form with Saint Augustine in the fourth. The traveler is Adam representing all mankind. Jerusalem is the heavenly city; Jericho is the fallen world. The robbers are demons who strip off Adam's immortality leaving him half dead. The priest and the Levite are the law and the prophets, while the Samaritan is Christ himself, who heals mankind with oil and wine, comfort and admonition. The inn is the Church; the innkeeper, the Apostles Peter and Paul; and the Samaritan's return is the Second Coming of Christ.

The allegory worked quite neatly and certainly pointed to something hidden in Jesus' parable. It made good sense in the fourth century but would have made no sense to Jesus' audience, who knew nothing of Paul or Christian theology. In such an allegory, the parable does not lead the hearer into a mystery but is a code for something already understood. One must know the story of the fall and redemption before one can decipher the code.

It is in the very nature of the parables, however, that they call forth more than one interpretation as different individuals in different times hear them. In the well-known parable of the "Prodigal Son" (Luke 15:11–32), the younger of two sons took his inheritance and traveled to a far country, where he squandered everything he had in loose living. When famine struck, he had nowhere to turn, and so he decided to return home. "But while he was yet at a distance, his father saw him and had compassion, and ran and embraced him and kissed him. And the son said to him, 'Father, I have sinned against heaven and before you; I am no longer worthy to be called your son.' " The father quickly forgave but the elder brother was angry and refused to rejoice in his brother's homecoming. "Lo, these many years I have served you, and I never disobeyed your command; yet you never gave me a kid, that I might make merry with my friends. But when this son of yours came, who has devoured your living with harlots, you killed for him the fatted calf." And the father replied, "It was fitting to make merry and be glad, for this your brother was dead, and is alive; he was lost, and is found."

Some interpreters have seen this story principally as a story of repentance and restoration for the younger son who left home. Others have thought Jesus was emphasizing the elder brother who stayed at home and was unable to forgive. Many have seen the father as the central character. The remarkable thing about Jesus' parable is that it has room for all three. In a few sentences, he created three characters who reveal by their interactions not only the breakdown of love and the degradation of life, but also the possibility of self-discovery, of restored love, and of joyous welcome. ✦

Joy and sorrow *are mingled in Rembrandt's touching representation of the Prodigal Son.*

307

✍ Key to the parables of Jesus ✍

THE PARABLES, Jesus said, contain "the secret of the kingdom of God" (Mark 4:11). This table shows how they overlap in the first three Gospels and in the recently discovered Gospel of Thomas, which may have preserved the parables independently. There are no parables in the Gospel of John, where Jesus says: "I shall no longer speak to you in figures but tell you plainly of the Father" (16:25).

	Matthew	Mark	Luke	Thomas
The sower	13:3-8	4:3-8	8:5-8	9
Seed growing secretly		4:26-9		
The mustard seed	13:31-32	4:30-32	13:18-19	20
The vineyard	21:33-44	12:1-12	20:9-18	65
The budding fig tree	24:32-33	13:28-29	21:29-31	
The doorkeeper		13:34-37	12:35-38	
Going before the judge	5:25-26		12:58-59	
Two houses	7:24-27		6:47-49	
Children in marketplace	11:16-19		7:31-35	
Return of unclean spirit	12:43-45		11:24-26	
Weeds in the wheat	13:24-30			57
The leaven	13:33		13:20-21	96
Hidden treasure	13:44			109
The pearl of great value	13:45-46			76
The dragnet	13:47-50			
The lost sheep	18:10-14		15:4-7	107
The unmerciful servant	18:23-35			
Laborers in the vineyard	20:1-16			
The two sons	21:28-32			
The great banquet	22:1-14		14:16-24	64
The thief in the night	24:43-44		12:39-40	103
The faithful servant	24:45-51		12:42-46	
The wise and foolish maidens	25:1-13			
Pounds and talents	25:14-30		19:12-27	
The two debtors			7:41-43	
The good Samaritan			10:29-37	
The friend asked for help at midnight			11:5-8	
The rich fool			12:16-21	63
The barren fig tree			13:6-9	
The narrow door			13:24-30	
Places of honor at a feast			14:7-11	
The tower-builder and the king going to war			14:28-32	
The lost coin			15:8-10	
The prodigal son			15:11-32	
The dishonest steward			16:1-13	
The rich man and Lazarus			16:19-31	
The servant's reward			17:7-10	
The unjust judge			18:1-8	
The Pharisee and the tax collector			18:9-14	

308

The Gnostic library *is one of the earliest*
examples of bound books ever found.

The thunderbolt of Nag Hammadi

Finding the Gospel of Thomas

I**N DECEMBER 1945**, two peasants from the village of Nag Hammadi, in southern Egypt, unearthed a cache of jars containing 52 manuscripts, bound into 13 books. Buried in the fourth century A.D., this cache is one of the most important manuscript discoveries of modern times. Among the manuscripts were a number of Christian texts that were previously unknown. One of these was the Gospel of Thomas. It has parallels in content to the Synoptic Gospels of the New Testament (Matthew, Mark, and Luke), and is believed by Bible scholars to come from a tradition as old as theirs.

The Gospel of Thomas consists of a collection of sayings, proverbs, and parables attributed to Jesus. Among the parables familiar to New Testament readers is the parable of the mustard seed: "The disciples said to Jesus, 'Tell us what the Kingdom of Heaven is like.' He said to them, 'It is like a mustard seed, the smallest of all seeds. But when it falls on tilled soil, it produces a great plant and becomes a shelter for birds of the sky.' " The chart at left shows which other parables the Gospel of Thomas has in common with the Synoptic Gospels.

Scholars believe that the Gospel of Thomas is based on a tradition of sayings that relate closely to the four canonical (official) Gospels of the New Testament, but had a different process of transmission. The Gospel of Thomas opens with the portentous words: "These are the secret sayings which the living Jesus spoke and which Didymus Judas Thomas wrote down . . . Whoever finds the interpretation of these sayings will not experience death."

While the narratives of Matthew, Mark, Luke, and John rely upon Jesus' death and resurrection as a means through which to understand his life and teachings, the Gospel of Thomas suggests a more mysterious route to enlightenment. In Thomas' Gospel, Jesus is depicted as a wisdom teacher, one who reveals the kingdom of God. And it is through a lifetime of the study of Jesus' sayings that one comes to enlightenment. According to this Gospel, it is not enough to recognize God, but one must come to recognize one's origins ("the light"), and one's final "repose." Thus, "Jesus said, If they say to you, 'Where did you come from?' say to them, 'We came from the light. . . .' If they ask you, 'What is the sign of your Father in you?' say to them, 'It is movement and repose.' "

Elsewhere in this intriguing book are passages that have no parallels in Scripture. Here is such a saying: "Jesus said, 'If you bring forth what is within you, what you bring forth will save you. If you do not bring forth what is within you, what you do not bring forth will destroy you.' " ✦

The twelve are chosen

Disciple, apostle, evangelist

*J*ESUS WAS NEVER a lonely prophet. Forming a community of people around him was fundamental to Jesus' ministry. The Gospels portray him as being besieged by people of all kinds and continually teaching and ministering to their needs. At some points, we are told, he could not even enter towns, but had to stay in the open country because of the press of people who "came to him from every quarter" (Mark 1:45).

Because of his miracles and his ability to heal the sick, villagers would often try to keep Jesus as a wonder-worker among them. Luke tells how crowds "sought him and came to him, and would have kept him from leaving them," but he insisted on going to other towns (Luke 4:42). Jesus wished for the throngs to understand that the miracles were a sign that the Kingdom of God was at hand, but that it was his teaching that was central to his ministry, not the miracles.

From the large group of disciples, Jesus created an inner circle to spread the news of his ministry. "Disciple" simply means one who learns from a teacher. As Mark 2:18 makes clear, John the Baptist and the Pharisees also had student-followers called disciples. The Gospels reveal at various points, that Jesus had several circles of disciples. The most intimate group consisted of three disciples, Simon Peter and the two sons of Zebedee, James and John; they were three of the four fishermen Jesus first called along at Sea of Galilee. The Gospels describe these three as being with Jesus at important moments such as the transfiguration and in the Garden of Gethsemane (Mark 9:2; 14:33).

The most important grouping was that known as "the twelve." Their number evidently was symbolic of the twelve tribes of Israel (Matthew 19:28). The exact number was sufficiently important that when Judas Iscariot betrayed Jesus, forfeiting his place among "the twelve," a replacement had to be named (Acts 1:15–26). It was made clear that the replacement must be one who had been a disciple during Jesus' mission.

The Gospels emphasize that the twelve did not simply volunteer for the mission but were selected by Jesus. From high on a mountainside Jesus summoned "those whom he desired" and appointed them "to be with him, and to be sent out to preach and to have authority to cast out demons" (Mark 3:13–14). The corresponding passage in Matthew (10:1–2) lists the twelve "Apostles" and elaborates on the commissioning and instruction of the twelve. "Apostle" literally means one sent out on a mission. So if a teacher deputizes a disciple for a mission, he becomes an apostle at the same time. Apostles were not always limited to twelve; in Acts 14:14 we find apostles Barnabas and Paul preaching the Gospel. Paul's authority to be an apostle and teacher of the gospel is based on his claim to have seen the risen Lord (Galatians 1:11-12).

The credentials of Jesus' followers were not impressive. The Book of Acts describes two of their leaders, Peter and John, as

The German artist *Hans Holbein the Younger*

"uneducated, common men," words that would evidently fit them all. But the group cut across some of the basic divisions of society. Among the twelve were Matthew the tax collector. As such he would have been despised by Jews as a collaborator with Roman oppression. Then there was Simon the "Cananaean" or "Zealot," who before his calling had probably been a man committed to the overthrow of Roman rule.

Although Jesus had chosen them, the Gospels repeatedly show that these disciples had great difficulties in understanding Jesus and his mission. Jesus was often exasperated with them: "Do you not yet perceive or understand?" he asked on one occasion. On another occasion, the disciples tried to prevent Jesus from blessing some children, apparently thinking it a waste of Jesus' time. Jesus overruled his disciples, and drawing the children to him, told the disciples that they had turned away the very ones to whom the kingdom of God belonged. Still, Jesus was forebearing towards the disciples. According to tradition, two of them, Matthew and John, would become evangelists—literally: one who proclaims "good news" or the gospel. The testimony of the apostle Peter was said to be recorded by the Evangelist John Mark. The remaining Evangelist was Luke, by tradition a friend of Paul's. Although these four came to be known as "the evangelists," in fact all apostles were evangelists, commissioned to proclaim good news.

The Gospel of Luke indicates that there was another wider circle, this one composed of 70 disciples, also commissioned by Jesus. Their number may allude to the 70 elders of Israel or the 70 nations of the world listed in Genesis. Both the twelve and the 70 were sent out on remarkable missions in Jesus' name. They were to "take no gold nor silver, nor copper in your belts, no bag for your journey, nor two tunics, nor sandals, nor a staff." Thus they traveled, two by two, from town to town, preaching the kingdom of God and healing the sick.

Yet another circle of disciples was a circle of women. These were women "who, when he was in Galilee, followed him and ministered to him." Luke indeed noted that these women provided for Jesus and his followers "out of their means." Amazingly, Luke reports that this group included one woman, named Joanna, whose husband was in the court of Herod. For a married woman of such station to leave home and follow a teacher like Jesus was certainly extraordinary. One of the more prominent of the women was Mary Magdalene, and the Gospels report that she was with the women at Jesus' crucifixion and was the first to receive a revelation of Jesus' resurrection. ✦

captures the solid, down-to-earth qualities of the twelve apostles, depicted with Jesus center.

The murder of John the Baptist

A gruesome vengeance

ONE OF THE MOST famous stories in the Gospel of Mark revolves around a banquet held by Herod to celebrate his birthday (6:21–29). While John the Baptist was imprisoned elsewhere, in the great hall there was food, drink, music, and merriment. Then Herod's stepdaughter performed a fateful dance. She so pleased the king that he promised her whatever she wished. The girl asked her mother, Herodias, what to request and was told the "head of John the baptizer." Although Herod was "exceedingly sorry," he could not go back on his promise, and in the scene immortalized in literature and opera, John's head was delivered to the girl on a platter.

Where did such a story come from? The disciples of John the Baptist believed that the reason for his arrest was his denunciation of Herod's marriage to Herodias. She had formerly been married to Herod's brother Philip: "It is not lawful for you to have your brother's wife" (Mark 6:18). The denunciation was also, of course, the reason for his execution. To John's followers, the purity of his moral stance explained his death, instigated by the vengeful Herodias.

The Jewish historian Josephus also told the story of Herod's execution of John. According to Josephus, John was put to death because Herod feared that John would instigate a popular rebellion. Nothing is said about his denunciation of Herod's marriage. But Josephus' account of John's execution immediately follows the detailed story of Herod's plans to marry Herodias. At the time, Herod was also married to the daughter of Aretas, the king of Nabatea. Aretas went to war partly to avenge his daughter's repudiation. When Herod's forces were defeated, Josephus says that many Jews interpreted the defeat as God's punishment for his treatment of John.

But who *was* Herodias' daughter? The Gospels do not give her a name. Josephus, who said nothing about the dance, did say that Herodias had a daughter named Salome. There are those who discount the historical accuracy of Mark's story precisely because it seems impossible that a daughter of royalty would have danced publicly.

A fascination with Salome should not blind us to the point of the story for early Jews and Christians. John the Baptist, the stern prophet who excited the masses by the power of his proclamation, met his end at the hands of a cruel ruler. For Mark, this foreshadowed the death of Jesus. ✦

"The Keys of the Kingdom"

Peter receives his commission

THE MOMENT ARRIVED when Jesus needed to reveal to his disciples the darker side of his ministry—the suffering and rejection that lay at its end. They were traveling in the north of Israel, near the source of the Jordan, at the city of Caesarea Philippi. There Jesus probed the disciples' grasp of who and what he was.

As Mark recounted the story, he focused on the crisis of that moment. Jesus began indirectly: "Who do men say that I am?" Opinions included a list of identities from the past: John the Baptist, Elijah, or one of the prophets. But then Jesus' probe became more pointed: "But who do *you* say that I am?" Peter responded for the group simply, "You are the Christ."

Those words were a vital step for the disciples, but Mark made it clear that the probe was by no means over. Jesus' only

Jesus gave to Simon *the name of Peter.*

response was sternly to command the disciples "to tell no one about him." They must first understand what that confession meant. Jesus immediately began to turn their image of a glorious Christ or Messiah (God's anointed king) on its head by teaching that he must "suffer" and "be killed" and "rise again." The crisis came to a climax as Peter, the confessor, began to rebuke Jesus for saying such things. Jesus' reply was scorching: "Get behind me, Satan! For you are not on the side of God, but of men." The crisis made clear that even an ancient title like *Messiah* or *Christ*, the meaning of which seemed clear, had to be transformed into something new and unexpected before Jesus would accept it.

Matthew's narrative built on Mark's but intensified the paradox of Peter's actions by stressing the greatness of his confession before Jesus' devastating rebuke (Matthew 16:13–23). When Simon Peter confessed, Jesus pronounced an exultant blessing on him, not because he had figured out Jesus' identity himself, but because God had revealed it to him. Then Jesus spoke of Simon's identity by using a play on words, "You are Peter (Greek, *petros*), and on this rock (*petra*) I will build my church and the powers of death will not prevail against it." Simon had been called Peter since he was first introduced in Matthew, but now the meaning of that name was revealed. He was the one through whom *God* revealed Jesus' identity, and thus, strengthened by that confession, he had become the rock on which *Jesus* would build his community. Further, Jesus promised to him "the keys of the kingdom of heaven," and whatever he bound or loosed on earth would be bound or loosed in heaven. The words seem consciously enigmatic. Some Christians have taken them to mean that Peter was given authority over the Church as a whole; other Christians find this too broad an interpretation. In any event, Jesus' words seem to foreshadow Peter's role as a principal leader of the early Church. ✦

313

The aura of the divine

The transfiguration of Jesus

A T THE MIDPOINT of his career, Jesus took his three closest disciples, Peter, James, and John, and went to a mountain. High on this unnamed mountain, a stunning event occurred—the transfiguration. According to all three of the Synoptic Gospel writers, Jesus suddenly took on a transcendent glory. His clothes became a brilliant, supernatural white and "his face shone like the sun" (Matthew 17:2). Alongside the radiant Jesus, two others appeared: "And behold, there appeared to them Moses and Elijah, talking with him."

Next, a cloud descended over them, and from out of the cloud a voice said, "This is my beloved Son; listen to him." The disciples fell to the ground in terror. When they looked up again, only Jesus was there.

The description of Jesus' transfigured appearance harks back to that of Moses coming down from Mount Sinai: "the skin of his face shone because he had been talking with God" (Exodus 34:29). Also, the joint appearance of Moses and Elijah is not without scriptural resonance. Together they represent the substance of scriptural revelation. Both were great prophets; both performed miracles. The transfiguration was therefore deeply rooted in sacred tradition.

The events of the transfiguration not only mirrored the past but also anticipated the future. There was a legend, current at the time of Jesus, that the two prophets were rejected and even martyred (Revelation 11:4–13). Elijah, moreover, was taken directly to heaven in the chariot of fire. Luke describes Moses as a rejected prophet (Acts 7:27, 35, 39), and Paul portrays Elijah as a prophet whose life was threatened by his own people (Romans 11:2–3). Still, Moses and Elijah are not portrayed in the Hebrew Scriptures (the Old Testament) as martyrs. Malachi promised that Elijah would return, and Moses declared that God would raise up a prophet like Moses himself. Both traditions converge in Jesus: thus Jesus is the prophet like Moses; furthermore, Jesus is identified by the returning Elijah—in the person of John the Baptist.

God's sudden tangible presence on the mountain also had complex biblical antecedents. Like the cloud in the Book of Exodus that indicated God's presence and protection of the pilgrim Israelites, the cloud that attended the transfiguration was a sure sign of God's special favor. "Listen to him," said the voice from the cloud. What did this command mean? As Jesus had not spoken a word at this time, the command must refer to something he had said earlier, most likely the prediction of his own coming death.

Scholars have long noted that theophanies (appearances of God) function as "commissionings" in the scriptural record. Moses at the burning bush was commissioned to lead Israel out of Egypt. Elijah on the mountain was commissioned to go to Damascus and to anoint Hazael. Now Jesus was being commissioned to pursue his work in Jerusalem. Moreover, this appearance balanced the earlier theophany at Jesus' baptism: "Thou art my beloved Son, with thee I am well pleased" (Mark 1:11).

Just as the latter theophany commissioned Jesus to preach and heal in the first half of the Gospel, so in the theophany at the transfiguration God was to authorize

"Whatever might have been the exact nature of this transfiguration . . . it was a high hour of vision which the disciples could trust. So the revelation on the mountaintop says to us, 'Trust your high hours. . . . The weather of the mind and spirit is varied. It runs from sunlight through dense fog to pitch darkness. Yet spiritual truth has its hours and days of high visibility. . . . Keep those hours in memory, both for the fortification and the measurement of life." —**Halford E. Luccock**
The Interpreter's Bible

The prophets Moses and Elijah *appeared beside Jesus on the mountain while Peter, John, and James slept (Luke 9:28–36).*

Jesus' mission—to die and to be raised from the dead. Mark's Gospel ends with a third proclamation of Jesus as "Son of God," when Jesus' centurion-executioner proclaims him a holy person at his death (Mark 15:39). In fact Mark patterned his book—beginning, middle, and end—around this key identification of Jesus as the Son of God.

That the transfiguration had to do with Jesus' future death and vindication in Jerusalem is borne out by the episode immediately preceding it: "And he began to teach them that the Son of man must suffer many things, and be rejected by the elders and the chief priests and the scribes, and be killed, and after three days rise again" (Mark 8:31). By his subsequent command that the disciples not speak of the transfiguration "until the Son of man is raised from the dead" (Matthew 17:9) Jesus revealed the connection between the transfiguration and the resurrection. However, the apostles did not grasp what Jesus meant by "resurrection." "So they kept the matter to themselves, questioning what the rising from the dead meant" (Mark 9:10). ✦

The raising of Lazarus

A death undone

RECOUNTED ONLY IN THE GOSPEL of John, the raising of Lazarus is considered by many to be the climax of Jesus' miracles. While the miracle at Cana, the healing of the official's son, and the multiplication of loaves and fishes were signs showing that Jesus was a prophet like the classical prophets of Israel who had multiplied food and raised the dead, it was by raising Lazarus that Jesus gave proof that he was indeed the giver of life.

The Lazarus story was much more than an illustration of Jesus' prophetic powers. The setting was one of crisis. A beloved disciple had died. Of the dying Lazarus, Martha sent word to Jesus, "He whom you love is ill," and the narrator made a point of noting that "Jesus loved Lazarus."

Lazarus was no insignificant person, but an intimate of Jesus. He ate the bread of life and was born again of water and the spirit. Yet it had been said: "Whoever believes in him should not perish but have eternal life" and again, "This is the bread which comes down from heaven, that a man may eat of it and not die. I am the living bread which came down from heaven; if anyone eats of this bread, he will live forever." Had the disciples misunderstood the words of Jesus? Such was the crisis when this beloved disciple became sick and died. Jesus merely said, "Our friend Lazarus has fallen asleep, but I go to awake him out of sleep."

> "All Jesus' miracles are signs of what he is and what he has come to give man, but in none of them does the sign more closely approach the reality than in the gift of life. The physical life that Jesus gives to Lazarus is still not in the realm of the life from above, but it is so close to that realm that it may be said to conclude the ministry of signs and inaugurate the ministry of glory."
> —Raymond E. Brown
> *The Gospel According to John* (1966)

Before the miracle could occur, there was much misunderstanding. Martha ran out to Jesus and bitterly exclaimed: "If you had been here, my brother would not have died" (11:21). This remark was repeated again, this time by Mary (11:32). And the other Jewish mourners said, "Could not he who opened the eyes of the blind man have kept this man from dying?"(11:37), underscoring the crisis that gripped the disciples.

Jesus had told Martha that her brother would "rise again" which she misunderstood as a reference to the resurrection at the end of time, saying "I know that he will rise again in the resurrection at the last day." Jesus then mysteriously stated, "I am the resurrection and the life, he who believes in me, though he die, yet shall he live, and whoever lives and believes in me shall never die." Thus Jesus proclaimed the way of understanding his promises of eternal life. The disciples would not be spared physical death, but they would not experience everlasting death. The implication is that persons who die in the faith will have life eternal—body and soul.

The Gospel makes the point that Jesus had full power over death, not just the death of a person who died just a few minutes earlier, but death that has already led to decomposition. The narrator emphasizes that Lazarus had already been in the tomb four days; according to popular belief, the soul hovered in the grave for three days in hope of reuniting with the body. At first sign of decay, said to be the fourth day, the soul departed. Thus, here is death at its strongest. Yet Jesus has power over it when he commands, "Lazarus, come out" (11:43).

The raising of Lazarus teaches the true meaning of Jesus' words: that he is the giver of life, he is truly "the resurrection and the life." But so great was his power that when the miracle became known to his enemies, it was Jesus' own death sentence. ✦

A triumphal entry into Jerusalem

The first Palm Sunday

THE FOUR GOSPELS all record that Jesus entered Jerusalem riding an animal in a triumphal procession a few days before his death. Matthew and Mark describe the crowds as holding branches—but only John says that they were from palms.

Although the stories in their present form are probably influenced by early church interpretations, the basic underlying event is easily discernible. Passover was one of the three pilgrim festivals of Judaism. In the days preceding the festival proper, thousands of pilgrims streamed into Jerusalem, transforming the roads into the Holy City into crowded highways. The pilgrimage was a sacred duty ordained by Scripture. Yet it was also a holiday, and no doubt a festive spirit pervaded the growing crowds as they approached the city.

Certain psalms were associated with the various festivals. One such song was Psalm 118, in which the word *hosanna* occurs, together with a reference to branches used in worship at the Temple. Celebrants sang verses from Psalm 118 at the feast of Tabernacles and at Passover. Words from that song seem directly related to the story of Jesus' entry before Passover. In Mark's version, which is probably the earliest, the crowds shout "Hosanna. . . Blessed is he who comes in the name of the Lord!" Here they are reciting lines from the Psalm (verses 25, 26).

There is, on the surface, nothing remarkable about the event as Mark tells it. Jesus and his disciples are but a few of many pilgrims entering Jerusalem for Passover. The pilgrims are chanting sacred psalms and carrying branches in their procession, a description that seems to evoke the feast of

*"**You will** find an ass tied."*

Tabernacles, in the fall, better than it does the spring festival of Passover.

Yet the stories say much more than this. In various ways, they all tell the reader that Jesus is not just one among many; he is unique, he is the Messiah-King entering his city. The very fact that Jesus rides on an animal points to Zechariah 9:9, a prediction of a humble king entering Jerusalem. Matthew and John explicitly cite the passage, while the other two Gospels indicate that the reader should hear the story with that passage in mind.

And while Mark suggests that the crowds are singing to and about Jesus, in Matthew they specifically acclaim Jesus to be "Son of David," in Luke and John, the "King." What on the surface is a simple event becomes a momentous messianic act. The main difference between Mark and the other Gospels is that for Mark the event remains a "secret," which is not objectively observable though understood by the reader. In the others, the meaning is perceived by the actors in the story itself.

Whether Jesus intentionally acted out the prediction from Zechariah to symbolize his claim to be Messiah or whether the messianic color given to the accounts is due to later Christian reflection upon the meaning of the event cannot be known with certainty. But this ride into Jerusalem has been transformed into one of the joyous celebrations of the Christian year. ✦

317

El Greco captures the high drama of Jesus' purification of the Temple.

Profiteering in the house of God

Jesus expels the money changers

THE ROLE OF MONEY CHANGERS comes dramatically into view in the Gospels. The time: soon after Jesus' triumphal entry into Jerusalem. The setting: the Jerusalem Temple. The event: Jesus' overturning of the banking tables and "cleansing" of the Temple.

Well might one ask why Jesus, who seems to have gone along with existing economic structures at other times in his career, should have reacted so violently against what was, after all, only a customary practice. Would he himself not say, "Render to Caesar the things that are Caesar's, and to God the things that are God's" (Mark 12:17)? Had he not used his special powers to provide the Temple tax for himself and Peter when the latter was questioned at Capernaum (Matthew 17:24–27)? Had he not recognized the practice of banking (Mat-

thew 25:27, Luke 19:23) in his teaching?

Ancient Israelite law permitted money-lending—interest could be levied on foreigners, but not on Israelites (Deuteronomy 23:19–20). Indeed, lending in Israelite law was governed by detailed and humanitarian principles which protected the poor. The laws were designed to protect against abuses. Jesus departed from Israelite law when he instructed his followers to lend even to enemies without expecting an earthly reward: The rewards, he said, come only from God. Nevertheless, his parables assumed that banking was a fact of life.

Money changers were necessary in the Israel of Jesus' time because of the bewildering array of different coinages, all of which enjoyed status as legal tender, subject to a variety of restrictions. For in addition to the official imperial money of Rome and the provincial coins from Antioch and Tyre, which were minted mainly according to Greek standard, the Jews of the Holy Land had their own local money.

The New Testament mentions numerous coins; one example is the Greek lepton, the widow's copper coin in Mark. It was the coin of least value in circulation. Other monies include the Greek drachma—the silver coin of Luke 15:8—approximately equivalent to the Roman denarius that Matthew mentioned in 20:2 as a day's wage; the shekel, being equal to four drachmas or four denarii, the coin taken from the fish's mouth to pay Jesus' and Peter's combined Temple tax (Matthew 17:27); the mina, or pound, equal to 100 drachmas; and the talent, equal to 6,000 drachmas.

The Temple tax had to be paid with coins from Tyre because their silver content was greater than that of the corresponding coins from Antioch. Priests cooperated with money changers who would provide the specified coins for Jewish visitors arriving from other lands with foreign money. They were also prepared to "make change" for larger denominations so that correct amounts would be in hand for the purchase of sacrificial animals or for other needs at the Temple. The money changers began to provide their services for Passover a month before the feast—a time when thousands of pilgrims traveled to Jerusalem—then moved their banking tables into the Temple's precincts, probably the Court of the Gentiles, as the feast neared.

A commission, (called in Greek the *kollybos*) had to be paid for services rendered; from this commission, the bankers received the name *kollybistes* or "money changers," as Matthew 21:12 terms them. The fee opened the way to excessive charging. Instances of profiteering in the sale of sacrificial doves are documented in the Mishnah. Abuses in lending can in fact be dated back several hundred years, to the time of Nehemiah, who had felt moved to urge the return of the one percent per month interest that Israelite lenders took from their countrymen (Nehemiah 5:7–11). Annual interest rates on loans of money and in kind were high in the ancient Near East, often exceeding a fifth of the loan, at times up to half.

Such commercialization of the worship area is the most likely explanation for Jesus' anger when he overturned the money changers' tables. They had made the Father's house "a den of robbers" and "a house of trade." They had destroyed its character as "a house of prayer for all the nations." The expulsion of the money changers may have also been a rebuke to priests who had maintained their dominance in Temple affairs by bribing or otherwise pacifying the Romans. It was thus not the legal use of banking and money—but their *abuse*—that was at issue. ✦

A tyrant rebuilds the Temple

The paradox of Herod's legacy

ISTORY SPEAKS of a First and a Second Temple. Both were destroyed, according to Jewish tradition, on the ninth of Av—in the years 587 B.C. and 70 A.D. respectively. In fact, the term "Second Temple" refers to two distinct structures, the earlier one constructed after the return from the Babylonian Exile, and dedicated in 515 B.C. The later Second Temple was that of Herod I ("the Great"), and was undoubtedly one of the outstanding engineering feats of the Roman Empire. Ironically, craftsmen had hardly put the finishing touches on the Temple when it was razed by the army of Titus, in the year 70.

The Temple was the ritual center of the Jewish people. Animal sacrifices were made there daily. On the three major festivals—Sukkot, Passover, and Shavuot—all adult males were obliged to attend Temple ritu-

In a remarkable scale model, *King Herod's Temple of Jerusalem comes to life once again.*

als. Estimates vary, but there may have been as many as two and a half million Jews living in Palestine in this period. During the festivals, the population of Jerusalem, which is estimated to have been 100,000–200,000, swelled by the thousands as pilgrims arrived. At these times, both pilgrims and resident Jews ascended to the Temple Mount. But as it had been rebuilt in the sixth century B.C., the Temple Mount could barely accommodate crowds of this size. An enlarged Temple was probably Herod's means of dealing with such throngs.

Perhaps the construction of the Temple was also a way to appease a suspicious priesthood. The Jews did not regard Herod as their rightful king. In 40 B.C. the Roman Senate had proclaimed Herod, the grandson of an Idumean who had converted to Judaism, King of Judea. But it took him about three years to subdue Antigonus, who was in possession of the throne. Soon after Herod had conquered Judea, he put to death 45 supporters of Antigonus who were members of the Sanhedrin (the Jewish supreme council, which, according to Jewish

for permission to construct this massive new structure. But because the Temple could possibly be used as a fortification, its construction could very well have caused concern in Rome.

The story we do have is in the Talmud, which relates that Herod sent a messenger to Rome to seek permission to pull down the old Temple and replace it with a new structure. The envoy is supposed to have departed with the instructions to take a year to reach Rome, remain there for a time, and take another year to make his way back with the answer. According to this legend, Herod got this response from the imperial city: "If you have not yet pulled it down, do not do so; if you have pulled it down, do not rebuild it; and if you have pulled it down and already rebuilt it, you are one of those bad servants who do first and ask permission afterward."

In fact, the construction of the new Temple, and its vastly expanded mount took 46 years. At the beginning, Herod did little more than assemble and train the 10,000 craftsmen and 1,000 priests who would prepare and construct the edifice. Masons spent years cutting, dressing, and transporting the stones for the Temple and its retaining walls. As prescribed, the stones used for the sacrificial altar were unhewn, so that no iron would touch it. Construction of the inner parts of the Temple had to be undertaken by members of a priestly family; this is supposed to have taken 18 months.

Herod solved the problem of space by enlarging the area surrounding the Temple. He doubled the area of the Temple Mount, building huge retaining walls that towered 30 meters above ground level, and were partly below ground level as well.

The old Temple continued to be in regular use all during the preparation. If Herod had proposed taking down the existing Temple before making ready for its successor, he would never have received the support of the priests, who would have assumed that he intended only to deprive the Jewish people of their ritual center. However, the daily sacrifices continued. ✦

writings, met at the Temple). This helped Herod consolidate his power, but it must have further decreased his legitimacy in the eyes of the religious leadership.

Around the year 20 B.C., Herod convened a national assembly and announced his plan to construct a new Temple. In his speech, Herod explained that the Temple then standing lacked 60 cubits in height, as compared with the Temple of Solomon, and that he intended to rectify this grievous situation, with the blessings of Rome. There is no record of Herod's application to Rome

An unscrupulous, powerful family

The Herodian dynasty

FOR MORE THAN A CENTURY in Palestine, political power revolved around the name of Herod. The distant Romans held ultimate control, but in the land itself the Herodian dynasty was the instrument of rule. These were the kings of the Jews.

Ironically, this most powerful Jewish family was not Jewish in its origins. Its members were Idumeans, descendants of the ancient Edomites, who inhabited the region south of Judea. In 125 B.C. Israel's Hasmonean king, John Hyrcanus, conquered the Idumeans and forcibly converted them to Judaism. Most Idumeans accepted the conversion and within a generation considered themselves wholly Jewish.

Under the later Hasmonean rulers one particular Idumean family emerged into prominence led by a man named Antipater. He successfully navigated the treacherous political waters when the Roman general Pompey conquered Palestine and the last Hasmoneans became puppets of Rome. Antipater was named procurator of the region and was able to promote the fortunes of his sons, including his brash and ambitious second son, named Herod.

From the start Herod was a man of bold action, obvious ability, and unswerving allegiance to Rome. When, in 40 B.C., Antigonus, the last of the Hasmonean rulers, regained the throne by joining forces with Rome's enemies, the Parthians, Herod fled for his life. In Rome he was supported by the most powerful men there, Mark Antony and Octavian. He was proclaimed king of the Jews by the Roman Senate and sent back to Judea to win his kingdom.

Herod reigned from 37 to 4 B.C.—a client of Rome, but very much the master of his land. He was ruthless in executing political opponents, confiscating their property, and imposing order in the land. He fostered economic prosperity by building on a grand scale. New and rebuilt cities, fortresses, and temples sprang up throughout his territory.

Herod's large family—including his 10 wives—was less a family than a murderous nest of dynastic struggle. Eventually Herod's three eldest sons were all executed for treason. When the fierce old king died in 4 B.C., Augustus divided his territory among three of his younger sons but granted none the title of king. Archelaus, who received the prize of Judea, along with Samaria and Idumea, was a brutal failure. Augustus banished him in A.D. 6, and Rome took over direct rule of Judea. Herod Philip ruled in obscurity over the northern regions of the kingdom until his death in A.D. 34. Between these two areas, Herod Antipas ruled over Galilee and Perea, which was east of the Jordan. It was he who had John the Baptist beheaded. Jesus derided him as "that fox," and, according to Luke, Antipas participated in the trial of Jesus (Luke 13:32; 23:6–12).

As each of Herod's sons passed from the scene, a grandson of Herod named Agrippa emerged as heir to the dynasty. Agrippa had been reared in Rome from childhood and became an intimate of Gaius Caligula, who ascended the imperial throne in A.D. 37. Caligula gave him Herod Philip's territory, then that of Herod Antipas, and finally, in the year 41, the new emperor Claudius reunited Herod's old realm under Agrippa, naming him king also of Judea. Unlike his grandfather, Agrippa maintained meticulous piety at home. He tried to suppress the newly emerging Christian sect by persecution, including, according to Acts, the execution of the apostle James and the imprisonment of Peter. He died suddenly after only a few years on the throne.

Agrippa left only a youthful son, Agrippa II, as his heir. He was eventually granted various territories. Though he supported Judaism, he was loyal to Rome and fought against the rebels in the Jewish war. With him the flame of the Herodian dynasty sputtered and was finally extinguished. ✦

Legend linked the mysterious Mary Magdalene to the anointing of Jesus.

"She has done a beautiful thing"

The anointing at Bethany

ESUS' CONTROVERSIES IN THE TEMPLE were over. The opposition to Jesus had now reached such a pitch that the chief priests and scribes were, as Mark recounts, "seeking how to arrest him by stealth, and kill him." The fateful Passover was approaching, and Jesus went to the village of Bethany to dine at the home of a man called Simon the leper (Mark 14:3).

That evening an unexpected event occurred that pointed enigmatically to the end of Jesus' life a few days hence. During dinner, as Mark tells the story, an unidentified woman entered the room carrying an alabaster flask filled with precious nard, a perfume imported from the far-off Himalayas. Without a word the woman broke the flask and poured the ointment over Jesus' head. The fragrance filled the room.

What did this mean? Since the woman said nothing but rather let the act speak for her, she was at the mercy of those who interpreted her deed. Some saw nothing but waste. The perfume was worth over 300 denarii—nearly a year's wages for a laborer. It should have been sold and the proceeds given to the poor. In some ways they were right, and Jesus indeed affirmed the continual need to care for the poor.

But in the woman's deed, Jesus saw something invaluable: "She has done a beautiful thing to me. . . .She has anointed my body beforehand for burying" (Mark 14:6, 8). The guests must have been dumbfounded by such a statement. But as Mark would reveal, Jesus was to be buried hastily without anointing. Before his friends could return with spices and ointments, he had risen. This woman's action was mysteriously and prophetically a sign of Jesus' death and also his resurrection. Thus, Jesus said, "wherever the gospel is preached in the whole world, what she has done will be told in memory of her" (Mark 14:9).

Though the Gospel of Matthew follows Mark's narrative closely, Luke and John have recorded distinctly different versions of this event. Still, in each Gospel, the story of the woman's deed was told and continues to be told to this day. ✦

The Last Supper

"Do this in remembrance of me"

THE MEAL THAT JESUS shared with his disciples the evening before his arrest created a sense of mystery and awakened hopes that were forever burned into the hearts of Jesus' followers. When the disciples looked back in later years, the events of that evening and the words Jesus spoke became laden with inexplicable power. It was the single moment of Jesus' life that they would reenact again and again. The disciples believed that by performing a ritual Last Supper, they expressed and somehow touched the heart and power of his life and death.

Within the Jewish community, the simple act of breaking bread with another person frequently signified an important event. Friendship, covenants, contracts, alliances, and marriages might all be sealed by shared bread. In addition, Israel's religious life was marked by feasts that celebrated God's blessings. The most important was the Passover meal. Thus it is not at all surprising that the mystery of Jesus' life and death was celebrated by his disciples through a commemorative meal.

Part of the enigma of the Last Supper arises from the various ways it was remembered in the early church. Each of the four Gospels gives it a prominent place, but as was often the case, each has a somewhat different version of the story. The greatest

divergence is between the Synoptic Gospels (Matthew, Mark, and Luke) and the Gospel of John. The Synoptics all explicitly describe the Last Supper as a Passover meal and focus on Jesus' words over the bread and wine (Mark 14:12—25). Just as explicitly, John states that the meal took place on the day before Passover (John 13:1; 19:14). But he makes no mention of the blessing of the bread and wine; instead, John describes Jesus' farewell conversation and prayer with his disciples.

The earliest written record of the Last Supper comes not from the Gospels but from the letters of the Apostle Paul, which date from approximately 20 to 40 years before the four Gospels. When he was instructing the church that he had established in the Greek city of Corinth, Paul recounted "that the Lord Jesus on the night when he was betrayed took bread, and when he had given thanks, he broke it, and said, 'This is my body which is for you. Do this in remembrance of me.' In the same way also the cup, after supper, saying, 'This cup is the new covenant in my blood. Do this, as often as you drink it, in remembrance of me.' For as often as you eat this bread and drink the cup, you proclaim the Lord's death until he comes" (1 Corinthians 11:23–26). Paul's story of the Last Supper gives us some insight into how the tradition was handed down in the early days of the church, until it ultimately became part of the Gospels.

Clearly the differing accounts of the Last Supper, as they appear in the New Testament, offer the historian numerous puzzles. Scholars have tried to establish whether the Last Supper was in fact a Passover meal but no consensus has been reached. However, it is clear that if the Last Supper was a Passover meal, it retained only the most basic elements from the feast.

The commemorative aspects of the meal have become part of Christian worship. The

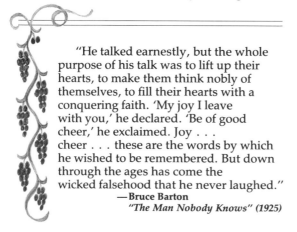

"He talked earnestly, but the whole purpose of his talk was to lift up their hearts, to make them think nobly of themselves, to fill their hearts with a conquering faith. 'My joy I leave with you,' he declared. 'Be of good cheer,' he exclaimed. Joy . . . cheer . . . these are the words by which he wished to be remembered. But down through the ages has come the wicked falsehood that he never laughed."
—Bruce Barton
"The Man Nobody Knows" (1925)

*"**Go and prepare** the passover for us, that we may eat it."*

layers of mystery that the early church found in the events of the Last Supper can be better understood by reading the individual accounts, rather than by trying to reconstruct the history behind them.

The most extensive of the narratives in the Synoptic Gospels is that in Luke 22. There, as in Matthew and Mark, the Last Supper came at the moment of crisis. Serious plots on Jesus' life had taken shape, and Judas Iscariot, one of the twelve apostles, joined the plots after "Satan entered into" him. Nevertheless, Luke portrayed Jesus in full control as he prepared for the Passover.

325

Jesus sent Peter and John to a particular room in the pilgrim-filled city, where they could eat together. "Behold, when you have entered a city, a man carrying a jar of water will meet you; follow him into the house which he enters, . . . And they went, and found it as he had told them; and they prepared the passover" (Luke 22:10–13).

Jesus began the meal by solemnly announcing that he had greatly desired to eat the Passover with his disciples, as he said, "before I suffer." But, he said, "I shall not eat it until it is fulfilled in the kingdom of God." A moment later he added, "from now on I shall not drink the fruit of the vine until the kingdom of God comes" (Luke 22:15–18). The purpose of the Passover was to bring the *past* vividly into the present; but for Jesus, the *future* was pressing into that moment. First there was the expectation of his own suffering; beyond that was the joyful future of God's kingdom.

In this context, Jesus offered the disciples bread from the meal and later the cup, with words that transformed them. The words transported the disciples out of that moment and into the future beyond the crucifixion, when Jesus would no longer be present. Jesus established a new covenant, sealed by the blood of that coming suffering: "This is my body which is given for you. Do this in remembrance of me." "This cup which is poured out for you is the new covenant in my blood."

Though Jesus did not explain them, these words remain as a living mystery of remembrance, anticipation, and unity at the heart of Christian worship. In later centuries Jesus' words came to be understood as a miracle that transformed the inner substance, but not the outer appearance, of the bread and wine into the actual body and blood of Jesus. To this day, a variety of interpretations of the mystery of the Last Supper persist.

However, Luke's narrative is darkened by the specter of human betrayal. When Jesus stated that a traitor was among the disciples, Luke dramatically described how they asked who among them would betray

In a tender act of love, *Jesus washed his disciples' feet.*

326

Jesus. Then they fell to wrangling over which of them was greatest. Jesus had to stop them and remind them of the values that made them disciples. He reminded them of the importance of humility in the life of service that lay ahead: "For which is the greater, one who sits at table, or one who serves? Is it not the one who sits at table? But I am among you as one who serves" (Luke 22:27).

Jesus spoke of the kingdom of God, but at the same time warned them of the real dangers that faced them as disciples. All would be sifted like wheat; even Peter, the most steadfast, would deny knowing Jesus. They would endure much suffering while trying to fulfill Jesus' mission.

John's Gospel emphasizes Jesus' divine nature. In his narrative, the Last Supper was the setting for a series of revelations in action and word that first manifested divine love and then drew the disciples into participation in that love. Jesus, as John relates, was aware that "the hour" had come for him to be glorified in his death and to depart from the world. He also knew that the betrayer was present. But as an expression of his love for his disciples, without a word he rose from the meal, took off his garments, wrapped a towel around himself,

and began to perform the menial tasks of a slave. He washed the feet of the disciples one by one.

We can feel the shock that this action caused when we hear Peter's bewildered response, "Lord, do you wash my feet? . . . You shall never wash my feet!" (John 13: 6, 8). Jesus explained that the disciple must accept Jesus' service if he was to have any part in Jesus. He was indeed their teacher and their Lord, but they must understand what kind of Lord. His action was an enduring example of love and service on which they were to pattern their lives.

Into the night Jesus talked with the disciples about his departure. Repeatedly he returned to the themes of love for one another and peace in the midst of tribulation. He promised them a counselor, the Holy Spirit, to guide and aid them. Jesus told his disciples, "These things I have spoken to you, while I am still with you. But the Counselor, the Holy Spirit, whom the Father will send in my name, he will teach you all things, and bring to your remembrance all that I have said to you." For John, the Last Supper was the moment when the disciples came into the circle of Jesus' mysterious unity with the Father, and prepared them for the arduous times ahead. ✦

The struggle in the garden

Jesus' prayer at Gethsemane

THE END WAS AT HAND. After the Last Supper Jesus retreated with the eleven remaining disciples to a place on the Mount of Olives called, from the Aramaic term for "Oilpress," *Gethsemane*. The site is traditionally associated with a grove of ancient olive trees. There in solitude Jesus struggled with his fate in prayer to God.

The Gospels of Mark and Matthew show that Jesus entered the grove in great distress: "My soul is very sorrowful, even to death." So distraught was he that he fell to the ground. Peter, James, and John, meanwhile, were charged to keep vigil, but in-

stead they slept, leaving Jesus all the more alone. It was at this moment that Jesus spoke the heartrending prayer: "Abba, Father, all things are possible to thee; remove this cup from me; yet not what I will, but what thou wilt" (Mark 14:36).

Jesus' prayer in Gethsemane echoes the prayer that Jesus had taught his own disciples to pray, now known as the Our Father or Lord's Prayer (Matthew 6:9–13). Jesus began by praying "Abba, Father." Then he prayed: "Not what I will but what thou wilt," the key petition of the Lord's Prayer: "Thy will be done."

While Jesus prayed, *Peter, James, and John slept.*

Just as the scene in Gethsemane revealed Jesus to be a model of faithfulness, so too it demonstrated the difficulty of remaining faithful. When Jesus returned to the three disciples whom he had told to watch, he found them sleeping. He woke them and urged them to pray also to avoid temptation. Again, they failed. The drama captured human frailty: "the spirit indeed is willing, but the flesh is weak."

Luke's account of the scene differs in detail from the other gospels. Mark says that Jesus prayed three times; Luke records only once. This suggests that Jesus quickly embraced God's will. It is from Luke 22:44 that the reference to the "agony" has come down to us. While modern readers tend to understand the word "agony" as meaning pain and fear, this is not what the word means in Greek, the language in which

Luke wrote. *Agon* in Greek means a contest or struggle. Luke may have seen Jesus, clearly God's holy and obedient son, as locked in combat with the tempter. Jesus had God's strength—"there appeared to him an angel from heaven, strengthening him"—but the struggle was so fierce that his "sweat became like great drops of blood falling down upon the ground."

In many important early manuscripts of the New Testament, the verses that refer to the angel, to Jesus' agony, and to his sweat being like blood do not occur. They were probably added to the original Lukan text by a Christian scribe. Therefore, some modern Bibles do not include them. The Gospels agree that in his struggle Jesus remained faithful to God. In Gethsemane, Jesus' Passion began. Through his prayer he was strengthened for the trials before him. ✦

The betrayal

The paradox of Judas' deed

THE NAME OF JUDAS Iscariot has become a byword for betrayal, and his kiss the symbol of treachery. The first time Judas is mentioned in each of the Gospels, he is identified as the traitor. The Gospel of John goes so far as to call him "a devil" (John 6:70). Yet Judas remains an enigmatic character. Who was he? Why did he betray Jesus? What became of him?

Though the name *Judas* was common in the time of Jesus, the puzzling designation "Iscariot" was not, and it perhaps holds a clue to Judas' background. The Gospel of John spoke both of "Judas Iscariot" and of "Judas the son of Simon Iscariot." Thus, the term perhaps applied to Judas' whole family. The most common guess at its meaning links it to a Hebrew phrase meaning "man from Kerioth," thought to be a town in southern Judea. If correct, this suggestion would mean that Judas was probably the only one of the twelve from Judea. Did he feel like an outsider among the disciples from Galilee? The ancient texts do not give us an answer to this.

Another suggestion is that "Iscariot" derives from the Latin word *sicarius* meaning "dagger-man," the designation of one of the most radical, anti-Roman of Jewish factions, a group that used terror tactics to deal with those who collaborated with Rome. If so, then perhaps Judas became disaffected because Jesus failed to take a radical stand against Rome and even approved the payment of Roman taxes (Mark 12:13–17). The greatest problem with this suggestion is that the ancient historian Josephus indicates that the *Sicarii* arose as a faction after A.D. 52, more than 20 years after the death of both Jesus and Judas. Other guesses have interpreted "Iscariot" to mean "man from Sychar" (a Samaritan), "carrier of the leather bag" (*scortea*), and "false one, liar" (an Aramaic Christian designation).

The Gospels provide no clear religious or political rationale for Judas' betrayal. Matthew suggested that his motive was simply greed by describing how he bargained with the chief priests for 30 pieces of silver—the recompense that the Torah required for the accidental killing of a slave. Mark and Luke, however, indicated that chief priests were the ones who first made the offer of money. John wrote that during Jesus' ministry Judas held the trusted position of treasurer for the twelve, and John accused him of stealing their funds. But when he wrote of the betrayal, John did not mention money.

For Luke and John, Judas' personal motives were less important than the assertion that it was Satan that brought about the betrayal. Still important for the Gospel writers was the fact that God's will determined the manner of Jesus' death (Mark 14:21). John indicated that the disciples suspected nothing when Judas quickly left the Last Supper to prepare for Jesus' arrest.

The deadly kiss of Judas, *here portrayed by Giotto.*

When the moment of arrest came, Judas led a large group to the garden of Gethsemane on the Mount of Olives. Since Jesus was a public figure, it is unlikely that Judas' kiss was needed to identify Jesus. Matthew, Mark, and Luke portray Judas leading "a crowd" of Jews, including many who had heard Jesus teach in the temple (Mark 14:43–49). On the other hand, John described Judas leading Jewish officers and a "band of soldiers." The term John used indicates a company of Roman troops.

What became of Judas? The New Testament provides two accounts. Matthew reported that he repented, returned the money, and in deep remorse went out and hanged himself. The priests used the tainted money to buy a burial ground for foreigners, a potter's field called the "Field of Blood" (Matthew 27:3–10).

The book of Acts recorded that Judas himself bought a field with the money and "falling headlong he burst open in the middle and all his bowels gushed out" so that his field was called "Field of Blood" (Acts 1:18–19). From his beginning to his horrible end, the dark character of Judas Iscariot remains an enigma. ✦

Jesus stands trial

The riddle of what happened

THE GREAT MYSTERY about the trial of Jesus lies in discovering what actually occurred. The Gospels are our only sources of specific information, but historians have come to widely differing conclusions regarding their content. The trial has also been a cause of intense and emotional dispute because for centuries the narratives were misused to justify the persecution of Jews by Christians.

Pontius Pilate was the Roman prefect or governor who ultimately crucified Jesus. He was notorious for his harshness toward the Jews and his contempt for their religion and customs. Philo, a Jewish contemporary of Pilate, wrote of "the briberies, the insults, the robberies, the outrages and wanton injuries, the executions without trial constantly repeated, the ceaseless and supremely grievous cruelty" that marked his rule. Ultimately Pilate was recalled to Rome to answer charges for crimes in office.

From the perspective of the evangelists, any criminal trial against Jesus would have been unjust. The New Testament narratives follow three basic patterns. The most controversial is the report given by both Mark and Matthew. They describe Jesus being led from his arrest on Passover evening to a night trial before the high priest and the whole Jewish court, the Sanhedrin. Mark states that they sought evidence against Jesus, but were unable to find two witnesses who could agree, as was required by Jewish law. Some "false witnesses" testified that Jesus had spoken against the Temple, but even they could not agree (Mark 14:55–59).

The trial might thus have collapsed, but the high priest confronted Jesus directly with a question that is a focal point for the entire Gospel of Mark: "Are you the Christ, the Son of the Blessed?" Jesus answered directly, "I am." That, Mark says, was considered blasphemy. The high priest tore his garments and Jesus was condemned by all the high priests "as deserving death" (Mark 14:61–64).

After another meeting of the Sanhedrin in the morning, Jesus was brought before Pontius Pilate. Thus, Mark wished to emphasize that it was Jesus' admission that he was "the Christ, the Son of the Blessed" that led to his condemnation.

Historical controversy arises because the Mishnah, the earliest codification of Jewish law, banned night trials in capital cases and required that a guilty verdict be delayed for one day after the trial. It also defined criminal blasphemy only in terms of pronouncing the ancient name of God. The Mishnah,

On the night of his arrest, *Christ appeared before Caiaphas.*

however, dates from more than a century and a half after Jesus; it is not known whether its rules were followed earlier.

Interestingly enough, Luke does not describe a night trial. According to Luke's Gospel, when Jesus was arrested, he was brought to the courtyard of the high priest's house and held there until morning. Peter followed the group who had arrested Jesus, and sat among them. As the night dragged on, Peter was three times accused of knowing Jesus. In the presence of his Lord, Peter denied knowing him. When the trial before the Sanhedrin was held on Passover morning, Luke mentions no witnesses or testimony, but only the demand of the council, "If you are the Christ, tell us." Jesus refused to answer. "Are you the Son of God, then?" they asked, and Jesus would only respond enigmatically, "You say that I am." Luke describes no formal verdict against Jesus, but only the decision that the council had heard enough to bring him before Pilate.

John omits specific mention of a trial before Jewish leaders. According to John's Gospel, Jesus was arrested on the night *before* Passover and taken to Annas, the father-in-law of the high priest Caiaphas, and questioned "about his disciples and his teaching." He was then taken to Caiaphas, presumably to stand trial before the Sanhedrin. However, John gives no details of the trial, and has no statement of charges or witnesses brought against Jesus, nor a verdict by any Jewish court.

According to Mark and Matthew, the fatal trial before Pilate was brief indeed. The notoriously harsh prefect asked the Galilean prisoner a single contemptuous question, "Are you the king of the Jews?" Jesus answered, "You have said so." The chief priests continued to hurl accusations at Jesus, and Pilate asked, " 'Have you no answer to make? See how many charges they bring against you.' But Jesus made no further answer, so that Pilate wondered" (Mark 15:2–5). If Philo's description of Pilate's cruelty was correct, the governor would have needed no more than Jesus' irritating behavior to convince him to get rid of a troublemaker.

Luke's narrative included further charges and an episode of Jesus being taken before Herod Antipas. He also stressed that Pilate and Herod found Jesus innocent of any capital charge, and thus made it clear that Pilate crucified an innocent man.

John's Gospel contained a more extended account of the trial before the governor (18:28–19:16). It included a three-way dialogue between Pilate, the chief priests, and Jesus. Pilate was revealed as weak, vacillating, and fearful. He was pushed by Jesus to contemplate questions of truth and power, but ultimately yielded his verdict to his political cowardice.

"Release to us Barabbas!" cried the throngs at Jesus' trial. It was the last chance for Jesus' rescue, the sealing of his fate. As described in all four Gospels, Pilate was to grant amnesty to one Jewish prisoner in honor of the Passover. The crowds were asked to choose between Jesus and Barabbas, a man under sentence of death for murder. They picked the murderer rather than the teacher whom they had praised just days before.

In Christian tradition, a fickle mob led by malevolent chief priests inexplicably chose to condemn an innocent man. Thus Pilate freed Barabbas and crucified Jesus. But was

Pilate washed his hands, *seeking to deny responsibility for Jesus' death.*

there more to it? Historians have searched in vain for any clear reference outside the Gospels to the custom of releasing a prisoner at Passover. The dearth of information, combined with the strange coincidence that the name Barabbas means "son of the father"—in contrast to Jesus as "son of God"—has led a few scholars to argue that the episode is a fabrication.

The key to understanding the choice of the crowd may lie in the description of the charges against Barabbas. Mark describes him as one of the "rebels in prison, who had committed murder in the insurrection." Luke says he was part of an "insurrection started in the city." John describes him with the Greek word *lestes*, which means bandit, insurrectionist, or revolutionary.

These descriptions may connect Barabbas with a group of relatively disorganized rebel fighters who harassed the Romans and urged the population to resist foreign domination, and to tolerate no ruler of Israel but God. Because of the massive presence of the Roman legions, however, these groups mainly existed as outlaw bands living in the hills. When the Romans caught them, they were charged as robbers and murderers, and were often crucified.

Barabbas may have been a leader in one of these outlaw bands. It is possible that Pilate, aware of Jesus' earlier popularity with the crowds, hoped that they would choose to condemn Barabbas, thus aiding Pilate in condemning an anti-Roman rebel. If this was his plan, it clearly backfired. The crowd cried for release of Barabbas. Along with Jesus, Pilate crucified two other men who, like Barabbas, are described with the term *lestes*, "insurrectionist" (Mark 15:27).

The Gospels interpret the cry to release Barabbas as a rejection of Jesus. But the episode may also illustrate a Jewish cry against Rome, and support of groups that were struggling against Roman rule. Jesus opposed such violent rebellion against Rome, but he ended his life in a row of crosses between two anti-Roman rebels. ✦

Crime and punishment in ancient times

A gruesome death

CRUCIFIXION WAS a form of capital punishment, but it was much more. It was a means of slow torture and public display, intended to shame and degrade the criminal and to deter others. Because of these added elements, its use throughout the Roman Empire was limited to slaves and non-Roman lower classes.

The basic procedures of a typical Roman crucifixion were certainly well known in ancient times, but there was considerable room for variation in practice. The condemned was scourged and usually forced to carry the cross-beam of his cross to the place where the upright part was fixed in the ground. He was stripped to his undergarments and nailed to the cross-beam with a four- or five-inch spike through the wrists. The cross-beam was hoisted up and attached to the top of the gibbet, usually forming a "T" shape. The weight of the body usually rested on a short crosspiece beneath the buttocks. This support helped prolong the torture, so that the condemned would not die quickly. The feet were nailed to the cross by a spike that was driven through both feet together. If the executioners wished to hasten death, the victim's legs could be broken, so that the body would slump down and constrict breathing.

The reality of this procedure has become particularly vivid through the recent discovery of a tomb near Jerusalem. Dating from the first century of our era, the tomb contained a partial skeleton of a man crucified perhaps during the census revolt of A.D. 6. The remains include the heel bones, still fastened together by a spike more than four inches long, and the lower leg bones, which showed that both legs had been broken.

Christ's anguished struggle up the hill of Golgotha is rendered by Tintoretto.

Without such a coup de grace to speed death, a victim might remain alive on a cross for several days until he died of starvation, exposure, or the effects of his wounds. Often the corpse would be left on public display until it became, as one ancient author wrote, "food for birds of prey and grim pickings for dogs." The grotesque realities of crucifixion were seldom spelled out in literature, but they provided a grisly show for the public in practically any city, and Jerusalem had seen its share.

The Torah did not specify crucifixion as a means of capital punishment, but it did allow for the corpse of a criminal, executed by stoning perhaps, to be hanged publicly for one day. The body had to buried by nightfall, however, because its continued exposure would defile the land, "for a hanged man is accursed by God" (Deuteronomy 21:23). This divine curse applied fully to crucified criminals and made the cross a particularly hateful form of execution among the Jews. ✦

The Crucifixion of Jesus

"Father, into thy hands I commit my spirit!"

WHEN CHRISTIAN PROCLAMATION first began, it quickly became clear that the fact of Jesus' crucifixion was a major problem. "We preach Christ crucified, a stumbling block to Jews and folly to Gentiles," wrote Paul, a Jewish Christian and an apostle to the Gentiles. A paradox of the Christian message is that what was most offensive became most central, as Paul went on to say, "I decided to know nothing among you except Jesus Christ and him crucified" (1 Corinthians 1:23; 2:2). Christian proclamation had to come to terms with the hard fact that Jesus was executed as a criminal by the Roman governor of Judea using the extremely harsh form of execution, crucifixion.

There was certainly never any expectation that God's Messiah would suffer such absolute degradation. There were traditions concerning the suffering of the righteous, but such suffering was what the Messiah would relieve, not what he would experience. Clearly the task of early Christians as they tried to make sense of a crucified Messiah was quite formidable. There was no need to emphasize the gruesome character of crucifixion—that was well known. But there was a need to illuminate the mystery of how such degradation could be the revelation of God.

Each of the four Gospels wrestled with this mystery, interpreting it in two ways. First, they gave emphasis to those details of the story that seem to fulfill patterns or prophecies of Scripture. Especially important here was Psalm 22, a psalm of lament to which all four Gospels refer. Second, they cited the words of Jesus from the cross.

The crucifixion narratives of Mark and Matthew are especially dark. Step by step, they show Jesus isolated and ridiculed. After he was condemned, the Roman soldiers scourged Jesus and mocked him as "King of the Jews." The scourging evidently so weakened him that he could not carry the beam of his cross; the soldiers forced Simon of Cyrene to pick it up.

Jesus, along with two other condemned men, was taken outside Jerusalem to the execution ground called Golgotha, meaning *skull*. Matthew and Mark say nothing about the crucifixion procedure of nailing Jesus to the cross, nor about the physical suffering, but mention seemingly lesser details: giving Jesus wine mixed with gall (hemlock) or myrrh; the executioners' casting lots for his clothes. Such details are signposts alluding to Scriptures and thus suggest that the crucifixion is the fulfillment of biblical prophecy. For example, Psalm 22:7 says, "All who see me mock at me, they make mouths at me, they wag their heads"; so also, Matthew notes that "those who passed by de-

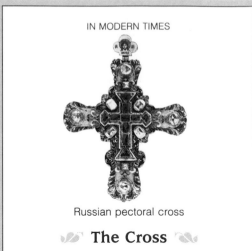

IN MODERN TIMES

Russian pectoral cross

❧ The Cross ❧

In the first three centuries after the crucifixion, the cross was an important symbol in private devotion, but Christians rarely used it openly. In the 4th century, the Roman emperor Constantine used the cross on his coinage. His devotion to the cross was reported to have come from a vision of Christ's cross emblazoned in the sky. With his help, the cross became the reigning symbol of the church.

It was during Constantine's reign, that the cross upon which Jesus was crucified was said to have been found, and numerous legends sprang up about the "True Cross."

The Latin cross of the early Christians took many forms, as they were embellished by craftsmen. Saints and martyrs were assigned their own symbolic crosses. The crucifix, with Christ's body on it, probably developed around the 5th century, but was not used on church altars until the 13th century.

| Latin | Greek | Patriarchal |
| St. Peter's | Maltese | Anchor |

rided him, wagging their heads." Moreover, when the chief priests mocked him by saying, "He trusts in God; let God deliver him now," they echo Psalm 22:8. Even the bandits crucified with him reviled him. His disciples abandoned him; Jesus was alone.

All this, however, is but preparation for the most somber mystery of the story. Matthew and Mark tell how at midday darkness covered the land for three hours. Then in the darkness Jesus cried aloud in the only words from the cross that Matthew and Mark record, " 'Eloi, Eloi, lama sabachthani?' which means, 'My God, my God, why hast thou forsaken me?' " (Mark 15:34). Abandoned by disciples, enemies, and onlookers, and now, in his word, "forsaken" by God, Jesus descended into the darkest experience that a human being can know.

Jesus' anguished cry also echoes the first words of Psalm 22, again showing the role that this psalm plays in the narrative. The Gospel writers did not try to tone down the anguish or explain the meaning of Jesus' cry. Instead they chose to show the consequences. First there was confusion as those around the cross completely misunderstood Jesus' words. The second was the declaration by the centurion who was executing Jesus. This unknown person became, especially in Mark, a focus of the whole Gospel. It was he who saw how Jesus died and was the first to exclaim, "Truly this man was the Son of God."

The focus of Luke's narrative was not on Jesus' anguish, but rather, his serenity and confidence. Luke knows that Jesus understood clearly the divine mystery that was occurring. Just after he was placed on the cross, Jesus prayed: "Father, forgive them; for they know not what they do" (Luke 23:34). The executioners acted in ignorance; only Jesus grasped what was happening. A little later, when one of the criminals defended Jesus against the reviling, Jesus promised him, "Truly, I say to you, today you will be with me in Paradise" (Luke 23:42). Luke was showing that even on the cross, Jesus had full competence to forgive sin and grant eternal blessedness. Death

The inscription "INRI" on the cross means "Jesus of Nazareth, King of the Jews."

held no threat at all to him. As in the Gospels of Matthew and Mark, the final words of Jesus are a quotation of Scripture, this time Psalm 31:5, "Father, into thy hands I commit my spirit!" (Luke 23:46). Here Luke lets us see the serenity that comes from understanding God's will and living it to the last moment.

The Gospel of John notes how quickly Jesus died. Like the Passover lamb, his bones were not broken, but his side was pierced after death, and blood and water came forth. John also records three distinctive sayings of Jesus from the cross, each of which emphasizes his control of events. In extremis, his love and concern for his mother moved him to care for her future by appointing the "disciple whom he loved" to act as her son (John 19:26). The last two sayings come in quick succession. John shows Jesus' desire to fulfill the Scriptures, and thus he says "I thirst." The reference is probably to Psalm 69:21, "For my thirst they gave me vinegar to drink." Though all the power of Rome is striving to kill him, Jesus is largely unaffected. It is only when that last deed is completed that the moment arrives to utter the words toward which his whole life has been moving; "It is finished." Then Jesus "bowed his head and gave up his spirit" (John 19:30).

Each gospel has its own voice and contribution. Together they reveal how for the early Christians a grotesque and brutal act of torture and execution became the mystery of God's love revealed in the world. ✦

Mary holds the body of Jesus: Pietà by Michelangelo.

A compassionate gesture

Joseph of Arimathea buries Jesus

THE DEPOSITION OF JESUS—that is, the removal of his body from the cross—is a cherished subject of Christian art. All four of the Gospels tell us that Joseph of Arimathea retrieved Jesus' body, and John records the additional presence of Nicodemus at the site of Jesus' burial. But in the Acts of the Apostles, the apostle Paul is reported to have said, in a speech given at Antioch of Pisidia, that the Jews—apparently meaning those hostile to Jesus—"took him down from the tree [the cross], and laid him in a tomb" (13:29).

Did Paul not know about Joseph of Arimathea? Luke, the writer of Acts, had written about Joseph in his Gospel as the one who had taken primary responsibility for the deposition of the body of Jesus (23:50–53). What could account for this apparent contradiction? It is possible that Joseph and Nicodemus were members of the Sanhe-

drin, the Jewish council that turned Jesus over to Pilate. Though Luke specifies that Joseph "had not consented to their purpose and deed," perhaps the Jews of Paul's speech were in fact these two men.

The death of Jesus came about the middle of the afternoon on the day of crucifixion. It was the custom to bury a body on the day of death. This was all the more urgent in the case of Jesus, not only because the Sabbath was approaching, but because the Law of Moses provided that someone put to death as a criminal should not be left to hang overnight. It would defile the land (Deuteronomy 21:22–23).

To save the body of Jesus from the indignity of remaining on the cross, and as an act of piety, Joseph of Arimathea got up his courage and asked Pilate for permission to take the body, so that he might arrange for the immediate burial of Jesus. Our accounts

338

tell us that Joseph was a good man and a secret follower of Jesus.

According to Mark, Pilate wondered if Jesus was already dead—victims of crucifixion often lingered for days. So he checked with the centurion in charge. On hearing that Jesus was indeed dead, he granted Joseph's request. Mark and Luke tell us that Joseph of Arimathea took the body down. Matthew and Luke say he took it away. He could hardly have done either alone. The wording allows us to deduce that he had the help of others. In fact, John suggests Nicodemus helped. There is no evidence that Jesus was not really dead when his body was removed from the cross. The spear thrust in the side (John 19:34), the testimony of the Roman centurion to Pilate, and the women who "saw the tomb, and how the body was laid" all emphasize that Jesus was, indeed, dead.

As for the actual burial of Jesus, we learn that he was laid in a new tomb which had been hewn into the rock. It belonged to Joseph of Arimathea and had never before been used. The opening for the tomb must have been rather low, as the "other disciple," Peter's companion when they arrived at the site Sunday morning, had to stoop to look in. There would have been a niche or ledge in the wall of the tomb, perhaps one of several, for placing the body. Finally, there was a large stone for covering the opening—probably a wheel-shaped slab that rolled in a groove.

Part of the preparation for burial was the provision by Nicodemus of a huge amount of myrrh and aloes—about 100 (Roman) pounds, or about 75 English pounds. Produced from plants not native to Palestine, these substances must have been extremely expensive. They were used by the Jews for preparing the body. John tells us that Joseph and Nicodemus bound the body "in linen cloths with the spices, as is the burial custom of the Jews."

While the Synoptic Gospels speak of a linen shroud for wrapping the body, it is not quite clear what John means by "linen cloths." It is possible that the term really means a single large piece of cloth. When the body of Jesus had been put in place, the stone was rolled over the opening.

The next day, according to Matthew, the chief priests and some Pharisees met with Pilate and told him they were afraid that Jesus' disciples would steal the body and then claim that he was raised from the dead. Pilate's reponse was, "You have a guard of soldiers; go, make it as secure as you can." So they sealed the tomb and left a guard on watch. It is not clear whether those assigned to this task were Roman soldiers or Jewish Temple guards.

The women who had followed Jesus from Galilee prepared spices for anointing his body. Thus they made ready to pay their final respects to their beloved master. By custom, they rested on the Sabbath (the modern Saturday). So through the night and the next day, the body rested in the darkness and silence of the tomb. ✦

A rock-hewn tomb, *secured by a massive, cylindrical stone.*

Pious hope or clever hoax?

The intriguing mysteries of relics

CENTURIES AFTER THE DEATH of Jesus, Christians sought to keep some direct contact with the physical remains of Jesus' life or that of the martyrs. Hence, as early as the second century, the veneration of relics became popular.

Legend relates that in A.D. 326, Helena, the aged mother of Constantine the Great, the first Christian emperor, was aided by divine guidance to find the True Cross and the crucifixion nails at Golgotha. The story was linked to the church that Constantine dedicated at the traditional site of Jesus' sepulcher in 335. The fragments of the cross became the most famous of the many treasured relics of the Passion.

The relics of saints were invested with supernatural powers. As St. Thomas Aquinas explained, "We are bound to hold in veneration the saints of God . . . to accord due honor to any of their relics, and this is primarily true of their bodies, which were the temples and instruments of the Holy Spirit, dwelling and acting within them . . .It is for this reason that God himself grants honour to their relics by performing miracles when they are present."

In the late Middle Ages, every new cathedral, chapel, and monastery in Western Europe sought to have at least one relic in its possession; having a relic had become necessary for the dedication of the altar. Relics also attracted a steady stream of pilgrims to pray and seek cures and, perhaps, to make substantial contributions to the building fund. Not surprisingly, a thriving trade in forged relics developed, as did a certain amount of thievery. The bodies of dead saints were even dismembered so that parts could be dispersed to various places. Periodically, ecclesiastical authorities attempted to bring order to the situation—the Council of Trent in 1546, for example, set down rules to ensure the authenticity of relics and to guard against corrupt practices. But the profits to be gained often outweighed the dangers.

The Shroud of Turin is probably the most famous and most controversial relic in present-day Christendom, and it continues to confound scientists and biblical scholars alike. Consisting of a length of handloomed linen cloth, 14'3" x 3'7", the Shroud carries the yellowish markings of what appear to be the front and back images of a crucified man. Traditional belief holds that this is the same cloth used by Joseph of Arimathea to wrap the body of Jesus before its burial in the "rock-hewn tomb." But many find no evidence that clearly links the image stained on the cloth to the crucified Jesus.

What little is known about the cloth begins in the mid-fourteenth century when it came into the possession of one Geoffrey de Charny, a French knight. De Charny

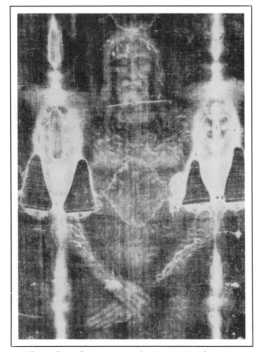

The ghostly trace *of a man's features and body on the Shroud of Turin.*

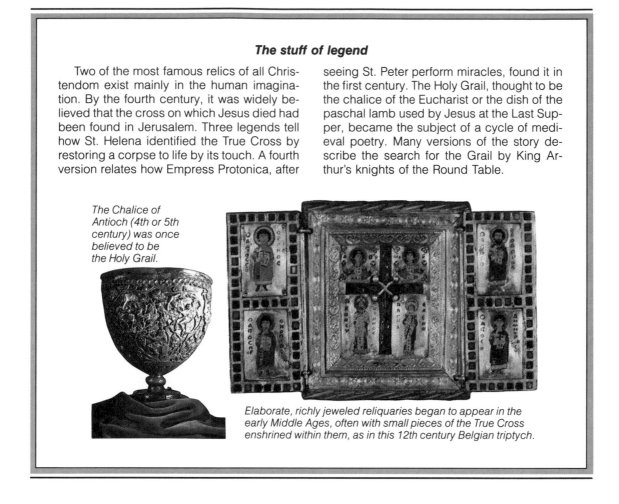
housed the treasure in a church that he founded, but the Bishop of Troyes denounced the Shroud's authenticity, claiming that it was a forgery, and that the artist who created it was known. He may have felt that de Charny was seeking the profits to be gained by turning his church into a pilgrimage site. However, the bishop's objections had little effect: Two centuries later, the Shroud was ceremoniously enshrined at the Cathedral of Saint John the Baptist in Turin, where it has remained ever since.

Given the supposed age and significance of this relic, church authorities have rarely permitted public exhibitions. But in recent times a number of scientists representing such disciplines as physics, aerodynamics, chemistry, electro-optics, and forensic medicine have been allowed to examine it. Using high-technology—analytical tools and techniques that can examine an object without causing damage to it—scientists have sought to determine, at the very least, whether the cloth is as old as believers say it is. They also hoped to discover whether any of the stains could be those left by the body of a crucified man. Because thousands of persons are known to have been crucified in antiquity, it is highly doubtful that any amount of "proof"—scientific or otherwise—will prove that the Shroud was the one that Jesus was wrapped in.

Among the conclusions that individual investigators have reached are these: The fabric is consistent in its herringbone weave and fiber content with that of linen used in the first century A.D. in the Middle East. The areas that appear to be stained with blood contain organic particles that are probably blood-related, and could not have been created by paint. Certain markings about the head, when greatly magnified, can reasonably be construed as having been produced by a crown of thorns; certain other dumbbell-shaped marks about the body are comparable in size and shape with those that would be produced by the blows of a Roman *flagrum*, a whip with metal or bone ends used to scourge prisoners. Still other marks conform to the shoulder abrasions that carrying a heavy crossbar would have produced, as well as to the spear wound in the side inflicted, according to the Gospel of John, by a Roman soldier. Finally, bloodlike stains appear at the wrists and feet.

One large question remains: What caused those parts of the body that were not wounded to leave something very like a photographic image on the cloth? Could it possibly have been caused by a burst of radiation, the "power . . . gone forth from me" that Jesus told his disciples he possessed (Luke 8:46)?

Two investigators have recently proposed another intriguing notion: that a naturally occurring chemical process called mercerization might be involved. As they see it, when Jesus' body was taken from the cross and wrapped in a burial cloth, it was probably exceedingly hot, perhaps over 108 degrees from the crucifixion and postmortem fever. When the body was laid on the damp limestone within the tomb, this heat may have speeded up or lengthened a natural acid-alkaline reaction, with the aragonite in the limestone attaching itself to the fibers of the shroud, thereby altering their color to a yellowish tone. If this theory holds up, the shroud with the haunting imprint could turn out to be not unlike a photographic

"Christ has made of death a narrow, starlit strip between the companionship of yesterday and the reunion of tomorrow."
— **William Jennings Bryan**
"The Fundamentals" (1923)

negative, preserving the image of a person who died in the time of Jesus, possibly even that of Jesus himself!

The Crown of Thorns is another well-known Crucifixion relic. And quite a bit of its history is known. In the first six centuries after Christ, few writers make reference to it as a known relic. However, there are exceptions. Saint Gregory of Tours wrote that the thorns in the crown were still green. The reputed crown was a venerated relic in Jerusalem for several hundred years before it was taken to Constantinople around 1063.

The Crown of Thorns was given to St. Louis, the king of France, in 1238 by Baldwin II, the Latin emperor of Constantinople. Ten years later, the Sainte-Chapelle in Paris was completed in order to house it; the Crown of Thorns remained there until the French Revolution. In 1806, it was moved to the Cathedral of Notre-Dame de Paris. A silver, bejeweled reliquary was made for it in 1862. The Crown of Thorns, as preserved today in the treasury of Notre-Dame, consists only of a band of rushes. The thorns themselves are elsewhere, and there are also many other thorns, thought to have touched the original thorns, that are venerated at other sites.

The origin of such items as the Spear of Longinus, the Holy Reed, the Holy Sponge, and bits of the wood and nails of the cross are somewhat more mysterious. All of these personal relics surfaced some time after the fourth century and reached the West during the Middle Ages and later.

For example, a spear, said to have been that used by the Roman soldier, called Longinus, to pierce the side of Jesus on the cross, was venerated in Jerusalem at the end of the sixth century. When Jerusalem was taken by the Persians in 615, the lance was broken into two parts. The shaft eventually found its way to Constantinople, but in 1492, the Ottoman sultan Bajazet II sent it to Innocent VIII. It was placed in one of the piers supporting the dome of St. Peter's Basilica. St. Louis, the 13th-century crusader and king of France, placed the head of the spear in the Sainte-Chapelle in Paris. It was lost during the French Revolution. ✦

An illuminated manuscript *of Jesus'*
resurrection dates from about 1420.

The miracle of the resurrection

Jesus walks the earth

E WAS CRUCIFIED IN WEAKNESS," wrote Paul concerning Jesus, "but lives by the power of God" (2 Corinthians 13:4). In those opposing faces—weakness and power; crucifixion and resurrection—early Christians found the mystery and vitality of their faith. The crucifixion was a hard reality for both believers and nonbelievers. For Christians, however, the resurrection marked the point of Christ's vindication, since God himself raised Jesus from the dead.

But what did the resurrection mean to the disciples? The Bible has many stories of the dead being brought back to life, whether by Elijah, Elisha, Jesus, or later, Peter and Paul. But the resurrection of Jesus was different; it was not simply a resuscitation, a coming back to life, but the beginning of a new age which would culminate with the resurrection of the dead on Judgment Day. Paul described Jesus as the "first fruits" of the final resurrection.

The Christians asserted that in Jesus' resurrection the victorious power of their faith had become a reality. Jesus promised that "I am the resurrection and the life; he who believes in me, though he die, yet shall he live, and whoever lives and believes in me shall never die" (John 11:25–26).

In spite of the intense interest in Jesus' resurrection, it is striking that no attempt was made in the New Testament to describe the moment of resurrection itself. In the Gospels, the resurrection narratives begin with women coming to an empty tomb. The resurrection itself occurred at some moment before Mary Magdalene arrived at dawn. The New Testament focuses instead on the appearances of the risen Christ to the disciples. These appearances had a profound effect upon Jesus' disciples, renewing and strengthening their faith.

The earliest written testimony to such appearances comes from Paul's first letter to the Corinthians. He presented a list of disciples who had seen the risen Christ: "For I delivered to you as of first importance what I also received, that Christ died for our sins in accordance with the scriptures, that he was buried, that he was raised on the third day in accordance with the Scriptures, and that he appeared to Cephas (Peter), then to the twelve. Then he appeared to more than five hundred brethren at one time, most of whom are still alive, though some have fallen asleep. Then he appeared to James, then to all the apostles. Last of all, as to one untimely born, he appeared also to me."

From the first, Jesus' resurrection was highly controversial. Scoffers could not produce Jesus' corpse as evidence of his death. But neither could believers present the risen Jesus in a public, demonstrable way that would erase skepticism. Everything was left up to the testimony of the disciples. The narratives that occur at the end of each of the Gospels share a basic unity; all bear witness to the resurrection of Jesus on the first day of the week following his death.

However, they are remarkably diverse in the specifics of their reports. For example, when Matthew and Luke wrote about the initial discovery of the resurrection, they evidently had the text of the Gospel of Mark before them. They might easily have echoed Mark's details: that three women (Mary Magdalene, another Mary, and Salome) went to the tomb and discovered that the huge stone in front of it had been removed. They entered the tomb, Mark said, and saw inside a young man dressed in white, and the youth told them of the resurrection.

Luke did not simply repeat the Gospel of Mark in his account; he revised some of the details. Luke indicated that more than three women entered the tomb, and when they did not find the body they were perplexed. At that point, "two men stood by them in dazzling apparel," and spoke.

Matthew described only two women going to the tomb, which, he said, was being guarded. He seems to indicate that the women saw an angel of the Lord descend,

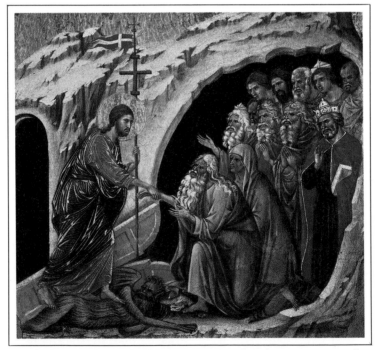

The harrowing of hell became a popular theme in art and literature of the Middle Ages. Above, a panel for a 14th century Italian cathedral depicts Christ in limbo, conquering Satan.

roll back the stone, and sit upon it. The angel's appearance was like lightning and immobilized the guards, but the angel reassured the women. "Do not be afraid; for I know you seek Jesus who was crucified. He is not here; for he is risen, as he said. Come, see the place where he lay" (Matthew 28:5–6).

In John, only one woman, Mary Magdalene, was mentioned. She simply saw that the stone was rolled away and she ran to tell Peter and the Beloved Disciple. Her encounter with two angels came later.

Differences continue throughout the resurrection narratives. For the evangelists, faith in Jesus' resurrection was not a matter of reconstructing a consistent story; rather, the narratives were themselves manifestations of the powerful and many-sided faith in Jesus that enlivened the church long before these accounts were written.

The shortest narrative, and certainly the most disconcerting one, was that in the Gospel of Mark. In its original form, the story evidently ended at Mark 16:8. Mark included no appearances of Jesus himself. The youth at the tomb told the women to tell the disciples that they would see Jesus in Galilee as he had promised. Like the faltering disciples earlier in the Gospel, the women fled, Mark said, "and they said nothing to any one, for they were afraid." And there Mark's Gospel ended, though whether more was intended is unknown.

Apparently, many in the early church were troubled by Mark's abrupt ending, and attempts were made to round off the narrative. Verses 9–20, which are not in the most ancient manuscripts, are thought to have been added to Mark in the second century as a compilation of material intended as a summary.

Matthew resolved the troublesome reticence of Mark's account. In Matthew's Gospel, the women received the message about going back to Galilee both from the angel and from Jesus himself, and they hastened to convey the command. The eleven returned to Galilee, and it was there on a mountain that Jesus met them. Majestically, Jesus asserted that God had given him all authority

IN MODERN TIMES

The lamb of God.

🐟 Christian symbols 🐟

Jesus is often depicted as a lamb, a symbol which probably derives from the Passover lamb of Exodus 12. The Gospel of John speaks of Jesus as the Lamb that takes away the sins of the world, and refers to the crucifixion of Jesus as a parallel to the ceremonial killing of the lamb eaten at Passover. How did the symbol of the fish evolve? The first Christians ate bread and fish at their communion meals. Many artistic representations of the Eucharist show fish as part of the meal. The epitaph of Abercius, a second-century A.D. bishop in Asia Minor, speaks of eating fish at the holy meal, as in the feeding of the five thousand with the loaves and fishes. In addition, the newly baptized are referred to by the church fathers as "little fish" because they are born again in the waters of baptism. In fact, a fish nearly became the universal symbol of Christianity. The Greek word for "fish," *Ichthus*, formed an acrostic for a phrase meaning "Jesus Christ, Son of God, Savior."

In the New Testament, the dove appears at the baptism of Jesus, symbolizing the Holy Spirit. As a dove announced to Noah the end of the flood, so for the first Christians, the dove symbolized faith. Representations of grapevines symbolized Jesus and the church: "I am the true vine, and my Father is the vinedresser . . . I am the vine, you are the branches."

in heaven and on earth. On that basis he sent them out to make disciples of all nations. Jesus said, "All authority in heaven and on earth has been given to me. Go therefore and make disciples of all nations, baptizing them in the name of the Father, and of the Son and of the Holy Spirit . . . and lo, I am with you always, to the close of the age" (Matthew 20:18–20).

In the Gospel of Luke and the Book of Acts, all the resurrection appearances occurred around Jerusalem. The women were not told to send the disciples to Galilee, but rather they bore witness to the disciples about the resurrection. Ironically, the disciples refused to believe their "idle tale." The same day, however, two disciples encountered Jesus near Jerusalem on the road to Emmaus; he allowed them to recognize him only as he broke bread for them. When they had returned to the disciples in the city, Jesus again appeared and assured them all of his resurrection by eating with them.

As Luke recounted, Jesus opened the minds of his disciples to understand the Scriptures, his suffering, and resurrection. He commissioned them as witnesses. They must, he said, stay in the city until they received "power from on high." Acts tells that Jesus' appearances continued in Jerusalem for 40 days.

John's is the only Gospel that asserts that Jesus made appearances to the disciples both in Jerusalem and in Galilee. On the evening of the resurrection Jesus appeared suddenly within the Apostles' closed room. He blessed them with peace, and commissioned them by breathing the Holy Spirit upon them. The Apostle Thomas was not present and refused to believe. Eight days later, Jesus again appeared. When Thomas saw the risen Jesus bearing the wounds of the Crucifixion, he exclaimed, "My Lord and my God!" Jesus said, "Blessed are those who have not seen and yet believe."

The final chapter of John tells of Jesus' mysterious encounter with seven disciples fishing on the Sea of Galilee. A miraculous catch of fish led to the disciples' recognition of the Lord. After again eating with them, Jesus challenged Peter to love him, to "feed my sheep," and to follow him.

Precisely through their variety, the Gospels reveal the diverse ways in which the experience of Jesus' resurrection transformed the lives of the disciples, helping them to grasp the mystery that "Death is swallowed up in victory." ✦

Caravaggio's Doubting Thomas: "Unless I see in his hands the print of the nails, and place my fingers in the mark of the nails, and place my hand in his side, I will not believe."

"God is love."

—1 John 4:8

Someone asked Karl Barth to sum up the message of his books on Christian theology. He unhesitatingly replied: "Jesus loves me—this I know, for the Bible tells me so." Barth's whimsical but deep reply goes to the heart of the matter: Love is what it's all about, and we are mere children. But if we love one another and love God, as God loves us, we will know God and become one with "the Love that moves the sun and the other stars," the infinite self-renewing source.

"Deepen Your love in me, O Lord, that I may learn in my inmost heart how sweet it is to love, to be dissolved, and to plunge myself into Your love. Let Your love possess and raise me above myself, with a fervour and wonder beyond imagination. Let me sing the song of love."

—**Thomas à Kempis**
The Imitation of Christ

"Of all strong things nothing is so strong, so irresistible, as divine love. It brought forth all the creation; it kindles all the life of Heaven: it is the song of all the angels of God. It has redeemed all the world; it seeks for every sinner upon earth; it embraces all the enemies of God; and from the beginning to the end of time the one work of Providence is the one work of love."

—**William Law (English mystic, 1686–1761)**

"God is love . . . and out of love he gives existence and life to every creature, supporting them all with his love. The color of the wall depends on the wall, and so the existence of creatures depends on the love of God. Separate the color from the wall and it would cease to be; so all creation would cease to exist if separated from the love that God is. God is love, so loving that whatever he can love he must love, whether he will or not."

—**Meister Eckhart**
(German theologian, c.1260–c.1327)

"The way to the love of God is foolishness to the world, but wisdom to God's children. When the world sees such love-fire in God's children, it says they are foolish; but to the children of God, this is the greatest treasure, for no life can express, nor can mouth describe, the fire of the inflaming love of God that is whiter than the sun, sweeter than any honey, more powerful than any food or drink, and lovelier than all the joys of this world. He who reaches this is richer than any king on earth, nobler than any emperor can be, and stronger than all might."

—**Jacob Boehme, *The Way to Christ***

"Divine Love crossed the infinity of space and time to come from God to us. But how can it repeat the journey in the opposite direction, starting from a finite creature? . . . How can we repeat the journey made by God when he came to us, in the opposite direction? How can we cross infinite distance? . . .

"It is only necessary to know that love is a direction and not a state of the soul. If one is unaware of this, one falls into despair at the first onslaught of affliction.

"He whose soul remains ever turned toward God though the nail pierces it finds himself nailed to the very center of the universe. It is the true center; it is not in the middle; it is beyond space and time; it is God. In a dimension that does not belong to space, that is not time, that is indeed quite a different dimension, this nail has pierced cleanly through all creation, through the thickness of the screen separating the soul from God.

"In this marvelous dimension, the soul, without leaving the place and the instant where the body to which it is united is situated, can cross the totality of space and time and come into the very presence of God."

—**Simone Weil, *Waiting for God***

*"**I am with you always,** to the close of the age."*

From humiliation to exaltation

The ascension

LATE IN THE EVENING of the day that Jesus was raised from the dead, as the Gospel of Luke tells, he led his disciples from Jerusalem to the village of Bethany, "and lifting up his hands he blessed them. While he blessed them, he parted from them and was carried up into heaven" (Luke 24:50–51). So ended a day that transformed the disciples and opened a new life before them.

The "ascension" of Jesus began a period in which the disciples would proclaim that Jesus was no longer dead but truly alive. Though physically absent, Jesus was present among them in the Spirit. They said that Jesus was not only raised from the realm of the dead, he was also elevated to the realm of God in heaven.

For the early Christians, the ascension marked the exaltation of Jesus, his final vindication and enthronement. Frequently quoted in the New Testament, Psalm 110:1 states: "The LORD says to my Lord: 'Sit at my right hand till I make your enemies your footstool.' " The Christians proclaimed that the crucified Jesus was summoned to God's right hand and there enthroned as "Lord and Christ" (Acts 2:33–36).

The Book of Acts began with another report of the ascension. Here Luke stated that Jesus continued to appear to his disciples for 40 days. At the end of that time he charged them to be witnesses from Jerusalem to the ends of the earth, and then, "as they were looking on, he was lifted up, and a cloud took him out of their sight." Two men appeared, like the two that spoke to the women at Jesus' tomb, and interpreted the event to them: "This Jesus, who was taken up from you into heaven, will come in the same way as you saw him go to heaven." Luke did not attempt to resolve the 40-day time difference between his two accounts; it was the meaning of the event that was crucial.

The Gospel of John also mentions Jesus' ascension, although he does not describe the event. When Jesus appeared to Mary Magdalene on the morning of his resurrection he told her, "Do not hold me, for I have not yet ascended to the Father; but go to my brethren and say to them, I am ascending to my Father and your Father, to my God and your God" (John 20:17).

The story of the ascension expressed a mystery that lay at the heart of the early Christian proclamation. The one who had been forsaken by all, and whom the Romans had crucified as criminal, was now exalted by God. ✦

PART VI

The Early Church

The Books of The Acts, Romans,
1 and 2 Corinthians, Galatians, Ephesians,
Philippians, Colossians, 1 and 2 Thessalonians,
1 and 2 Timothy, Titus, Philemon,
Hebrews, James, 1 and 2 Peter, 1, 2, and 3 John,
Jude, and Revelation

*Empowered by the spirit of Jesus Christ,
a handful of men went forth to spread the good
news of salvation. Undaunted by persecution
and suffering, the apostles and disciples
of Jesus established small communities of the
faithful. In their fervor, these few forged
the structure of the great Christian church and
"turned the world upside down."*

The first Pentecost

The spirit came among them

GREEK-SPEAKING JEWS referred to the Jewish spring harvest festival of *Shabuoth* as Pentecost (Greek for *fiftieth*) because it occurred 50 days after Passover. Today, Pentecost is more often associated with the day on which Jesus' closest followers received the Holy Spirit and became for the first time an *ekklesia* (Greek for *assembly*), or a church.

According to Luke's account in Acts, this event coincided with that year's celebration of *Shabuoth*. Luke reports that the Spirit's coming was perceived by the kinfolk and disciples of Jesus as a miracle that was accompanied by something "like the rush of a mighty wind" and the appearance of "tongues as of fire, distributed and resting on each of them" (Acts 2:2–3).

Upon feeling themselves suddenly gifted with a new vitality, Jesus' family and friends began to praise God with loud voices; but instead of their native Aramaic, their words came out in a variety of languages that were previously unknown to them. As a result, many of the pilgrims to the festival from other countries expressed astonishment that they could understand what the Galileans were saying. Some observers, on the other hand, heard only babbling and concluded that the enthusiastic worshippers must be drunk. To clear up the confusion, Peter stepped forward and announced to all of them that this exuberance was none other than the fulfillment of a prophecy by Joel that God would send the Holy Spirit upon "all flesh" as a sign that the world's last days had come.

The mysteries surrounding Pentecost are numerous. The New Testament furnishes only a small amount of information about it. The lack of details is paradoxical in view of the fact that all New Testament writers, with Paul and John leading the way, lay great stress upon the presence of the Holy Spirit in the faith and life of believers. Yet only Luke tells how the experience of the Spirit came to be a distinctive mark of Christian identity.

Luke places his emphasis on Peter's explanation to the crowd, which was apparently made in a common language that everyone understood. If the event itself was unusual, Peter's interpretation was straightforward enough. For him, it was the risen Jesus who had sent the Spirit, and he expected that same Spirit to descend upon all who repented of their sins and presented themselves for baptism in Jesus' name.

From a purely historical point of view, one must assume that something close to this speech and its prediction actually did take place, for the new community quickly grew in sufficient numbers to draw the attention of the religious and political authorities. Prior to Pentecost, these leaders had assumed that the execution of Jesus would suffice to check the danger of a popular messianic uprising against Rome. But now the authorities had to deal with a renewed group of Jesus' followers that was growing in spite of the founder's death (Acts 4:1–4).

"In 1787 the Constitutional Convention meeting at Philadelphia was near failure because the 13 former colonies could not agree on a form of effective national government. When the deadlock appeared too great for human power to break, 81-year-old Benjamin Franklin rose to his feet. All his life, he said, he had been convinced that the Psalms were right in saying, 'Except the LORD build the house, they labor in vain that build it.' He moved that the delegates begin the next day's meeting with a prayer offered by a Philadelphia clergyman. The motion carried. So dramatic was the improvement in legislative temperaments and efficiency that Congress still observes Franklin's precedent."
—**James Daniel**
The Psalms - Hymnbook of Humanity

Their faces upraised in ecstasy, *the apostles, gathered in Jerusalem, received the Holy Spirit—and were henceforth transformed.*

Here again, the question arises as to how the followers of Jesus could acquire such a sense of mission and a community life that attracted significant numbers of Jerusalem's pilgrim visitors and citizens. Luke's answer is that it all came about through a dramatic descent of the Holy Spirit.

From the moment of its birth until its departure from Jerusalem shortly before the Jewish war with Rome (66–70), this community—the early church—considered itself not a new religion but rather a renewal movement within Judaism. So it was that church members continued to observe the

Speaking in tongues

The ecstasy, joy, and intimacy with God that many early Christians felt because of their new faith took expression in a remarkable phenomenon—speaking in tongues, sometimes called glossolalia. The New Testament shows that this experience was mysterious even to the early Christians.

To understand what tongues meant in the early days of the church, it is worthwhile to study two passages in the New Testament. The first, in the book of Acts, is the description of the coming of the Holy Spirit at the great pilgrim feast of Pentecost. Some 50 years after it occurred, Luke described it as a mighty miracle in which the Spirit came with a great sound of wind and the appearance of tongues like fire. Suddenly, the confusion of languages, which had troubled humanity since the tower of Babel, was overcome. Peter and the other apostles could speak, and people of any language could "hear them telling in our own tongues the mighty works of God" (Acts 2:11).

The second major passage in the New Testament concerning speaking in tongues appears in Paul's first letter to the church in Corinth. What the Corinthians and Paul were experiencing so joyously was ecstatic speech, which they understood as speaking directly to God. Paul wrote that "one who speaks in a tongue speaks not to men but to God; for no one understands him, but he utters mysteries in the Spirit" (1 Corinthians 14:2).

Early church authors refer to the continuation of the phenomenon of tongues until the end of the second century. After that time the experience of ecstatic speech was sporadic until the beginning of the 20th century when the Pentecostal and charismatic movement began to grow in America and elsewhere. In the movement's many forms and denominations, it has grown to become one of the largest religious movements in the world.

Jewish laws and worshipped regularly in the Temple. What distinguished them from other Jews was their conviction that Jesus as the promised messiah would soon reappear to restore the kingdom of Israel.

From its inception, the church was a missionary organization, for when its leaders told stories of their experiences with Jesus, they expected their listeners' hearts to become filled with the Spirit. The practical consequence of such a coming to faith was an initiation into the church through the rite of baptism. Since there is no record of Jesus' disciples having been baptized with water, students of the Bible may wonder why the practice became standard for everyone else. An altogether satisfactory explanation has yet to be found. Less obscure in their origin were the common meals held by members of the church, for they recalled similar events in Jesus' ministry, especially his last supper with the disciples.

The missionary preaching of the church sometimes included criticisms of Jerusalem's leaders, but its positive stance toward the Jewish people as a whole, coupled with its attempts to serve them in the name of Jesus, produced a certain confusion among those charged with keeping the public order. The church may have mystified some of the authorities by showing itself to be at one and the same time steadfastly but not traditionally Jewish.

Surprisingly, it was James rather than Peter, the bold spokesman for the twelve disciples, who became the chief leader of the church in Jerusalem. According to tradition, it was after the execution of James by a hostile high priest that the church emigrated from Jerusalem, the city of its origin, to a town called Pella on the other side of the Jordan River. Some reports indicate that a message from Christ in a vision prompted the departure.

But then an unaccountable thing happened—the first and most influential of all Christian churches faded from the pages of history. In its demise as well as in its birth, the Jewish church of Jerusalem remains an enigma down to the present day. ✦

A blinding light on the road to Damascus

The conversion of Saul

IT WAS AN AGITATED man who approached Damascus at the head of a small delegation from Jerusalem, just a year or two after the death of Jesus. Apparently on his own initiative, Saul of Tarsus had persuaded a high priest in Jerusalem that followers of Jesus who were members of synagogues in Damascus ought to be sought out and brought to trial, even when they lived outside Jerusalem itself.

The trip to Damascus was a large operation, and Paul carried letters to the synagogues as proof of his authority. This move against the people called Nazarenes (a name deriving from Jesus' hometown in Galilee) was odd on at least two counts. For one thing, most Jews in Jerusalem took no offense at the infant church. Secondly, Paul belonged to a group within Judaism called the Pharisees, whose leaders were not known for persecuting other sects.

What convinced Saul that the Nazarenes were something other than a harmless sect whose members happened to believe that Jesus was the Messiah? It might have been Saul's presence at a speech by Stephen, one of the more zealous followers of Jesus. Stephen denounced the Jerusalem Temple (as an aberration of God's will) and attacked his critics as murderers of the prophets. He concluded by announcing that he had just seen a vision of Jesus in heaven standing at the right hand of God.

That disclosure was enough to incite a mob action that led to Stephen's death by stoning according to the Acts of the Apostles. Luke reports that the "witnesses" to Stephen's death, who seem to have taken an active role in the stoning, "laid down their garments at the feet of a young man named Saul . . . And Saul was consenting to his death" (Acts 7:58; 8:1).

Did Saul conclude from Stephen's speech that all Nazarenes opposed the Temple and set themselves up as judges over their brother and sister Jews? Was it the claim that Jesus ruled at God's right hand that proved ultimately offensive? Or was it

Blinded before the light of Jesus, *Saul, overwhelmed, fell to the ground on the road to Damascus. He was blinded for three days.*

the last words that Stephen is remembered to have cried out just before his death, as if to a god: "Lord Jesus, receive my spirit . . . Lord, do not hold this sin against them"? In any event, something burned in Saul as a result of his contacts with followers of Jesus, and he became their hunter. His own words put the matter succinctly: "I persecuted the church of God violently and tried to destroy it" (Galatians 1:13). As he approached Damascus to search out the local Nazarenes, Saul must have been in a state of high agitation.

What happened next is reported in ways that do not dovetail with one another. According to three separate accounts in Acts (9:1–22; 22:4–16; 26:9–18), Saul saw a great light that seemed to fall about him from heaven. Immediately he fell to the ground and heard a voice say, "Saul, Saul, why do you persecute me?" No doubt terrified, the smitten man could only ask, "Who are you, Lord?" And the reply came back: "I am Jesus, whom you are persecuting."

When he managed to stand up and open

In his final, *agonizing moments, Stephen forgave his tormentors.*

his eyes, Saul discovered that he could see nothing, and he had to be led by the hand into Damascus. He languished there, eating nothing for three days, not knowing what to do. At the end of this period, he was visited by a Jewish believer named Ananias, who in a vision was instructed by Jesus to heal Saul by laying hands upon him. Reluctantly and fearfully, Ananias obeyed this command. When he touched the stricken man, "something like scales fell from his eyes and he regained his sight. Then he arose and was baptized" (Acts 9:18).

After his baptism, Saul was still called by his Hebrew name. Later, as an apostle to the Gentiles, he was called Paul, a Roman name he probably carried from birth as a Diaspora Jew.

There are several references to Paul's transforming experience in his letters. Although these are more fragmentary than the stories in Acts, they have the advantage of being firsthand reports. Moreover, they were all written around the middle of the first century, whereas Acts is usually dated around A.D. 80 or 85.

In his letter to the Galatians, Paul said that God changed his life by revealing his Son to him, which suggests that his experience as a whole could be understood as a conversion of the heart. Probably another reference to the Damascus event is Paul's rhetorical question to his Corinthian readers: "Am I not an apostle? Have I not seen Jesus our Lord?" (1 Corinthians 9:1) and his grouping of himself with all the other disciples to whom Jesus first "appeared" (1 Corinthians 15:3–9).

Paul did not perceive his conversion as the giving up of one religion for another but as a call to carry out a new mission by the God he had always worshipped. The church Paul joined in Damascus was an altogether Jewish institution. Even later, when Gentiles as well as Jews held membership, Paul continued to consider himself Jewish. While he uttered some harsh words against his co-religionists, one of his last extant letters shows that he believed all Jews to be God's chosen people, destined for salvation (Romans 11:17–36). ✦

Paul the great trailblazer

Proclaiming the word of God

LIKE MANY OTHER educated people of his day, the Apostle Paul traveled a great deal. A century before, the Roman general Pompey had cleared the Mediterranean of pirates, making sea voyages safe. Roman roads had made land travel less burdensome, and many towns had some sort of accommodations for travelers and their animals.

Although much of the travel was commercial, authors intrigued readers with their tales of exotic places. India, for example, was already the mysterious East. And professional guides plied their trade at some of the more popular tourist attractions— among them, the pyramids of Egypt, the Temple of Apollo at Delphi, and the site of the ancient city of Troy.

Paul, however, did not travel for pleasure. Rather, he traveled to found communities devoted to the worship of Jesus Christ, Lord of the world. Paul's letters do not reveal whether he appreciated the beauty of that world, or what he saw of the aesthetic achievements of artists and architects. Instead, he seems to have been single-mindedly focused on carrying his gospel to as much of the Roman world as he could.

Paul was not a solitary traveler. Whether by land or sea, his missionary journeys were undertaken with others (some are named in his letters). They carried with them the necessary food, drink, and clothing, and, on trips through mountainous territories, they used pack animals.

These travels obviously involved both

planning and expense. How did Paul finance these journeys? One theory is that Paul supported his missionary activity by his own labor. However, his letters reveal that he sometimes accepted church support for his endeavors. It is difficult to imagine that Paul's earnings could have paid for the extensive itinerary and the men and supplies involved. It is more likely that the new congregations provided financial support whenever it was necessary.

Paul reported that he traveled to many of the major cities and several provinces of the Roman Empire, including Damascus, Antioch, Troas, Ephesus, Philippi, Thessalonica, Athens, and Corinth. And from his letters, it is clear that he anticipated a trip to Rome. Among the provinces he visited were Syria, Cilicia, Galatia, Macedonia, Achaia, and Illyricum. Thus, in his missionary work, Paul covered many cities in the northeastern part of the Roman Empire.

Paul may also have been preparing to travel to the West. In one letter he mentioned a possible trip to Spain. Whether he ever achieved that goal is questionable; he was arrested in Jerusalem and imprisoned in Rome. Though he was rumored to have been executed by Nero, there is no explicit historical evidence that this happened. Thus, it is possible that Paul completed more of his missionary plans than the record shows.

Paul's mission was not simply to establish Christian communities. As a true minister, he was concerned that the churches be firmly rooted and settled in their faith. According to Acts, his founding visit often lasted months or years, and when possible, he paid return visits.

Part of Paul's strategy of maintaining contact with the fledgling churches was his letters. To the Corinthian church he wrote, "I write this while I am away from you, in order that when I come I may not have to be severe in my use of the authority which the Lord has given me for building up and not for tearing down." The Corinthian letters suggest that Paul visited the church at Corinth at least three times and perhaps more.

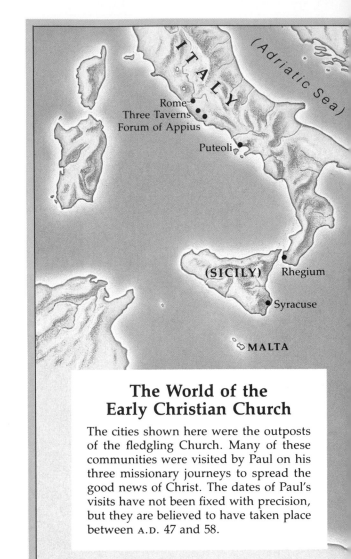

The World of the Early Christian Church

The cities shown here were the outposts of the fledgling Church. Many of these communities were visited by Paul on his three missionary journeys to spread the good news of Christ. The dates of Paul's visits have not been fixed with precision, but they are believed to have taken place between A.D. 47 and 58.

In the Book of Acts, Paul's missionary journeys are described as three large, circular tours that began and ended at some major city in the East, Antioch or Jerusalem. However, Acts was probably written a number of years after these trips occurred, and its author may not have known all of the details of Paul's extensive itinerary. In his own writings, Paul mentioned or implied having visited a number of places which Acts does not discuss.

But the true meaning of Paul's travels

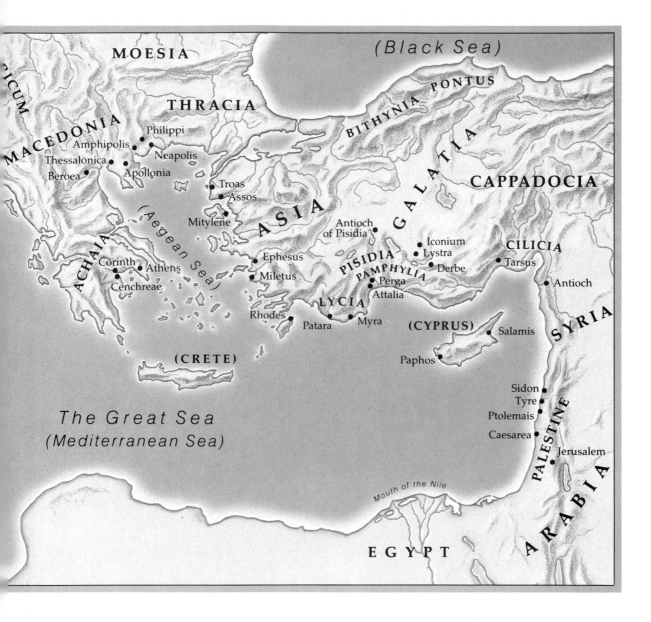

lies beyond the exact details of his itinerary. Clearly he covered an impressive amount of territory despite frequent setbacks. These included not just privation from scant supplies, the rigors of weather, raging rivers, and attacks by highwaymen, but such extraordinary hardships as being shipwrecked three times. He was hounded by both Jew and Gentile adversaries, captured, beaten, and cast into prison.

On one ignominious occasion, Paul made a remarkable escape from his enemies. He wrote, "At Damascus, the governor under King Aretas guarded the city of Damascus in order to seize me, but I was let down in a basket through a window in the wall, and escaped his hands" (2 Corinthians 11:32–33).

Paul's story is one of human struggle, much of it painful and all of it challenging. The mystery and meaning lie in the courage and stubborn faith of the Apostle, who refused to quit despite obstacles that would have forced a lesser man to retreat. ✦

Marshaling Christian forces

The founders of the church

IN THE MONTHS and years following the execution of Jesus, the religious movement he began spread throughout the Roman Empire. The flourishing of this new faith was at least partly attributable to the early leaders who gave their lives to it.

In the earliest days, the apostles who had remained together in Jerusalem were the leaders of the church. But soon a few men came to the fore. By about A.D. 53, Paul mentioned three principal leaders of the original church in Jerusalem, "James and Cephas and John, who were reputed to be pillars" (Galatians 2:9). Only two of these "pillars" of the church were from the original twelve—Cephas, or Peter, and John the son of Zebedee.

When these men were arrested by the Jewish leaders in Jerusalem, and their judges "saw the boldness of Peter and John, and perceived that they were uneducated, common men, they wondered; and they recognized that they had been with Jesus" (Acts 4:13). This fact set them apart. It meant that they could never go back to their lives as simple fishermen.

While the ministry of Peter ranged widely from Jerusalem to Antioch, across Asia Minor, to Rome, John is believed to have labored for decades in the city of Ephesus.

The third "pillar," called by Paul "James the Lord's brother," devoted his life to leading the Jerusalem church. He was not one of the twelve and indeed had evidently not even been a believer during Jesus' lifetime. In tradition, he was also called James "the Righteous." He ended his life as a martyr—thrown from a parapet and beaten to death with a club.

The fourth great leader was Paul, who, like James, was not one of the twelve. Perhaps the unlikeliest of all the early leaders, he had been an implacable enemy of the church. Acts, however, designates him as literally Christ's "chosen vessel" or, in modern terms, his "chosen instrument" to take the Gospel to the Gentiles.

Amazingly, within 50 years, Christianity had spread across the Roman Empire and perhaps beyond. The New Testament attributes this spread first and foremost to God who empowered and guided the growth of the faith. But it also recognizes the role of those who gave their lives to it. ✦

The early Christian *evangelists were often perceived as a threat to Rome, and thus were punished. Here, Paul visits Peter in prison.*

Artemis of Ephesus

IN HIS THIRD MISSIONARY journey (about A.D. 53–58), Paul went to Ephesus, the capital of the Roman province of Asia; he spent nearly three years there, teaching "both Jews and Greeks" (Acts 19:10). Ephesus was in ancient times a major port on the trade routes between Greece and Asia Minor. It was there that Paul caused "no little stir" (19:23) among members of one of the most venerated pagan cults, that of Artemis.

The city of Ephesus was probably founded in the 11th century B.C. by Ionian Greeks, but even before their coming, the cult of a goddess identified with Artemis existed in the area. It is likely that the worship of Artemis spread outward along the trade routes.

The Ephesian Artemis was a form of the ancient Asian and Anatolian mother-goddess; as such, she was revered throughout much of the Mediterranean world. The Greeks identified her with their Artemis (Roman Diana), daughter of Zeus and Leto and sister of Apollo. But she was actually quite different from this virgin huntress, moon goddess, and protector of chastity. Rather, the Ephesian Artemis was a patroness of fertility. She was represented in sculpture as having what seem to be numerous breasts, and her garments were adorned with animals and birds.

Though Artemis was revered in many parts of the Roman Empire, the most important center for her worship was in Ephesus. In the sixth century B.C., the Cretan architect Chersiphron erected a great marble edifice in honor of Artemis. After this structure burned down in the fourth century B.C., it was rebuilt and was even larger and more splendid than before. The temple became famous as

The fertility goddess, Artemis of Ephesus.

one of the seven wonders of the ancient world. Acts 19:35 calls Ephesus "temple keeper of the great Artemis, and of the sacred stone that fell from the sky." This stone may have been a meteorite associated with the goddess and kept in her shrine.

The Book of Acts recounts St. Paul's difficulties in bringing his message to Ephesus (19:23–41). The silversmiths and craftsmen there, whose livelihood depended on the sale of silver objects associated with the worship of Artemis, feared that Paul's preaching of a rival religion would threaten their jobs. Worse, it appeared to them that Christianity threatened the goddess Artemis herself by denying her divinity: "she may even be deposed from her magnificence, she whom all Asia and the world worship."

On one occasion, the opponents to Paul and his missionary companions nearly started a full-scale riot, which would of necessity have involved the Roman authorities. This was averted through the intercession of the town clerk, who succeeded in pacifying the mob that had gathered. However, perhaps because his mission to the pagan population of Ephesus could no longer be safely pursued, Paul left for Macedonia.

The temple of Artemis at Ephesus endured well into the third century A.D., but its importance began to lessen with the expansion of Christianity. The temple was finally destroyed by the Goths around A.D. 262, and very little of it remains today. Around the fifth century, a statue of the goddess near the marketplace was taken down by a Christian and replaced with a cross. On the base was an inscription stating that he had "removed the deceitful image of the demon Artemis."

The greatest city *in the world went up in flames as the terrified populace fled.*

The burning of Rome

A catastrophe that kindled persecutions

IN THE EARLY HOURS of July 19, A.D. 64, a catastrophic fire broke out in Rome; fanned by the wind, it swept through much of the city. When the fire started, the Emperor Nero hurried from his villa in Antium, 33 miles away, to direct the fire fighting. Still, the fire burned for nine days, destroying much of the city.

In spite of his apparent concern, a rumor spread that at the height of the blaze Nero sang a song about the sack of Troy—that he "fiddled" while Rome burned. Another story claimed that he himself had ordered the fire set in order to provide space in Rome for some ambitious building projects. Indeed, after the fire, Nero began to build himself a grandiose palace on some 200 acres of prime city land, much of it expropriated from the fire-devastated area.

Nero's notorious ambition, coupled with his monstrous cruelty (he had arranged for the murder of his own mother), made such rumors credible. Still, it is unlikely that Nero started the fire. He was, after all, far from Rome when the fire broke out. Also, the moon was bright—a condition that would hardly allow such extensive arson to go undetected.

Nero made scapegoats of the Christians. The first to be interrogated implicated other Christians. Many were put to death in bizarre ways: some were dressed in animal skins, and savage dogs were set upon them; others were crucified; still others were made into human torches in Nero's own garden. Tradition has it that in the period of persecution following the burning of Rome, the apostles Peter and Paul were put to death.

360

We do not know how large the Christian community was at the time of Nero's reign (A.D. 54–68). But some time after Nero became emperor, Paul wrote his letter to what was then a flourishing community of Christians in Rome.

Rome was not the only place where the early Christians were persecuted, nor was Nero the only public official who persecuted them. There is abundant evidence in the New Testament and other sources that Christians suffered for their faith throughout the Roman world.

In Jerusalem, the Sanhedrin, an administrative and judicial council of the Jews, forbade Peter and John to speak in the name of Jesus (Acts 4:1–21). When they persisted, they were arrested and jailed, escaped, were re-arrested and beaten. They were told not to continue teaching and were then released (5:17–42).

About A.D. 44, Herod Agrippa I, then ruler of Judea and other parts of Palestine under the Romans, lashed out savagely against the Christians. He had James, son of Zebedee and brother of John, killed—and then arrested Peter, who later escaped from prison miraculously (Acts 12:1–11). In his *Jewish Antiquities*, Flavius Josephus wrote that, around A.D. 62, James (the brother of Jesus) who was a leader of the church in Jerusalem, was put to death at the instigation of Ananus, the high priest.

According to tradition, Peter died by crucifixion. Yet the details of his martyrdom are actually a mystery. In the *First Epistle of Clement to the Corinthians*, from about A.D. 96, Clement of Rome, one of the Apostolic Fathers, wrote: "Peter was subjected to tribulation, not once or twice but many times; it was in that way that he bore his witness, ere he left us for his well-earned place in glory." A passage in the Gospel of John is often read as a reference to Peter's death: Jesus said, "When you are old, you will stretch out your hands, and another will gird you and carry you where you do not wish to go" (John 21:18–19). The widely held idea that Peter was crucified head down may have been invented by the author of the apocryphal *Acts of Peter*, probably written in the second century.

Did Peter's death take place in Rome? Mention of "Babylon" in 1 Peter 5:13, which is most likely a cryptic reference to Rome, is often taken to point to Peter's presence there. He is widely believed to have died in Nero's garden in the vicinity of the Vatican. It is here, in fact, that he is believed by many to have been buried.

In the aftermath of the persecution under Nero that followed the burning of Rome, the Christian community was badly shaken. Scholars believe that some of the New Testament books were written to encourage and support the fledgling faith.

The stage was set for the more systematic and widespread persecution of Christians that followed in the next centuries, as the Christian movement grew. ✦

Thousands of Christians *were martyred in the Colosseum.*

Was Nero the "beast" of Revelation?

Exploring the eerie legend

THE FAMOUS "number of the beast," 666, in Revelation 13:18 can be understood in reference to the violent Roman ruler Nero. In Hebrew and other ancient languages, the letters of the alphabet were used as numbers, and thus every letter had a numerical value. The number of the beast is best explained as code for "Neron Caesar." If this name is written in Hebrew, the sum of the letters equals 666. If the Latin form, Nero Caesar, is used, the result is 616—a variant number actually found in some manuscripts of the Greek text of Revelation.

The Book of Revelation contains a description of a beast. "One of its heads seemed to have a mortal wound, but its mortal wound was healed" (13:3). This gruesome image may be another veiled reference to Nero. After the emperor committed suicide by stabbing himself, some believed that he had not really died, but had gone into hiding. It was feared that he would one day reappear to resume his bloody career. A later variation of this belief was that he had indeed died but would come to life again. An allusion to this resurrected Nero, identified with the Antichrist, occurs in 17:8: "the beast . . . was and is not and is to come." ✦

The destruction of the Temple

The end of an ancient institution

JUDEA'S GREAT REVOLT against Rome broke out in A.D. 66 and lasted for four years, pitting several of Rome's disciplined legions against the poorly organized Jewish rebels. This challenge to Rome's authority had to be suppressed to avoid flare-ups in other lands. Under the command of Vespasian, Rome's legions recaptured most of Palestine. The war culminated in the siege of Jerusalem in the year A.D. 70. During the fall of the city, Judaism's holiest site, Herod's Temple, went up in flames.

Josephus, the renowned first-century Jewish historian and soldier, devoted two books in his work *The Jewish War* to an account of the lengthy siege of Jerusalem and its eventual conquest by Rome. Titus (who had replaced his father, Vespasian, in Judea when Vespasian left to become emperor) commanded the legions' bloody capture of the city. The Jewish defenders made a valiant effort to save the Temple.

The triumphal Arch of Titus, in Rome, commemorating the Roman victory over the Jews, depicts soldiers carrying off the Temple Menorah.

According to the Talmud, it was on the 9th day of Av—the traditional date of the destruction of the First Temple—that the Temple gates were set on fire. While the Temple was burning, the Jewish defenders were slain. "Most . . . were civilians, weak and unarmed people, each butchered where he was caught," Josephus wrote.

The last holdout, the Upper City, fell to Rome a month later. Titus ordered the destruction of the city and its walls, leaving just three towers standing as a reminder of past glory and as a fortress for the 10th Legion, which was left to guard the city.

Jerusalem's fall was celebrated by Titus as a great victory, and a commemorative arch was erected in Rome to mark the occasion. For the Jews, however, the 9th of Av became a day of mourning and prayer. In subsequent generations, the Western Wall (the portion of the western supporting wall of the Temple Mount that remained intact) became a site for pilgrimages and prayers for the Jewish people. It became associated with the Western Wall of the Holy of Holies and therefore with the Divine Presence.

One part of the wall in particular became the site of worship and mourning. It is called the "Wailing Wall," or, in Hebrew, the *Kotel*. To this day, many pilgrims to Jerusalem leave notes—prayers and requests—tucked in between its stones.

No trace has ever been found of the Temple's holy vessels, carried off to Rome by Titus and depicted on the arch in Rome. The Ark of the Covenant probably disappeared before or during the destruction of the First Temple in the sixth century B.C.

The destruction of the Temple eliminated the focal point of ancient Jewish worship. Judaism adapted to the harsh new realities. The Jews were now a people without a homeland. But new leaders arose to replace those who had perished in the revolt against Rome. The town of Jabneel, near the coast, became the center of Jewish learning and law. The *bet midrash*, or house of study, was founded, and prayer in the synagogue became more important. Judaism, deprived of its cult center, developed a new, yet more spiritual, dimension. ✦

IN MODERN TIMES

❧ The Wailing Wall ❧

Orthodox men praying at the Wall.

Throughout the centuries, Jews have returned to the Temple Mount to remember, to mourn, and to pray. Under some rulers, Jews were forbidden to enter the Holy City, except on the Day of Atonement. When the Old City of Jerusalem, which encompasses the Temple Mount, came under Jewish control in 1967, the age-old dream of countless Jews came true.

The Wailing Wall is the holiest site in the Jewish world. It is in fact only one section of the Western retaining wall that Herod the Great built to enlarge the Temple Mount. The debris of the centuries covers much of the lower layer of the Wall, and today only the top tiers are visible. The area in front of the Wall is cleared, accommodating the large number of people who come there to worship. It is divided down the middle into two sections, one for women, and one for men. On *Shabbat* (the Sabbath), *bar mitzvot* are performed there; this ceremony, during which a boy of 13 is called to read a portion of Torah, marks his new role as a full member of the Jewish community.

Last stand against Roman oppression

The siege of Masada

SOLDIERS OF THE TENTH LEGION burst upon the horrifying carnage within the rocky fortress of Masada on May 2, A.D. 73. There lay the bodies of 960 men, women, and children. These Jewish rebels known as Zealots, who believed in "no rule but the Law—no King but God," had chosen death rather than the shame of the galleys, the Egyptian mines, or the slave quarters of wealthy Roman households.

Never mentioned in the Bible, Masada was the last remaining Zealot stronghold in the Jewish revolt against Rome that began in A.D. 66. Set atop an isolated rock between the eastern edge of the Judean Desert and the Dead Sea, Masada was virtually impregnable. Approximately 330 feet high on the west and some 1,300 feet above the Dead Sea on the east, it was approachable only by steep pathways.

Who were the Zealots?

The Zealot movement was founded in A.D. 6 or 7 by Judas the Galilean and a Pharisee named Zadok after the Romans ordered a census of the Jewish population for taxation purposes. Called the "fourth school of Jewish philosophers" by the Jewish soldier and historian Josephus, the Zealots were marked by their absolute insistence that no one except God be honored as "king" or "Lord." Thus, any foreign rule over Israel was rejected, and the paying of taxes to the emperor was considered to be idolatry.

Although the census revolt led by Judas the Galilean was easily suppressed, the movement was not. While many scholars believe it was the Zealots who held Masada until A.D. 73, others believe it was the Sicarii, thought by many to be a splinter organization.

Masada was settled as early as the fourth millennium, and some scholars believe that it was originally fortified by Alexander Janneus in the first century B.C. It did not assume importance, however, until the reign of Herod the Great. This isolated and fortified rock was used by Herod as a refuge for his family when he fled from the Parthians in 40 B.C. It was manned by a force of some 800 soldiers.

When Herod returned from Rome, he enhanced the fortifications of Masada, ensuring that any retreat in the future would be comfortable and secure. A double wall 4,590 feet in circumference was erected around the top of the site; it featured some 30 towers, 70 rooms, and 4 elaborately built gates. Within, he built an official palace of some 36,000 square feet, a large bathhouse in the Roman style, storehouses for food and other supplies, and lesser residential and administrative buildings. But probably most remarkable of all was Herod's private villa, a three-tiered palace with royal living quarters on the top terrace and two lower terraces carved into the rock.

A Roman garrison held the fortress after Herod's death, but Zealots captured it in A.D. 66 and slaughtered the Romans in cold blood after they had surrendered. This atrocity marked the opening of the first Jewish Revolt, which was to embroil Palestine for over four years, as tens of thousands of Jews were put to death by Roman troops or driven from their homes by mobs of Gentiles. It was in this turmoil that Jerusalem fell and the Temple, then a Zealot stronghold, was razed in A.D. 70.

Even as the rest of Palestinian Jewry was cruelly subdued, however, Masada held out. Nearby, other Zealots were routed from the desert fortresses of Herodium and Machaerus by the Roman army, but this last remaining outpost of Zealots did not yield.

The Zealots of Masada, under the guid-

An aerial view of Masada *shows why it was impregnable to attack for so long.*

ance of their leader Eleazar, adapted Herod's showplace to suit their needs. To accommodate their numbers, they partitioned living quarters within the fortress walls. Stores of dried food left from the time of Herod's occupancy a century earlier and rainwater collected in huge cisterns built during his reign were sufficient to sustain the people. The Zealots built two *mikvahs*, or ritual baths, and a synagogue.

The Romans failed to rout the Zealots from their stronghold until, under the Tenth Legion's commander, Governor Flavius Silva, a massive assault was launched. A ramp was constructed on which their battering ram could hammer Masada's impressive outer wall. The ramp was some 645 feet long and more than 200 feet high. Roman catapults bombarded Masada with enormous stones. Finally, on the eve of May 2, A.D. 73, the wall was breached, and a secondary wall was set on fire. The Romans settled in for the night thinking that the next day's assault would be victorious.

What they could not know was that Eleazar had gathered together the surviving Zealots and, in a moving speech later described by Josephus, painted a lurid but no doubt accurate picture of the dishonor and indignities to come. In conclusion, Eleazar persuaded his people to take matters into their own hands. Each man killed his own family, and then, by lot, 10 men were chosen to kill the others. Also by lot, one of these 10 was selected to dispatch the remaining 9 and then commit suicide. Personal belongings and the great palace were torched, but food supplies were purposely left intact, as proof to the Romans that the Zealots had chosen death before dishonor. When the conquerors finally broke into the stronghold the next morning, they found alive only two women and five children who had hidden. Their story was the sole basis of all later accounts.

Masada remained a Roman garrison for at least the next 40 years. In the fifth and sixth centuries A.D., a community of monks lived there. The site was then unoccupied, except for brief periods of exploration, until large-scale excavations began in the 1960s. It is now an historical shrine in Israel. ✦

Penetrating the mysteries of the Apocalypse

The Revelation to John

NO OTHER WRITING in the New Testament is so intentionally mysterious as the Revelation to John, also called the Apocalypse. Within its pages one reads of a scroll eaten from the hand of an angel, a woman clothed with the sun pursued by a great red dragon, a beast with ten horns and seven heads. Exotic symbols and riddles abound. All these are part of a vision that John says he saw "in the Spirit."

Revelation is a vast pageant set on a visionary stage spanning heaven and earth. The message was directed to Christians who were faced with persecution by the Roman state, and it gave them a vision in which the powers of the world were measured by a new scale.

For example, the mighty Roman Empire, which presented itself as the keeper of ancient values, the fountainhead of order and law, appears in the vision as nothing more than a beast or a harlot, or the demon-filled ruin of a once awesome city: "Fallen, fallen is Babylon the great!" (18:2). By contrast, the church becomes "a great multitude which no man could number, from every nation, from all tribes and peoples and tongues, standing before the throne" (7:9). It is not seen as it in fact was—a tiny and mostly poor minority within a hostile or indifferent society. The narrative is intended to thrill and captivate its readers as it circles about its central vision of a world transformed by God's power.

Although to modern tastes Revelation, with its exotic images, may seem bizarre, it was in fact following a common pattern within Jewish literature of its time. Numerous examples of such writings have survived, including the Book of Daniel in the Hebrew Bible and 2 Esdras in the Apocrypha. Scholars call these works "apocalyptic literature" after the Greek word *apocalypsis* which means "revelation."

John introduced his book as "The Revelation of Jesus Christ, which God gave him to show to his servants what must soon take place; and he made it known by sending his angel to his servant John." Apocalyptic literature often described the way in which the present evil age of human history would be overthrown by God, who would then create a new, perfect age from which evil would be banished.

The visions in this literature were ascribed to many of the ancient figures of the Bible: Adam, Abraham, Moses, Ezekiel, Daniel, Ezra, and others, though almost all were written from about 200 B.C. to A.D. 200. These great men of earlier centuries were typically said to have received a revelation that either took them on a visionary journey or symbolically laid out the course of human history until its end.

Seven-headed *beasts of Revelation.*

Death, on a pale horse, *leads ghostly battalions.*

Revelation is closely related to this literature but differs in that it was not attributed to a figure from ancient times. Instead its author was a Christian named John, who was probably known to the readers of the book. Most scholars have concluded that this John was not the apostle John, but was a Christian leader living near the end of the first century.

Toward the end of the reign of the emperor Domitian (A.D. 81–96), John had evidently been exiled to the small island of Patmos in the Aegean, as he says, "on account of the word of God and the testimony of Jesus" (1:9). Although we know little about John, the churches to whom he was writing knew him. And they knew this to be a document composed in their own time, with direct importance for them.

To Christians of John's time, Revelation was startling but recognizable. Though John never expressly quotes the Scriptures, Revelation is full of biblical images and language. John depended on his readers' knowledge of the Scriptures to catch these resonances. For example, in John's description of "four living creatures" that surround God's throne, each creature had a different face. The first had a face like a lion, the second an ox, the third a man, the fourth an eagle (4:6–8). John's readers would hear echoes of Ezekiel's vision of God's throne, in which Ezekiel also saw four creatures, each with those four faces (Ezekiel 1:5–10).

The Book of Revelation is structured around the number seven, a number that in the ancient world usually symbolized completeness and perfection. The words that begin John's strange journey come to him from a "voice like a trumpet" that says, "Write what you see in a book and send it to the seven churches" (1:10–11). The seven churches, all from western Asia Minor, are symbolized by seven lampstands. The churches have seven angels symbolized by seven stars, and each is sent a highly stylized letter. These are addressed not from John to the church but from Christ—with his face "like the sun shining in full strength"—to the angel of the particular church. The letters are specific and direct in dealing with problems in the churches, and they suggest that all is not well.

Christ praised some of the congregations for faithfulness and endurance under persecution, but others were beset by idolatry and heresy. He rebuked the church at Ephesus because they had "abandoned the love" they had at first (2:4). He harshly told the church at Sardis, "you have the name of being alive, and you are dead" (3:1). And the church at Laodicea was so "lukewarm," he said, "I will spew you out of my mouth" (3:16). These were clearly churches that needed a vision to lift their eyes above their struggle. The message was for all: "He who has an ear, let him hear what the Spirit says to the churches" (3:22).

After the letters, John was summoned through "an open door" in heaven and ascended to see the throne of God and the glory surrounding it (Revelation 4:1–11). In his right hand God held a scroll, sealed with seven seals. John's vision centers not on the content of the scroll, but on the opening of its seven seals. No one was found worthy to open the seals but Christ, who was introduced enigmatically as "the Lion of the tribe of Judah" and also as a "Lamb standing, as though it had been slain." The Lamb was acclaimed by the heavenly court and proceeded to open the seals as a demonstration of his universal authority.

As the Lamb opened the first four seals the thundering vision of the famous "four horsemen" was revealed: conquest, war, famine, and death. The opening of the fifth seal rang with the cry of martyrs. With the sixth seal the overthrow of earth and sky was revealed, and all the people of earth, even the most powerful, were reduced to scurrying among the rocks like rodents be-

At the opening of the sixth seal:

fore "the wrath of the Lamb." What more could the seventh seal bring?

Rather than continue the progression of seals, however, John paused to reveal "the seal of the living God," a vision that depicts the salvation of the faithful. The number of the faithful is given explicitly as 144,000.

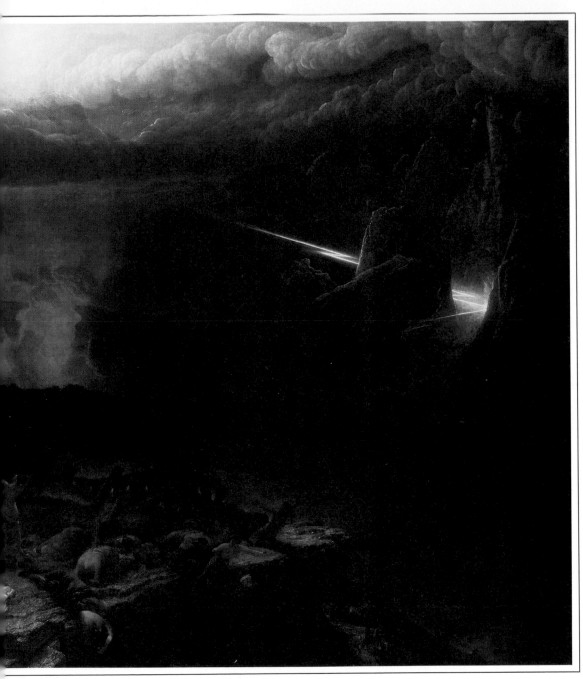

"Behold, there was a great earthquake; and the sun became black as sackcloth."

This number represents all of the redeemed, who are also portrayed by a numberless throng who shout, "Salvation belongs to our God who sits upon the throne, and to the Lamb!" (7:10). When John finally described the seventh seal, it seems an anticlimax: "there was silence in heaven for about half an hour." But this was simply a pause before the next series of visions.

The new visions repeat and embellish the themes that were established in the opening of the seals: persecution and martyrdom; judgment and punishment on the forces of evil in the world; and the triumph of God and Christ and the salvation of the faithful. The seven trumpets of woe follow the opening of the seven seals. Between the sixth and seventh trumpets two visions intervene. The final trumpet brings a celebration because "The kingdom of the world has become the kingdom of our Lord and of his Christ; and he shall reign for ever and ever."

The visions that follow continue the same themes but focus on the Roman state as the enemy of God and his people. John saw a woman in heaven, who evidently represented the people of God. She was "clothed with the sun" and about to bear a child. A "great red dragon" identified as "that ancient serpent, who is called the Devil and Satan" pursued her, ready to devour her child at birth. When she bore a son, "who is to rule all the nations with a rod of iron," he was caught up to God, but she fled to the wilderness of earth, still pursued by the dragon.

The dragon then empowered two beasts: one that rose from the sea and a second that rose from the earth. The sea beast represented the Roman Empire, and the second beast represented the emperor and the emperor worship that was common throughout the Empire. Christians from Ephesus might especially have recognized this "beast." Their city had built a huge temple for the emperor Domitian housing a colossal statue of this emperor who styled himself "Lord and God." The first beast made war on the saints and the second required everyone, on pain of death, to worship an image of the first beast. In Domitian, John evidently saw the rebirth of the evil embodied in the late emperor Nero, who is represented by the number of the beast, 666 (13:1–18).

"We do not need complicated arguments to prove that the Bible is more than a human book, that it is divinely inspired. Its very durability over the centuries supports Isaiah's claim: 'The grass withereth, the flower fadeth, but the word of God shall stand forever.' "
—Rev. Billy Graham
What the Bible Says to Me

John's vision describes a total conflict between the church and the Roman Empire and its ruler cult. The vision of seven plagues shows God's punishment of this "great Babylon" just as he had sent plagues on Egypt long ago. John portrays their opposition to God as the dragon and beast gather "the kings of the whole world" for battle "at the place which is called in Hebrew Armageddon" (16:13–16).

This mysterious word, Armageddon, is usually thought to mean "Mount Megiddo" in Hebrew, since Megiddo was the site of many famous battles. But since there are no mountains located in Megiddo, some scholars see in it a veiled reference to Jerusalem. Visions and hymns celebrate the fall of "Babylon the great, mother of harlots and of earth's abominations" and the lamentation of all who supported her (17:1–19:10).

Thus the visions return with new emphasis to Satan's defeat and the supremacy of Christ's rule. The cry of the martyrs that had been heard in the opening of the fifth seal was finally answered. Satan is bound and the resurrected martyrs reign with Christ for a thousand years. As the great white throne of God opens to John's sight, all the dead stand and are judged before the throne "by what was written in the books, by what they had done." The "book of life" records the names of the faithful; anyone not there is condemned to the lake of fire.

John's last chapters breathe a sense of exhilaration and peace as he sees a new heaven, a new earth, a new Jerusalem. God is tenderly present with his people to "wipe away every tear from their eyes" (21:4). Paradise has been regained in a visionary city of "pure gold, clear as glass," and a perfect communion with God.

John wrote Revelation for a community of people struggling to survive against the threats of a hostile empire. Despite their strangeness, the visions were clear in their message. Satan and his Roman beasts would continue to war, but not a single faithful heart would be lost. Thus they could be confident: " 'Surely I am coming soon.' Amen. Come, Lord Jesus!" ✦

The souls of the dead stand before the awesome throne of God at the Last Judgment. The cataclysmic end of days is heralded by an angel "coming down from heaven, holding in his hand the key of the bottomless pit."

Index

Page numbers in **boldface** type refer to the illustrations.

Israelites exiled in, 129, 146, 166,
201–202, 238, 244, 247–248,
262–263, 266, 319
Judah destroyed by, 198–201, 248
Persian conquest of, 201–202
Bahrdt, C. F., 182
Balaam, **100**
Balthasar, 278
Baptism, 10–11, 266, 352
of Jesus, 9–10, 11, 269, 272, 285,
285, 288
Barabbas, 332–333
Barak, 106, 107
Bar Kappara, 152
Barnabas, 310
Barth, Karl, 347
Barton, Bruce, 324
Baruch, 242–244
Bathsheba, 129, 146, 147–149, **148,** 276
Beatitudes, 300–301
Bedouins, 107, 186, 286–287
Beersheba, 39
Bees, 117, 121
Begats, 40
Bel and the Dragon, 242
Belshazzar, King, 258, **258**
Belteshazzar. *See* Daniel.
Bene Israel, 263
Ben-hadad, King, 186
Benjamin (son of Jacob), 62, 66–67, 145
Benjamin, tribe of, 82, 144, 262
Benjamin of Tudela, 263
Ben Lakish, Simeon, 204
Ben Sira, Joshua, 36, 181
Berytus (Beirut), 167
Bethany, 323
Bethel, 184
as sanctuary, 58–59, 163, 236–237
Bethlehem, 125, 126, 260, 276, 279–280
Beth-shan, 124, 142
Beth-shemesh, 137
Bethuel, 127, 129
Bible
authorship of, 12
chronology in, 12
English translations of, 14, 40, 63, 90
facts about, 14
foreign texts and, 215, 220, 223, 228, 252
language of, 14, 355
Latin Vulgate, 14, 227, 269, 299
as literature, 12, 214–230, 235–236
manuscripts of, **40,** 286–287, 309
musical legacy of, 214–217
oldest text in, 106
oral tradition of, 269
recurring themes in, 108, 246
sacred numbers in, 92–93, **92, 93,**
367–370, **368**
traditional sources combined in, 9, 12,
58, 87, 137–139, 215, 220, 224, 239, 254
translations of, 9, 13, 14, 83, 87, 130,
139, 266, 269
wisdom of, 217–225, **221,** 227
See also Gospels; New Testament; Old
Testament; Torah.
Biblical scholars, 12, 91, 98, 105, 157,
158, 192, 218–219
Bickerman, Elias, 204, 259
Bildad, 210–212
Bilhah, 60
Bitter Lakes, 77
Blanton, Smiley, 223
Blessings, 208–209

of Jesus, 300–301
patriarchal, 57–58, **57,** 67
Blood, 81, 93
Blood feuds, 108
Boaz, 125–126, **126,** 146
Boehme, Jacob, 84, 240, 347
Boils, 196
Bones
dry, 248–249, **249**
of Elisha, 188, **188**
jawbones, **117,** 119, 121
of Joseph (Jacob's son), 76
Bonhoeffer, Dietrich, 133, 289
Book of the Law, 199
Book of the Twelve, The, 260–261
Boswellia tree, **278**
Bowie, Walter Russell, 276
Bread, breaking of, 324, 346
Breastpieces, 136, **136,** 141, 233
Brown, Raymond E., 316
Bryan, William Jennings, 342
Buber, Martin, 85
Bulls, 173
worship of, 79, **79, 80,** 81–82, **81**
Burial, 150–151, 323, 335, **339**
of Jesus, 338–339
Burning bush, 72, **72,** 314
Burnt offerings, 116, 145, 159, 186
Buttrick, George A., 303
Byblos, 167

C

Caiaphas, 330–332, **331**
Cain, 28–29, **28, 29,** 49, 92, 130
Caleb, 94, 95
Calendars, 39, 67
Caligula, Emperor, 322
Calkins, Raymond, 76, 179, 185
Cana, wedding feast of, 37, **292,** 293,
316
Canaan, 44, 45, 58, 66, 67, 79, 94–95,
114, 215
iron chariots of, 106, 107, 124
Israelite conquest of, 98–107, **98,**
105, 124, 129, 144–145
Israelites subjugated by, 106, 107
Philistine invasion of, 122–124
religion in, 12, 166, 199, 246
Candelabra, 83. *See also* Menorahs.
Canon, 13, 299
Capernaum, 318
Caphtor, 123
Caravans, 58, 64, 127, 161, 278, 282
Carchemish, Battle of, 243
Carew, Thomas, 229
Cedars of Lebanon, **157**
Censuses, 68, 96, 280, 364
Cephas. *See* Peter.
Ceres, 121
Chaim of Volozhin, Rabbi, 218
Chaldeans, 46
Chalice of Antioch, **341**
Chariots
of fire, 179–181, **180,** 183, 186
iron, 106, 107, 124
Pharaoh's, 77, **77**
Chemosh, 156, 186
Cherubim, 79, 86, 157
Christ
name of, 14, 283
See also Jesus.

Christianity, 356–357 (map)
baptism and, 10–11
Book of Jonah and, 251–252
early suppression of, 322, 357–358,
358, 360–361, **361,** 366, 367
importance of Last Supper in, 324–326,
352
Judaism and, 275, 351–352
Messiah tradition in, 240–241, 259
missionary aspects of, 352, 355–357
Pentecostal movement in, 352
pillars of, 268, 358
relics of, 340–342, **340, 341**
rise of, 263, 350–351, 355–358, 360–361
role of Paul in, 355–358, **358**
role of Peter in, 313, 350, 358
shrines of, 297
Song of Solomon in, 228, 230
symbols of, **336,** 345, **345**
Christology, 270
Chrysostom, Saint, 152
Circumcision, 50–51, 73, 99, 265, 271,
275, 282
City of David Archaeological Project,
90, 194
Claudius, Emperor, 322
Clement of Alexandria, 84
Clement of Rome, 204, 251, 361
Codices, 286
Coins, 89–90, **89, 93,** 96, 131, 318–319
Coliseum, **361**
Commentary
on the fear of God, 27
on God's love, 347
on grief, 152
on marriage, 133
on prayer, 197
on signs and wonders, 182
on suffering, 213
Concubines, 50, 60, **129,** 130, **130,** 132, 156
Constantine, Emperor, 297, 336, 340
Constantinople, 342
Corinthians, Paul's epistles to, 9, 115,
200, 324, 343–344, 352, 356–357
Corpses, 88, 115, 116, 121, 190, 294
Covenants, 80–82, 181, 192, 269
Cowper, William, 62
Creation of the universe, 16–18, **18, 19,**
21–26, 270
Crete, 79, 123
Crosses, 333, **336.** *See also* "True
Cross."
Crown of Thorns, 342
Crucifixion, 55, 271, 272, 333–337,
337, 341–343
Cuneiform, 44, **129,** 170, 192
Curses, 208–210
Customs
gift giving, 58, 61, 126, 127, 131
of hospitality, 53, 107
mourning, 115
religious, 61
taboos in, 96
Cynics, 223
Cyrus, King, 201–202, 205, 239

D

Dagon, 122, 124, 136–137, 166
Dagon, Temple of, 118, **120,** 121, 122, 124
Damascus, 186, 192, 291, 314, 354–355, 357
Dan, 60, 163

Dan, tribe of, 82, 262–263
Dance, **216,** 217
Daniel (Belteshazzar), 232, **233,** 254–259
  in lion's den, 242, 256, **256–257,** 296
Daniel, Book of, 254–259, 261
Daniel, James, 350
Darius I, King, 202
Darius III, King, 264
David, House of, 128, 137, 146, 148,
  191, 201, 202, 262, 280, 283
David, King, 96, 129, 136, 137–139,
  138, 142
  ancestors of, 60, 126, 129, 139, 146,
    146
  Bathsheba and, 129, 146, 147–149, **148,**
    276
  death of, 149, **149**
  dynasty established by, 128, 137, 146,
    146, 148, 191, 201, 202, 262, 280, 283
  Goliath and, **6,** 137–139, **139,** 155
  Judah ruled by, 144–146, 163
  leadership of, 113, 122, 124, 137–139,
    141, 144–151
  poetic and musical skills of, 137,
    143, 147, 214, 216–218
  psalms associated with, 143, 147, 214,
    217–218
  Saul and, 124, 136–137, **138,** 214, 218,
    283
  united Israel ruled by, 147–148, 156,
    262
  wives and concubines of, 130, 132,
    146, 147–149, **148**
Day of Atonement, 83, 87, 88, 157, 363
Day of Yahweh, 236
Dead Sea, 236, 266, 284, 286, **287,** 364
  earthquakes affecting, 53
  pillars of salt in, **53**
Dead Sea Scrolls, 286–287, **286,** 290
Death, 141, **367**
  burial and, 150–151, 323, 335,
    338–339, **339**
  by crucifixion, 55, 271, 272, 333–337,
    337, 341–343
  love and, 229–230
  martyrdom and, 353–354, **354,** 358,
    360–361, **361,** 370
  mourning and, 150–152, **150, 151**
  power of Jesus over, 316, 346
  resurrection and, 151–152, 187–188,
    188, 346
  by stoning, 353–354, **354,** 361
  suicidal, 142, **142,** 144, 147, 365
  visions of, **367, 371**
Deborah, 106–107, **106,** 121, 217
De Charny, Geoffrey, 340–341
Deities
  animals as, 79, **79, 80**
  astral, 199
  Babylonian, 246, **246,** 248
  Canaanite, 108, 122, 124, 166–167,
    166, 169, 171–173, 195, 199, 246
  demons and evil spirits as, 177–178,
    178
  Egyptian, 79, 95, 246
  fertility, 166, 172, 195, 246
  golden calves or bulls as, 79, **80,**
    81–82, **81,** 163, 175
  Hellenistic, 79
  Mesopotamian, 178, **178**
  pagan, 12, 64, 79, **79,** 81, 95, 108,
    121, **122,** 124, 136–137, 156, 163,
    186, 195, 246, 265

Pharaohs as, 74
  Roman, 359, **359**
  statues of, 60–61, **60,** 79, 136–137,
    178, **178,** 255, **255**
  Syrian, **60,** 79
  See also Baal; Yahweh.
Delilah, 118–119, **119,** 121
Delphi, 355
Demons, 11, **154,** 178, **178,** 293–295, **294,**
  296
Deutero-Isaiah (Second Isaiah), 239, 241
Deuteronomic Law, 132
Deuteronomy, Book of, 12, 95, 98, 102,
  115, 151, 199, 208–209
Diaspora, 266, 291, 354
Dinah, 60
Disciples
  of Jesus, 268, 272, **290,** 292–293,
    310–315, 324–327, **326,** 343–346,
    348–352
  of John the Baptist, 284
  women as, 311, 323, **323,** 339, 343–346,
    348
Diseases, 88, 150, 189–191
Dishonest Steward, parable of, 306, 308
Divided Kingdom, 56, 59, 144, 156, 162
  (map), 163, 165, 262
Divination, 232–234
Djoser, Pharaoh, 67
Dome of the Rock, 55, 156
Domitian, Emperor, 367, 370
Donne, John, 133, 152
Dostoyevsky, Fyodor, 17
Dothan, 64
Doves, 32, 34, 345
Dreams, 63, 65, 141, 145, 153, 232–234
  of Abraham, 50, 234
  apocalyptic, 258–259
  of Daniel, 258–259
  of Jacob, 58, **58,** 234
  of Joseph (Jacob's son), 63, 65, 66,
    105, 141, 234
  of Joseph (Mary's husband), 274,
    276–278, 279
  of Nebuchadnezzar, 232, **232–233**
  of Pharaoh, 65, **65**
  prophecy in, 58, **58,** 65, 105, 110,
    141, 145, 153, 232–234
  of Solomon, 145, 153
  warnings in, 60, 234, 279
  of wise men, 279
Droughts, 67, 172

Ꙫ

Ea, 32–34, 178
Earthquakes, 53, 99, 100, 175, 299, **369**
Ecclesiastes, Book of, 153, 223–225, **225**
Eckhart, Meister, 303, 347
Eclipses, 104–105
Edom, 155, 185–186, 260, 322
Egypt, 44–45, 65–67, 164–165, 192, 194
  Assyrian dominance of, 164
  deities of, 79, 95, 246
  hair styles of, 113, 114
  Holy Family in, 272, 279, **280,** 283, **283**
  Israelites in, 69–76, **70–71,** 98–99, 176
  Joseph (Jacob's son) in, 62, 64–67
  Judah invaded by, 163
  language and culture of, 72, 215, 220,
    223
  Macedonian conquest of, 264

Philistine invasion of, 123
  Ptolemaic rule of, 264, 291
  ten plagues of, 74–76, **74,** 370
El, 166, 167
Elah, King, 169
Elah, Valley of, **139**
Elamites, 44
Elath, 154, 159, **159,** 161
Eldad ha-Dani, 262–263
Elders, 135, 137, 159, 177, 248, 311
Eleazar (exorcist), 295
Eleazar (Zealot leader), 365
Eli, 124, 134, **135,** 136
Eliezer of Tarnegrod, Rabbi, 182
Elihu, 212
Elijah, 162, 168, 171–176, **174, 176,** 292
  Ahab vs., **168,** 172–173, 177
  ascent into heavens of, 179–181, **180,**
    183
  Elisha and, 169, 175, 179–180, **180,**
    183–185, 187, 314
  Jesus linked to, 181, 185, 314, **315**
  mantle of, 175, 179, 183
  on Mount Horeb, 174–176, 186
  prophecy of, 168, 171, 175, 179, 234
  prophets of Baal and, 166, 171–175,
    171, 173, 183, 187
Elimelech, 125, 126
Eliphaz, 210–212
Elisha, 169, 175, **184,** 216, 292
  death of, 180, 188
  Elijah and, 169, 175, 179–180, **180,**
    183–185, 187, 314
  miracles of, 183–185, **183,** 187–189,
    187, 188, 190
  political revolutions instigated by,
    186–187
Elizabeth, 274–275, **275,** 284
El Jib, 144–145
Elkanah, 134
Ellison, H. L., 85
Enlil, 32, 34, 178
Enoch, 30, 181
Ephesus, 356, 357 (map), 358–359, 368,
  370
Ephods, 110, 141, 233
Ephraim, 65, 67, 68
Ephraimites, 82, 111, 112
Epic of Gilgamesh, 32–34, 44
Epicureans, 223
Erech, 41
Eretz Israel, 56
Esau, 56–58, **57,** 61, **61**
Essenes, 11, 265–266, 286–287, 290
Esther, Queen, 203–204, **203**
Esther, Book of, 14, 203–204
Ethbaal, King, 167, 172
Ethiopia, 67, 161, 263
Eucharist, 341, 345
Euphrates River, 24, 32, 43, 47
Evangelists, 268–272, **268, 271,** 311,
  358. *See also specific Evangelists.*
Eve, 22–28, **22, 23, 26, 49,** 92
Exodus, 44, 76–78, 80, 83, 98–99
Exodus, Book of, 44, 69–78, 80–83, 86,
  173
Exorcism, 293–295, **294**
Ezekiel, 217, 232–233, 254
  visions of, 247–249, **247, 249,** 271, 367
Ezekiel, Book of, 116, 247–249
Ezion-Geber, 154, 161
Ezra, 130, 202, 205–206, 252, 263
Ezra, Book of, 130

374

ministry of, 9–10, 269, 271, 272, 285, 288, 290–333
miracles of, 37, 185, 272, 283, **292,** 293, 294, **295,** 296–299, **298,** 316, 345
money-changers expelled by, 318–319
Moses and Elijah as link to, 181, 185, 314, **315**
multitudes fed by, 272, 297–298, 316, 345
name of, 14, 283–284
nature commanded by, 292, 296–299, **298**
parables of, 90, 170, 269, 271, 298, 304–308, **304, 305, 306, 307**
passion of, 10, 328–337, **334**
prophecies prefiguring, 55, 241, 252, 260
raising of the dead by, 272, **295,** 316
resurrection of, 252, 269–270, 309, 310, 315, 343–346, **343**
sermons of, 269, 272, 300–308, **300**
as "Son of David," 128, 146, 276, 280, 283, 317
as "Son of God," 10, 269, 282, 288, 315, 332–333, 345
as "Son of man," 10, 259
as "Son of the Law," 281–282
teaching of, 10, 291–295, 297, 300–308
in the Temple, 272, 280–282, **282,** 318, **318**
temptation in the wilderness of, 272, 288–289, **288**
terminology of, 301
tomb of, 297, 339, 343–345
transfiguration of, 181, 272, 310, 314–315, **315**
triumphal entry into Jerusalem of, 272, 317, **317**
universal message of, 252, 271, 292
washing of disciples' feet by, **326,** 327
water changed to wine by, 272, **292,** 293, 316
Jethro, 72
Jewish law
codification of, 330–331
Deuteronomic, 132
dietary, 88, 255
first-born males in, 56, 126, 179
graven images in, 80, **113**
Hellenization of, 264–265
Leviticus as source of, 87–88, 190
marriage in, 128–133
ritual purity in, 87–88, 190–191, 287
status as a Jew in, 128, 263
taboos in, 96, 129–130, 132, 284, 330–331
Jewish War, 287, 333, 351, 362–364
Jewish War, The (Josephus), 362
Jews, **176**
Abraham as model for, 55
circumcision of, 50–51, 73, 99, 265, 271, 275, 282
derivation of term, 200
dispersion of, 266, 291, 354
Egyptian, 13
Ethiopian, 263
Hasidean, 286
Hellenistic culture among, **114,** 264–266, 355
Israelites as, 263
Orthodox, 115, **363**
persecution of, 263, 330, 364–365

Persian, 203–206
status as, 128, 263
Jezebel, Queen, 166–170, **168,** 234
Ahab and, 167–169, 170, 172, 174, 177, 187
Baal worship fostered by, 167, 169, 174
death of, 168, 187
Jezreel, Valley of, 141, 142
Joab, **144,** 145, 149
Joanna, 311
Joash (father of Gideon), 108
Joash (Jehoash), King of Israel, 180, 188, 236
Joash, King of Judah, 191
Job, 208–212, **209, 210, 211,** 254
Job, Book of, 18, 115, 208–212, 296
Joel, 234, 260, **260,** 350
Joel, Book of, 260
John, Gospel of, 9, 14, 170, 268–272, 276
John, Revelation to. See Revelation, Book of.
John Hyrcanus, King, 322
John the Baptist, 181, 269, 270, 271
birth of, 274–275, 280
circumcision of, 275
disciples of, 284, 310
as "forerunner" of Jesus, 288
Jesus baptized by, 9, 10–11, 285, **285,** 288, 290
murder of, 285, 312, 322
parents of, 274–275, 284
preaching of, 284–285, 293
John the Evangelist, 93, 230, 268–272, **268,** 292, 310–311, 314, **315,** 358
symbol of, 270, 271, **271**
Jonah, 200, 250–254
mission to Gentile states of, 250–252
and the whale, **4,** 11, **247,** 251–252, **253,** 254
Jonah, Book of, 250–252, 260
Jonathan (priest), 287
Jonathan (son of Saul), 142, 150–151, 233
Joram, King, 187, 238
Jordan River, 49
baptism in, 284–285, 288
bathing in, 189, **190**
earthquakes affecting, 99
parting of, 99, 175, 183–184
Joseph (husband of Mary), 128, **277,** 280, 282
as a carpenter, **281,** 283, 297
dreams of, 274, 276–278, 279
Joseph (son of Jacob)
birth of, 60, 62
bones of, 76
brothers' betrayal of, 62, **62, 63,** 64, 66–67, **66**
death of, 67, 69
dreams of, 63, 65, 66, 105, 141, 234
in Egypt, 62, 64–67, **64**
Jacob's preference for, 45, 62–63, 68
multicolored coat of, 63, **63,** 64
wisdom embodied in, 62
Joseph of Arimathea, 338–339, 340
Josephus, Flavius, 72, 114, 134, 139, 161, 172, 195, 262, 284–285, 286, 291, 295, 312, 362, 364–365
Joshua (priest), 202
Joshua (son of Nun), 94, 206, 233
angel's appearance to, 100, **100**
Battle of Jericho and, 99–101

death of, 95, 98
five kings demolished by, 103–105, **103, 105**
Gibeonite trickery of, 103, 144, 150
Israelites led by, 78, 98–101, 144
sun and moon stopped for, 103–105, 144
Joshua, Book of, 98–105
composition of, 98
holy war defined in, 102
Josiah, King, 199–200, 243
Jubilees, Book of, 30, 48–49
Judah (son of Jacob), 59, 60, 64, 67, 200
Judah (kingdom), 118, 124, 125, 154, 162 (map), 163, 165, 185–186, 198, 262
Assyrian dominance of, 163–164, 192–201
Babylonian destruction of, 198–201, 248
creation of, 56, 262
David's reign in, 144–146, 163
decline of, 191, 239, 243–244, 261
Edomite connection to, 185, 260
Egyptian invasion of, 163
vassal status of, 236
Judah, tribe of, 82
Judaism, 60, 202, 263, 294
astrology and, 201
Christianity and, 275, 351–352
Elijah traditions in, 176, **176,** 181
exclusivism vs. universalism in, 252
holy days of, 75–76, **75,** 83, 87, 88, 93, 99, 157, 195, 206, 224, 265, 319–320
rabbinic, 227, 261, 262
ritual purification in, 88, 115, 116, 159, 190–191, 195, 287, 294–295
Second Temple, 262–263
symbols of, 155
synagogues central to, 291
theology of Ezekiel in, 248
Torah as central to, 265–266
Judas Iscariot, 90, 233, 325, 329–330, **329**
Judas Maccabeus, 265, **265**
Judas the Galilean, 364
Judea, 276, 284
under Roman Empire, 320–322, 361
Judges, 121
Samson as, 119, 121
Samuel as, 134–135
Judges, Book of, 106, 108, 112, 117, 119, 121, 124, 135, 166
Jupiter (planet), 9

K

Kadesh, **11,** 94, 95
Karun River, 25
Kenan, 40
Kenites, 107
Kenyon, Kathleen, 101
Kerr, Hugh Thomson, 228
Ketuvim, 12
Kierkegaard, Soren, 55, 213
Kimhi, David, 152
King James Bible, 14, 40, 63, 90
Kings, First Book of, 153, 154, 172
Kinnors, **217**
Kircher, Athanasius, **33**
Knight, George A. F., 219
Koheleth, 223

Serapis, 79
Sermon on the Mount, 269, 300–301, **300**
Sermon on the Plain, 300
Serpents
  Aaron's rod and, 73, 74
  in Garden of Eden, 23–25, **23**, 296, 370
Seth, 30, 40
Seti, Pharaoh, 69–72
Seven Pillars of Wisdom, 93
Seven Seals, 368–369, **368–369**
Shabuoth. *See* Shavuot.
Shadrach (Hananiah), 255, **255**
Shalmaneser III, King, 163
Shalmaneser V, King, 238
Shavuot, 319–320, 350
Sheba, 160–161
Sheba, Queen of, 159–161
Shechem, 49, 64, 163
Sheep, 60
Shem, 36, 40, 46
Sheol, 64, 151–152, 229–230
Shepherds, 218, 227, **277,** 280
Sheshbazzar, 202
Shibboleth, 112
Shiloh, shrine at, 103, 134, **135,** 136, 243
Shinar, 41
Shishak, Pharaoh, 163
Shofars. *See* Rams' horns.
Shrine of the Book, **286**
Shroud of Turin, 5, 340–342, **340**
Shunem, 187–188
Sicarii, 329, 364
Sidonians, 156, 167, 172
Signs and wonders (commentary), 182
Silver, 89–90, 96, 155, 161
  thirty pieces of, 90, 329
Simeon, 59, 66
Simeon, tribe of, 82
Simon of Cyrene, 335
Simon Peter. *See* Peter.
Simon the Zealot, 311
Sinai desert, 78, 83, 87, 94–96
Sins
  of Adam and Eve, 23–25, **23,** 28, 36
  of David, 147–148, **148**
  litanies of, 236
  repentance of, 248, 251, **304**
  scapegoats offered for, 88, **88**
  of Sodom and Gomorrah, 52–53, 126
Sisera, 106, 107, **107**
Sizoo, Joseph R., 99
Slaughter of the innocents, 279, **280**
Slavery, 16, 132, 246
  of Israelites, 49, 50, 70–73, **70–71,** 93
  of Joseph (Jacob's son), 64–65
Smith, Robert Houston, 105
Sneezing, 188, 189
Sockman, Ralph W., 116, 182, 244
Sodom, 49, 52–53, **52,** 54, 126
Solomon, King, 146, **149,** 295
  building projects of, 79, 87, 91,
    154–159, **154,** 167
  death of, 155, 163
  dream of, 145, 153
  merchant fleet of, 154–155, 161
  Queen of Sheba and, 159–161
  reign of, 149, 153–161, **160,** 163
  reputed mines of, 159
  wisdom of, 153–154, **153,** 156, 220,
    223, 234
  wives and concubines of, 130, 132, 156
  See also Song of Solomon; Temple of
    Solomon.

Somalia, 154–155
Song of Deborah, 14, 106, 107
Song of Hannah, 134, 275
Song of Solomon (Song of Songs), 115,
  132, 153, 217, 226–230, **226, 229**
  authorship of, 228
  as holiest of scriptures, 226, 227
  metaphorical interpretations of, **226,**
    227–228, 230
  nature references in, 227
  works of art influenced by, 227, **229**
Spear of Longinus, 342
Spices, 38, 323, 339
Spies, 94, **94,** 186
Standard of Ur, 47
Star of Bethlehem, 9, 278, **279,** 280
Star of David, 155, **155**
Stations of the Cross, 297
Statues, 38
  of deities, 60–61, **60,** 79, 136–137,
    178, **178,** 255, **255**
  Nebuchadnezzar's, 255, **255**
  Rachel's theft of, 60–61, **60**
Stephen, 353–354, **354**
Stoics, 223
Suffering (commentary), 213
Sukkoth. *See* Feast of Tabernacles.
Sultan of Egypt, 297
Sumerians, 43–44, 46–47, 92, 178,
  299
Susa, 204
Synagogues, **201,** 216–217, 266, 270,
  290–291, 363
Synoptic Gospels, 269–270, 288, 304,
  309, 324–325
Syria, 79, 155, 165, 177, 186, 188,
  264–265, 280

T

Tabernacle of Moses, **82,** 83, 87
Talents, 89, 306, 319
Talents, parable of, 306
Talmud, 27, 116, 133, 152, 202, 291,
  321, 363
Tamar, 276
Tanak, 12
Targum, 230
Taxation, 271, 280, 318–319, 329, 364
Tax collectors, 271, 311
Taylor, Jeremy, 197
Temple, Herod's, **320**
  banking and money-lending in,
    318–319, **318**
  building of, 319–321
  Court of the Gentiles in, 319
  destruction of, 216, 263, 266, 291,
    319, 362–363
  pilgrimages to, 281–282, **282,** 317
  taxation for, 318–319
Temple, Second, 206, 239
  building of, 202, 205, 261, 263
  destruction of, 319
  historic period of, 262–263
  pagan worship in, 259, 265
  rededication of, 265–266
Temple Mount, 320, 321, 363
Temple of Solomon, 239
  architecture and decoration of, 79,
    91, 157–159, **158**
  Ark of the Covenant in, 87, 154,
    156–157, 363

Babylonian destruction of, 156, 200,
  206, 245, 248, 319, 363
building of, 55, 87, 154, **154,** 156
dimensions of, 91, 157
Isaiah in, 239, **241**
Jeremiah in, 243
plunder of, 244
religion centered in, 156, 163, 195,
  199, 363
Temples
  of Apollo, 355
  in Babylonia, 17
  in Bethel, 59
  in Canaan, 17, 79
  in Egypt, 17, 123, 159
  pagan, 246, 359
Ten Commandments, 5, 80–86, 87, 92,
  136, 154, 157–158, 220
  on the meaning of, 84–85
  scroll of, **286**
Ten lost tribes of Israel, 262–263,
  262, 271
Tent of meeting, 103
Terah, 40, 46–48
Teraphim, 60–61, 60
Teresa of Avila, Saint, 303
Tertullian, 302
Testament of Solomon, The, 154
Tetragrammaton, **21,** 284
Thebes, **91**
Theophanies, 72, 314–315
Theophilus, 271
Theseus, 79
Thomas, 346, **346**
Thomas, Gospel of, 308–309
Thomas à Kempis, 347
Thomas Aquinas, Saint, 84, 340
Thummim, Urim and, 136, 141, 233
Tiglath-pileser III, King, 164, 238
Tigris River, 24, 26, 43, 47
Time Line 1000 B.C.–500 B.C., 164–165
Time, reckoning of, 9–10
Timnah Valley, 159
Tishbe, 171
Tithing, 206, 236
Titus, Emperor, 319, 362–363
Tombs, 38, **46,** 339, **339**
Tongues, speaking in, 350, 352
Tools, 38, 43
Torah, 12, 14, 133, 181, 233, 265–266, 282,
  329. *See also* Pentateuch.
Tower of Babel, 41–43, **42,** 352
Trade, 236
  Phoenician, 167
  under Solomon, 154–155
Trade routes, 47, 124, 154–155, 161, 278
Tree of knowledge, 23–24, **23**
Tribute, payments of, 185, 192, 194,
  198, 238, 243
"True Cross," 297, 336, 340–341, **341**
Tunnels, 90–91, 192, 194–195, **194–195**
Twelve tribes of Israel, 60, 68, **82,** 93,
  103, 136, 155, 173, 200, 262, 310
Twenty-third Psalm
  on the meaning of, 218–219
Tyre, 154, **157,** 167, 200, 217, 319

U

Ugarit, 166, 246
Underhill, Evelyn, 197, 302
Unmerciful Servant, parable of, 306, 308

Sources

Hundreds of publications were consulted in the course of preparation of MYSTERIES OF THE BIBLE, notably *The New Oxford Annotated Bible with the Apocrypha,* Oxford University Press, Inc.; *The Interpreter's Dictionary of the Bible,* Abingdon Press; *The Encyclopaedia Judaica,* Keter Publishing House Jerusalem Ltd.; *The Interpreter's One-volume Commentary on the Bible,* Abingdon Press; *The Interpreter's Bible,* Abingdon Press; *New Catholic Encyclopedia,* McGraw-Hill Book Company; *Harper's Bible Dictionary,* edited by Paul J. Achtemeier, Harper & Row, Publishers, Inc.; *Encyclopedia of Archaeological Excavations in the Holy Land,* Prentice-Hall, Inc.; *The History of Israel,* by Martin Noth, Harper & Row, Publishers, Inc.; *Old Testament Theology,* by Gerhard von Rad, Harper & Row, Publishers, Inc.; *Theology of the Old Testament,* by Walther Eichrodt, The Westminster Press; *A History of Israel,* 3rd ed., by John Bright, The Westminster Press; *Understanding the Old Testament,* 4th ed., by Bernhard W. Anderson, Prentice-Hall, Inc.; *Ancient Israel: Its Life and Institutions,* by Roland de Vaux, McGraw-Hill Book Company, Inc.; *The Hebrew Scriptures,* by Samuel Sandmel, Oxford University Press, Inc.; *Archaeological Encyclopedia of the Holy Land,* edited by Avraham Negev, G. P. Putnam's Sons; *Eerdmans' Handbook to the Bible,* edited by David Alexander and Pat Alexander, William B. Eerdmans Publishing Company; *The Illustrated Bible Dictionary,* Tyndale House Publishers; *The New Unger's Bible Handbook,* by Merrill F. Unger, Moody Press; *The New Testament Era: The World of the Bible from 500 B.C. to A.D. 100,* by Bo Reicke, Fortress Press; *Understanding the New Testament,* 4th ed., by Howard Clark Kee, Prentice-Hall, Inc.; *ArtScroll Tanach Series: A traditional commentary on the Books of the Bible,* Rabbis Nosson Scherman/Meir Zlotowitz, General Editors, Mesorah Publications, Ltd.; *Commentary on the Holy Bible,* by Matthew Henry and Thomas Scott, Thomas Nelson, Inc.; *Handbook on the Pentateuch,* by Victor P. Hamilton, Baker Book House Company; *The Macmillan Bible Atlas,* by Yohanan Aharoni and Michael Avi-Yonah, Macmillan Publishing Co., Inc.; *Rand McNally Bible Atlas,* by Emil G. Kraeling, Rand McNally & Company; *Josephus,* translated by William Whiston, Kregel Publications; *Legends of the Bible,* by Louis Ginzberg, The Jewish Publication Society of America; *Ancient Near Eastern Texts Relating to the Old Testament,* 3rd ed. with supplement, edited by James B. Pritchard, Princeton University Press.

Credits and Acknowledgments

We wish to express our gratitude to the artists, photographers, picture collections, and private collectors who have contributed to this book. We would like to give particular thanks to Steven Schindler who designed the decorative border on our title page and part openers, and to Ray Skibinski who designed the decorative elements on our Commentary pages, "Words from Scripture" pages, as well as the borders on the brief quotes throughout Mysteries of the Bible.

4 Sonia Halliday Photographs. **6** Scala/Art Resource, N. Y. **8** Bibliothèque Nationale, Paris. **10** Michael Zohary. **11** Scala/Art Resource, N. Y.

PART I: THE PENTATEUCH

16 The Pierpont Morgan Library. **18** The New York Public Library, Rare Book Division. **19** Palazzo Doria-Pamphili, Rome. **21** The Ancient Art & Architecture Collection. **22** Scala/Art Resource, N. Y. **23** Mary Evans Picture Library. **24** Musée du Louvre, Paris. **25** George Buctel, based on a map created by Marsh Communications, Inc., Mt. Kisco, N.Y. **26** Scala/Art Resource, N. Y. **28** Sonia Halliday Photographs. **29** Reproduced from *The Doré Bible Illustrations* published by Dover Publications, Inc. in 1974. **31** The Granger Collection, New York. **32** Musée du Louvre, Paris. **33** Michael Rowe/© *Discover* 1985, Family Media, Inc. **35** Mary Evans Picture Library. **37** *left* Scala/Art Resource, N. Y.; *right* Erich Lessing/Magnum. **38** *left* British Museum/© Michael Holford; *right* The Granger Collection, New York. **39** British Museum/© Michael Holford. **40** The New York Public Library, Picture Collection. **42** Erich Lessing/Magnum. **44-45** George Buctel. **46** British Museum/© Michael Holford. **47** The University Museum, University of Pennsylvania. **48** Scala/Art Resource, N. Y. **50** Victoria & Albert Museum/© Michael Holford. **51** Mary Evans Picture Library. **52** The Metropolitan Museum of Art, Bequest of Mrs. H. O. Havemeyer, 1929, The H. O. Havemeyer Collection. **53** John Lewis Stage/The Image Bank. **54** Historical Pictures Service, Chicago. **57** The Ancient Art & Architecture Collection. **58** Picturepoint, London. **59** Leicestershire Museums and Art Galleries, Leicester. **60** Erich Lessing/Magnum. **61** The Ancient Art & Architecture Collection. **62** Historical Pictures Service, Chicago. **63** National Museums and Galleries on Merseyside, Walker Art Gallery, Liverpool. **64** Scala/Art Resource, N. Y. **65** Bibliothèque Nationale, Paris. **66** The Ancient Art & Architecture Collection. **68** Figures designed by Larissa Lawrynenko. **69** The New York Public Library, Picture Collection. **70-71** Bridgeman/Art Resource, N. Y. **72** Kunsthistorisches Museum, Vienna. **73** The New York Public Library, Picture Collection. **74** By courtesy of the Board of Trustees of the Victoria & Albert Museum. **75** Mary Evans Picture Library. **77** & **78** Scala/Art Resource, N. Y. **79** Private Collection. **80** Gemäldegalerie, Staatliche Museen Preussischer Kulturbesitz, West Berlin. **81** The Granger Collection, New York. **82** Mary Evans Picture Library. **83** Georg Gerster/Rapho/Photo Researchers. **86** Jewish Museum of New York/Art Resource, N. Y. **88** Counsel Collection. **89** Zev Radovan, Jerusalem. **90** *bottom center The Emergence of Man/The Persians*, Photograph by Dmitri Kessel © 1975 Time-Life Books Inc.; *remainder* Zev Radovan, Jerusalem. **91** © Michael Holford. **92** Sonia Halliday Photographs. **93** Zev Radovan, Jerusalem. **94** & **95** Scala/Art Resource, N. Y. **96** Bodleian Library, Oxford.

PART II: HISTORY

98 Culver Pictures. **100** The Ancient Art & Architecture Collection. **101** Jewish Museum of New York/Art Resource, N. Y. **102** *left* Museum of Anatolian Civilizations, Ankara; *right* Jewish Museum of New York/Art Resource, N. Y. **103** Reproduced by courtesy of the Trustees of the British Museum. **104-105** & **106** Culver Pictures. **107** Rijksmuseum, Amsterdam. **109** By courtesy of the Board of Trustees of the Victoria & Albert Museum. **111** The New York Public Library, Picture Collection. **113** *left* Scala/Art Resource, N. Y.; *right* Rijksmuseum van Oudheden. **114** *bottom left* Iraq Museum; *center* C. M. Dixon; *upper right* The Robert Harding Picture Library. **117** The New York Public Library, Picture Collection. **118** Sonia Halliday Photographs. **119** The Pierpont Morgan Library. **120** Reproduced from *The Doré Bible Illustrations* published by Dover Publications, Inc. in 1974. **122** Culver Pictures. **123** Courtesy of the Archaeological staff officer of Gaza; Photo: Israel Museum/David Harris. **124** Erich Lessing/Magnum. **125** The New York Public Library, Picture Collection. **126** The Tate Gallery, London. **127** Jewish Museum of New York/Art Resource, N. Y. **128** Bodleian Library, Oxford. **129** *left* Holman Pictorial Collection of Biblical Antiquities, Holman Bible Publishers, Nashville, TN; *right* Reproduced from *The Doré Bible Illustrations* published by Dover Publications, Inc. in 1974. **130** Roger-Viollet. **131** *left* Jewish Museum of New York/Art Resource, N. Y.; *right* Biblioteca Apostolica Vaticana. **135** Wadsworth Atheneum, Hartford, Ella Gallup Sumner and Mary Catlin Sumner Collection. **136** Ray Skibinski based on an illustration from the Counsel Collection. **138** Jewish Museum of New York, Gift of the heirs of Jacob H. Schiff/Art Resource, N. Y./Photography by James A. McInnis. **139** & **140** Scala/Art Resource, N. Y. **142** Reproduced from *The Doré Bible Illustrations* published by Dover Publications, Inc. in 1974. **144** The University Museum, University of Pennsylvania/Photo by Dr. James B. Pritchard. **146** Figures designed by Larissa Lawrynenko. **148** Scala/Art Resource, N. Y. **149** Fitzwilliam Museum, Cambridge. **150** National Sculpture Society. **151** British Museum/© Michael Holford. **153** National Gallery of Scotland. **154** Reproduced from *The Picture Book of Devils, Demons, and Witchcraft* published by Dover Publications, Inc. in 1971. **155** *top* James A. McInnis. **157** Reproduced from *The Doré Bible Illustrations* published by Dover Publications, Inc. in 1974. **158** Mary Evans Picture Library. **159** The Ancient Art & Architecture Collection. **160-161** "The Visit of the Queen of Sheba to King Solomon" by Sir E. J. Poynter, Collection Art Gallery of New South Wales. **162** George Buctel based on a map by Hal and Jean Arbo as it appears on Plate VI from *The Westminster Historical Atlas of the Bible* (Revised Edition), edited by George Ernest Wright and Floyd Vivian Filson; © 1956 by W. L. Jenkins; adapted and used by permission of The Westminster Press, Philadelphia, Pa. **166** The Louvre, Paris/© Michael Holford. **167** Ray Skibinski based on a model from the

Collection of the National Maritime Museum, Haifa, Israel. **168** Culver Pictures. **170** Israel Department of Antiquities and Museums. **171** Jean-Loup Charmet. **173** Reproduced from *The Doré Bible Illustrations* published by Dover Publications, Inc. in 1974. **174** The New York Public Library, Picture Collection. **176** *left* Jewish Museum of New York, Gift of Dr. Harry G. Friedman/Art Resource, N. Y.; *right* Erich Lessing/Magnum. **178** *upper left* Musée du Louvre, Paris/Photography by Denise Bourbonnais; *center* Giraudon/Art Resource, N. Y.; *bottom right* Dr. Mary Boyce. **180-181** National Gallery of Art, Washington, Samuel H. Kress Collection. **183** The New York Public Library. **184** Reproduced from *The Doré Bible Illustrations* published by Dover Publications, Inc. in 1974. **186** Zev Radovan, Jerusalem. **187** Leighton House, London. **188** Culver Pictures. **190** Reproduced by courtesy of the Trustees of the British Museum. **193** Alte Pinakothek, Munich/Artothek. **194** *left* City of David Archaeological Project; *right* David Harris. **195** Zev Radovan, Jerusalem. **196** Culver Pictures. **198** Courtesy of the Oriental Institute, University of Chicago. **201** Sonia Halliday Photographs. **203** Scala/Art Resource, N. Y. **205** Jewish Museum of New York, Gift of the heirs of Jacob H. Schiff/Art Resource, N. Y./Photography by James A. McInnis. **206** Ray Skibinski.

PART III: POETRY AND WISDOM

209 Reproduced from *The Doré Bible Illustrations* published by Dover Publications, Inc. in 1974. **210** Städelsches Kunstinstitut/Artothek. **211** *left* Historical Pictures Service, Chicago; *right* Courtesy of the National Gallery of Art, Washington, Rosenwald Collection. **215** Beuroner Kunstverlag/Artothek. **216** Scala/Art Resource, N. Y. **217** *left* British Museum/© Michael Holford; *right* Ray Skibinski based on a reconstruction from The Haifa Museum of Music and Ethnology, Israel. **220** Sonia Halliday Photographs. **221** The Metropolitan Museum of Art, Purchase, Funds from Various Donors, 1902. **222** Norman Tomalin/Bruce Coleman Inc. **225** Giraudon/Art Resource, N. Y. **226** Culver Pictures. **229** The Granger Collection, New York. **230** *Observer* Magazine/Transworld Feature Syndicate.

PART IV: PROPHECY

232 The Pierpont Morgan Library. **233** Gift of Mrs. Robert Homans, 27.354 Courtesy, Museum of Fine Arts, Boston. **234** British Museum/© Michael Holford. **235** Counsel Collection. **237** Reproduced by courtesy of the Trustees of the British Museum. **239** Giraudon/Art Resource, N. Y. **241** The New York Public Library, Picture Collection. **242** *left* SEF/Art Resource, N. Y.; *right* Alinari/Art Resource, N. Y. **243** Bibliothèque Nationale, Paris. **245** Rijksmuseum, Amsterdam. **246** The Granger Collection, New York. **247** "Ezekiel's Vision," miniature from Bible de Sens, 14th century, Biblioteca Reale di Torino (cod. 483/V), Archivio Edizioni Paoline. **249** Mary Evans Picture Library. **250** Sonia Halliday Photographs. **253** Alte Pinakothek, Munich/Artothek. **255** The Bettmann Archive. **256-257** National Museums and Galleries on Merseyside, Walker Art Gallery, Liverpool. **258** Reproduced by courtesy of the Trustees, The National Gallery, London. **260** Winchester Cathedral. **261** Private Collection. **262** Kunstsammlungen der Veste, Coburg. **264** Musée du Louvre, Paris/Photography by Denise Bourbonnais. **265** Musée de la Renaissance Ecouen/Photography by Denise Bourbonnais. **266** Ray Skibinski.

PART V: THE GOSPELS

268 Alte Pinakothek, Munich/Artothek. **271** *left* Ray Skibinski based on illustrations from The New York Public Library, Picture Collection; *right* Scala/Art Resource, N. Y. **273** Nimatallah/Art Resource, N. Y. **275 & 277** Scala/Art Resource, N. Y. **278** Uni-Dia Verlag. **279** Reproduced from *The Doré Bible Illustrations* published by Dover Publications, Inc. in 1974. **280** Jean-Loup Charmet. **281** Scala/Art Resource, N. Y. **282** Courtesy of the National Gallery of Art, Washington, Rosenwald Collection. **283** Musée Condé, Chantilly, France. **285** The Granger Collection, New York. **286** *upper* The Ancient Art & Architecture Collection; *bottom* David Harris. **287** The Ancient Art & Architecture Collection. **288** Courtesy of the National Gallery of Art, Washington, Ailsa Mellon Bruce Fund. **290** Scala/Art Resource, N. Y. **292** The Barber Institute of Fine Arts, The University of Birmingham. **294** Hessisches Landesmuseum, Darmstadt. **295** The Fund of the Guard's Chapel. **296** *left* St. Mary's Church, Fairford, Gloucestershire, England; *right* Scala/Art Resource, N. Y. **298** The Granger Collection, New York. **300** The Brooklyn Museum, Photography by John Neitzel. **302** Ray Skibinski. **304** Scala/Art Resource, N. Y. **305** The Pierpont Morgan Library. **306** Reproduced by courtesy of the Trustees, The National Gallery, London. **307** Teylers Museum, Haarlem. **309** Institute for Antiquity and Christianity, Claremont, California. **310-311** Stift Seitenstetten, Niederösterreich. **313** Reproduced by permission of the Trustees, The Wallace Collection, London. **315** Scala/Art Resource, N. Y. **317** The Metropolitan Museum of Art, The Cloisters Collection, 1955. **318** Copyright The Frick Collection, New York. **320-321** Marvin E. Newman. **323** Delaware Art Museum, Samuel and Mary R. Bancroft Memorial Collection. **325** Lee Boltin. **326** Mary Evans Picture Library. **328** Musée des Beaux Arts, Tours/Giraudon. **329** Scala/Art Resource, N. Y. **331** The Granger Collection, New York. **332** Museo Christiano, Brescia. **334** Scala/Art Resource, N. Y. **336** *top* The Granger Collection, New York; *bottom* Ray Skibinski. **337 & 338** Scala/Art Resource, N. Y. **339** The Robert Harding Picture Library. **340** Vernon Miller. **341** *right* The Pierpont Morgan Library. **343** The Pierpont Morgan Library. **344** Scala/Art Resource, N. Y. **345** Giraudon/Art Resource, N. Y. **346** Staatliche Schlösser und Gärten Potsdam-Sanssouci. **348** Scala/Art Resource, N. Y.

PART VI: THE EARLY CHURCH

351 Sonia Halliday Photographs/Photo by Laura Lushington. **353** The Bettmann Archive. **354** Reproduced from *The Doré Bible Illustrations* published by Dover Publications, Inc. in 1974. **355** Israel Department of Antiquities and Museums. **356-357** George Buctel. **358 & 359** Scala/Art Resource, N. Y. **360** Giraudon/Art Resource, N. Y. **361** The Bettmann Archive. **362** Scala/Art Resource, N. Y. **363** Mondadori Press. **365** Zev Radovan, Jerusalem. **366** Sonia Halliday Photographs. **367** Reproduced from *The Doré Bible Illustrations* published by Dover Publications, Inc. in 1974. **368-369** The National Gallery of Ireland. **371** Scala/Art Resource, N. Y.